Ian Douglas is Emeritus Professor of Geography in the School of Environment and Development, Manchester University. He is Past-President of the Society for Human Ecology; President of the International Council for Ecopolis Development; Past-Chairman of the UK UNESCO MAB (Man and the Biosphere) Urban Forum; and Co-Chairman of the UNESCO SCOPE Expert Group on Urban Futures. He is a member of the editorial boards of Catena, Ecological Processes, Geographical Research, and Land Degradation and Development. His books include *The Urban Environment* (1983), *Humid Landforms* (1977) and (as co-editor) *Companion Encyclopaedia of Geography* (2007) and *Routledge Handbook of Urban Ecology* (2011).

D0139980

From the ancient glories of Bam and Varanasi to the teeming conurbations of Tokyo and São Paulo, cities are amongst our greatest creations. Yet at the start of the twenty-first century, with cities now home to more than half the world's population, there is increasing concern over their unchecked expansion and the detrimental effect this is having on the planet. This unfettered growth is affecting every ecosystem on Earth, from the deepest oceans to the highest mountains, as induced climate change and ever increasing demands upon the world's resources take effect. As the pace of urbanisation quickens, especially in the developing world, how can we make the world's cities more sustainable? How can we prepare new urban areas for future environmental challenges?

Ian Douglas tells the story of cities. Drawing on examples ranging from the cities of the classical world to the megacities of today, he shows why they exist, how they have evolved, and the problems they have encountered. He shows how, from the very beginning, environmental management played a key role in urban life. He examines the concept of the city as an ecosystem and the holistic ideas that guided some planners, architects and urban managers in their responses to the worst consequences of the nineteenth-century urban development. He addresses specific problems associated with urban life, such as noise and air pollution, water supply and waste management, as well the vulnerability of cities to hazards such as earthquakes and flooding. And he considers strategies to make cities more sustainable and help them to adapt to climate change, such as waste recycling, energy conservation, dual water systems, sustainable housing, as well as initiatives to reduce commuting and food miles and attempts to retrofit existing cities.

As we seek to adapt cities to climate change, to make them greener, energy-efficient and sustainable, *Cities: An Environmental History* highlights the essential relationship of humans to their physical world in urban areas. Written by an acknowledged international authority, this unique volume will be welcomed by students and specialists in environment, planning, geography, ecology and the built environment.

ENVIRONMENTAL HISTORY AND GLOBAL CHANGE SERIES

This important new series provides a much needed forum for understanding just how and why our environment changes. It shows how environmental history – with its unique blend of geography, history, archaeology, landscape, environment and science – is helping to make informed decisions on pressing environmental concerns and providing crucial insights into the mechanisms that influence environmental change today. The focus of the series will be on contemporary problems but will also include work that addresses major techniques, key periods and important regions. At a time when the scale and importance of environmental change has led to a widespread feeling that we have entered a period of crisis, the *Environmental History and Global Change Series* provides a timely, informed and important contribution to a key global issue.

IAN DOUGLAS

Cities

An Environmental History

I.B. TAURIS
LONDON · NEW YORK

Published in 2013 by I.B.Tauris & Co Ltd
6 Salem Road, London W2 4BU
175 Fifth Avenue, New York NY 10010
www.ibtauris.com

Environmental History and Global Change: 5

ISBN: 978 1 84511 795 5 (HB)
        978 1 84511 796 2 (PB)

A full CIP record for this book is available from the British Library
A full CIP record is available from the Library of Congress

Library of Congress Catalog Card Number: available

Typeset by Free Range Book Design & Production Limited

Contents

Figures and Tables

FIGURES

TABLES

Acknowledgements

The writing of this book has been inspired by contacts with, and the work of, many scholars. I have a particular debt to the writings and advice of Abel Wolman, Joel Tarr, Sabine Barles, Ian Simmons, David Goode, Rusong Wang and Marina Fischer-Kowalski. I owe a special debt to my colleagues in the Centre for Urban and Regional Ecology at the University of Manchester for their encouragement and advice, especially Joe Ravetz and Nigel Lawson. I am most grateful to Ana Monteiro of the University of Porto for her constructive comments on the air pollution chapter. I thank Ian Whyte for inviting me to write this book and David Stonestreet for his encouragement, forbearance and reminders. As ever, my greatest thanks are due to my wife, Maureen, the best critic, proofreader, and source of common-sense advice anyone could wish for. Any deficiencies, faults and errors in this work are my responsibility.

Introduction

Cities are now the home and the habitat of most of the world's people. Many countries are urbanized societies where most people spend most of their time in a built-up environment, which often seems removed from nature. However, few cities escape from nature's extremes, whether they are dust storms in Dubai, snow in New York or floods in Paris. Nature exerts its influence in towns and cities and adapts to the opportunities provided by cities, from breeding sites for disease vectors, such as the anopheles mosquito, to the invasion of exotic species, from the Oxford ragwort to Himalayan balsam. Any account of the environmental history of urban areas has to examine both the impacts of nature on people in cities and the way urban people modify natural systems and change the biogeochemistry of the urban habitat. That modification is expressed in a multitude of ways, from the type of housing to the water supply and sanitation systems to parks and gardens and the air pollution from traffic, industry, commerce and domestic activities. Counteracting the problems that arise from the modifications depends on culture, politics, technology, scientific understanding, community concern, human aspirations and financial and energy resources. Behind all the major improvements are political decisions, engineering skills and daring, financial risk taking and campaigning, lobbying, community action and local champions to push innovative ideas forward into practical action.

Cities and towns are also dependent entities, originally relying on their immediate surroundings for food and materials resources, but increasingly dependent on an ever widening base, nationally and internationally, for supplies to feed the people, sustain manufacturing and facilitate trade and exchange. These flows of goods and materials are part of the urban metabolism supporting life in towns and cities and justifiably should form part of urban environmental history. However, the environmental impact that urban areas have exerted on rural landscapes has not been included in this book. The discussion of the role of the footprint of cities fits more sensibly with the environmental history of the rural landscape with accounts of changes caused by farming, forestry and mining. The urban impacts on the oceans, from the debris thrown overboard from cargo ships, to oil

1

spillages and overfishing, remain a relatively untold story that is beyond the scope of an urban environmental history.

The development and growth of cities has been the subject of many excellent studies from Lewis Mumford[1] to Peter Hall.[2] The urban environment received little attention until the 1970s following Abel Wolman's stimulating article on urban metabolism.[3] Urban environmental history is even younger, Melosi[4] having to argue in 1993 that it was imperative for environmental historians to study not only the built environment, but also the impact of the city's built environmental on the natural environment. Hays[5] at about the same time was convinced that environmental historians must study all the means by which people have organized themselves to act upon the environment over time, which included examining nature's role and place in the history of urban life.

Fellow geographer Ian Simmons' brief account of the environmental history of England and Wales[6] says little about urban areas, being essentially a landscape history, as is John Sheail's review of ecological history studies in Britain.[7] Bill Luckin[8] has criticized some of this type of work as having little to say about the ways particular groups at particular points in the past had dealt with community-threatening urban disasters, such as huge fires, disease carried by water, and major smoke-laden fog episodes and their health impacts.

Simmons provides an account of urban environmental history in his 2001 volume[9] and in his 2008 work[10] takes a broader view of the impact of globalization since 1950 on all the community and social structures that had previously modified natural environments, especially through the growth of cities, in different ways in different parts of the world. Indeed, we might wonder whether all the cultural and social diversity that makes the world so fascinating and cities such wonderful places to visit is being lost under the pressure of international commerce, fashion, media and multi-national institutions such as the International Monetary Fund. Some streets of Shanghai now have facades that could be in New York, Paris, or Sydney. However, the much altered natural features, such as the Huang Pu waterway, and the historic buildings along the Bund, help to retain a sense of place. Here is the essence of urban environmental history, an amalgam of the local changes made by a particular culture and the consequences of ever-wider external links. Trade has greatly shaped cities, as have power and religion, which have often been conflated to the disadvantage of many people.

In writing an overview of environmental history, my background as a physical geographer leads me to look closely at the changing role of ecological and earth surface processes in urban areas, recognizing that they involve both natural changes, such as the direct impacts of falling rain or the spread of weeds, and people-modified processes, such as the watering of lawns with treated water originating in a distant reservoir or the deliberate planting of exotic garden flowers. I find it important to understand both what is altered as natural processes are modified by urban development and why people made changes the way they did. I also want to know how the natural environment affects life in towns and cities and how people respond to events like earthquakes and floods. In the chapters that follow I endeavour to set out how matters like water supplies, drainage, noise and odours have been managed since the foundation of the earliest urban settlements and how some basic technologies have persisted up to 2012.

However, the final two chapters (9 and 10) and my 'final thoughts' examine ways to make cities better places in which to live. For hundreds of millions of poor people in cities of all sizes, from megalopolises to towns of a few thousand inhabitants, life is hard, insecure and full of risks. For many others air pollution, traffic congestion, noise, crowded housing and flood or earthquake risks cause regular anxiety. Yet people have always had ideas on how to make cities better, how to cope with problems of smoke, fire hazard and drainage. These ideas are still relevant at the start of the twenty-first century as we seek to adapt cities to climate change, lower greenhouse gas emissions, make cities greener and build smart, energy-efficient, sustainable cities. As ever, demographic realities, political indecision, hangovers from the past and lack of public awareness and imagination make most cities slow to change. Nevertheless, the environmental history of cities shows that great improvements can be made and that the innovative adventurous ideas of one generation can become the standard practices of the next (or, more likely, the next but one). In this way environmental history can show that there is ample precedent for being adventurous in city design, planning and management, providing the essential relationship of humans to their physical world in urban areas.

THE DIMENSIONS OF URBAN ENVIRONMENTAL HISTORY

Rosen and Tarr[11] proposed four dimensions of urban environmental history:

1) analysis of the effects of cities on the natural environment over time;
2) analysis of the impact of the natural environment on cities;
3) the study of societal response to these impacts and efforts to alleviate environmental problems;
4) examination of the built environment and its role and place in human life as part of the physical context in which society evolves.

The first dimension has been well examined in terms of urban metabolism and industrial ecology, but is now multi-dimensional with the reliance by all cities on ever growing supply chains delivering goods, materials and services from, and to, other parts of the world. In this book it is addressed in terms of urban metabolism and through consideration of water supplies, wastewater disposal and biodiversity (Chapters 3, 5, 6 and 9).

The effects of the natural environment on urban areas are examined in terms of urban climate, hydrology, geomorphology and ecology (Chapters 4, 8 and 9), but it is remembered that over time aspects of the natural environment become so modified by human action that subsequent urban generations are coping with urban air, rivers, land surfaces, floristic and faunal assemblages that differ greatly in character from those that existed before the first foundations of their city were laid.

Examination of societal response is also multi-dimensional, from responses of individuals to immediate situations such as noise and smells to global efforts to counter greenhouse gas emissions. For most urban people the responses that matter are those made by municipal and national governments, such as flood protection or air pollution controls. In this way, the changes made to cities reflect a constant interplay between public and private interests, whether these interests be those of royalty or religion or of business and municipal enterprise. Improvements for public welfare were often driven, or at least triggered, by circumstances or events that impinged on those in power. This dimension comes into all parts of the book, but is particularly evident in discussions of environmental challenges, greening cities and sustainable cities (Chapters 2, 7, 9 and 10).

The role and place of the built environment in people's lives and the physical context of human evolution remain a constant theme of public health, social stability, causes of violence, and habitats for all kinds of organisms, benign or threatening. Here it is addressed primarily in terms of public health and safety, the latter being associated with the increased risks posed by the built environment in areas prone to geophysical hazards, such as earthquake, volcanoes and floods (Chapters 2 and 8). However, there are other urban hazards from industrial chemicals, self-inflicted ill-health, traffic accidents, and fire that have to be remembered when examining human vulnerability in the urban environment.

MAKING CITIES HABITABLE: CULTURE AND DIVERSITY

The search for urban environmental sustainability has proved to be a hard struggle. Some small and medium sized cities with particularly enterprising and committed environmental leadership have achieved more than their bigger counterparts. All too often, many 'solutions', have merely created a fresh set of problems. Nevertheless, much has been achieved. As Melosi[12] shows, by the second half of the twentieth-century North American and European cities possessed efficient environmental services, surface water quality had improved, the incidence of communicable diseases had declined, air pollution had diminished, and most city people lived longer and healthier lives than their forebears. In addition, in Europe a further great step forward in environmental quality has been made as a result of European Community Directives requiring member countries to reach higher standards of drinking water quality, reducing river pollution, taxing vehicle CO_2 emissions and recycling. Improvements to sewage treatment across the member countries have been particularly striking.

Today also, there is a growing view that cities are part of a landscape continuum from the wildest places on Earth, where human influence is minimal, yet always present, even if just through climate change and fall-out of atmospheric aerosols, to the artificial landscapes of shopping mall interiors, the atriums of luxury hotels and the manicured greenspaces between blocks of apartments in densely built-up Asian cities. The urban patchwork of habitats and ecological niches, affecting biodiversity in cities merges into the suburban mosaic of gardens, trees and public open spaces, to urban fringe smallholdings, and thence to agricultural landscapes, rangelands and forests and grasslands. In some cases, the seas and oceans provide an abrupt edge to a city, in others, mountain ranges limit building in some directions, but in every case, the city is merely an intrusion into the natural world where nature still responds to opportunities just as the urban business entrepreneurs, artists, trades people and rubbish dump scavengers all do. Understanding cities needs awareness both of how society, economy and technology function and of how all the ecological and geophysical processes that fashion the landscape and its wildlife work.

Adaptation and interaction with nature is modified by power, ethnicity and culture.[13] It is also affected by human preferences. Urban gardeners among populations whose cultural history reflects migration only a few generations previously vary greatly in their decisions to plant native or exotic species.[14] This suggests diversity in modifying the environment at the scale of the individual urban landholding or house plot. The environmental history of cities tries to go some way towards explaining that diversity in the development and modification of city environments.

Despite all the impacts of economic and cultural globalization and global environmental change, the stark contrasts between the shining glass, steel and concrete towers and the drab social housing or informal settlements of the poor remain. Life in cities is unequal, and often unfair. So too is the impact of environmental quality. In reading about how the world's cities have evolved, recognizing the many great achievements, especially in terms of public health and safety, an impression is gained that making cities fit for all their inhabitants is not only an unfinished task, but one that is getting bigger by the day. If this environmental history helps to inform that task and encourage others to tackle it with increased vigour, it may do some good.

1

Trading Village to Global Megalopolis

The Origins and Expansion of Cities

Now that more than half the world's people live in cities we are becoming increasingly aware that we need to understand the origins, present dynamics and future trends of urban development in much more detail than ever before. Not only has international and intra-national migration made the social character of cities more diverse and complex than previously, but also patterns of international trade and globalization have led to large urban centres taking on something of a familiar pattern everywhere, with the same multiple stores and similar middle-class housing, motor vehicle congestion and urban rapid transit conditions in cities across all continents. The environmental history of cities examines how these changes in cities have impacted upon the environment, how they have aggravated or produced environmental problems and how city governments and communities have endeavoured to deal with these problems.

The earliest human settlements were clusters of families engaged in subsistence hunting and gathering. Later they became involved in sedentary agriculture, and sometimes found they had occasional surplus production which could be traded for obsidian to make tools, copper ornaments, better seeds or other types of food. Some settlements began to develop specialized tool-making and ornament-making, others became trading posts where goods were exchanged. These were the beginning of urban functions. In some cases there were needs for military protection behind walls, and, quite often, the need for special structures for religious activities. In such ways the settlement began to meet some of the pre-conditions for an urban entity including: permanent settlement in dense aggregations; non-agricultural specialists; taxation and wealth accumulation; monumental public buildings; and a ruling class. Such phenomena are usually associated with the existence of: writing techniques; predictive science; artistic expression; trade for essential materials; and a decline in the importance of kinship.

It was not always thus. Compared to the existence of *Homo Sapiens* in Africa 164,000 years ago and the migration from Africa to other continents about 50,000 years ago,[1] the development of cities has been short-lived, but dramatic. Cities, or more probably towns and urban settlements, where a specialization of labour and some form of social hierarchy emerged, began to develop 9000 to 6000 BC. Nearly all this rural to urban transition began with agriculture and trade. The first towns were essentially overgrown villages associated with trade routes and water management. During the Neolithic, trade in obsidian became important in villages to the north of the Tigris and Euphrates rivers. Copper was worked into ornaments that were also traded. Centres began to produce pottery, but there is no evidence of the development of strong government or political authority. Çatalhöyük and Jericho (Table 1.1) are usually regarded as 'precocious' urban-like developments. However, they like their successors all involved enormous human effort to modify the environment to create building sites and reliable water supplies. Çatalhöyük was built on a large artificial mound, while Jericho had huge rock-cut ditches to carry its water (Table 1.1). The hydrological and geomorphological changes will have affected surrounding areas and changed the local biota. The cities also had to deal with their rubbish, usually by piling it up nearby. Not surprisingly, archaeologists often find many layers of garbage accumulated over centuries, interspersed with periods of new building after fire or temporary abandonment of the settlement. Records of destruction by fire or by war also emerge as do changes in the types of food used and the remnants of changing technologies. Soon metals begin to appear in the waste, indicating new forms of urban consumption and technology. It is therefore good to look at how the technologies of the earliest cities have ramifications for today's cities. The basic water supply system of the palace at Knossos, Crete in 1700 BC is highly similar to that of today. Aqueducts bring water in and it is stored in local distribution reservoirs. The wastewater is removed by one drainage system, stormwater in another. Many of the more deprived city dwellers of the twenty-first century AD do not benefit from such water supply and sanitation.

ÇATALHÖYÜK

Çatalhöyük in Anatolia (Turkey) flourished due to its rich obsidian deposits from around 6500 to 5550 BC. Neolithic Çatalhöyük is important both in terms of its record of symbolic expression and cultural complexity and as one of the best-studied of the first wave of agricultural settlements to appear in South-west Asia and the Balkans.[2] Çatalhöyük thus demonstrates that cities may have developed outside the so-called Fertile Crescent, for long thought to have provided a unique environment for the creation of the first Near Eastern cities.[3]

The detailed multi-disciplinary investigations at Çatalhöyük reveal the close relationship between the environment and human activity at the beginnings of urbanization. Neolithic Çatalhöyük was located in an extensive alluvial wetland with a strongly seasonal climatic regime that produced a spring flood that surrounded the settlement mound by water for up to two months of the year (Figure 1.1). The seasonal wetlands provided a range of environmental resources from the protein-rich tubers of club-rush and wildfowl to marl clay for wall plaster, while the Çarşamba River, then flowing past the site, provided a key means of transport and communication.[4] However, unless planted in late spring as flood-recession farming, the local alluvial soils cannot have provided the locus for cereal crop cultivation. Archaeobotanical data indicate that most of these crops were dry-farmed in non-alluvial soils located too far from Çatalhöyük to have been visited on a daily basis. The dry-farming would have been supported by the wetter and more reliable rainfall regime of Neolithic times.

Many of the themes found in symbolism and daily practice at Çatalhöyük occurred early in the processes of village and town growth. These themes include a social focus on memory construction; a symbolic focus on wild animals, violence, and death; and a central dominant role for humans in relation to the animal world.[5] These themes are integral to the development of settled life and the domestication of plants and animals. Human settlements and early urbanism were thus part of efforts to overcome environmental difficulties, to have protection against the annual floods, to achieve adequate food supplies by seasonal engagement in dry-farming some distance from the settlement, and so extend the ecological footprint of the settlement. Eventually the site was transformed from a village into a town. This transformation must have been associated with an element of expansion and spreading of influence, perhaps under the leadership of a dynamic leader, family or group.

THE NORTE CHICO REGION OF PERU

In South America, urban settlements developed independently of those elsewhere. Caral and Aspero (Table 1.1) in Peru, date back to 5000 BC and provide a distinct counter-example to the concept of human conglomerations coming about due to war alone. The settlements are devoid of all signs of warfare; they have no walls, no defensive battlements, no weapons or mutilated bodies have been found and there are no artistic depictions of battle. Both enjoyed the benefits of trade between farmers and fishermen. They constructed large mounds to support ceremonial buildings. Baskets made of reeds were found beneath some of these earthworks, indicating how labourers had carried stones and earth on their backs. These settlements grew into major cities. Altogether, 20 sites in the region, sharing certain basic characteristics, including large-scale monumental architecture, extensive residential architecture and a lack of ceramics, demonstrate the development of a major cultural complex in the Norte Chico region of Peru by 3000 to 1800 BC.[6]

Table 1.1: Key early cities and their characteristics and environmental features

Approx-imate date BC	Locality	Country and continent	Characteristics	Environmental issues
9000	Çatalhöyük	Turkey, Asia	Over 150 dwellings; trade in obsidian; settled farming community producing surplus, early pottery abundant	Built on a large mound above a wide marshy plain, season variations in flow of local river
9000	Jericho	Israel, Asia	Pre-pottery, Neolithic settlement, re-occupied later	Huge rock-cut ditch and stone wall
6500	Tell Zaidan	Syria, Asia	Centre of major trade routes along Euphrates River; eight large kilns for firing pottery	Three large mounds on the east bank of the Balikh River
5400	Eridu	Iraq, Asia	At junction of three different ecosystems with different lifestyles, needing agreement about water use in a desert environment; impressive temple complex	Large mound and temple; water security a serious problem; eventually affected by encroaching desert dunes and rising saline water table
5000	Bago, Indus Valley	Pakistan, Asia	Village-like settlement with strong evidence of trade	River channel changes
5000	Caral	Peru, South America	Six pyramids, 20 m tall; craft workshops; rich trading environment; irrigated agriculture; cotton traded for fish	Built on earth and rock mounds; massive earth and rock movement to create bases for pyramids
5000	Aspero	Peru, South America	Coastal seafaring community; some evidence of agriculture and trade, but mainly dependent on marine resources	Two huge platform mounds; 15 other smaller mounds; and also plazas, terraces and large refuse area covering 14 ha in total
4500	Hamoukar	Syria, Asia	Trade centre for obsidian; tool and pottery manufacture; specialized mass production	Late Chalcolithic city that was destroyed by fire around 3500 BC; reoccupied subsequently
4000	Uruk	Iraq, Asia	Important religious and government centre with specialized workshops	Organization of water supply and transport on the Euphrates important

Table 1.1 (continued)

4000	Cheng Tou Shan	China, Asia	Fortress site containing shrines and administrative buildings	Irrigation system for surrounding fields, with reservoir pools; earth wall around city
3700	Liangzhu	China, Asia	Producer of jade, pottery and lacquer ware; much trade	At junction of two rivers and of mountain landscape with plains; raised foundations on compacted earth
3500	Maadi	Egypt, Africa	Basically farming community but with locally produced, hand-built jars and evidence of the specialized construction of copper tools, stone vases and tabular flint tools	On a rocky ridge next to the Nile River flood plain, many sequences of garbage deposits and occupation layers
3000	Ur	Iraq, Asia	Became the largest city in the world from 2030 to 1980 BC	Drought, river channel change, and silting of the waterways leading to the Persian Gulf
3000	Memphis	Egypt, Africa	Royal city with population that rose to 40,000 at its peak; hierarchical social organization, workshops for crafts; trade	Responded to environmental changes by moving eastwards as Nile channel shifted and sand dunes advanced
3000	Knossos	Crete, Greece, Europe	Rapid population growth transforms Neolithic settlement into town; palace developed after 1750 BC	Palace had separate drainage systems for stormwater and waste-water, and a piped water supply fed by 10 km long aqueducts
2650	Dholavira	Gujarat, India, Asia	Built of stone (unlike other Harappan cities); huge structure of bricks may be a tomb	Series of mounds on Khadit Bet Island surrounded by water in monsoon season; sophisticated water conservation using cisterns cut into rock
2500	Mohenjo-Daro	Pakistan, Asia	Regular grid pattern; lower town residential; citadel for religious and administrative purposes	Importance of changing river channels; mud brick embankment 13 m wide; drainage system
2500	Harappa	Pakistan, Asia	Differentiated living quarters, flat-roofed brick houses, and fortified administrative and religious centre	Grid city layout; effective sewer and drainage systems

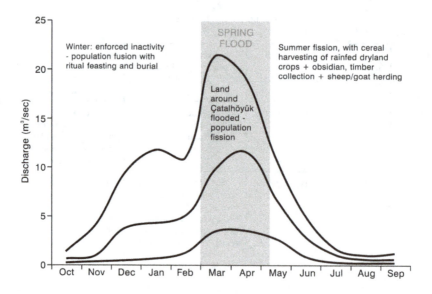

Figure 1.1: River flood regime annotated to show possible fission and fusion of Çatalhöyük's population, along with seasonal activities located close to and more distant from the site. Lines show maximum, mean, and minimum monthly water flows of the Çarşamba River at Bozkir for the period 1964–80 (after Roberts and Rosen, 2009)

THE TIGRIS–EUPHRATES RIVER BASIN (ESPECIALLY MESOPOTAMIA)

From 6500 BC onwards urban settlements that combined defensive, commercial and religious functions began to develop both in Mesopotamia proper and along the trade routes of the upper Euphrates. Places like Tell Zaidan (Table 1.1) and Halaf, in the extreme northern river basin of the Euphrates in present-day Syria, became important. Specialist skills became concentrated in urban settlements. Religious leaders and rulers developed their power in the larger settlements and protected their interests by building defensive walls. These cities were primarily concerned with security and commerce. Many also had religious functions. Most of them changed the local environment by building mounds for the main structures.

By 3500 BC many prosperous cities, such as Uruk (Table 1.1), each surrounded by irrigated fields and villages, existed in the Tigris–Euphrates basin. They shared several key characteristics. They were governed by male priests, initially serving a female deity. Cultivated land came right into the city: many townspeople being part-time farmers who lived just outside the walls, within walking distance of the fields. The poor lived at the periphery but inside the walls. Merchants and craftsmen had homes closer to the centre, while the nobility, priests and warriors lived at the centre which had imposing ceremonial structures, the ziggurats and temples. The great surge in urban development led to the near abandonment of the surrounding countryside. Probably, most of the part-time farmers were people who had left their homes in isolated villages and moved into the city.[7] Warfare is also a possible cause of the abandonment of rural settlements. Another might be that the kings of Uruk wanted tighter control of their subjects,[8] perhaps in order to be able to coerce them to work on major construction projects.

However, these cities were vulnerable and plagued by major problems, including fires from out of control cooking fires; disease, linked to poor sanitation; famine in years when the annual floods were reduced in extent; and the threat of invasion by enemies. The famines were also associated with the impact cities had on their environment. The farmers had no drainage channels to carry excess water away from their fields. Thus salt built up as the excess water was evaporated, forcing farmers to switch from wheat to the more salt-tolerant barley (as at Eridu, Table 1.1). Eventually the salt levels were too great even for barley and the fields had to be abandoned. This legacy of saline soils still constrains agriculture in Iraq today.[9]

THE EARLIEST EGYPTIAN CITIES

Around 3500 BC, the village of Maadi was established about 15 km south of present-day Cairo, probably as a trade centre, with warehouses, silos and cellars. Maadi was at the end of an overland trade route to Palestine, and was probably inhabited by middlemen from the Levant at that time, trade items including copper and bitumen from South-west Asia being found at the site. Other artifacts linking the site with Upper Egypt suggest that Maadi was a junction of trade routes for the upper Nile and the Levant.

By 3000 BC, the first Egyptian kings consolidated their power at Memphis, developing a royal ideology that bonded all the districts to the person of the ruler. Although an important population centre throughout three millennia of pharaonic history, Memphis responded to environmental changes by moving eastwards as the Nile channel changed and sand dunes moved towards the city. At the peak of its development, the population of Memphis was probably below 40,000. Further south Thebes (the site of modern Luxor) reached a similar size, but most ancient Egyptian towns, such as Illahun, Edfu, Hierakonpolis and Abydos had from 1,400 to 3,000 inhabitants. Their residents included rural people, such as farmers and herdsmen who worked the fields every day. The kings, nobles and the temples possessed estates that employed a variety of personnel, many of whom were rural workers on the agricultural land. As in Mesopotamia, these cities and towns had a hierarchical organization, with palaces, mansions and temples for the elite, and more humble housing for workers, as well as workshops, granaries, warehouses, shops and local markets: all the institutions of residential urban life. As in Mesopotamia and at Çatalhöyük, the annual flood was both a challenge and a blessing. The agriculture was supported by the watering of the soils and the deposition of silt, but the floods could disrupt both urban and rural activity.

EARLY CITIES AROUND THE INDUS VALLEY

The greater Indus region was home to the largest of the four ancient urban civilizations of Egypt, Mesopotamia, South Asia and China. It emerged around 2500 BC along the Indus River in what is now Pakistan. The most important cities were Harappa, and Mohenjo-Daro. The most distinctive feature of the Indus civilization was its intricate urban planning. The cities were distinguished by a well-planned grid-iron pattern layout of straight streets and stone or brick buildings and sophisticated construction. Within the cities, precincts/areas were distinguished by specific economic activities. The cities, unlike those of Mesopotamia, had highly developed sanitation systems with sewers and waste collection systems. Most houses had water wells and bathrooms with drains. The streets also had drains.[10]

Harappa may have had 50,000 people at times. Some cities were composed of two sections surrounded by walls, the 'Citadel' and the 'Lower Town'. The Citadel was the administrative and religious centre with public buildings such as the 'Great Bath' and the 'Granary', and the 'Lower Town' was primarily a residential area. However, Dholavira had a threefold division: an acropolis or upper town consisting of a massive 'castle' and an adjacent 'bailey', a middle town (including a huge ceremonial ground), and a lower town, a large part of which was occupied by a series of reservoirs (Figure 1.2).

These cities show response and decline in relation to environmental change. The Indus culture probably gradually spread from west to east, with sites towards central and southern India flourishing after Harappa and Mohenjo-Daro had declined. The drying up of the ancient Saraswati or Ghaggar-Hakra River, east of and parallel to the Indus, may also have affected the civilization. Such a possible explanation of the decline of the Indus civilization is provided by an environmental deterioration theory. The decay of the sites in and around Gujarat was affected both by colder and drier weather and by diminished port capability associated with a falling sea level.[11]

THE EARLIEST CITIES OF THE LOWER YANGTZE, CHINA

One of the oldest urban settlements in China is said to be Cheng Tou Shan (Table 1.1), established about 4000 BC. Situated on the Yellow River (Huang He), it is a fortified settlement, enclosed within a clay wall and protected by water ditches. The latter, however, may be older than the city because rice cultivation in the area began about 10,000 BC and the ditches may have been part of the irrigation system. Although, in China, the early agriculture from which the

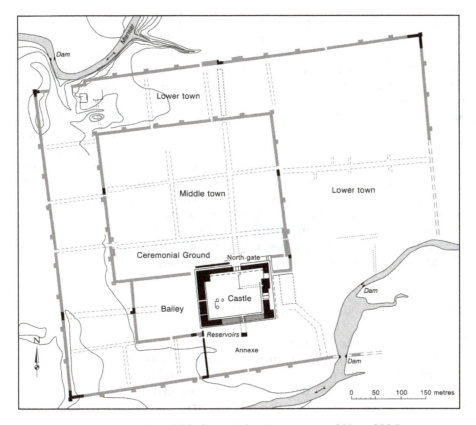

Figure 1.2: Plan of Dholavira (after Teramura and Uno, 2006)

city sprang was concentrated around the area where the Yellow River emerges from the Loess Plateau on to the great plain of northern China, settlements began to develop in the Yangtze delta shortly before 5000 BC.

Continuous records of biostratigraphy, sedimentology and geochemistry suggest climate change seriously affected the Neolithic cultures in the Yangtze Delta.[12] During the warm and humid period 7240–5320 BP, a higher sea level than at present rendered the region unsuitable for permanent settlement. By 5320 BP the sea had withdrawn from the region, but cold and humid climatic conditions resulted in the expansion of water bodies that lasted for about 800 years. After this event, the civilization migrated to the region and began to reclaim the plain. The city of Liangzhu developed after 3700 BC (Table 1.1) giving its name to the culture of the period. The significant 33.8 km² Liangzhu site, 16 km north-west of modern Hangzhou, contains 119 heritage sites where high quality jade carvings, textiles, sculpture and black pottery artifacts have been uncovered. There are also a tomb, a sacrifice altar, a military garrison wall and dikes for irrigation and water management.[13]

At the late stage of the Liangzhu Cultures, rapid expansion of water bodies occurred. The high lake levels and high water tables caused the civilization to vanish and human settlement migrated to the higher landscapes of the western Yangtze Delta. Later, the Maqiao Cultures emerged, but during a late stage of the Maqiao Cultures, expansion of water bodies caused by cold and humid climatic conditions again led to a rapid collapse of settlement in the delta. Settlement of the region resumed during the Tang Dynasty (AD 618–907) when climatic conditions again became more favourable for agriculture in the region. Overall, in the Yangtze Delta, there were five declines in human civilization during the Holocene (the shaded zones a–e in Figure 1.3), which match the five periods of high sea level, increased development of peat and burial of trees by floods. These environmental variations exerted tremendous impacts on human settlements and the development of human civilization.[14] This long-term vulnerability of cities and human settlements generally to climate change raises questions for those considering how cities will adapt to climate changes in the twenty-first century.

THE EARLIEST SETTLEMENTS OF CRETE AND GREECE

Mycenaean and Minoan cities emerged after 3000 BC, Knossos, Crete (Table 1.1), beginning the transition from a village to a town at about that time, although Athens did not become truly urban until about 800 BC. Minoan cities were connected by stone-paved roads, formed from blocks cut with bronze saws. The streets were drained and water and sewer facilities were available to the upper class, through clay pipes. They usually had a radial structure, with streets starting at the centre and extending straight outward like the spokes of a wheel. Environmental vulnerability in this region includes the effects of the great eruption of Thera (modern Santorini) which affected Crete by both ash fall and a tsunami, but many believe that the ultimate decline of Knossos was due to invaders as much as to the difficulties posed by the eruption and the impact of deforestation of Crete through urban consumption.

The eighth century BC saw Greek city-states develop from Sicily to Anatolia (Figure 1.4). The Polis, or city-state first developed in places such as Smyrna on the west coast of Asia Minor.[15] The situation of the cities, surrounded by non-Greeks, meant that they had walled, defendable settlements. Most of the cities of the time on the Greek mainland focused on the citadel (acropolis) which was the temple area and a place of refuge in times of trouble. By 630 BC, colonists from Thera, no longer able to support its population, founded Cyrene in Cyrenaica and significant new trade routes opened up. The earliest Greek foundation in Italy was Pithekouassi on Ischia, which was probably a centre for iron-working using ores brought from Elkba.[16] These townships were much involved with meeting the needs of cities in Greece, their mineral and agricultural trade indicating the growth of the

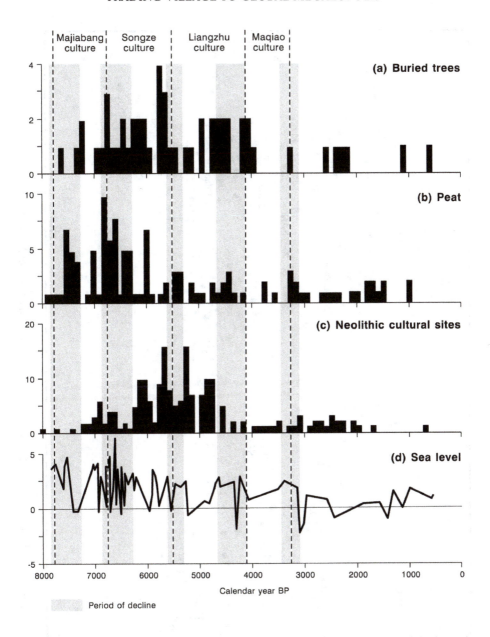

Figure 1.3: Temporal relationships between sea level, frequency of dates of the buried trees, peats, and number of Neolithic sites in the Yangtze Delta. (A) frequency of dates for buried trees; (B) frequency of dates for peat; (C) frequency of dates for Neolithic cultural sites; and (D) sea level changes (in metres) reconstructed from shell ridges and peat. Shaded zones indicate the periods of cultural decline. Dashed lines separate the different cultural periods (after Zhang et al., 2005)

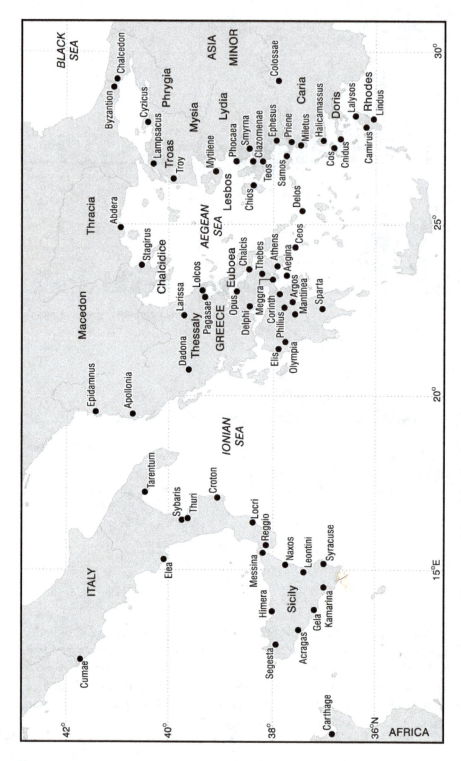

Figure 1.4: Map of the Greek city states in the 8th century BC (after Morkot, 1996)

urban footprints, while the need to migrate from Thera suggests how an island population can readily exceed the carrying capacity of its environment.

ROMAN CITIES AND THE ENVIRONMENT

Many ancient cities used the agricultural products and natural resources of their hinterlands, and deposited their wastes on nearby land, without thinking about the environmental consequences. Soil fertility was depleted and products were harvested and taken to distant cities. The Romans achieved great feats of engineering, carrying water great distances along aqueducts and capturing soil washed off hillsides behind small valley bottom dams. This increased the possibility of provincial governors meeting agricultural targets imposed centrally from Rome, but left an increasingly denuded environment.

Rome became one of the largest cities of the ancient world, with an estimated one million people by AD 100. These people were supported by supplies from the whole Roman Empire, but especially from North Africa. The rare timbers of North Africa were highly prized and forests were cut down to provide both high quality timber and fuel-wood. By 50 BC, Africa produced 500,000 tonnes of grain annually, and by AD 20 it was meeting 65 per cent of Rome's wheat needs.[17] Large olive tree plantations were established in North Africa, supplying olive oil to Rome. Eventually, three to four centuries later, these systems broke down, some people arguing that the soils had become so degraded that they could no longer support the large urban communities that had developed in the towns and cities of the African provinces, but it may simply be that the whole Roman system broke down and the provincial centres were unable resist the advance of other societies. However, the Roman Empire really does emphasize the security and commercial roles of cities.

The legacy of Roman urban consumption and landscape transformation is readily visible today from one extreme of the Roman Empire to the other. In northern England, debris of Roman lead mines in Teesdale and the Lake District still lies on the surface of the ground and lead is leached from it into the rivers. In central Tunisia, the centuriated fields, olive presses and ruined walls of large scale Roman agriculture remain prominent in the landscape. This evidence of the metabolism of ancient cities indicates how deep rooted is the environmental history of cities.

THE SPREAD OF WORLD RELIGIONS AND THEIR IMPACT ON URBAN ENVIRONMENTAL ISSUES: THE EXAMPLE OF ANGKOR THOM, CAMBODIA

By AD 400, Christianity had begun to become established over a large part of Europe, as cathedrals and abbeys were built in subsequent centuries they sometimes changed the nature of urban settlements, religious orders not only controlling much agriculture but also intervening in the regulation of urban food

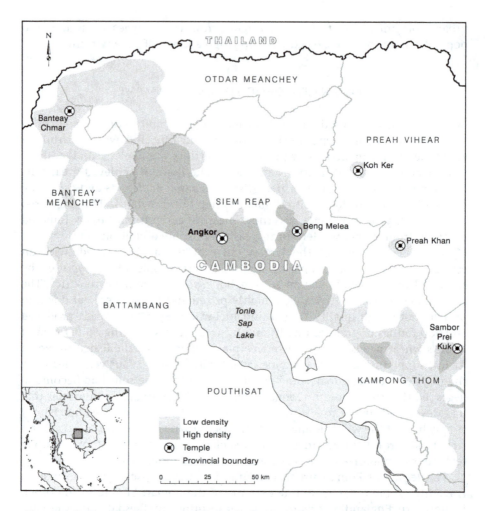

Figure 1.5: Approximate extent of temple-and-pond-based agricultural settlements of the Angkorian and pre-Angkorian periods on the basis of an analysis of Landsat imagery and the spatial coverage of recent archaeological maps (based on data in Evans et al., 2007)

markets. From about AD 300 there was increasing adoption of Hindu and Buddhist cults among the local rulers of South-east Asia. Hindu temples were constructed at Angkor Borei on the Mekong River downstream of Phnom Penh in the seventh century. From the ninth century AD temples incorporating both Hindu and Buddhist elements began to be built at Angkor north of the Tonlé Sap (Figure 1.5). Here ability to control water resources was crucial, in order to be able to grow sufficient food to support all the workers, priests and others involved in what became the largest monumental religious building complex of the ancient world.

Agriculture long remained a major factor in the development of cities. Among the large Asian cities around AD 1000 is Angkor Thom, sometimes said to have had over a million people and claimed to have been the largest pre-industrial city. While undoubtedly based on a complex hydraulic infrastructure, there is uncertainty as to whether it was an urban area or an area of dense agrarian occupance supporting a number of urban nodes and spiritual functions: a complex of agriculture and temples. Remote sensing throws some light on this, Evans et al.[18] stating that 'Even on a quite conservative estimate, Greater Angkor, at its peak, was therefore the world's most extensive pre-industrial low-density urban complex.' It can now be seen as a vast, flimsy, low-density dispersed urban complex spread over about 1000 km² from the Tonlé Sap to the Kulen hills and their associated ranges.[19]

Angkor is visibly an infrastructural network, along which people also lived, imposed on the regional pattern of the residential landscape north of the Tonlé Sap. The large-scale infrastructure gave coherence to the scatter of traditional residential units and 'created' Greater Angkor as a corporate entity. The key question is the extent of the low-density urban complex. The critical point is that the smaller components of the settlement pattern (the local temples, the occupation mounds, the ponds, and the durable and highly structured web of agricultural space that binds them) occur with remarkable consistency within 15–25 km of the current high-water mark of the lake. Furthermore, an analysis of the Landsat data shows that this form of small-scale, low-density occupation continues essentially uninterrupted, forming a contiguous, even lower-density occupation across a large swathe of the Cambodian landscape (Figure 1.5). Although there are areas of somewhat more concentrated occupation, there is, at this stage, no particular spatial or temporal pattern that lends itself to a convenient boundary definition.[20]

Angkor Thom was enclosed by a wide moat some 13 km in circumference and a formidable laterite wall, supported on an enormous earth embankment. Five stone causeways crossed the moat and gave access to the city through five monumental gates, with towers surmounted by enormous gigantic heads with four human faces. The causeways themselves were flanked on each side by balustrades formed by rows of giants holding on their knees a naga, whose seven heads rose fanwise at each end of the causeway.[21] At its greatest scale of activity, at the end of the twelfth century, Angkor Thom and the surrounding intensive agricultural zones producing three or four rice harvests per year, were stretched to the utmost by the king's building programme. Thousands of villages were assigned for the upkeep of the great temples, while tens of thousands of officials and hundreds of dancers were employed in their service. In addition great armies of labourers, sculptors and decorators were required for the construction activities.[22] Through these enormous demands on the population the king impoverished the Khmer society, neglecting the hydraulic infrastructure on which the whole system depended.

The city itself, far from being an urban agglomeration, was a collection of waterworks stretching far and wide beyond the palace and its immediate temples, with a considerable population densely settled along its causeways and canals, and much of its land cut up into cultivated holdings.[23] Groslier considers the labour bestowed on the irrigation works as 'Far more impressive than the building of the temples, which were merely chapels crowning a cyclopean undertaking.'[24]

URBAN PROGRESS: SURVIVAL OR DECLINE

Perhaps Angkor should be regarded as an early example of urban sprawl, a sprawl dominated by flows of water, rather than flows of motor vehicles. It was a city dependent on a hydraulic system but driven by the need to support a great religion. In a way the decline of the irrigation system has a parallel to the decline of the Easter Island society: too much building for rituals exhausting the population and over straining the local environment. This echoes some of the evidence used by Gordon Childe who talks of 'mechanisms of accumulation'[25] and the squandering of most of the surplus production of Mesopotamian farmers and artisans on 'unproductive luxuries or futile ceremonial'[26] associated with the building of ever more elaborate temples. For some this would also find a parallel in modern cities, but with the building of ever more elaborate and costly hotels and shopping malls from Las Vegas to Dubai rather than ceremonial structures. Many great cities have lasted far longer than Harappa, Uruk, Memphis or Angkor. However, is it possible that a megalopolis such as Istanbul or Cairo can survive indefinite growth and expansion?

Much of the environmental history of cities can be ascribed to the determination of particular individuals or elites to gain power, influence or wealth. Some individuals deliberately founded new cities, others changed the local, national or even international roles of cities. The overcoming of environmental problems, such as those affecting health, was often due to perspicacious and determined individuals. We know little, if anything of these individuals in Neolithic times, but much is known of the roles of people such as Alexander the Great, Hadrian, Sir Christopher Wren and Haussmann.

Although little is known of the key individuals and government decisions of the times, the environmental outcomes of the growth and decline of cities and their vulnerability to environmental change are becoming increasingly understood. The chapters that follow will carry forward the messages and lessons learned (or forgotten) from ancient cities to examine in greater detail how the environment within and around modern cities has been managed, damaged, restored and conserved in many different ways. The chapters are arranged to deal with some major environmental issues: public health, urban consumption, air pollution, water supplies, solid and liquid wastes, noise and odours, landforms and water circulation. The final two examine progress made over the centuries towards greener and more sustainable cities.

2

Communities Responding to Disasters and Threats

Vulnerable and Resilient Cities

Throughout history, extreme events, be they caused by natural processes or by human behaviour, from earthquakes to fire, volcanoes to the spread of disease, have given rise to changes in the urban environment, largely through rebuilding or retrofitting new infrastructure, but sometimes by the relocation of urban settlements. Sometimes the reconstruction has been on a new site, sometimes new city plans have been made and the old urban structure has been replaced by a more modern, healthier, safer city plan. In other cases, the redevelopment of the city has been guided by new, tighter building regulations and health and safety requirements, but with properties still occupying the spaces of former land ownership. In many instances, despite forward thinking ideas and plans for building a better city, the patterns of tenure and ownership have caused the city to continue to have a street layout unchanged from previous centuries. Thus the attraction of the future is delicately balanced against the desire for the possessions and heritage of the past, as indicated by the careful rebuilding of the centres of many European cities after bombing in the Second World War. However, many responses to disaster have set cities on new paths of development that in turn have created their own legacies, often of inequality and environmental injustice.[1]

In extreme cases, towns and cities are abandoned. Settlement abandonment may be envisaged as a multi-stage process of increasing vulnerability, transition from population increase or stability to instability and population decline, and growing out-migration that reinforces the erosion of adaptive capacity among the remaining population (Table 2.1).[2]

23

Table 2.1: Generalized view of the settlement abandonment process (after Porter, 1997)

	Stage 1 Rising vulnerability Population rising or stable	Stage 2 Transition to population decline	Stage 3 Abandonment
Exposure to drivers	Anthropogenic and/or environmental drivers emerge or increase in frequency and/or severity	Extended duration, increased severity, synergistic effects of multiple drivers Potential emergence of additional drivers May be magnified by inadequate and/or inappropriate institutional responses	Existing drivers persist or intensify Additional drivers may emerge Out-migration reduces adaptive capacity and itself becomes a driver
Adaptation responses	*In-situ* adaptation responses dominate, either by institutions or autonomously by residents	*In-situ* adaptation resources become increasingly strained Other settlement destinations become increasingly attractive Autonomous temporary or permanent out-migration emerges Population instability and decline follows	*In-situ* adaptive options become exhausted Autonomous out-migration increases Temporary migration becomes indefinite Population decline accelerates Institutional decisions become critical in determining outcomes

PLAGUES, EPIDEMICS AND CHRONIC DISEASES AS DRIVERS OF URBAN ENVIRONMENTAL CHANGE

Infectious diseases have long been tackled by isolating the sick, whether they have leprosy, bubonic plague, tuberculosis or yellow fever. This avoidance of contact with the unaffected population gave rise to leper colonies, plague villages, tuberculosis hospitals and yellow fever islands. Cholera spread came to be controlled by inspections of ships en route and the establishment of quarantine stations close to key ports and sea routes. This pattern of segregating those with disease from the rest of the population was gradually extended as local governments and colonial powers moved those thought to be more susceptible to, and more likely to catch, the disease away from the rest of the population. In some places this initiated a path of segregation and differentiation of urban environmental quality that persists until the present day.

Plague

Although originally used as a term for any widespread disease causing high mortality, plague now refers to a specific infectious fever caused by *Yesinia pestis* (also called *Pasteurella pestis* or *Bacilluspestis*). Plague has always been a threat to city populations. A great plague struck Athens from 430 to 427 BC.[3] Plague decimated the human population of Europe and North Africa during two pandemic waves called Justinian's plague (AD 541–767) and the Black Death (1346–nineteenth century).[4] The latter provoked a lasting demographic crisis. Thousands of villages were abandoned and by 1427 Florence's population had fallen by 60 per cent from over 100,000 to about 38,000.[5] Many believed the plague was sent by God to punish sinners. If so, only prayer and fasting could be effective against the plague. Flagellant bands wandered from town to town, whipping each other and denouncing Jews. This denunciation encouraged persecution of the Jews who were accused of poisoning wells. In Basel, Jews were penned up in a wooden building and burnt alive; 2000 were said to have been slaughtered in Strasbourg and 12,000 in Mainz, while in July 1349 the flagellants led the burghers of Frankfurt into the Jewish quarter for a wholesale massacre.[6] Eventually moves were made by magistrates, nobles or councils to try to control the disease by restricting the movement of the sick, enclosing plague victims in their houses and leaving them to die, and even by killing dogs and cats, not knowing that they would have killed the rats that carried the plague.

Ultimately, cities established quarantine measures. In 1377, Ragusa (Dubrovnik, Croatia) made anyone arriving from an affected area spend up to 40 days in isolation on a nearby island.[7] Within 100 years, Lucca, Florence and Venice had set up Boards of Health to take environmental and other measures to reduce the incidence of plague. Thus began the role of municipal health officials in improving the urban environment.

Modern plague achieved global importance after 1894, when *Y. pestis* was spread by marine shipping from Hong Kong during a third pandemic wave.[8,9] By this time, strong public health awareness had permeated most urban administrations, not the least those of the new cities of the European colonial empires. For example, the planning of the Leopoldville in the then Belgian Congo was marked by two distinct parts: 'European and Congolese ... separated by a *cordon sanitaire* of uninhabited ground ... designed to prevent the spread of African disease into the white residential areas.'[10] In South Africa, especially in Natal and Transvaal, fear of plague, and also of epidemic cholera and smallpox, prompted and rationalized efforts to segregate Indians and Africans in urban areas from the 1870s onward. The municipality of Durban, for example, attempted, in the 1870s, to establish a new settlement for Indians in order to remove the 'breeding haunts and nursery grounds of disease, misery and discomfort' that were thought to menace the town.[11]

The third pandemic of plague reached South Africa in 1900 during the Anglo-Boer War. The port cities of Cape Town, Port Elizabeth, East London and

Durban were vulnerable to infection, burdened by wartime commerce, swollen with refugees from the interior and large numbers of migrant African labourers.[12] In Cape Town, the first affected city, medical officers and the emergency Plague Administration focused on the presence of the Africans whom they directly and inherently associated with the poor social and unsanitary conditions that harboured the plague. The Plague Administration sought to remove Cape Town's African population en masse, even though fewer Africans contracted the plague than did either whites or coloureds.[13] The Cape government set up a native location under the Public Health Act at a sewage farm called Uitvlugt, some 10 km east of the town on the Cape Flats. Worry that the plague might cause a medical disaster triggered a social policy that changed the physical character of the built environment of Cape Town. Urban blacks would remain migrant labour segregated in compounds and distant locations away from white society, lest they corrupt and be corrupted.[14] 'The sanitation syndrome', equating black urban settlement, labour and living conditions with threats to public health and security, became fixed in the official mind, reinforcing a desire to achieve positive social controls, and rationalizing white race prejudice in terms of the popular imagery of medical menace.

In West Africa between 1917 and 1920, plague epidemics hit urban colonial society in Saint-Louis-du-Senegal mainly affecting the poor, who lived in appalling unhygienic conditions. The medical authorities refused to compromise between their plans to prevent further contagion and desire of the poor to practise traditional cultural and religious practices, especially funeral rites. This led to popular disquiet and a disobedience campaign which lasted several months. While the medical authorities advocated the use of force against the rebels, some politicians tried, but failed, to reconcile the two sides. Worry that the epidemics would reach the better-off classes pushed the authorities to declare a state of emergency; to force those continuing the tradition practices to move to the quarantine zone; and to set fire to the contaminated areas. Those who were displaced remained homeless until their part of the town was rebuilt.[15]

Malaria

Malaria has long been recorded, Hippocrates reporting on three types, quotidian, tertian, and quartian, in the fifth century BC. Malaria is closely associated with poor drainage, stagnant water and the storage of water in open vessels, all of which provide opportunities for mosquitoes to breed. It is thus readily harboured in a multitude of urban locations. Concern over malaria involved both taking appropriate prophylaxis and avoiding being bitten by mosquitoes that had been in contact with carriers of malarial parasites.

Even before these risks were understood, in India, colonial administrators had ensured the segregation of military cantonments and European civilian residential areas from places where Indians lived. This form of spatial segregation again formed part of the anti-malarial strategy in Africa with European quarters being built on high ground to the windward of areas occupied by Africans and expressed itself in colonial planning decisions in many parts of Africa. From May 1900, the UK Colonial Office's pamphlet of instructions recommended dealing with malaria by: elimination of Anopheles mosquitoes; personal protection against mosquito bites (not screening of houses); and residential segregation of the European population.[16] This ultimately led to varying segregation patterns in the colonial cities in Africa, but usually distinct environmental zonation, with the Europeans frequently to the windward and on the highest ground. Ill-drained low-lying sites were avoided, but as more and more Africans moved into the cities such hazardous sites frequently became occupied by informal settlements and remain hazardous places today, at risk of flooding and harbouring water-borne diseases.

Cholera

In the fifth century BC, Thucydides described what may have been cholera in Athens. However, Susrata made the first record of cholera in India in the seventh century AD. Jacobus Bontius described cholera in the Dutch East Indies (modern Indonesia) in 1629 and Chinese writers have said that cholera arrived in China from India in 1669. Long rooted in South Asia, cholera did not spread worldwide until the beginning of the nineteenth century. As early as 1814 the celebrated Parisian public health reformer, A.J.B. Parent-Duchâtelet, wrote his thesis about cholera.[17] In 1816, a severe cholera epidemic in Bengal began to spread, occurring throughout the subcontinent and beyond to China[18] by 1820. By 1824 it reached the Philippines, Japan and the borders of Russia. In the west it spread into the Persian Gulf, through Persia and into the Ottoman and Russian empires, but, although reaching the western Caspian, it did not go further into Europe. However the second pandemic, starting in 1829, spread through North Africa and Europe, reaching Sunderland, in north-east England, in 1831[19] and London and Edinburgh in 1832. Thence it moved on to New York the same year, reaching the western seaboard of the USA and Mexico in 1834. A third cholera pandemic began in 1852 and was particularly severe, over 2.5 million Russians being affected, with more than a million dying.

The fourth cholera pandemic started in 1863 and lasted to 1875. This time it arrived in Europe after being carried by Islamic pilgrims returning to Alexandria, whence it was carried by sea to Italy and Marseilles. It also spread in the aftermath of the Austro-Prussian war (1866) and spread south across Africa. The fifth pandemic, in 1881–96, caused severe deaths in Hamburg, Germany.

These cholera pandemics spurred action among both victims and public health officials. Isolation cordons, quarantines and other segregation devices failed and from St Petersburg to Paris, riots occurred as people feared that magistrates and doctors were conspiring to poison them. In Britain, where cholera victims were isolated in the infirmaries of workhouses, rioters accused the medical profession of using the epidemic as an opportunity to seize bodies for dissection.[20]

After the 1832 cholera epidemic, Parent-Duchâtelet was a member of the commission investigating the causes of cholera in Paris. He challenged the old theories about occupational health and disease,[21] especially the belief that miasma, emanations from rotting vegetation and filth, caused disease. He critically assessed the social causes of sickness related to living conditions and argued vigorously for improvements to public health, morality and administration.

Cholera was one of many factors, such as population pressure, which forced the issue of public health reform.[22] Such issues contributed to the pressure for Poor Law reform, Edwin Chadwick being secretary to the Poor Law Commission through which a new Poor Law was enacted in 1834 that effectively led to public responsibility for the sick poor, a move that eventually became the basis for the British National Health Service. This led to further related reforms in the following decade with Chadwick urging construction of effective sewerage and drainage and the need for a central public health authority to direct local boards of health in the provision of drainage, cleansing, paving, drinking water and the sanitary regulation of buildings, nuisances and offensive trades.[23] Thus began a series of public health and urban planning and housing reforms that greatly improved environmental conditions in cities. The moves also helped to set paths that led to the large scale centralized sewerage systems, well-spaced housing, and standards of drinking water treatment that characterize many western cities today. However, it did not happen easily. Two more cholera outbreaks occurred, in 1848 and 1865, before the 1866 Act compelled local authorities to provide sanitary inspectors and allowed the central government to insist upon the removal of nuisance, the provision of sewers and a good water supply.[24]

Yellow fever

Yellow fever virus (YFV) is the prototype member of the genus *Flavivirus*, a group of viruses that are transmitted between vertebrates by arthropod vectors. The virus is found in tropical regions of Africa and South America and is transmitted to primates by mosquitoes: *Aedes* spp. in Africa and *Haemagogus* and *Sabethes* spp. in South America. Molecular epidemiologic data suggest there are seven genotypes of YFV that are geographically separated, and outbreaks of disease are more associated with particular genotypes.[25] From nucleotide-sequence data and phylogenetic analyses, it seems that YFV may have originated in East and central Africa, extended its range to West Africa, and was then transported from West Africa to South America.[26] Three cycles of yellow fever (YF) are recognized in Africa: jungle, savannah and urban. In the first two YF is passed by mosquito bites from monkeys to humans, but in urban areas it is from human to human.

Paris

Long a major problem in Africa, YF reached Cuba in 1648 and Brazil in 1685. Thence it spread throughout the American tropics from Buenos Aires to the east coast of North America.[27] YF control set precedents for disease management in African cities.[28] It occupied a special place in the minds of French West African colonial officials who developed a belief that Africans were natural carriers of the disease and thereby justified social segregation. YF struck Saint-Louis-du-Senegal several times in the second half of the nineteenth century and produced thousands of casualties. Two theories dominated local ideas about the cause of the spread of the disease at the time: localism and contagion.

The localists argued that YF had to do with local environmental conditions, both natural and human-made. They thought that epidemics were caused by noxious miasmas emitted by decaying organic matter in cemeteries; stagnant pools after the torrential rains that transformed the streets of Saint-Louis into infected ponds; and the flat, swampy environment at the mouth of the Senegal River and the mixture of salt and freshwater adjacent to the city. Frequent, strong summer southerly winds were also believed to contribute to the spread of diseases.

The contagionists thought that YF was caused by a kind of poison that could be transmitted through contacts between people or through infected buildings, clothing, and other materials, regardless of the local sanitary conditions. Contagionists believed that YF did not arise locally but was brought to the city from Sierra Leone, Gambia, or Portuguese Guinea.

The YF policy of the mid-nineteenth century was formulated from an environmental and narrow contagionist perspective. Health authorities first targeted Saint-Louis's marketplace, which was transferred to Ndar Toute. They then targeted unsanitary housing, removing the shacks in the city centre that were seen as breeding grounds for the disease, and deciding to move all Africans out of the city centre. This 'bataille de la paillotte' (war on shacks or thatch-roofed houses) continued from around 1850 to 1874.[29] Criticism of the practice of smoking fish on the periphery of the city led to the removal of much of the fishing activity, dozens of fishermen moving away to become pilots or boatmen on the Senegal River. Here again, the sanitation syndrome, described by M. Swanson in South Africa, was at work.[30] When another outbreak of YF occurred in Saint-Louis in 1900, the authorities moved swiftly to identify the people who had introduced and spread the disease and to impose strict quarantine. Despite protests from traders and others about being unable to obtain goods and materials, the outbreak was far less severe than previous ones. Better sanitation, salubrious housing, the provision of clean drinking water and the general improvement in living conditions reduced exposure to pathogenic micro-organisms in Saint-Louis. While similar in achievement to the reforms of Edwin Chadwick and others, such progress however, was, in Africa, also associated with segregation, forced evacuations and tight police control that led to considerable social and environmental injustice.

Today, the risk of urban YF, owing to transmission of the virus by *Aedes aegypti*, is increasing in Africa, as is the potential of urban YF returning to

South America. Both present serious potential public health problems to large population centres.[31]

Despite the availability of an effective vaccine, YF is considered a re-emerging disease owing to its increased incidence in the past 25 years.

Sanitary segregation and socially and environmentally divided cities

The series of global pandemics and the spread of disease that was facilitated by the much increased trade and human movement with revolutions in land and sea transport in the nineteenth century also set new standards and patterns of town planning that had lasting implications for urban environmental change. In the broad sweep of African urban history, then, the desire for sanitary segregation played a role in the formation of residential patterns, but the motivation of racial and cultural segregation was no less important than precedents of the Indian cantonment system, the North African *funduq* (a hostelry or shelter often reserved for non-Muslims, particularly Jews), the southern African mining compound and 'native reserve', and even broader European ideas about governmental and private controls over urban development. Although its influence was strong, medical thought was neither alone nor dominant in giving shape to the cities of tropical Africa. It is perhaps more interesting as an illustration of the way both doctors and administrators tried to solve problems of life and death in an alien environment, with the help of science interlarded with race prejudice, political convenience, and economic advantage – all of this in the middle of an important paradigm change in the history of Western medicine.[32]

The role of public health reformers in improving the urban environment

Beginning in the 1840s, as indicated above, people concerned about unsanitary environments such as J.B.R. Parent-Duchâtelet in France, Edwin Chadwick in the UK and John H. Griscom and Lemuel Shattuck in the USA argued that environments with contaminated water and much rubbish and dirt, rather than individual morality, determined the likelihood and course of epidemic diseases such as cholera.[33]

Chadwick wrote in his 1842 Sanitary Report:[34]

> ... the various forms of epidemic, endemic and other disease caused, or aggravated, or propagated chiefly amongst the labouring classes by atmospheric impurities produced by decomposing animal and vegetable substances, by damp and filth, and close and overcrowded dwellings prevail amongst the population in every part of the kingdom, whether dwelling in separate houses, in rural villages, in small towns, in larger towns – as they have been found to prevail in the lowest districts of the metropolis.

After brief service as New York City Inspector during the early 1840s, Griscom worked steadily for some 20 years for a systematic public health programme that included the basics of careful vital statistics reporting, improvement of slum housing, and general cleansing of the city's environment.

In 1845 Griscom wrote that the pauper classes are more affected than other classes,

> ... because they live in situations and circumstances which expose them more to attacks of disease. They are more crowded, they live more in cellars, their apartments are less ventilated, and more exposed to vapors and other emanations, & c., hence, ventilation, sewage, and all other sanitary regulations, are more necessary for them, and would produce a greater comparative change in their conditions.[35]

At the same time, in Boston, MA, Lemuel Shattuck immersed himself in politics and in the analysis of public problems through statistics, developing guidelines for improving the vital statistics of the city of Boston and the state of Massachusetts, and for conducting the model census of Boston in 1845.[36] In his views he was stimulated and influenced by the activities and ideas of contemporary British and French sanitary reformers. In his 1850 survey of sanitary conditions throughout the state, the *Report of the Sanitary Conditions of Massachusetts*, which was commissioned by the state legislature, Shattuck proposed the creation of a permanent state-wide public health infrastructure. He also recommended establishing health offices at the state and local levels in order to gather statistical information on public health conditions. Although the legislature did not adopt his comprehensive plan, his specific proposals became routine public health activities over the course of the twentieth century.

However, in the 1880s and 1890s, German and French bacteriologists soon discovered the microscopic pathogenic organisms responsible for diseases such as tuberculosis and cholera, among others. Peterson states, 'As this new public health approach gradually took hold, it shifted attention away from the root premise of sanitary reform – that most infectious disease had its source in the visible environment.'[37] Thus, preventative measures such as isolation, immunization, disinfection, and antitoxins became more important than sanitary reform. Sanitary scientists developed methods of filtration and chlorination of water, allowing polluted water to become purified. Although sanitary reform eventually lost momentum in the face of microorganisms and filtration, the movement sparked valuable innovations in sewerage and city planning as ways of avoiding many of the worst environmental and human health consequences of urbanization during the nineteenth century.

Concern about the spread of disease in urban areas led to many strict measures by medical authorities in the second half of the nineteenth century. Local authorities were often highly pro-active in control measures, but sometimes they ran into difficulties with local cultural traditions. In Saint-Louis, Senegal, the French colonial authorities sought to vaccinate the whole urban population, especially the children, against the disease, but met resistance from large numbers of African slum dwellers who considered western medicine to be harmful and who were persuaded by traditional healers that there were other ways of dealing with smallpox.[38]

OPPORTUNITIES PROVIDED BY FIRE, DISASTERS AND WARS TO RESHAPE AND REDESIGN THE URBAN ENVIRONMENT

Major disasters can create opportunities to redesign and rebuild cities. Sometimes the opportunity is taken. More often it is not, the problem mainly being inertia of land tenure rather than the finances of rebuilding. Planning of large damaged zones assumed that the local authority was powerful enough to expropriate private property wholesale. Even in these cases, however, officials still had to come to terms with the owners in order to prevent them from settling elsewhere.[39] However, one of the greatest risks following a natural disaster or conflict in cities is the ensuing social chaos or breakdown of order. Failed cities, such as parts of New Orleans following Hurricane Katrina in 2005 and Baghdad following the 2003 war in Iraq, can be viewed as socio-ecological systems that, as a result of disaster or conflict coupled with lack of resilience, have 'collapsed into a qualitatively different state that is controlled by a different set of processes'.[40]

Some argue that cultural diversity within a city helps in post-disaster recovery and resilience. However, there are many resilient cities in which cultural diversity was not a factor, including Tangshan China following the 1976 earthquake, Guernica following Franco's collusion with the Germans to bomb this Basque stronghold, and Tokyo following earthquakes, fires, and war. In these cases, either strong governments or private industry played a major role in rebuilding, often with the express purpose of setting a political agenda (such as demonstrating a more open economy following the death of Mao in China, or destroying Basque culture in Guernica). On the other hand, new immigrants have been instrumental in rebuilding North American cities after disaster, including Irish and German immigrants following the 1835 fire in New York City, and Latin American immigrants following civil unrest in the 1990s in Los Angeles.[41] It may equally be argued that people displaced from eastern Germany to the west of the Iron Curtain considerably helped in the post-1945 reconstruction of cities in West Germany.

Fire following earthquake is an extremely variable phenomenon. Losses from such fires can vary from insignificant (as in the 1999 Chichi earthquake, Taiwan) to serious (1995 Kobe earthquake, Japan) to disastrous (1923 Kanto earthquake, Tokyo, Japan). A similar picture emerges from New Zealand where post earthquake fire damage ranges from no reports,[42] to little damage as in the Wairarapa earthquake of 1942, where one house was destroyed by fire and there was minor fire damage to a few others.[43] However, in one other case, the Hawke's Bay earthquake of 1931, there was a major conflagration that destroyed most of the Napier business district.[44]

The 1905 San Francisco earthquake caused fires that raged for three days. Even though building codes were eventually strengthened in the face of public demand, unstable filled land was swiftly reoccupied once the wreckage was cleared even though it would shake when the next earthquake occurred. In fact, more unstable fill was created when the rubble was dumped in a topographic basin on the north side of town.

After the 1666 Great Fire of London, detailed plans by both John Evelyn and Sir Christopher Wren for reconstructing the city with a series of wide streets and piazzas were debated in parliament and at the Royal Court. Parliament reached no conclusion, while the Privy Council, despite the king's enthusiasm, hesitated because of the cost of the whole scheme. As Wren's son wrote, the grand plan was not adopted 'because the Generality of the Citizens and Proprietors insisted on having their Houses rebuilt on their old Foundations, without any deviation'.[45]

In sharp contrast, Finnish authorities expropriated all private land following the 1827 fire in Turku. They auctioned off new sized lots at five times their prior value. One of the consequences of this fire was a full realignment of the parcels of land. The same happened again in Finland after the fire of 1852 in the town of Pori.[46]

After Hamburg's great fire of 1842, city planners and rebuilders were given a free hand to redesign the city, and radically modernize the infrastructure. A new city plan was made and the streets were widened. Most importantly the city acquired Europe's first modern water supply and sewerage system.

Chicago was rapidly rebuilt after the great 1871 fire had swept the ground clean, through a rapid response by land speculators and business owners. The need for office space in a physically circumscribed central district was the pressing problem. The economics of real estate and escalating land values required faster construction that also made possible new construction cheaper. The growth of the steel industry provided material and techniques. The creative intellectual vision of the founders of the Chicago School developed the skyscraper out of these needs and possibilities. However, Americans did learn a practical lesson from the Chicago fire, for shortly thereafter they began to build their cities more carefully.[47] Perhaps the significance for all the USA was the way the Chicago fire became a national media event, covered in detail by newspapers throughout the land. Even the most casual readers could discern in the accounts of the fire almost any lesson that suited them, be it the need for a spiritual revival, the case for scientific planning, the superiority of genteel eastern ways of life, or the unstoppable progress of the West.[48] Greater safety, stronger buildings and a better urban environment thus arose out of Chicago and many other horrific city fires. In Chicago, fire regulations and building codes were greatly tightened, giving rise to the fire proofing systems that were an important prerequisite for building skyscrapers. The opportunity for steel framing to come to the fore arose from the need to rebuild the business district of Chicago.

Rebuilding after the Second World War bombing in the UK

In the 1930s the impact of the great economic depression was strongly felt in the UK. People were looking forward to a better future that was beginning to be expressed in some of the new garden suburbs that were expanding on the edges of many cities. However, the onset of the Second World War brought all that to an end and the Blitz of 1940–1 saw the bombing and destruction of much of the centre of many great cities. Some realized that the pre-war hope for a better future should be strengthened and that rebuilding was an opportunity to create better living conditions and city centres adapted to modern life. A few cities took that opportunity, particularly Plymouth and Coventry. The achievement of the reconstruction goals was not easy.

On 4 July 1941, just four months after the destruction of most of the city centre by bombing in March 1941, Lord Reith, the UK government's reconstruction chief advised Plymouth to 'go ahead, planning boldly and comprehensively, go on with good planning and bank on getting financial help' (i.e. from central government).[49] In May 1941 the city council decided to prepare a Redevelopment Plan, which was completed by September 1943, its basic principles being approved by the council in August 1944. The plan provided for urban neighbourhoods and traffic separation, with fairly self-contained neighbourhood community centres, insulated from arterial roads, with their own schools, libraries, shops, swimming pools and cinemas. Political expediency in this heavily-damaged area led to speedy implementation. On 29 April 1946, a public inquiry into the first compulsory purchase order began. The main opposition came from the Chamber of Commerce and the Order was taken to the Court of Appeal. This was the first such public inquiry in England. On 12 May 1947 the Court of Appeal allowed the Minister of Town and Country Planning to issue a Compulsory Purchase Order approval to Plymouth City Council. Like many of the other plans made in other UK cities for post-war reconstruction, the plan was idealistic and far-sighted. Over time, several changes were made to the plan in the course of implementation, often for reasons of economy. Plymouth moved, in the course of a decade, from the idealism of 'plan boldly' to 'plan modestly' and finally to 'plan for essentials' (from a reviewer of the city's 1950s Development Plan).[50]

Coventry's innovative city architect and planner, Donald Gibson, involved members of the council and the general public in thinking about town planning ideals. Even before the Second World War began he had given councillors copies of Lewis Mumford's the *Culture of Cities*.[51] When the air raid of 14/15 November affected 50,000 of the city's 75,000 rated properties, Gibson responded to the disaster by drawing up a redevelopment plan inspired by Le Corbusier, Mumford, Abercrombie and Tripp, but also by Thomas Sharp's belief that 'good town planning would succeed or fail on the basis of what the buildings looked like – the third dimension'.[52] Gibson's plan for a city 'designed for future health, amenity and the convenience of citizens'[53] had a shopping zone with a series of traffic-free arcades, with galleries overlooking the central precincts. Supported by all but one of the Labour Party councillors in charge of the city, the plan was accepted, but saw external opposition from more traditional elements, partly on the basis of cost and partly from the Chamber of Commerce. Nevertheless, skilful politics by the local council and its officers saw the plan through, although the 150-odd firms formerly located in the area of the new city centre had to be placated. Eventually the implementation of the plan moved slowly, only accelerating once the 1947 Town and Country Planning Act gave the city wider powers to direct development. Budgetary constraints forced the council to make agreements with major retailers to finance some of the initial blocks in the shopping precinct. Overall this slow progress disappointed some citizens, but Coventry emerged with one of the most outstanding city centres of the 1950s. There was no wholesale departure from the Gibson proposals. The council's ability to overcome obstacles was to a large extent the result of its local popularity rather than any response to central government pressure.[54]

Reconstruction of German cities after 1945

Rebuilding of cities in western Germany after the Second World War appeared to visitors from the UK to have proceeded at a rapid rate. Many historic town centres were restored by 1955, while large parts of many British cities were still bomb sites. In Germany, significant intangible legacies from the early twentieth century contributed profoundly to the reconstruction effort.[55] A complex heritage of urban planning concepts and practice was readily tapped; a 20-year old debate on building regulations could be drawn upon; a continuing exchange of views on architectural styles and methods could influence new building; and the many experienced planners, architects, professionals, entrepreneurs, property owners and concerned citizens were able to guide and question the reconstruction process.[56]

The damage to German cities was immense. Masses of people were employed to clear, sort and recycle the great piles of rubble (Table 2.2) created by wartime bombing and shelling. No city was rebuilt as an exact copy of what had been destroyed. Most of the buildings now date from after 1945, many newer buildings having been built behind historic facades. The nature of post-war buildings has to be understood in the context of ideas that existed before Hitler's 12-year long Third Reich. Germany's rapid reconstruction after the disaster of 1939–45 drew heavily on ideas, methods and experience from the first 32 years of the twentieth century.[57] Nonetheless, many praised the post-1945 reconstruction for replacing the worst housing and sanitary facilities that had been left over from the rapid nineteenth century industrial expansion of many German cities.

Table 2.2: Volumes of rubble in leading German cities
at the end of the Second World War (data from Diefendorf, 1993)

City	m³ of rubble
Berlin	55,000,000
Hamburg	35,800,000
Cologne	24,100,000
Dortmund	16,177,100
Essen	14,947,000
Frankfurt am Main	11,700,000
Nuremburg	10,700,000
Dusseldorf	10,000,000
Bremen	7,920,000

Reconstruction of Dresden, Germany, after the Second World War bombing

Dresden, Germany reveals another pattern of reconstruction with attention to some significant historic buildings, but the neglect of others. In the first years after the war, the city centre was cleared of the enormous masses of rubble, with the assistance of tens of thousands of volunteer helpers. In 1949, the Communist German Democratic Republic's Ministry for Reconstruction was given the right of free expropriation of formerly private property. Instability and uncertainty continued to hinder an integrated approach, as the occupying governments pursued divergent recovery policies within their respective sectors and government funding was diverted to war reparations. At the start of the 1950s, reconstruction began with residential and representative buildings in the city centre. However there was a long debate, under the Communist regime, as to how far the historic core should be rebuilt and how far the city should be reformulated with a new order, and new spatial structures reflecting the new socialist society.[58]

The reconstruction of selected architectural monuments was prioritized from the start: the reconstruction of the Swinger was completed in 1964. Further important buildings, such as the Court Church, Johanneum, Albertinum, the Royal Mews and the Semper Opera House, were also restored, though at the same time the valuable remains of other monuments were demolished. In practice, the East Germans were quite architecturally conservative and retained damaged historic buildings where Western planners and developers often seized the opportunities to clear away such inconveniences. Communist East Germany came to make a virtue of conservation. As the newspaper *Neues Deutschland* declared in June 1950: 'We are defending our national heritage against its destruction by imperialist American ideology and against its barbarization by Boogie-Woogie culture.'[59] However, despite certain important successes, subsequent concentration on industrial construction technologies and increasing economic difficulties left the overall rebuilding of the city incomplete and unsatisfactory.

After the unification of Germany in 1989, Dresden once again became the capital of the State of Saxony. Extensive building work since then has transformed the face of the city. The greatest achievement was the accurate reconstruction of the Frauenkirche using the original building materials, and superb craftsmanship, so helping to make Dresden once more one of the most attractive cities in Germany.

The general urban environmental legacies of war and civil conflict

Some cities of great international and historic significance have experienced successive waves of war and civil disturbance. In Beirut, separating the warring factions has been one objective of reconstruction planning. The 'Green Line' between communities was envisaged as a potential open space. Separating potentially troublesome residential areas from the main international business centre was another objective, but this would marginalize the importance of daily journeys to work and social relations of the great bulk of the city's people. Segregation of this type would lead to social disorientation and further heighten existing feelings of alienation.[60]

Another issue for post-war reconstruction is the extent to which the ruins of iconic buildings should be allowed to remain as part of the historic heritage, as Coventry Cathedral and Berlin's Brandenburg Tor have done. In Beirut there seems to be reluctance to do this. These examples seem to show that in many instances, war damage, even if extensive, is but a temporary interruption to city growth. For example, in an analysis of the variation and persistence of Japanese regional population density over the last 8000 years, Davis and Weinstein[61] investigate whether or not the bombing of Japanese cities during the Second World War had a permanent or only a temporary effect on Japanese city growth in the post-Second World War period. They found, at most, a temporary impact on relative city growth in Japan. Japanese cities completely recovered from the war and were back on their pre-war growth path quite soon.

For Germany as a whole the impact of bombing on relative city size has been significant but temporary. This conclusion holds for western German cities taken in isolation, but not for the smaller group of eastern German cities in the former German Democratic Republic (GDR) that was separated from the west in 1949. Here the Second World War and the ensuing establishment of the GDR had a permanent impact on relative city size.[62] Incentives for reconstruction were lacking in East Germany. The state's priority for rapid industrialization used up scarce investment funds. Furthermore, the Communist Party wanted to destroy the remnants of the old Germany, and left the war-struck inner cities to decay.

The switch from a market economy to a planned economy implied that market forces that were possibly relevant for West German city growth, were no longer or at least less relevant for East German city growth after the creation of the GDR. Thus the finding that the Second World War shock had a permanent impact on East German city growth results from not only the war itself but also from East Germany becoming a centrally planned economy after the war.[63] However, overall these observations from Japan and Germany support urban growth theories that predict that large, temporary shocks will have at most a temporary impact. However, the worst shocks with permanent health hazards, such as the Chernobyl nuclear explosion, are always likely to have permanent impacts on future human settlement.

Rebuilding after the atomic bombs in Japan and after nuclear accidents

Reconstruction after the nuclear bombs on Hiroshima and Nagasaki in Japan in 1945 was more rapid, partly because the local flora made a surprisingly rapid recovery from radioactive pollution, but the human costs of the two bombs are still being counted.[64] The mayors of Hiroshima provided important leadership in the reconstruction of the city and its urban forests. They pushed for a comprehensive redevelopment plan that the local residents, often unemployed and without housing, did not fully support. Illegal squatters occupied public open spaces including the Peace Park covering 12.21 ha of land near the centre of Hiroshima, which was a memorial to those killed in the bombing and a statement against the use of nuclear weapons in the future.[65]

In 1954 the then mayor, Shinzo Hamai, asked the mayors of other cities to donate trees to plant in Peace Park. Later in 1957 the succeeding mayor, Tadao Watanabe, persuaded communities neighbouring Hiroshima to donate large trees for the Peace Park and other parks. In this way, the city not only spent considerable political capital in convincing landowners to exchange land for parks and the Peace Boulevard, but also initiated a successful urban greenery movement (Figure 2.1).

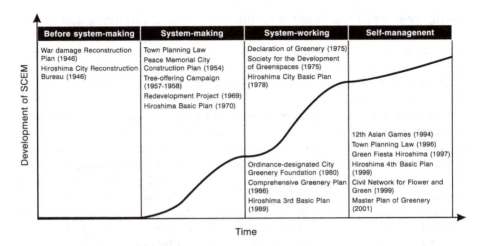

Figure 2.1: Urban planning and green issues in Hiroshima: the process of development of social capacity for environmental management (SCEM) (after Nakagoshi et al., 2006)

On the other hand, following the Chernobyl nuclear accident in Russia, when the radiation released from the plant was roughly equivalent to 1,000 Hiroshima bombs, no reconstruction has occurred and the risks of exposure to radioactivity remain high. Chernobyl remains an indicator of the worst kind of risk that supplying energy to cities can imply and much of why and how the disaster occurred remains unexplained.[66]

Reconstruction of New Orleans after Hurricane Katrina

Over its 300-year history, New Orleans evolved a flood defence system through a series of decisions made over a long period of societal responses to hazard events that led to better protection from relatively frequent events, and increased vulnerability to large, rare events.[67] The levees protecting New Orleans are also what have made it vulnerable by confining the Mississippi River in its channel, removing the flood overbank flows that historically provided the freshwater and sediments that were deposited to offset the city's subsiding soils and maintain the coastal wetland buffers that protect it.[68] This meant that in 2005, Hurricane Katrina's truly catastrophic consequences for New Orleans included the deaths of well over 1,300 people and $40–50 billion in monetary losses.

When Hurricane Katrina struck land 75 km to the south-east of the city on 29 August, 2005, a six metre storm surge caused levee failure and flooding to over 75 per cent of the city.[69] The storm surge pushed up the Industrial

Canal, overtopped the levee protecting the Lower Ninth Ward and caused a 250 m failure of the levee near N. Claiborne Street releasing a torrent of water that pushed residential structures off their foundations and caused catastrophic damage to nearby homes. Water carried 125 buildings onto the roads. Homeowners later voluntarily demolished another 1,000 homes that had heavy structural damage.[70]

Katrina was both a tragedy and an opportunity to improve New Orleans.[71] However, despite many of the poorest people with fewest choices being black, white affluent residents disproportionately returned to the city in the first two years after the hurricane. In the first year only 1,600 Housing Authority of New Orleans (HANO) social housing families had returned to the city, and another 400 units stood ready to be occupied. But HANO had also, by that time, contracted for the demolition of some 4,500 apartments in four remaining large projects. Government officials had determined, quite rightly, that it needed to take the opportunity to give up its policy of concentrating the poor in massive, segregated, and decaying projects in favour of more mixed developments. But these housing blocks did provide a certain comfort level despite the poverty, crime, and other dangers found there.[72] After Mayor Nagin won the 2006 local election, it quickly became apparent how lightly his racial ties bound him. He continued to take counsel from many of the same white developers, businessmen, and civic elites that supported him before the disaster.[73] Although the seven-member New Orleans City Council had become majority black in 1985, the first post-Katrina body to be sworn in had whites outnumbering blacks by a 4:3 margin. It seemed unable to live up to expectations of a quick return to reconstruction and efficient government and to 'fall in the realm of visceral reactions, the application of long-nursed grudges, and the utter inability of leadership to overcome the burden of the past even as unprecedented circumstances demanded it'.[74]

Events in the city council created some of the problems of public trust in government environmental officials in Louisiana. A second area issue was the lack of planning for debris disposal, and the possibility that this may create future public health and environmental injustice sites. Residents trying to clean up and rebuild after the storm, particularly the poor and working class, faced particular difficulties. These were exacerbated during the rebuilding of New Orleans' 20 historic districts, particularly through tensions between local knowledge and the federal response to the disaster.[75] Because levee protection must be funded at the federal level, under-funding has remained a constant threat.[76] The limited protection offered by the current levee system, affects resident confidence, not only about rebuilding, but also over home insurance premiums, which increased dramatically in 2006, by 22 per cent statewide, but by considerably more in coastal and flood hazard parishes.[77] Residents' difficulties of access to recovery capital also critically affected the speed of recovery.

Additional burdens faced by less affluent returning residents of the Lower Ninth Ward included restrictions on entering the Ward, the lack of potable water and electricity until a full 14 months after the storm, which slowed recovery and restricted residents' ability to place the trailer caravans released by the Federal Emergency Management Agency (FEMA) in the Ward.[78] Many residents could not afford to rent accommodation in the temporary housing market. Because much of the flooding in the Lower Ninth Ward was outside the designated FEMA flood zone, many did not have the flood insurance that enabled others to start recovery activities in other parts of New Orleans.[79]

LAGGING RECOVERY FROM DISASTER IN MARGINALIZED SUB-POPULATIONS AND ITS ENVIRONMENTAL CONSEQUENCES

As after both Hurricane Andrew in Florida, and the Loma Prieta and Northridge earthquakes in California,[80] lagging recovery in marginalized sub-populations has significant historical, social and economic components unrelated to the damage. The experience in long-term post-disaster recovery is that often the standard of living for minorities and low income households falls.[81] When all residents do not have equal capacity to begin to rebuild, the act of rebuilding does not measure preferences or plans. Slow recovery in the Ninth Ward may reflect the non-viability of a laissez-faire approach to post-disaster housing recovery, rather than the non-viability of the neighbourhood's housing stock or social fabric.[82]

Hurricane Katrina exposed the tragedy, 'enduring ghettos' and 'crisis' that are endemic in African American social, economic, and political life. Although poor, old, frail and young whites were victimized by the storm, blacks were disproportionately represented among those who died or lived to face the worse ravages of the flooding.[83] Over 40 years before the onset of Katrina, poor and working-class whites vacated the flood-prone Lower Ninth Ward for the suburbs, leaving the area to an African American population with few alternatives for improving their living space within the city. Although the disaster hit predominantly white suburban communities, other outlying white communities escaped the huge loss of life and property that accompanied the storm's arrival in the inner city. Six years on much of the Lower Ninth Ward still appeared half-abandoned, with damaged buildings still not repaired, and vacant lots where others had been demolished.

ENVIRONMENTAL IMPROVEMENTS AS PART OF CHANGING LABOUR RELATIONS; IMPACTS OF INDUSTRY ON THE PUBLIC SAFETY AND HEALTH ASPECTS OF THE URBAN ENVIRONMENT

Every technology entails a particular ecology and has its own set of human and environmental consequences. Often solutions to one problem lead to new problems, either in the same place or elsewhere. Successful technological innovation often requires a change in social organization, particularly in the way people arrange their lives. New organizations may demand different hours of working, different relationships with fellow workers, and exposure to new hazards, some of which even the employer may not be aware of at the time, as was the case with risks from asbestos or to some fumes from hydrocarbons. Accidents and disease are thus an ecological consequence of that industrial organization and process system, no less than soil erosion is a consequence of the economics of agriculture or fishery depletion has its roots in the regulatory structure of fishing. Technology thus shapes the ecology of the workplace in three ways: by posing hazards directly, by shaping the social organization that exposes workers to risk, and by influencing society's awareness of danger to its working population.[84]

Machines of ever-greater complexity thoroughly transformed the ecology of the workplace with the spread of industrialism and the division of labour in the nineteenthth century. The worker came to be no longer individually important, but an abstract factor of production, to be bought at a price determined by impersonal market forces and combined with capital and resources at the will of the entrepreneur. Nineteenth-century writers described the worker's body as a mere appendage to the machine. To Friedrich Engels, in Manchester in 1844,[85] this transformation of the nature of work expressed itself in the poverty, ill-health and workplace injuries of the labouring population.

As technology advanced and sources of energy changed, the hazards that people faced in the workplace altered. Industrial health and safety came into sharper focus with the emphasis on the role of accidents, of unforeseen consequences, and of complex interaction, in history and social life, as well as in the natural world. Re-emphasizing the significance of industrial accidents in urban factories and workplaces reveals the hidden truth that labour is not merely an economic activity, but is also an expression of the worker's life and humanity. Protection against these hazards through working procedures and health and safety regulations is as important for urban life as good sanitation and safe transportation. However, experience with toxic chemicals and radiation since 1950 has shown that a workplace is a biological environment no less than is a national park.

Major accidents involving toxic chemicals do occur. Such critical events often lead to government action to improve regulations that affect the environment. The explosion caused by the failure of a temporary pipe at the Nypro chemical plant at Flixborough, UK, on 1 June 1974, killed 28 workers and a further 36 suffered injuries. The number of casualties would have been more if the incident had occurred on a weekday, as the main office block was not occupied. The incident provided the main impetus for the setting up of an Advisory Committee on Major Hazards. Their first report was published in 1976 and in 1978 the UK Health and Safety Commission issued a Consultative Document on Hazardous Installations (Notification and Survey) Regulations.[86]

The 'Seveso' accident in 1976 at a chemical plant in Seveso, Italy, manufacturing pesticides and herbicides released a dense vapour cloud containing tetrachlorodibenzoparadioxin (TCDD) from a reactor, used for the production of trichlorofenol. Commonly known as dioxin, this was a poisonous and carcinogenic by-product of an uncontrolled exothermic reaction. Although no immediate fatalities were reported, kilogram quantities of the substance, which is lethal to humans even in microgram doses, were widely dispersed which resulted in an immediate contamination of some 20 km^2 of land and vegetation. More than 600 people had to be evacuated from their homes and 2,000 were treated for dioxin poisoning.[87]

The Seveso accident prompted legislation aimed at the prevention and control of such accidents that had been increasing rapidly around the world in the previous 20 years (Figure 2.2). In 1982, the EU issued its first so-called Seveso Directive, which was replaced by a newer version in 1996 and extended further in 2003. The Seveso II Directive applies to some thousands of industrial establishments where dangerous substances are present in quantities exceeding the thresholds in the directive.

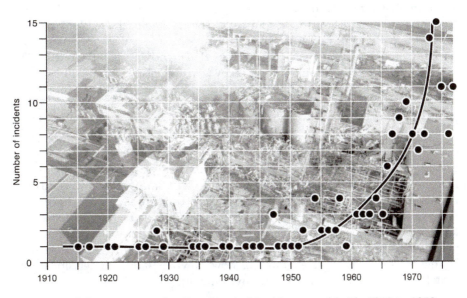

Figure 2.2: Frequency of major chemical incidents worldwide 1910 to 1979
(after Carson and Mumford, 1979)

The Seveso II Directive contains land use planning guidance as a result of the 'lesson learnt' from the 1984 Bhopal, India, leak of methyl isocyanate gas and other chemicals from a large fertilizer plant, that the land-use planning implications of major-accident hazards should be taken into account in the regulatory process. Member states are obliged to pursue the aim of the directive through controls on the siting of new establishments, modifications to existing establishments and new developments such as transport links, locations frequented by the public and residential areas in the vicinity of existing establishments. In the long term, land-use planning policies should ensure that appropriate distances between hazardous establishments and residential areas are maintained.[88]

This does not always follow, however. In November 1986, a fire broke out at the Sandoz chemical plant at Schweizerhalle, near Basel, Switzerland. The water that firefighters used to put out the fire flushed huge amounts of insecticides and pesticides into the River Rhine, triggering an environmental catastrophe. As a consequence, public pressure was put on manufacturers to take tougher action against pollution. In September 2000 a referendum was held on the introduction of a levy on nonrenewable energy and an ecological tax reform. However, a rise in fuel prices prior to the referendum contributed to its defeat. The defeat of the referendum slowed down Switzerland's once-ambitious environmental programme.[89]

It was in the light of industrial accidents after 1999 (the 2001 explosion at Atofina's Grande Paroisse fertilizer plant in Toulouse, France; the 2000 Baia Mare, Romania, cyanide spill; and the 2000 Enschede, Netherlands, fireworks explosion) and studies on carcinogens and substances dangerous for the environment, that the Seveso II Directive was extended. The most important extensions were to cover risks arising from storage and processing activities in mining, from pyrotechnic and explosive substances and from the storage of ammonium nitrate and ammonium nitrate based fertilizers.

This European example shows that managing environmental risks from industrial chemicals requires constant improvement to legislation and even greater attention to the location of plants, in relation to existing urban land uses, and to regulating the use of land surrounding chemical industrial installations. Some hazardous sites are locations where chemicals have been made and stored for decades, or even more than 100 years. Occupation of the land around may have changed over that time, and the materials used, the products manufactured, and the nature of the industrial hazards may have changed. This is another example of how previous land use decisions have long-lasting impacts on the urban environment.

HEALTH BENEFITS AS A CONTINUING FACTOR IN DEBATES ON URBAN ENVIRONMENTAL QUALITY

Despite all the improvements made to public health in cities, there is still much to do as The UK Royal Commission on Environmental Pollution's 26th Report in 2007, which is concerned with the urban environment, says:

> Much more can be done to make health concerns central to the development of new and renewed urban areas and to recognize that the

health of individuals and communities is affected by a range of interacting environmental, social and economic factors.[90]

The Commission also recommends:

That the UK government promotes the concept of exposure reduction for reducing the overall health impacts of outdoor air pollutants and actively pursues such measures in domestic, EU and international policy on air quality.[91]

Conditions in the cities of the United Kingdom are highly variable and much improvement is indeed needed. However, many other cities, especially in the developing world, face even greater problems and challenges. The consequences of the past are still with us and our infrastructure can be highly vulnerable and supply chains are readily disrupted. Just in time delivery may have increased economic efficiency, but it makes systems vulnerable. The neglect of key infrastructure, especially those parts of it that are out of sight and out of mind, brings greater risks and merely delays problems for the future. Past habits of merely moving environmental problems somewhere else also leave significant public health worries, such as those that arise from the dumping of toxic chemicals in inappropriate places. These concerns grow with the increasing size of cities. The overall issue is well expressed by Gandy:

All modern cities face an invisible threat of system failure. Although cities are dependent on elaborate technological networks, the politicization of urban infrastructure has tended to be associated with failure rather than success, whether it be the disease outbreaks of the 19th century or the climate-change-induced flooding of the 21st century. The political history of urban infrastructure has been one of crisis, reconstruction, and neglect, a cycle that becomes ever more worrying in relation to the twin threats of climate change and the denigration of the public realm.[92]

Despite this, cities are currently surviving wars: both Damascus and Kabul were suffering bomb attacks in 2012, but seemed likely to be able to be rebuilt. Epidemics are usually able to be managed in twenty-first-century conditions, even if the numbers who suffer are high. The scenarios that are frightening are those that stem from a combination of threats such as a major earthquake in a war-torn city that causes both fire and epidemics and perhaps also a tsunami. Again the resilience of the local population will be severely tested and their survival may depend on just how much outside help is available.

3

Foods, Goods, Materials and Ornaments

The Metabolism of Cities

Metabolism in the sense used in this chapter is concerned with the material turnover by human society. Prehistoric societies probably required about 6 tonnes per capita (t cap.) of material input annually (t cap^{-1} yr^{-1}), breathed out 5.1 t cap^{-1} yr^{-1} of gas, and had about 0.8 t cap^{-1} yr^{-1} of excreta. Their stock of materials was zero and they produced about 0.1 t cap^{-1} yr^{-1} of solid waste. Modern society on the other hand uses about 89 t cap^{-1} yr^{-1}, emits 19 t cap^{-1} yr^{-1} of gases, and 61 t cap^{-1} yr^{-1} of excreta. Present-day society has a stock of around 260 t cap^{-1} yr^{-1} of materials and creates 3 t cap^{-1} yr^{-1} of solid waste.[1] These great increases in per capita use of materials are largely a product of urbanization, of trade in goods produced by agriculture, mining, fishing, forestry and manufacturing. The driving force is the power of the consumer, the people with the ability to purchase materials and manufactured goods, either for themselves or for the organization for which they work.

The process of urban consumption began with the first traced links between cities and rural producers, but remained at a relatively low level until urban areas began to expand as political power was extended over larger and larger areas. When empires came into being, elite groups were able to enjoy the benefits of trade with distant areas and expressed their power through collections of artifacts and displays of wealth. Sometimes wealth was concentrated by religious organizations, expressed in temples, churches and mosques. Elsewhere it accumulated in palaces, while the majority of the population used scarcely more resources than pre-urban society.

In this chapter, urban metabolism is considered in three ways: 1) in terms of the materials flows and stocks in urban areas; 2) in terms of the sources of goods supplied to cities and the expansion of the trade networks that bring them to the cities, including the growth of the ecological footprint of urban areas; and 3) in terms of the socio-political forces driving urban metabolism and

46

affecting its direction. Subsequent chapters examine the impact of aspects of the processes of metabolism on the urban environment and the many attempts made to cope with them and to mitigate their effects.

THE CONCEPT OF URBAN METABOLISM

The concept of urban metabolism helps us to understand and analyse the way cities use resources, energy and land, all elements of the environmental system, for maintaining and reproducing themselves. Urban systems concentrate economic, reproductive and distributive functions in certain locations, while using and exchanging resources from much larger areas, especially in a global economy context. The way cities and urban areas are built, in spatial and technological terms, greatly influences the quantities and qualities of resources being used in maintaining urban life. The nature of this exchange with the environmental system, the extraction of specific resources and sources of energy as well as the return of waste and exhaust to the environmental system, can be, but need not be, increasingly damaging.

Understanding the nature of urban metabolism in any particular urban settlement involves exploring the interrelated web of social relations that create social differences and inequities and also develop biophysical diversity. It also involves linking urban environmental problems to larger socio-ecological solutions.[2] The modified and people-made flows and stocks of goods and materials in urban settlements are politically and economically mobilized and socially appropriated to produce environments that embody and reflect positions of social power.[3] Urban metabolism is essentially the process by which urban accumulation occurs and discarded urban materials are recycled or returned to the external environment. It is the product of food supply chains, trade, warfare and plunder, leading to accumulation of materials by wealthy elite and powerful organizations and individuals through the efforts of working people. The task of this chapter is to analyse how the complexity of urban metabolism has arisen, how cities have sought goods and materials from wider and wider areas, to such an extent that the citizens of some cities need a land area tens, even hundreds, of times the size of the space occupied by their city to supply all their needs. This 'urban footprint' is a highly approximate indicator of the pressure of a city on the rest of the planetary environment.

In the environmental sociology of urbanization, the concept of metabolism is central.[4] A city is a concentrator of resources and a generator of residues.[5] The concept of metabolism emphasizes the idea that material and energy are consumed by cities and cities are embedded in larger ecosystems. Isolated communities rely on local natural resources. Modern urban growth is positively associated with 'the dispersion of the objects of consumption'[6] and bringing supplies into built-up areas from neighbouring and more distant producers. An international cross-national analysis showed that urbanization is positively associated with meat consumption and negatively associated with fish consumption. However, within the United States, no statistically significant association was found between urban location and total meat consumption, perhaps because people living in rural areas tend largely to live urban lifestyles and consume food and goods like their urban counterparts. Rural–urban differences are much greater in other parts of the world. All modern urban areas have an ecological footprint larger than the built-up area representing their boundaries.[7] Even in cities where urban agriculture is well developed, such as some in Africa, locally grown food meets only a third, at most, of the urban food requirements.

THE EARLY STAGES OF THE EXPANSION OF URBAN METABOLISM

As cities have increased in size and complexity they have increasingly needed to access their hinterlands (near and far) to meet the needs of their metabolism. Their very survival therefore depends on the continuing effectiveness and integrity of these support systems, which are stressed if not overwhelmed by these demands.[8] The Early Bronze Age (third millennium BC) cities along the Euphrates Valley (modern Turkey, Syria and Iraq) illustrate this point. The cities in the portion of the Euphrates closest to the sea grew to a much greater size, the centre of Early Bronze Age Uruk covering some 400 ha, than those of the middle Euphrates, where Sweyhat covered 40 ha,[9] partly because they had access to a wider area of potential suppliers of food and materials. The irrigation systems of southern Mesopotamia permitted higher and more reliable crop yields. Boat transport on the river could bring bulk quantities of food and other materials right up to the cities. Further upstream, in what is now northern Syria, conditions were harsher. Crop yields from dry farming were lower and less reliable due to a variable rainfall regime. The local terrain limited the extent of dry farming.[10] Hunting of wild animals and expansion of cultivation and grazing all reached a maximum when the local population was greatest. This suggests that at that time all available productive habitats were being exploited to the greatest possible extent.[11] Possibly, the demands on the ecosystems became too great. Shortly after Sweyhat reached its maximum urban extent, it underwent some form of collapse, resulting in contraction of the settlement, the cessation of occupation of public buildings and fortifications, and a loss of population.[12]

In the lower Euphrates and Mesopotamia generally, the larger cities built up powerful trading relations. Allegedly unequal,[13] these transactions involved imports of metals, timber, ivory, pearls, conch shells and beads from places to the north-east, as far away as Iran and beyond. From localities around the Persian Gulf, such as Dilmun and Magan, and even as far away as Meluhha, near the mouth of the Indus, dates, timber, copper, ivory, lapis lazuli, and metals came by ship to ports at the mouths of the Tigris and Euphrates (Figure 3.1). The main exports were grains such as barley, wool, textiles and manufactured goods.

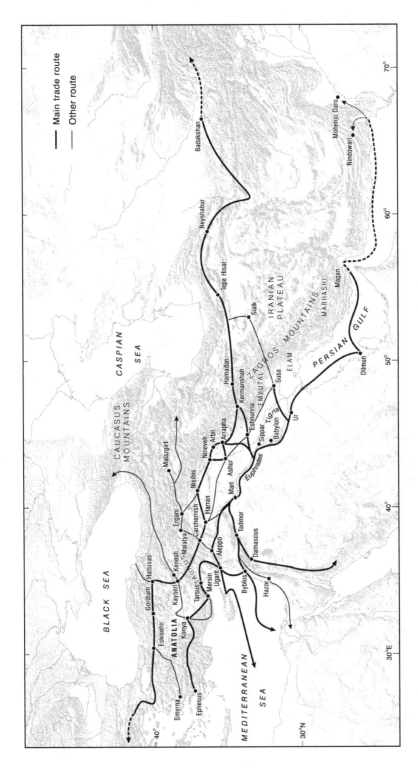

Figure 3.1: Major trading routes linking Mesopotamia to the east and to the Mediterranean (after Hunt, 2004)

The Indus Valley Bronze Age cities of Harappa and Mohenjo-Daro had similar trading relationships extending into Baluchistan, Afghanistan, Iran, central Asia, peninsular India and the Persian Gulf and southern Mesopotamia. Gold, silver, lead, copper, tin and semi-precious stones were acquired through trading posts the Harappans established in outlying areas to facilitate the movement of goods and materials.[14] Timber was gathered from as far away as Gujarat and the foothills of the Himalayas, but in addition to local use, it was also exported to Mesopotamia. The Indus delta to Tigris–Euphrates delta trade route became more important than the central Asian land route in the third millennium BC, but began to decline towards the middle of the second millennium BC.

These cities were supported by an elaborate local irrigated agricultural system on the alluvial soils of the Indus Valley. Local sources of the basic food needs were also influenced by the exploitation of clays, gravels and rock for the construction materials needed for the expansion of the elaborate and well-designed cities that had some of the finest street layouts and drainage systems of any urban areas of their epoch. Their urban metabolism was thus dependent on local sources for daily essential needs and more distant sources for the luxury goods used by the elite for ornaments and decoration.

In Crete, the human transformation of the landscape, which began in the seventh millennium BC, accelerated with the growth of Knossos from the fourth millennium. The city was small, but had considerable storage capacity for nearly 250,000 litres of olive oil and much grain. The plains of Messara had sufficient land to provide for the whole island population of about 250,000, but soil erosion occurred and declines in yield could have become a problem.[15]

Conquests by the Athenians in the fifth century BC brought new luxury goods to the city. Carpets and cushions came from Carthage, fish from the Hellespont and figs from Rhodes.[16] By the fourth century BC, the urban metabolism of Athens depended considerably on the mining of silver and the export of olive oil.[17] Silver mines were owned by the state but worked, using slaves, by private individuals through a system of leases. Olive oil and silver exports paid for the import of wheat from Egypt and the Crimea. Olive trees did not grow to the north of the Black Sea, but the area sent hides to Athens where leather goods were made.[18]

URBAN METABOLISM IN THE ROMAN EMPIRE

Cities and towns have always depended on the surrounding countryside for food and materials. The inhabitants of ancient cities farmed land outside the city, or were closely involved with agriculture. In Roman Britain there were farms or 'suburban' villas directly adjacent to the city, where many advantages of both town and country were obtained. With the cost of transport high, land for horticulture and pasture also was a valuable asset for a city to have in its immediate neighbourhood, to supply it with vegetables, fruit and other produce for the table. Many cities would have had vegetable gardens within their walls.[19]

In the ancient world, probably only Rome, Constantinople, Alexandria and one or two others were large enough cities to have a life largely divorced from the countryside. Both Rome and Constantinople had a state-organized, free or heavily subsidized, food supply that allowed their urban proletariats to exist without being supported by work on the land but by the employment now given in cities by modern industry.[20] Supplying the million inhabitants of ancient Rome with food involved a complex trading system that extended far beyond the city and across the Mediterranean Sea into North Africa. Rome was a vast and wealthy market. In the provinces, previously largely devoted to subsistence farming producing only a small surplus for trading, many landowners were encouraged to change the ways in which they managed their farms, to concentrate on producing goods that were in demand in Rome.[21] In Rome, a million people required at least 150,000 tonnes of grain annually. The amount actually imported was probably greater than that. Equally vast quantities of staples like wine, oil, vegetables and fruit were needed, along with more luxurious foodstuffs like meat and spices, and wood for fuel and building work, marble and innumerable other commodities.

Egypt, Libya and Tunisia in North Africa were major sources of grain for Rome, shipping cereals directly to Ostia, the official port of Rome. Within Rome, about 275,000 male citizens received free grain. Yet sometimes supplies were disrupted and food riots occurred in Rome. Thus penalties for disruption of the most direct grain supply routes included deportation or execution. Once delivered to Ostia, the grain was weighed, checked for quality, and then sent up the Tiber River on barges to Rome, where it would be repacked for distribution throughout the empire.

While the production and transportation of foods dominated the trading industry, there was also a vast exchange of other goods from all parts of Europe, Asia, and Africa. The prosperity of the empire and many of its citizens generated a need for luxurious and exotic imports. Silks from China and the Far East, cotton and spices from India, ivory and wild animals from Africa, vast amounts of mined metals from Spain and Britain, fossilized amber gems from Germany and slaves from all over the world were all part of the urban metabolism of ancient Rome. Romans thrived off of its imports, and importers were among the wealthiest citizens of the empire.[22] The overall metabolism of Rome had impacts not only on the distant provinces, but also on the countryside of Italy. Scholars argue as to whether Rome took supplies from wherever they were easiest to obtain and failed to stimulate local producers or whether the growth of sophisticated urban tastes gave local farmers around Rome and throughout the peninsula, new opportunities for crop production and trade.

Ancient Rome is an exception to these historic limits. With a population that rose to almost one million, Rome was only able to maintain its system through continual colonization. The population would have been unable to maintain itself without the vast supply of slave labour, intensive agricultural techniques, grandiose irrigation and water works, and the imperial armies. In other words, the entire known world had to be subjugated in order to overcome the natural limits imposed by Rome's agricultural energy base. When Rome initiated its urban expansion, it started a battle that was lost even before it began. The continual expansion of the city required increasing quantities of energy; the disorder that ensued was directly proportional to the quantity of energy absorbed, the institutional infrastructure set up to deal with this grew larger and larger and this process became unsustainable. The energy supply given to the army became so small that the military ended up by absorbing more energy than it delivered to the city. The intensive exploitation of the land resulted in a reversal of the agricultural system and it became too expensive to keep slaves. The bureaucracy could not be sustained because its disproportionate growth imposed very high running costs. The over-stretched city fell in ruins and, after it was captured, it returned to an ecological equilibrium with its energy supply.[23] After its fall, Rome counted a mere 30,000 inhabitants.

URBAN METABOLISM IN EARLY CHINESE CITIES

Rome is not the only city whose metabolism has been criticized for draining the life-blood of the countryside.[24] In the third century AD the Chinese city of Chengdu was using timber from forests up to 300 km away.[25] The surroundings of the city were an immense garden sustained by the diversion of water from the Min River into irrigation channels across the Sichuan plain. Chengdu was also a 'commercial suction pump that drew goods from a wide hinterland'.[26]

In the eleventh century, K'ai-feng, now in east-central Henan province, central China, then the capital of the Northern Sung, had around a million inhabitants. As the imperial capital, it housed the court with the emperor's extended family and well over a thousand servants and retainers.[27] Together with the army and the imperial officials and their families, this all amounted to many tens of thousands of people to be supported by the labour of others, both in the city and the surrounding countryside. Although the rice supplies and other food requirements of the imperial court came in the form of tithes and taxes, there was in the urban hierarchy a growing interest in agricultural technology including improvement to irrigation and the production of padi rice.

TRADE AND URBAN METABOLISM IN MEDIAEVAL EUROPE

In mediaeval Europe the greatest cities thrived on trade. For basic foodstuffs, such as grain and meat, the suppliers sending goods to the cities needed to have easy access to the sea or the banks of navigable rivers. In France, Picardy and the adjacent Vermandois exported grain to Flanders by the Scheldt and to Paris by the Oise, while Champagne and the nearby Barrois sent

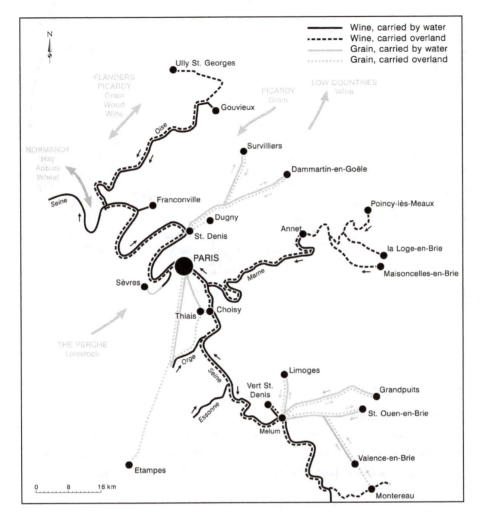

Figure 3.2: Sources and routes of supplies to Paris illustrating the role of navigable waterways (after Braudel, 1988)

grain via Vitry-le-François down the Marne to Paris.[28] Other commodities came to Paris from neighbouring regions, by horse, by cart and by river. Grain and wine came from the surrounding countryside, both by barge and by horse cart (Figure 3.2).

At this time, the metabolism of Paris drove environmental change within and beyond the Paris basin. Supplies of water and building materials came from immediately beyond the city walls, but as the urban area expanded, the sources reached further and further afield. Aqueducts were built 20 m below ground to deliver water when the River Seine often dried up in summer.

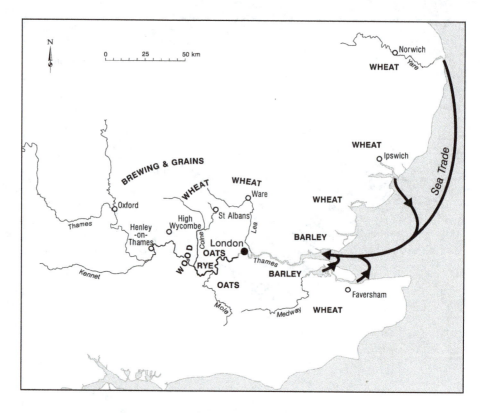

Figure 3.3: Areas supplying grains and wood to the London Market in the 14th century. Fruit and vegetables were grown immediately adjacent to the city. The towns named were major centres for the purchasing of grain by corn merchants (based in part on data in Galloway and Murphy, 1991)

Construction material for Paris originally came from places close to the mediaeval city. Until the fourteenth century, limestone was quarried on the Left Bank from Place d'Italie to Vaurigard. Sands and gravels came from Bercy, Porte d'Italie, Grenelle, Billancourt, and Cergy. Later sources of limestone were Sevres, Saint Cloud, Calmart, Bagneux, Ivry, Charenton, St. Maurice, and L'Île Ceam. The modern sources of limestone are Saint-Leu-d'Esserent, Saint-Maximin, St. Vaast-less-Mello, while sand and gravel now come from the Seine Valley between Juvisy and Paris and from Villneuve-la Garenne, Gennevilliers.

Mediaeval London's metabolism took dairy and perishable horticultural products from the farmland closest to the city, followed by fuel produced from the woods of Middlesex, while arable and pastureland products came from further away. The presence of the London market encouraged specialization in wheat production on suitable soils.[29] Grain for London was carried overland from places up to around 35 km away, but water transport enabled it to be carried up to 100 km (Figure 3.3). By the late thirteenth century the woodlands around London were carefully managed, some manors specializing in fuel supply. Straw, animal fodder, wood, charcoal and coal were all used as fuel. Approximately 22 per cent of the fuel was used for baking and brewing. Coal was coming to London in the thirteenth century, primarily for use in limekilns.[30]

THE GLOBAL TRADING SYSTEMS AND URBAN GROWTH IN THE SIXTEENTH TO EIGHTEENTH CENTURIES

Trade already brought goods from distant shores prior to 1500. In the following two centuries, the ecological footprint of Paris grew rapidly. Not only were there the supplies of food from within France, such as butter from Normandy, cheese from Brie, Normandy, Auvergne, Touraine and Picardy, but cod was brought in from the eastern Atlantic and Channel fisheries through Dieppe, Honfleur and Le Havre.

However the European voyages to the Americas in the sixteenth century brought new products to the towns and cities of Europe. Coffee was introduced to Paris in 1643, with famous cafés such as the Café de la Régence (1681) and the Café Procope (1686) being established 40 years later.[31] The first coffee house in London in St. Michael's Alley off Cornhill opened in 1652, followed by a second in 1655.[32] In 1700 there were 1000 of them in London.[33] By 1716, coffee was being planted on La Réunion and later in Cayenne (1722) and Martinique (1723–30). By the eighteenth century, increasing amounts of sugar from the West Indies (Martinique, Guadeloupe, Jamaica and Santo Domingo) reached France. By 1788 consumption of sugar in Paris was around 5 kg per capita per year (it fell to 3.62 kg by 1846).[34] Around 1707 almost 70,000 cattle were being sold annually in the Paris markets, with long distance supplies from eastern Europe supplementing local and regional trade.[35]

Paris had huge demands for energy, mainly from burning wood. After 1549, logs were floated down the Cure and Yonne tributaries of the Seine. In the sixteenth century charcoal was brought to Paris from the forest of Othe, some 250 km to the north-east. By the eighteenth century it came on carts, packhorses and boats from all available forests. Demand grew such that in 1789 some 2 million tonnes of wood and charcoal were consumed in Paris, a per capita consumption of two tonnes per year.[36] The demands of Paris drove a transformation of the countryside as the urban population grew.

By the end of the eighteenth century, many British walled towns still had gardens within the walls, as the 1801 maps of Chester and Colchester show.[37] Immediately beyond the walls, much of the area was closely cultivated for horticulture or cereal crops. However, the trade of the manufacturing towns had greatly expanded. By the end of the sixteenth century Manchester was sending specialized woollen goods to France, Spain and Portugal. With the expansion of the market, raw materials were brought from Cumbria, the Midlands and Ireland.[38]

In the early seventeenth century the Manchester textile trade entered a new phase. Wool weaving declined being replaced by the manufacture of small wares where the warp was of linen yarn, but the weft of worsted (often called fustian), for which cotton was substituted later in the century.[39] Raw cotton was imported from eastern Mediterranean countries, such as Syria and Egypt. Importing raw materials required improved transport. By 1730 the Mersey and Irwell were made navigable up to the centre of Manchester. Roads leading to neighbouring towns and into Yorkshire were turnpiked in the following 30 years. The opening of the Bridgewater canal in 1764 made it possible to bring in coal much more cheaply, but it was the extension to Runcorn on the Mersey estuary that enabled West Indian and American cotton to be easily imported.[40] These improvements enabled Manchester to expand its ecological footprint as the industrial revolution advanced. The canalized rivers allowed iron ore and metals to be brought to the new foundries and blast furnaces where the steam engines for the mills were built.

THE NINETEENTH CENTURY BEGINNING OF MASS CONSUMERISM THROUGH THE EXPANSION OF THE GLOBAL MIDDLE CLASS

In Britain, the industrial revolution saw an increase in the number of doctors, chemists, engineers and other professionals. Trade and commerce gave rise to an increase in merchants and retailers. In 1797, the reformer William Wilberforce chided the 'upper and middle classes' for their lack of concern for Christianity.[41] This recognition of a tripartite society acknowledged that there was an important social group between the nobility and the poor. Already buying homes in the prosperous streets of Georgian houses of London, Bath, Edinburgh and other cities, the middle class became politically significant when the 1832 Electoral Reform Act gave men with property with a rateable value of ten pounds the vote.[42] The new middle-class voters included the people controlling the development of the country's wealth through manufacturing and commerce. Their new purchasing power altered the consumption patterns in towns and cities. Consumption is one of the key cultural dynamics of middle-class life. How class formations relate to goods, and how goods are imbued with social meanings, have been recurring themes in social theories of class from Marx and Weber onward.[43] The same happened in all the countries benefiting from the new industrial technology and the manufacturing and wealth creation that it facilitated.

In the nineteenth century, rising personal incomes and an expanding array of consumer goods, displayed in attractive downtown shops, produced striking changes in the habits and lifestyles of many urban Americans, leading to 'a revolution of expectations regarding luxuries and comforts'.[44] Around 1850, some New York people forthrightly lived an extravagant life, ignoring their ancestors' firm belief in the virtue of plain living. During the second half of the nineteenth century in the United States and western Europe the definitive formation of the present-day consumer society occurred. Although the seeds of commercialization were sown at the end of the eighteenth century, the national and international markets for mass-produced consumer goods only emerged 100 years later. Demographic factors, particularly the rapid growth of cities, innovations in the production process, rising wages and improved means of transport, particularly railways, made the advent of the mass market possible.[45]

In 1846 the first floor of Alexander Stewart's 'marble Dry Goods Palace' opened on Broadway, with the full store opening two years later and becoming 'the place to be' in New York.[46] In Chicago, Potter Palmer copied Stewart's idea in opening a dry goods store in 1852. That store was taken over by Marshall Field and Levi Leiter in 1865. Rowland Macy opened a small store in New York in 1858 which rapidly expanded into a flourishing department store. Later, John Wanamaker opened a 'new kind of store' in Philadelphia in 1877, and then took over the defaulting Stewart business in New York in 1896.[47]

Department stores came to Paris a little later, the first building specifically designed as a department store being 'Au Coin de la Rue' opened in 1864 but closed in 1880. However, others followed rapidly from 1867 onwards. Eventually by 1890–1914, Toulouse, Bordeaux, Lyon and Le Havre all had their *grands magasins* housed in impressive buildings. Britain and Germany developed their big stores later around the turn of the century. These were the 'temples of consumption' of their day, the day out destinations equivalent to the out-of-town megamalls of the end of the twentieth century. In terms of urban metabolism, they reflected an upsurge of per capita middle-class consumption, vastly increasing the size of the per capita ecological footprint, and enhancing global sourcing of supplies by the more affluent people of wealthy countries. This was paralleled by a great increase in urban infrastructure, transport development and energy consumption, particularly of coal, with its consequent local and global atmospheric impacts.

In London, one aspect of the growth of the middle class and the change of the relationship between home and workplace, made possible by railways, was the great expansion of restaurants in the second half of the nineteenth century. The Café Royal opened its doors in 1865 and the Criterion restaurant in 1874.[48] Women began to use restaurants, with lunch in town becoming a key part of a weekday shopping trip. The new demands of the expanding middle class were superimposed on the huge demand for construction materials, basic foods and clothing to house, feed and clothe the expanding urban populations of London and the industrial towns and cities of Britain. Further construction materials were needed for the dams, water works, sewage systems and wastewater treatment plants to deal with the public health systems to maintain the urban water and drainage works. Coupled to this were the enormous earthworks needed for the new railways, their stations and infrastructure. Thus all cities enjoyed a great increase in their per capita materials flows. Nevertheless many retained and expanded systems of resource recycling that had begun centuries earlier.

Environmental consequences of nineteenth-century urban metabolism

The manufacturing industries of Manchester caused many environmental problems, particularly in terms of the waste discharged into rivers. However, there was considerable re-use of urban raw materials, from the 'night soil' exported by canal and railway to the moss lands to the west of the city, to the re-use of waste fibres from textile manufacturing. The sales value of a cotton mill's waste often represented the difference between a profit and a loss for the mill. There were at least 30 types of waste and each could be sold for further use. It was almost essential for every mill to have an outlet for its waste and many secondary industries had a symbiotic relationship with the spinning and weaving mills.[49]

By the nineteenth century Paris had developed an internal recycling of materials that kept a large population occupied in collecting, processing and re-using urban by-products. These urban raw materials alone enabled Paris's newly established industries to expand and to meet demands from its dense and rapidly growing population. One example was the trade in rags of vegetable origin, for unless men and women clothed themselves, unless used cloth existed, paper could not be produced. Paper making created a huge demand for rags: 1.5 kg of rags was needed to make 1 kg of paper. Mechanization of paper making led to the reorganization of the rag trade.[50]

Bones formed 20 per cent of animal wastes and had many uses in fancy goods, gelatine, glue, and phosphorous-match making. Bone charcoal was used to process sugar beet during the Napoleonic Wars. It was later used in refining cane sugar from the French colonies, with the manufacture of 1 kg of sugar requiring 1 kg of charcoal. Rags and bones were collected together by the 'rag and bone' men who were still walking the streets of European cities until the 1950s. Woollen rags were used in agriculture.[51]

Coupled with this was the peri-urban agriculture that depended on urban organic waste as a fertilizer. In the 1820s, Paris was a rich source of human wastes that were converted to compost, or dried or pulverized and taken out of the city to nearby farms. Waste collection relied on residents sorting material and putting it out for collection. Compost making took too long to deal with the volumes of waste available.[52]

By the late nineteenth century, sewage sludge was fertilizing 17,000 of the 28,000 ha of farmland in the Departement of Seine around Paris. This use of urban waste had become insignificant before 1930 and by 1952 there were only 7,000 ha of agricultural land left in the Seine Departement. Similarly rags gradually declined in importance as a raw material for paper making, their use becoming confined to the highest quality papers.

THE TWENTIETH-CENTURY EXPLOSION OF MATERIAL FLOWS AND ENVIRONMENTAL IMPACTS

In the twentieth century, the European metropolis became the classic example of the consumer city, its huge population supported by the surplus production of the rest of the country.[53] Throughout the century the mass of material consumed per capita in highly urbanized countries grew (Figure 3.4). New technologies and new machinery set up demands for new materials, such as the rare earths used in making IT equipment. Above all the enormous expansion in the number of motor vehicles transformed the urban environment. Once a country moves into the stage of modernized road transport, its consumption of basic infrastructure materials like concrete expands exponentially.

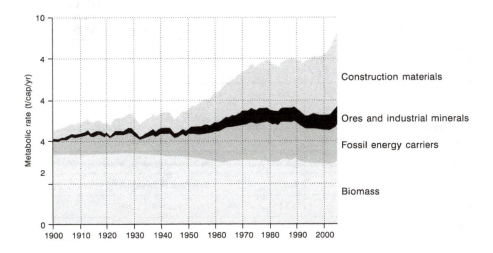

Figure 3.4: Growth in global consumption as indicated by the metabolic rate (materials use in t/cap/year) 1900–2005 (after Krausmann et al., 2009)

The consequence of this exponential upsurge in urban metabolism is that cities became material hot spots containing more hazardous materials than most hazardous landfills. Huge stocks of plastic material now exist in cities. At the end of the century about 500,000 tonnes of fuel oil equivalent in plastic materials was being dumped in Austrian landfills every year.[54] About 50,000 tonnes of packaging plastics were being recycled at an extremely high cost. In 1987 most chlorofluorocarbons (CFCs), which were then being widely used as refrigerants, propellants (in aerosol applications), and solvents, were banned by the Montreal Protocol.

Table 3.1: Estimates of urban ecological footprints
of cities of varying size around the world

Country	City	Ecological footprint ha cap⁻¹	Source
Canada	Calgary	11.0	Wilson, 2001
Canada	Edmonton	10.4	Wilson, 2001i
USA	Sonoma County	8.90	http://www.sustainablesonoma.org/quotes.html
UK	Belfast	8.59	Walsh et al., 2006
USA	Santa Monica	8.46	http://www.smgov.net/Departments/OSE/Categories/SustainabilitySustainable_City_Progress_Report/Resource_Conservation/Ecological_Footprint.aspx
Australia	Woolahra, Sydney	8.31	Lenzen and Murray, 2003
Australia	Waverley, Sydney	7.97	Lenzen and Murray, 2003
Australia	Aurora eco-development	7.03	www.epa.vic.gov.au/ecologicalfootprint/casestudies/aurora.asp
Australia	Randwick	6.95	Lenzen and Murray, 2003
UK	York	6.79	Best Foot Forward, 2002
UK	London	6.63	Best Foot Forward, 2002
UK	Winchester	6.52	Calcott and Bull, 2007
Netherlands	The Hague	6.36	Best Foot Forward, 2002
Ireland	Limerick	6.32	Walsh et al., 2006
UK	Liverpool	5.47 4.15	Best Foot Forward, 2002 Barrett and Scott, 2001
Norway	Oslo	5.44	Best Foot Forward, 2002
Singapore	Singapore	5.3	http://www.wildsingapore.com/vol/footprint.htm
UK	Birmingham	5.22	Calcott and Bull, 2007
China	Hong Kong	4.86	Kou et al., 2006
Germany	Berlin	4.06	Pacholsky, 2003
Finland	Helsinki	3.45	Hakanen, 1999
Chile	Santiago de Chile	3.52	Best Foot Forward, 2002
China	Shanghai	3.42	Kou et al., 2006
UK	Salisbury	5.01	Calcott and Bull, 2007

Table 3.1: (continued)

China	Beijing	3.07	Kou et al., 2006
China	Tianjin	2.96	Kou et al., 2006
China	Guangzhou	2.5	Guo et al., 2005
China	Qingdao	2.26	Kou et al., 2006
China	Shenyang	2.04	Kou et al., 2006
China	Shenzhen	2.02	Kou et al., 2006
China	Chongqing	1.31	Kou et al., 2006
China	Xi'an	1.07	Kou et al., 2006
India	Delhi slum dweller	0.8	http://www.hardnewsmedia.com/2006/11/652

However, by then huge stocks of CFCs had accumulated in cities. The largest component of the stock was made up of building insulating materials. Other foams, coolants and fire extinguishing agents accounted for about half the CFC stock and household refrigerators for less than 3 per cent.[55] If these stocks were not properly disposed of when they were finished with, for example when they were removed during building demolition, extension or reconstruction operations, the degradation of the ozone layer would still continue. This type of legacy within the urban materials stock poses problems for future generations.

While the European city was the classic metropolis, towards the end of the century the modern megacities of Asia and Latin America emerged. In these rapidly changing cities, and throughout the urban communities of Africa, Asia and Latin America, the growing middle-class consumption is less about *having* or *possession* than it is about *being* and *belonging*.[56] For example, Kathmandu's emerging middle class is itself a response to, and active purveyor of, a now globalized capitalist market and commodity regime. Members of Kathmandu's middle class are precisely those who have hitched their local sociocultural lives to an ever growing world of goods.[57]

THE TWENTY-FIRST CENTURY OPPORTUNITY TO DECOUPLE GROWTH FROM MATERIALS AND ENERGY CONSUMPTION

The material throughput of a modern city is about an order of magnitude larger than that in an ancient city of the same size.[58] Houston, Texas, is a global city that has articulated a model of the growth machine in the service of the world oil industry, also encouraging mass consumption and suburban sprawl. On the other hand, Havana, Cuba, is a global city struggling to articulate a radical approach to the urban socio-ecological metabolism, in the form of community gardening and urban agriculture.[59] At the beginning of the twenty-first century, international activity was encouraging all cities to improve their environmental performance. In 2004, the OECD asked member countries to improve information and knowledge on material flows and resource productivity and to develop common methodologies and measurement systems, with emphasis on areas in which comparable and practicable indicators can be defined. In early 2008, the OECD's second *Recommendation on Resource Productivity* recommended member countries to develop analysis of material flows and their environmental impacts and policies concerning the improvement of resource productivity.[60] The EC Thematic Strategy on Urban Environment was launched in 2006. The Chinese Law on Promoting Circular Economy early in 2009 defines the circular economy as 'reducing, reusing and recycling activities conducted in the whole process of production and consumption'.[61]

Among the many techniques used to quantify the resource flows involved in urban metabolism, the ecological footprint[62] provides a vivid expression of how much pressure each person in a given city or country puts on the global environment. Although there are some variations in the precise methodology used and the allowance made for double counting through the multiple uses of some resources, the per capita ecological footprint shows the range of variation between cities, not only across the globe, but within a single country (Table 3.1).

At the global and national scales, the decoupling of resource input from growth in GDP is apparent. Industrialized economies have the lowest material intensities (or highest eco-efficiency), with Western Europe being world-leader with around 1 tonne per 1,000 US$ GDP in the 1980s and improving to 0.6 tonnes by 2000. Although North America has high levels of per capita resource extraction, material intensity is still low and declining.[63] However, it is not clear whether these trends apply in cities, as much manufacturing now takes place outside cities and, in many cases, in a different country from the city being studied.

Analyses of changes in urban metabolism from around 1980 to about 2005 reveal interesting contrasts. In Budapest, Hungary, the changing political scene is reflected in resource efficiency. The period from 1955 to 1980, was the extensive socialist development phase of the metropolis, during which energy, water and food consumption all increased significantly. The next period, from 1980 to 1990 was the pre-transition period characterized by temporary stagnation of resource use (Figure 3.5 A). After 1990 a robust improvement in resource efficiency can be explained by notable decrease of population, transformation of the consumption patterns of the city, and more use of the 'user pays' principle.[64]

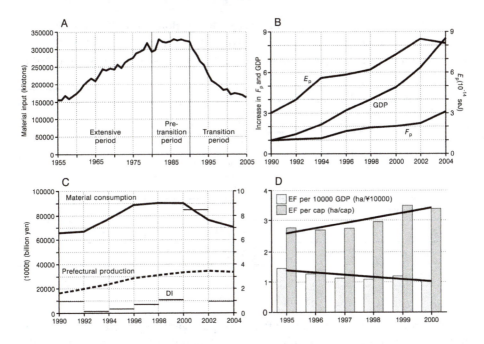

Figure 3.5: Illustrations of increased resource use efficiency and decoupling materials use from GDP: (A) Material input into the Hungarian economy 1955–2005 demonstrating increasing resource use efficiency (Pomazi and Szabo, 2008); (B) Beijing: indicators of increased resource use efficiency: both resource efficiency (Ep) and metabolic flux(Fp) increasing less rapidly than GDP after 1996 (Zhang et al., 2009); (C) Aichi Prefecture, Japan: decoupling of material consumption from prefectural production after 1996 (Tachibanaa et al., 2008); (D) Guangzhou: resource use per unit GDP decreasing after 1995, while per capita efficiency increases (Guo et al., 2005)

Hong Kong, the subject of one of the earliest studies of urban metabolism, provides a comparison between urban metabolism in 1971 and 1997. Population grew from nearly 4 million to 7 million in the period. By 1997, net material resources input into Hong Kong was 46.5 million tonnes (Mt), or 7,027 kg cap^{-1}. Per capita food supply in 1997 was 1.86 kg day^{-1} (679 kg yr^{-1}, or about 3,200 kcal cap^{-1} day^{-1}), a rise of 20 per cent from 1.55 kg day^{-1} in 1971. Since 1971, per capita consumption had risen for meat (+ 68 per cent), fruit (+ 53 per cent), sugar (+ 128 per cent), alcoholic beverages (+ 56 per cent) and milk (+ 142 per cent), but consumption of cereals (– 24 per cent) and vegetables (– 32 per cent) fell.[65] Between 1971 and 1997 all material resource inputs per capita increased (Table 3.2). There was no sign of decoupling energy use from the rate of growth, even though some manufacturing companies had adopted much leaner forms of production.[66]

Table 3.2: Trends in per capita materials flows in Hong Kong 1971 and 1997 (Note Hong Kong's population increased from 3.94 million at the end of 1971 to 6.62 million at the end of 1997) (based on data in Warren-Rhodes and Koenig, 2001)

Type of material	1971 kg cap^{-1} yr^{-1}	1997 kg cap^{-1} yr^{-1}	per cent change
Food	570	680	+20
Fossil fuel	1000	2000	+100
Construction materials	1000	3800	+280
Other goods	250	530	+112
Total solid waste	762	2086	+174
Sewage	73115	102311	+40
CO$_2$ emissions	2285	4776	+119
Air pollutants	65	50	-23

In Toronto, Canada, urban metabolic inputs generally increased at higher rates than outputs between 1987 and 1999. Inputs of water and electricity increased marginally less than the rate of population growth (25.6 per cent), while estimated inputs for food and gasoline increased by marginally greater percentages than the population. With the exception of CO$_2$ emissions, the measured output parameters grew more slowly than the population; residential solid wastes and wastewater loadings decreased in absolute terms over the 12 year period from 1987 to 1999.[67] This indicates a slight trend to greater environmental efficiency, particularly in terms of waste management, which reflects changes in the local government policies for recycling and waste disposal.[68]

In Limerick, Ireland, although total material consumption and waste production increased between 1996 and 2002, metabolic inefficiency decreased by 31 per cent from 0.13 in 1996 to 0.09 in 2002.[69] The overall reduction in metabolic inefficiency in this period was largely due to the increased consumption of construction materials in Limerick in 2002 and the fact that construction and demolition (C&D) waste produced showed little change. The results are highly affected by the construction industry, as construction materials accounted for 76 per cent of material and product consumption in 1996 and 83 per cent in 2002, which implies that construction is heavily dominant in total consumption. At the household level there was little increase in environmental efficiency. Similar small gains are noted in Malmö, Sweden, where relative decoupling seems to appear in some important cases such as in the total energy consumption.[70] In Aichi prefecture, Japan, which had a population of over 7 million in 2007, over 2.1 million of whom were in the city of Nagoya, some decoupling of production and material input occurred after 1996[71] (Figure 3.5 C).

In Beijing, from 1990 to 2004, the metabolic flux (Fp) increased, but at a dramatically slower rate than the increase in GDP (Figure 3.5 B). The trend is thus of a slight decoupling of resource consumption from GDP in Beijing's metabolic system, but an absolute decoupling of pollution discharge from GDP.[72] A slight increase in environmental efficiency is also apparent in Guangzhou where the total environmental footprint and the footprint per capita increased from 1995 to 2000, while environmental efficiency per unit GDP decreased[73] (Figure 3.5 D). Since 1990 Shanghai's rapid growth has been accompanied by greater efficiency in the use of energy and water, and the quality of wastewater. Policies of removing polluting industries from the centre to new suburbs have also reduced emissions. This greater eco-efficiency may explain some of the improvement of the overall environment quality in Shanghai after 1990.[74]

CONCLUSION

Throughout their history, cities have relied on the surrounding countryside, originally the area within a few hours' walk, to supply much of their needs, but by the end of the nineteenth century most of them in the industrialized world used materials from almost all continents. However, luxury goods and precious metals were always traded over longer distances, as ancient Athens and Rome showed. Sustaining the city has relied on easy access to bulk materials and basic foods with opportunities for wealthy elites to acquire valuable goods from more distant markets. Spices and precious stones began to be carried long distances early in human history. Shipping made bulk transfers of grain, oil and wine easy by the time of the great civilizations around the Mediterranean. Later mechanized land transport began to transform the supply of food and raw materials to urban markets, leading to a transformation in retailing and the globalization of people's shopping habits. Yet even though the world's middle-class shops in malls that carry the same retailers' names as their counterparts in other global cities, and groceries are ordered online and delivered by national and international companies, perhaps almost 50 per cent of the world's urban people buy their food in traditional markets, such as those of Lusaka or Phnom Penh.

Consumption per capita remains highly unequal, the ecological footprint of the wealthiest being 10 to 100 times greater than those of the poorest. However, as the urban middle classes of the newly industrializing countries grow, rates and magnitudes of urban consumption will increase and the entire infrastructure to manage the stocks and flows involved will have to increase, including the huge warehouses and distribution depots for the virtual department stores used by internet shoppers. The supply lines of such large-scale retail systems are potentially vulnerable, perhaps as much from labour dispute and war, as from flood and drought. Reliance on large scale producers can also lead to price volatility, as occurred in the first decade of the twenty-first century when the expansion of biofuel production caused competition for food crops such as corn. Equally, weather and climate change increases the risk of supply failures. The impacts of such extremes on the urban poor are particularly marked.

4

Smoke, Fumes, Dust and Smog

Changing the Atmosphere of Cities

Urban air pollution depends on the local topography, the structure of the atmosphere above the city, the size of the built-up area and the distribution of green areas and water bodies within the city, as well as on the nature of the industrial activity and the fuels used for heating, transport and power generation. A big issue is whether or not inversion layers occur naturally over the city. Such temperature inversions can trap rising warm air containing pollutants and help retain fogs and smoke. Casablanca, Santiago de Chile, Los Angeles, Mexico City and Chongqing are among urban areas experiencing major inversions.[1] A second important factor is the presence of weather systems that help to retain polluted air over a city. Localities in dry mid-latitude regions such as those of Mediterranean-type or semi-desert climates often experience high-pressure systems when the air is still and a local urban heat island and associated dust dome build up. Local mountain or sea breeze diurnal wind patterns affect the movement of polluted air across urban regions. The actual pollutants vary considerably, depending on local sources, weather conditions and industrial, domestic, commercial and transportation forms of energy use (Table 4.1).

URBAN SMOKE IN ANCIENT AND MEDIAEVAL TIMES

Long regarded as a problem and as a health risk, urban smoke, the visible particulate clouds emitted from chimneys and vehicles, has been difficult for governments to control, partly because it is difficult to measure and partly because there have always been strong lobbies from powerful economic interests to avoid limiting productivity and employment by placing restrictions on fires and furnaces. Measurement technology has improved since 1960 and fine particles of fractions of a millimetre in diameter can be detected, enabling the components of haze and vehicle exhausts that most threaten human health

Table 4.1: The major air pollutants

Pollutant	Nature and impacts
Smoke	A collection of airborne solid and liquid particulates and gases emitted when a material undergoes combustion or pyrolysis, together with the quantity of air that is entrained or otherwise mixed into the mass. Highly visible and a product of burning wood or coal, it was familiar to all people in historic and prehistoric times.
Sulphur dioxide (SO_2)	Gas formed when sulphur is exposed to oxygen at high temperatures during fossil fuel combustion, oil refining, or metal smelting. SO_2 is toxic at high concentrations, but its principal air pollution effects are associated with the formation of acid rain and aerosols.
Nitrogen oxides (NO and NO_2, referred together as NO_x)	Highly reactive gases formed when oxygen and nitrogen react at high temperatures during combustion or lightning strikes. Nitrogen present in fuel can also be emitted as NO_x during combustion.
Carbon monoxide (CO)	An odourless, colourless gas formed by incomplete combustion of carbon in fuel. The main source is motor vehicle exhaust, along with industrial processes and biomass burning.
Volatile organic compounds (VOCs)	Hydrocarbons (C_xH_y) and other organic chemicals emitted from a wide range of sources, including fossil fuel combustion, industrial activities, and natural emissions from vegetation and fires. Some anthropogenic VOCs such as benzene are known carcinogens.
Aerosols or particulate matter (PM)	Solid and liquid particles that are suspended in the air. These particles are referred to as aerosols in the atmosphere. They typically measure between 0.01 and 10 micrometres in diameter.
Ground-level ozone (O_3)	A pernicious secondary air pollutant, toxic to both humans and vegetation. It is formed in surface air (and more generally in the troposphere) by oxidation of VOCs and carbon monoxide in the presence of NO_x.
Smog	A generic term for any kind of air pollution that reduces visibility, especially in urban areas. Usually described as industrial smog or photochemical smog.
Industrial smog (also called grey or black smog)	Develops under cold and humid conditions. Cold temperatures are often associated with inversions that trap the pollution near the surface. High humidity allows for rapid oxidation of SO_2 to form sulphuric acid and sulphate particles.
Photochemical smog	Forms when NO_x and VOCs react in the presence of solar radiation to form ozone. The solar radiation also promotes formation of secondary aerosol particles from oxidation of NO_x, VOCs, and SO_2. Photochemical smog typically develops in summer (when solar radiation is strongest) in stagnant conditions promoted by temperature inversions and weak winds.
Lead (Pb)	In the past, motor vehicles were the biggest source of lead. But where leaded gasoline has been phased out, lead emissions have decreased by about 98 per cent. Metal processing has become the biggest source of atmospheric lead, with the highest air concentrations being found close to ferrous and nonferrous smelters and battery manufacturers.

Table 4.1 (continued)

Mercury (Hg)	A toxic pollutant whose input to ecosystems has greatly increased since 1900 due to anthropogenic emissions to the atmosphere and subsequent deposition. Mercury is ubiquitous in the environment and is unique among metals in that it is highly volatile. When materials containing mercury are burned, as in coal combustion or waste incineration, mercury is released to the atmosphere as a gas.
Other heavy metals	Any metallic chemical element that has a relatively high density and is toxic or poisonous at low concentrations. Cadmium and copper, in addition to lead and mercury, are among the most important for human health. Humans are exposed to heavy metals through inhalation of air pollutants, consumption of contaminated drinking water, exposure to contaminated soils or industrial waste, or consumption of contaminated food.
Acid rain	Precipitation with pH values below 5, which generally happens only when large amounts of man-made pollution are added to the atmosphere. Acid rain damages vegetation and corrodes metals in buildings and infrastructure.

to be determined. However, strong social arguments have insisted that, despite the health concerns, people should be free to use the most economical fuels for cooking and heating. Equally, people enjoy their motor vehicles and the majority are only likely to be encouraged to move to those that are least polluting for economic reasons.

In the cities of antiquity, smoke and soot were the two main air pollutants. Smoke so stained marble, that the ancient Jews, among others, introduced several laws.[2] Many people recognized the impact of smoke and particulates in and around Rome. Pliny the Younger wrote to Domitius Apollinaris that at his new farm in Tuscany, 'the atmosphere is clearer and the air purer' than in Tusculus, Tivoli and Praenestes near Rome.[3] The greyish tone of smoke-affected marble annoyed several classical poets, including Horace (65 BC to AD 8) who wrote that Roman buildings were turning increasingly dark from smoke. In the first century BC, Vitruvius, recognizing the importance of air circulation for human health, advocated wide streets and openings in buildings to promote sufficient air flow to disperse smoke.[4] Seneca (4 BC to AD 65), the teacher of Emperor Nero (AD 37–68), was in poor health all his life and his physician frequently advised him to leave Rome. In one of his letters to Lucilius in AD 61, he said that he had to escape from the gloomy smoke and kitchen odours of Rome so that he could recover.[5]

Civil claims over smoke pollution were brought before Roman courts almost 2000 years ago. According to the Roman law, cheese-making premises should be established in such a way so that their smoke would not to pollute other houses. Rules set out under the Roman emperor Justinian in AD 535 and later used as texts in law schools include a section 'Law of Things' which states:

> By the law of nature these things are common to mankind – the air, running water, the sea, and consequently the shores of the sea. (Lib. II, Tit. I: Et quidem naturali iure communia sunt omnium haec: aer et aqua profluens et mare et per hoc litora maris).[6]

As towns expanded in China, the Mediterranean and in North Africa, from about AD 1000, more and more people lived in smoky and sooty surroundings. Maimonides, the philosopher and physicist (1135–1204), who knew the Mediterranean towns of that time, from Cairo to Cordoba, said the urban air was 'stuffy, smoky, polluted, obscure and foggy'.[7] In Britain, references to coalmining occurred in 1180 and to coal deliveries in London in 1228. Burning coal in towns and cities soon started to cause a nuisance. When staying in Nottingham in 1257, Queen Eleanor of England found the smoke so annoying that she moved out of the city to lodgings in nearby Tutbury.[8]

In London, England, as early as 1306, a royal proclamation was issued, forbidding the use of coal in London, followed by a commission to punish miscreants 'for the first with great fines and ransoms, and upon the second offence to destroy their furnaces'. A further proclamation issued in Elizabeth I's reign made illegal the burning of coal during periods when parliament was sitting. Nevertheless its use continued, as wood was becoming both scarce and more expensive as the English woodlands were being depleted, largely as a result of increasing demand for timber for shipbuilding and urban construction. In 1648 Londoners unsuccessfully petitioned parliament to prohibit the importation of coal from Newcastle on account of the injury suffered from smoke.

In 1661 John Evelyn published his brilliant indictment of London's smoke: *Fumifugium: or the smoke of London dissipated*.[9] He discussed ways of alleviating the smoke with King Charles II, but while agreeing that much could be done, the king took no action. In 1700, Timothy Nourse commented on how the recently built St Paul's Cathedral in London was becoming discoloured by smoke and urged the re-introduction of wood burning to ease the problem. By the end of the eighteenth century, William Murdoch had begun to make gas from coal and in 1832 there were 300 gas-making plants in Britain. This move towards more efficient use of coal had little impact on the colossal expansion of coal consumption by a rapidly growing urban population. From one tonne per capita in 1800, coal output rose to six tonnes per capita in 1900.[10] Air quality deteriorated even further.

In 1819 the UK parliament appointed a committee to enquire into reducing smoke from steam engines and furnaces. Despite there being good practices that could have been adopted, little was done. In 1843 a Select Committee recommended legislation to try to eliminate black smoke from households and non-industrial premises. Progress need not have been hampered by a shortage of potentially useful devices, for the committee found over 60 devices available on the market and a further 30 under development.[11] A further committee in 1845, however, stated that no law could yet be introduced that might reduce atmospheric pollution from household coal burning. Nevertheless, legislation in 1845, 1853 and 1856 incorporated several clauses relating to smoke abatement. In the meantime action was being taken locally in many cities, of which Manchester was a leading example.

TACKLING SMOKE IN NINETEENTH-CENTURY MANCHESTER

As elsewhere, Manchester's prosperous middle classes moved away from the city centre to enjoy the cleaner air and brighter skies of suburbs situated upwind of the major smoke emitting factory and domestic chimneys. They left the city's most vulnerable inhabitants to face the brunt of such health problems as bronchitis, pneumonia, and rickets. While the health risks associated with coal smoke were distributed unequally between the classes, the human labour at home and work impacts of polluted air were divided unequally along gender lines. The all-pervasive smoke and soot filtered through the narrowest cracks and fissures to soil everything within the home. Time-consuming and strenuous house cleaning and clothes washing pushed legions of women into a never-ending round of drudgery.[12]

In early nineteenth-century Manchester there were three main avenues open to those actively trying to curb air pollution by legal means: the Common Law, the Court Leet, and the Police Commissioners. With the expansion of industry using coal-fuelled steam power and increasing economic prosperity, smoke was usually seen as an inevitable and probably unavoidable consequence of manufacturing success. The traditional nuisance law came to be interpreted in different ways by the courts. Nuisance law judges faced a dilemma over how to reconcile the often conflicting goals of environmental quality and business growth, the benefits of abating smoke being thought to be less than the negative repercussions of pollution injunctions for industrial growth.[13]

The Tory mercantile and manufacturing elite that dominated the court shared the economic beliefs of their Liberal rivals. When the latter finally broke the Tory stranglehold on Manchester's political institutions in 1838, the attitude that effective action against smoke pollution might damage the expansion of trade and industry did not change.[14]

The business community also controlled the Manchester Police Commissioners that seldom used their powers to require steam engine owners to construct furnaces and chimneys in a manner that would consume smoke effectively. Right up until they surrendered their responsibilities to the new Borough Council in 1843, the Commissioners remained disinclined to take action against those who caused serious smoke problems.[15]

On 26 May 1842, the Manchester Association for the Prevention of Smoke (MAPS) was founded, partly to draw the smoke issue to the attention of the eminent scientists gathered at the British Association for the Advancement of Science in the city in the next month. MAPS concentrated on finding reliable 'smoke consuming' devices and techniques to ensure more complete combustion of coal during the steam raising process:[16] a technical solution to pollution that has its parallels in the search for more efficient motor vehicle engines in the twenty-first century. The reformers believed that, eventually, improved combustion technology would both save manufacturers money and provide a reliable solution to the smoke problem. However there was relatively little change in air quality. Many small manufacturers were slow, unwilling or financially unable to buy improved furnaces. While many industrialists built tall chimneys to increase the efficiency of their furnaces, MAPS was concerned that unless factory owners installed larger boilers much of the heat generated by the improved combustion would be lost up these smokestacks.[17]

Often, the open domestic fire was believed to perform a key hygienic function in ensuring the circulation of fresh air in crowded working-class homes.[18] This helps to explain why MAPS (and later anti-smoke societies) found it difficult to persuade local and national governments to promote alternative smokeless technologies in the home.

Campaigning by MAPs helped to ensure that, well ahead of any national legislation, a new smoke-control clause was included in the Manchester Police Act of July 1844. However, even at the time, it was commented that similar clauses had failed to see smoke abatement in Leeds, Bradford or Derby. The same happened in Manchester.[19] Reasons for this included the lack of an accurate means of measuring the intensity of smoke, the poor training of smoke inspectors, the trifling nature of the penalties imposed (£2 as opposed to fines of £100 imposed by the Court Leet 40 years earlier), and the links between local magistrates and the business elite.[20]

The Manchester and Salford Sanitary Association (MSSA) established in 1852 to reduce the appalling mortality rates in the two cities, when campaigning against smoke, ran into the same business establishment opposition as MAPS did. It was more successful in fighting for better sewers, drainage, clean water and efficient waste collection. However, by 1876 when a Royal Commission began investigating air pollution from chemical works, some MSSA members became concerned about the problems caused by noxious vapours from alkali and other chemical works. They helped to form the Manchester and Salford Noxious Vapours Abatement Association (NVAA) whose work soon became focused on the local issue of the role of coal smoke in air pollution. Apparently unaware of the work done by MAPS, the NVAA tried to promote more efficient coal burning apparatus, campaigned for better legislation and regulation for smoke control and endeavoured to heighten public awareness of the adverse effects of smoke pollution.[21]

In addition to promoting efficient furnaces, the NVAA tried to improve the techniques used in stoking existing furnaces so that coal was applied evenly and did not create sudden bursts of smoke. However, the Chamber of

Commerce was reluctant to pay higher wages to boilermen who managed their furnaces in the ways the NVAA desired. When in the 1880s the NVAA tried to promote the use of gas engines, the Manchester Corporation was charging a high price for gas, hitherto used almost entirely just for lighting.

Gas production had its own pollution problems, gasworks using soot-producing bituminous coal in gas-producing ovens. Gas workers risked burns, respiratory ailments, and cancer. Their families suffered as well. Gasworks, like other offensive and polluting industries, were typically built in poor working-class neighbourhoods where land was cheap, labour plentiful, and residents had little power to oppose such projects.[22] Despite some businesses with large buildings to light supporting an NVAA campaign for cheaper gas, cheap bituminous coal continued to be the manufacturers' fuel of choice.

[handwritten margin note: poor people getting the worst again]

Coal remained householders' fuel of choice for heating and cooking and was thought by some reformers to account for up to 50 per cent of the smoke pollution in Manchester. The NVAA promoted closed stoves and smokeless grates, but even the few middle-class households that had them found problems in getting their servants to use them properly.[23]

AIR POLLUTION ALLEVIATION IN BRITAIN AFTER 1875

Between 1875 and 1926 English law relating to the excessive emission of smoke from industrial chimneys, with the exception of London, was administered under clauses in the Public Health Act 1875. London was covered by very similar but somewhat more severe provisions in its own Public Health (London) Act, 1891, while certain modifications of the general clauses of the act of 1875 were introduced in local acts. Scotland also had separate legislation.

For almost two decades 'The local authorities merely winked at the pollution of the atmosphere rather than taking meaningful action to discourage the production of industrial smoke.'[24] In 1894 the NVAA led the setting up of a new pressure group, the Smoke Abatement League, with a key goal of enforcing 'the law prohibiting unnecessary pollution of the air by coal smoke'. The League's promotion of private prosecutions resulted in ineffective small fines. It failed to get parliament to ensure that local government had technically competent officials to regulate smoke pollution. Overall, despite the educational efforts of the NVAA, the League and some public health officers, there was little sign of any change in the prevailing positive image on Manchester's coal smoke.[25]

Bronchial diseases quietly became the most significant cause of death in Britain's factory towns, but, at the end of the nineteenth century, the working people en masse showed no inclination to campaign against coal smoke.[26] For them, a town of smoking chimneys was a town of full employment and regular wages. Governments were not prepared to intervene to remove the right of every British family to enjoy a bright household coal fire,[27] that provided heat, light, ventilation, hot meals and boiling water, while the 'cheerful' glow of the hearth denoted warmth to contemporaries in every sense of the word.[28]

SMOKE ABATEMENT IN BRITAIN IN THE TWENTIETH CENTURY

Early twentieth-century legislation was still based on the act of 1875, modified by the Public Health (Smoke Abatement) Act 1926, which was largely the outcome of the work of the departmental committee on smoke abatement. Domestic grates were exempted, but power was given to make by-laws requiring the provision in new buildings other than private dwelling houses of such arrangements for heating and cooking as might be calculated to prevent or reduce smoke emission.

The Public Health Act of 1936 allowed two or more local authorities to combine together to carry out their functions under the Act. The Sheffield–Rotherham Statutory Committee so formed began to advance practical measures to alleviate the severe problems in its area. Advisory committees in several English districts, including Manchester and District, the West Riding of Yorkshire and the Midlands were established just before the Second World War brought all smoke abatement activity to an end in 1939.[29] Smoke remained a key problem after the war. In 1945 Manchester and Liverpool residents said that smoke was the greatest planning issue facing local people.[30]

Under some of the subsequent local acts, several towns made plans for establishing 'smokeless zones' in which all emission of smoke would be prohibited; and one local authority was planning to subsidize the installation of modern domestic appliances. Town gas from coal and coke made in municipal gasworks was the main alternative to using coal for cooking and heating. Well into the 1950s, many households still had a coal-fired stove with a side oven and back boiler that provided hot water and also could be used for cooking. Usually this stove was supplemented by a gas cooker. More modern houses, typically the semi-detached houses built in the great suburban expansion of the 1920s and 1930s, had a coke or anthracite-fired boiler for hot water and a gas or electric cooker in the kitchen. Although gas and coke reduced domestic emissions, the emissions from the gas works added to air pollution and their legacy of contaminated land affected both soil and water quality beyond 2000.[31]

Indeed it was not until the great London smog that persisted for several days in December 1952 (Table 4.2) that government, itself affected by the event, felt it had to take steps to reduce the burning of coal, something that Manchester and Salford had already campaigned for when they gained permission for the first urban smokeless zones in the late 1940s. The Clean Air Act, 1956, went into force in1958 making dark smoke emission or lack of dirt and grit arresting equipment offences. The local authorities could declare smoke control areas in which smoke emission was an offence.

Table 4.2: Some major urban air pollution events

Year	Location	Cause	Impacts
1930 December	Meuse Valley, Belgium	Intense fog over Belgium at the start of December; temperature inversion over the deeply incised Meuse Valley; emissions from many industrial works on the valley floor.	After three days, throat irritation, vomiting, eye irritation and watering; particularly among old people and those in ill-health; presence of toxic substances in patient's blood; bronchial disease definitely caused by the event.
1948 October	Donora, USA	Temperature inversion and high pressure over Pennsylvania; dense fog developed close to the steel-making area of Pittsburgh.	20 deaths in five days from the polluted air; 8,457 days of work lost; young children, the elderly and those suffering from asthma, chronic bronchitis, emphysema and heart disease fared worst during the event.
1950 November	Poza Rica, Mexico	Leakage of hydrogen sulphide gas for 25 minutes from a broken pipe at a natural gas plant; gas trapped in an existing fog over the town that was held down by a temperature inversion above.	Produced similar bronchial tract symptoms in the local population; lack of wind allowed gas to concentrate around residents' homes; 22 people died and 320 treated in hospital.
1952 December	London, England	Anticyclonic conditions and urban smoke under a light easterly drift (worst direction for carrying industrial smoke into London) combined to create extremely thick fog, visibility of less than 2 m in places, persisted for four days over the London area.	People suffered runny noses, sore throats, breathing difficulties, tight chests, vomiting and bronchitis; men over 45 suffering the most; much higher hospital admissions than normal; over 4,000 excess deaths.
1954 October	Los Angeles, USA	Five days of extreme smog under warm high pressure system.	Schools and industries shut down for most of month; severe eye irritation; smog said to have caused 2,000 car accidents in a single day; people blamed everything from burning rubbish to industrial companies and politicians for the emissions.
1985 January	Ruhr, Germany	Five days with 24 hour averages of SO_2 as high as 0.8 mg m^3 and particles up to 0.6 mg m^3; due to fossil fuel burning in steel works and other industries.	Daily death rate increased by 8 per cent; hospital admissions for respiratory and cardiovascular problems up by 15 per cent.

Ironically one consequence of the 1956 Clean Air Act that was stimulated by the 1952 industrial grey smog was the far greater admission of sunlight into the streets, just in time for it to interact with the emissions of nitrogen oxides from the rapidly increasing number of cars to form dangerous photochemical smogs (Table 4.1). From 1954 to 1967 a steady decrease in overall emission of smoke occurred in Britain, reflecting the combined effects of changes in energy sources, methods of fuel burning, and the implementation of the 1965 Clean Air Act. Emission of smoke from domestic appliances fell after 1957 through the impact of smokeless zone legislation. However, domestic smoke emission still exceeded that from industry in the early 1970s.[32] Smoke concentrations in large urban areas, such as London and Greater Manchester, in the mid-1960s, tended to be higher over suburban areas than over the central business districts and large industrial estates. Subsequent gradual extension of smoke-control zones in the next 20 years saw the smoke problem greatly reduced. However, the process of declaration of zones was political, patchy and prolonged. Where miners' families received free coal, local politicians were reluctant to declare smokeless zones. Wigan, for example, was the last part of Greater Manchester to become smoke free.

However, the smoke problem was not totally removed. Power stations, cement works, incinerators and metal smelters installed tall chimneys that forced smoke and pollutants higher into the atmosphere, whence it was carried by prevailing winds to cause acid rain in regions downwind: the urban areas exporting their pollution to rural regions, often in other countries. The sulphur in the smoke became acid rain (Table 4.1). Thus British emissions carried by the prevailing westerly winds into Scandinavia and France, Germany and the Benelux countries, affecting trees in urban areas as much as the forests and woodlands of Norway and Germany.

By the end of the twentieth century, local authorities in Great Britain were required to carry out air quality reviews and assessments, with the aim of identifying local hotspots where national air quality objectives were not likely to be met. Approximately 120 Air Quality Management Areas were declared, for which the local authorities, in partnership with others, were required to write and implement an action plan outlining remedial measures to improve the air quality situation in these areas.[33]

SMOKE CONTROL IN GERMANY

German industrialists seldom opposed smoke abatement because the regulatory environment made such a position counterproductive. Smoke regulation became a compromise between the interests of business entrepreneurs and the other parties involved.[34] German businessmen were not brought into discussions on smoke abatement. Failure to include them weakened the efforts of such organizations as the Hamburg Society for Fuel Economy and Smoke Abatement. German businessmen, however, faced a strong bureaucracy that never wavered in considering excessive smoke production unlawful.

When the urban smoke nuisance emerged in the last two decades of the nineteenth century, German bureaucrats were prepared to meet it. The legal foundations of smoke abatement were laid early in the course of German industrialization. For example, Dresden, Stuttgart and Braunschweig all passed smoke ordinances in the 1880s, when, in the USA, Chicago was the only city seriously dealing with the issue. Moreover, unlike American smoke ordinances, until after the First World War most German smoke laws changed little once passed. The Prussian Ministry of Commerce promulgated the most important German smoke regulation, the so-called 'smoke clause' in 1853, almost 30 years before Chicago passed the first American smoke ordinance. Referring to the contemporary situation in London, where the Smoke Nuisance Abatement Act was passed the same year, the Ministry ruled that Prussian officials should take precautions in case a smoke nuisance of the London type developed in Prussian cities. Consequently, future licences of steam engines and other large furnaces had to include a clause which made smokeless combustion mandatory and enabled officials to demand alterations if the plant defied the law and produced smoke. When the Prussian system of licensing plants became national law after German unification, states adopted the smoke clause as well, making it one of the most important legal instruments of smoke abatement around 1900. Never seriously contested, the smoke clause, invented by a Prussian ministry when Germany was still a largely agrarian state, was one of the pillars of the smoke law until after the First World War.

Not all German governments were as far-sighted as Prussia when it invented the smoke clause. The law on the smoke nuisance was a conglomeration of municipal ordinances, building codes, the smoke clause and several other regulations, with a variety of weaknesses and idiosyncrasies on the eve of the First World War. The bottleneck of German smoke abatement was not passing legislation, but enforcing it. Guidelines for enforcement gave German officials considerable leeway. While legal theory supposed that every offensive emission of smoke could be prevented, most officials felt that they fulfilled their duties by investigating the citizens' petitions. In doing so, most officials embraced a routine practice that combined, though in a somewhat haphazard way, a cooperative spirit with a rigid legalistic attitude.[35] In general, cooperation and bureaucratic legalism intermeshed surprisingly well, mainly because they were arranged sequentially. When investigating complaints, officials first adopted the cooperative approach; only if that failed, did they proceed rigidly according to the letter of the law.[36]

Germany lacked a civic anti-smoke movement. While smoke abatement was the object of fierce agitation by reform groups in the US, the involvement of urban residents in Germany was low. Occasionally, citizens filed complaints against specific smoke producers, but protest against the smoke nuisance in general was rare. Even more important, there was not a single group of citizens that organized a smoke abatement association, as in American cities.[37]

SMOKE CONTROL IN THE USA

The mainly small early US cities generally used wood until the nineteenth century. However, once they started to burn coal the inhabitants of these cities began to suffer from industrial smog. The problem, that was called the 'smoke evil' after 1860, became more and more severe in midwestern cities that relied on bituminous coal for fuel, whereas cities on the eastern seaboard that mostly used anthracite coal (e.g. Philadelphia) were largely smog free.[38] Even until the First World War, New York City, Philadelphia and Boston were cited as examples of smokeless cities. Thus agitation about smoke began mostly in midwestern communities.

In the mid-nineteenth century, St Louis, Missouri, passed an ordinance regulating the height of chimneys, and the first smoke case recorded in any US court occurred in that city in 1864, when a citizen was awarded $50 damages in the local court, which declared smoke to be a nuisance. The case was appealed to the Missouri Supreme Court which upheld the lower court's decision.

Chicago

Chicago began to be concerned about smoke as early as 1874, when a citizens' association interested itself in the problem. The first smoke ordinance in the United States was adopted by the Chicago City Council and took effect on 1 May 1881. It made the emission of dense smoke from the smokestack of any boat or locomotive or from any chimney anywhere within the city a public nuisance. The penalty for violation was not less than $5 and not over $50. In 1892, several of Chicago's business leaders organized the Society for the Prevention of Smoke. Their goal was to persuade the city's business community to put smoke control equipment on their boilers and furnaces in order to eliminate the dark, dirty, smelly, heavy coal smoke pouring from the chimneys and smokestacks of buildings and factories in downtown Chicago. Like their Manchester UK counterparts, the Society's members set out to prove to sceptical citizens that a range of technologies existed that could in fact reduce smoke emissions.[39] However, the Chicago Society may have met with more success. In July 1892, the Secretary of the Society reported that the engineering staff had investigated 430 smoking steam plants and had sent out over 400 reports to owners about how to curtail the smoke. He stated that about 40 per cent of the owners of smoking buildings had voluntarily followed the engineers' recommendations and had 'practically cured their smoke nuisance'. Some 20 per cent of the others had voluntarily installed abatement equipment, but were either not using the equipment correctly or not stoking their fires properly and so were still causing a smoke nuisance. Only 40 per cent had done nothing to reduce the pollution emitted from the chimneys on their buildings. Tugboat owners also had done nothing, but several railroads had installed abatement equipment on their locomotives. One of the motivating factors that led to business people taking action was their belief that Chicago must get rid of the smoke nuisance before the World's Fair opened in 1893. However, a variety of factors account for why some members of the business community felt it was in their interest to abate smoke, while others did not. The personal values that led people to invest time, money, and energy in the anti-smoke campaign were products of family upbringing, education, life experiences, and temperament.[40]

Again, as in Manchester UK, even when factory owners were prosecuted for breaking the smoke regulations and convictions were won, the courts had often refused to impose fines. In 1891 none of the 331 $50 fines imposed were collected. While business reformers blamed corruption and machine politics for this failure, others simply could not explain such shameless failure to enforce the law. As in Manchester, many people associated smoke with business and prosperity.[41] In part this was seen as a general reluctance of the courts to take action in terms of the culture of a young, expanding, enterprising economy,[42] 'public policy' being more important than private property.[43,44]

Although the Chicago leaders of Society for the Prevention of Smoke failed to impress visitors to the World's Columbian Exposition with Chicago's smoke-free skies, this did not hurt the city's reputation. It actually heightened admiration for the business community's accomplishments at the fair grounds, visitors being awed by the incredible contrast between the beautiful, glisteningly clean, harmoniously laid out neoclassical buildings of the 'White City', and the blackened buildings and smoky pall of the surrounding metropolis.[45]

In September 1908, the women of Chicago declared war on smoke, Mrs Charles H. Sergei and her Anti-Smoke League turning a technical debate among policy experts into a mass political movement. The women took to the streets and promised to go on strike, vowing to halt domestic routines such as cleaning house, washing children, playing bridge and shopping.[46] Although the women's threatened strike was tongue-in-cheek, their crusade was real enough. They chose the perfect enemy, the Illinois Central Railroad Company (IC), which ran its belching locomotives along the lake-front neighbourhoods of the well-to-do on the city's south side. Unlike the pollution rising into the atmosphere from the city's 17,000 factory chimneys, train smoke suffocated people and befouled their clothes at the street level.

Getting the support of the Health Commissioner and 40,000 signatures on its petition in less than a month, the Anti-Smoke League campaign eventually persuaded the council to take the offensive. By refusing permission for Illinois Central to build a new railway line the council initiated a long-term policy which led to the electrification of all steam railroads within the city.[47] Chicago in 1907 was the first city to refuse permits for new fuel-burning plants or their reconstruction unless approved by the city. In 1930, Chicago established annual inspections to assure that plants were properly maintained.

However, in the early stages of smoke control, Chicago, like Manchester in England, suffered from lack of capacity among council staff to carry out adequate inspections. Because they were responsible for enforcing all the city's sanitary laws, from those covering alley and manure-box cleaning to those covering sewerage, the Sanitary Inspectors lacked the time to monitor the smoke problem and rarely identified violators.[48]

The campaign mounted by Chicago's Anti-Smoke League demonstrates the links among gender, science, and the reformulation of environmental policy. Although not the first civic crusade devoted to removing dirty air, it represented a striking departure from the past, emphasizing gendered perceptions of the health hazards associated with coal smoke and its environmental impact. These progressives placed greater emphasis on recent chemical, biological, and medical research in demanding clean air as a public right, as opposed to technical engineering matters.

Pittsburgh

The strong cultural attitudes to smoke were well marked in Pittsburgh where acceptance of smoke was regarded as a rugged, backwoods, pioneer attitude. A nineteenth-century Pittsburgher genuinely weary of the city's smoke might not be rugged enough for the frontier or virtuous enough for the republic.[49] From around 1880 Pittsburgh used local supplies of natural gas, but by 1920 they were largely depleted. People feared the return of the smoky days of the mid-nineteenth century.[50] By 1914, many of Pittsburgh's heavy industries had already improved combustion technologies in ways that reduced smoke. Local mills, for their own reasons, had converted from heavily polluting beehive coke ovens to waste-reclaiming by-product coke ovens, and the largest mills saved fuel by using automatic stokers. An important 1914 Pittsburgh study confirmed the link between smoke and pneumonia deaths, adding that pneumonia not only killed the poor, but 'many of our most useful business men on whom most has been spent on education'.[51]

In 1916, Pittsburgh officials reported that they had reduced the city's smoke by 46 per cent just four years after adopting a new smoke ordinance. This relied on industries making capital investments in improved technology, continuing to operate their furnaces with care and attention, and burning costlier and cleaner anthracite or the better grades of bituminous coal.[52] Pittsburgh's smoke ordinance was expanded in 1917 to include the city's mills only in the context of such investments. During the First World War, Pittsburgh's smoke regulators resisted federal government urgings to lift restrictions on smoke out of concern that they might impede maximal industrial productivity. But eventually wartime transport difficulties and shortages of clean coal and skilled labour caused them to relax restrictions.[53]

The appointment of Herbert Meller, a mining engineer and Dean of the School of Mines at the University of Pittsburgh, to head the city's smoke control department led to a decade of scientific and regulatory advance in smoke control during the 1920s.[54] Between 1910 and 1950, talk about smoke in Pittsburgh alternated between claims of success and calls for control.

The newly appointed (18 February 1941) Pittsburgh Mayor's Commission for the Elimination of Smoke drafted a smoke control ordinance that was to serve as the cornerstone of civic revitalization. It was passed on 7 July, 1941, but its implementation for domestic consumers would eventually be postponed until six months after the end of the war.[55] Both new and old smoke abatement efforts in Pittsburgh relied on Mellon family initiatives. The Mellon Institute had long been the local centre for work on the relationship between air pollution and health. Anti-smoke campaigners had tried to establish convincing evidence of the impact of smoke on health. The Mellons, the most powerful industrial and business family in the city, themselves had extensive post-war plans – for Pittsburgh and for their own business ventures.[56]

In 1940, 81 per cent of Pittsburgh households burned coal for heating purposes and 17 per cent used natural gas. In 1946, however, cheap south-western natural gas reached the Pittsburgh region via pipeline, and householders and businesses began a rapid conversion to this superior fuel. By 1950, only 31 per cent of households used coal and 65 per cent used gas. Almost all conversions had occurred after 1946. The decrease in the percentage of Pittsburgh homes that utilized coal as a fuel was therefore approximately 50 per cent, as compared with 44 per cent in Cincinnati, 40 per cent in Cleveland, 23 per cent in Chicago, and 20 per cent in Milwaukee. During the same decade, the percentage of coal used nationally for residential and commercial space heating dropped from 67 per cent to 46 per cent.[57] Smoke control policy in Pittsburgh was successful because it set limited goals and stressed cooperation and community cohesion rather than conflict. The unpredicted availability of large supplies of cheap natural gas, however, resulted in a larger degree of success for the policy than would have been possible under the original fuel supplies.[58]

Other US cities

Cities such as New York, and St Louis were just as pro-growth as Chicago and Pittsburgh in the late nineteenth century. As a means of pacifying the public on the issue of air quality, they simply passed smoke ordinances that went largely unenforced. Other symbolic actions on air pollution by political elites included token enforcement efforts and rhetorical commitments to smoke abatement.[59] By 1886 in Cincinnati, the three biggest killers were tuberculosis, bronchitis and pneumonia. Some American physicians thought smoke had psychological effects, but data from Germany and England linking smoke to lung disease gradually began filtering into the USA. A 1905 German study found more acute pulmonary illness in smoky areas than elsewhere, and also discovered that animals infected with tuberculosis died more quickly in smoky air.

The 1902 anthracite miners' strike in Pennsylvania emphasized the difference between the clean, anthracite burning cities such as New York, Philadelphia and Boston and the dirty bituminous using ones like Pittsburgh, Chicago, St Louis, Cincinnati and Birmingham. In New York City, as the strike-induced shortage caused anthracite prices to rise, more and more coal users turned to bituminous, violating city laws and alarming city residents. Some allegedly switched to bituminous after dark when smoke would attract less attention. June 1902 saw a *New York Times* headline 'Smoke Pall Hangs over the Metropolis'. Andrew Carnegie, the steel magnate whose bituminous-burning mills added to smoke warned that 'If New York allows bituminous coal to get a foothold, the city will lose one of her most important claims to pre-eminence among the world's great cities, her pure atmosphere.'[60]

At this time Americans were creating national parks, protecting nature in its wildest state, but the growing anti-pollution movements 'emerged not from the forests but from the kitchens'.[61] Women took their home cleanliness principles beyond their front steps and into the community at large in what was called the 'municipal housekeeping' movement.

Middle and upper middle-class women joined civic clubs like the Ladies Protective Association of Pittsburgh and the Wednesday Club of St Louis. For them, 'smoke abatement' was part of a much larger reform movement also focusing on water supply, sewage disposal and solid waste removal. While not cheap, huge publicly funded infrastructure could solve these problems, but for coal smoke, governments tried to do something much harder: persuade those putting the smoke into the air to find and finance their own solutions.[62] The women's clubs successfully lobbied for new municipal laws banning dense smoke; by 1916, 75 cities had adopted smoke abatement orders.[63] As a result of this pressure and the consequent ordinances, some cities claimed substantial improvements in air quality.

In 1915 the city of Des Moines prosecuted a laundry plant for violation of the city smoke ordinance that became effective 6 September 1911. After conviction, the laundry appealed to the US District Court, southern district of Iowa, that the Des Moines smoke ordinance should not be enforced in their case. When this was turned down, the laundry appealed to the US Supreme Court, which affirmed the district court's decision.

For many years, the US Bureau of Mines acted as a clearing house for smoke prevention activities. In 1924 the bureau, in co-operation with the national engineering societies, drew up a standard smoke ordinance as a guide for law-making bodies. In the late 1920s and 1930s there was agitation for more strict smoke legislation and some standard on dust concentration to combat the increase in emissions of soot, fly ash and cinders. Late in 1939, the American Society of Mechanical Engineers appointed its model smoke law committee, to recommend a standard or model ordinance. This committee was composed of leading fuel and combustion engineers. After many years' work by the Committee, the 'Example Sections of a Smoke Regulation Ordinance' was adopted by the ASME and published in 1949. These sections were used as a guide in writing or revising more than 100 ordinances.

The economic costs of smoke were always high. In 1911, the city's smoke inspector estimated that the annual cost of Chicago's smoke nuisance was at least $17,600,000, and possibly two or three times this sum. The same year, the

US Geological Survey estimated that in the aggregate, the large and medium sized cities in the US as a whole lost over $500,000,000 per year from smoke.[64] Lewis Mumford noted the costs of cleaning in Pittsburgh in 1940: $1,500,000 for extra laundry work, $750,000 for extra general cleaning, and $60,000 for extra curtain cleaning. This estimate, some $2,310,000 a year (in 1940 values) does not include losses due to the corrosion of buildings or the increased cost of painting woodwork, nor the extra costs of lighting during periods of smog.[65]

After an especially severe smoke episode, the city of St Louis passed the nation's first law requiring in the home either mechanical stoking or smokeless fuels on 8 April 1940.[66] This was a daring step, and city officials knew their careers were on the line, so through the fall and winter they strove to enforce the law and to ensure sufficient quantities of low-smoke fuel were available at reasonable prices. The effort worked; the winter heating season of 1940–41 in St Louis was a landmark for its improved air quality.[67]

The 1948 Donora PA industrial smog disaster (Table 4.2) resulted in greatly increased interest in prevention of smoke all over the USA. Agitation for preventive measures was voiced in scores of communities. Many municipalities adopted smoke ordinances or made existing ones stricter. In general, greatest progress was made by those communities with the larger budgets. However, after 1945, an amazing thing happened, the long-intractable smoke problem suddenly and permanently retreated. The many St Louis-style ordinances passed across the country undoubtedly helped, but the real reason was more subtle – the sudden (and unexpected) availability of a completely smokeless fuel, natural gas.[68] As in Britain, disastrous smoke events often triggered legislation, but the technical change followed the availability of an alternative that was more convenient and simpler to use.

LEAD POLLUTION

Lead poisoning is among the most prevalent and serious preventable diseases of occupational and environmental origin. Many sources contribute to human exposures, and the residues from past uses continue to present risks due to contamination of dusts, soils, and drinking water. In many aspects, lead poisoning is a local-scale problem, and factors in specific environments and workplaces, as well as characteristics of specific populations, determine the nature and extent of disease. However, lead is also a global pollutant: emissions from stationary and mobile sources are transported across boundaries and even oceans; lead-containing products are traded extensively; and lead-containing wastes such as batteries also move internationally.[69] Like many heavy metals, lead finds its way into the environment, including the urban atmosphere, by a variety of routes. People are exposed to lead in food and drink due to such practices as cooking in lead-lined or lead glazed pots and the supply of water through lead pipes. Lead in paint has been of a particular concern with regard to the exposure of children who might ingest small fragments of paint in their houses. In the past, lead was widely used in tooth fillings by dentists. Some communities living in areas where there is natural lead occurring in the local rocks are exposed to higher levels.[70] Although lead is toxic to adults and affects virtually all organ systems, adverse effects on cognitive development and behaviour in children (2–5 years old) are of special concern.

At the start of the nineteenth century, occupational lead poisoning had become a serious problem, with children of workers exposed to lead often suffering high infant mortality or retarded growth and development.[71] By 1900 'toxicity of habitation' had been recognized, this being due to exposure to lead paint and the view that 'the house formed a simple lead trap'.[72] Concern over lead poisoning has been documented since the 1920s.[73] Considerable work in hospitals in the USA recognized that children ingested paint chips in their household environment and the lead in that paint produced the poisoning. Because paintwork may be many tens of years old in some circumstances, especially in older multi-occupancy buildings in run-down districts, children continued to be exposed to lead from this source, years after the awareness of the problem reached national prominence.

After 1950 lead became used as an additive to improve the anti-knock quality of petrol. However, the combustion of petrol containing lead produces particles containing this element that affect the alveoli and move into the bloodstream, causing serious health problems. In the mid-1960s, lead poisoning, a preventable illness, was occurring in epidemic proportions in many inner city slums. Mass screening in the USA began in Chicago in 1966 and other cities quickly followed. The subsequent unexpected discovery of thousands of children with elevated blood lead levels caused health workers to realize the need to detect undue lead absorption in children and the risk of possible toxic effects of lead in the young. The key issue was that lead was accumulating in the bloodstream, but not yet producing any noticeable symptoms in the majority of affected children. In the early 1970s the problem of lead in the environment was seen as more pervasive, the lead in dust in the streets and gardens coming from a variety of sources, including emissions for chimneys and motor vehicles. The 1971 Lead-Based Paint Poisoning Prevention Act authorized federal assistance through the Department of Health, Education and Welfare for screening and treatment programmes required the Department of Housing and Urban Development to determine the nature and extent of the problem in the USA; and prohibited the use of lead-based paint in residential structures constructed or rehabilitated with federal assistance.[74] However, the Environment Protection Agency (EPA) failed to fulfil a congressional demand to issue an air standard for lead of 1.5 $\mu g\ m^{-3}$ averaged over a calendar quarter for urban areas with over 500,000 population until 1978.[75] Some claimed that scientists advising the EPA were biased towards the lead industry and that the reduction of the permitted lead content in gasoline (petrol) was unnecessarily delayed.[76] In the US lead-free gasoline became widely available in 1974. From 1975, new cars had to have catalytic converters to control emissions. However, it took several more years for the lead content of all gasoline to be reduced. Some of this may help to explain why during the 1980s and 1990s, surveys still found high blood lead levels in children in many US cities.

In 1984, an estimated 200,700 US children living in standard metropolitan statistical areas (SMSAs) had blood-lead levels of greater than or equal to 25 ug/dl, the Centers for Disease Control and Prevention's (CDCP's) current definition of an elevated blood-lead level for use in screening programmes for children. Growing evidence indicates that levels of blood lead in the range of 10–15 ug/dl and above have adverse neurobehavioural effects in children (3–5); in 1984, an estimated 3 million children in SMSAs had blood-lead levels of greater than or equal to 15 ug/dl. In 1988, a total of 796 cases of childhood lead poisoning were identified through surveillance by the New York City Bureau of Lead Poisoning Control (BLPC), about 3 cases identified per 1000 children screened. Because of incomplete screening, false negative results, and lack of information on children with lower but potentially harmful levels of blood lead (10–24 micrograms/dl), the magnitude of excessive lead absorption in New York City children was underestimated. These surveillance data indicate that lead poisoning among children is a persistent public health problem in New York City.[77] Nevertheless, there was an overall decline in the general blood lead levels in the US population following the removal of lead from petrol (Table 4.3).[78] The drop of 40 per cent in blood lead levels,[79] compared to the almost complete elimination of lead from petrol suggests that there was residual lead in the blood and that other sources were important.

Table 4.3: Relationship between lead in petrol (gasoline) and blood levels in the US population (after Silbergeld, 1997)

Year	Lead used in petrol (10⁶ kg)	Median blood lead level
1976	186.47	14.6
1980	51.59	9.2
1990	0.47	2.8

Many studies have highlighted the levels of lead in urban street dust[80] and deposited on roadside soils and vegetation and the lead content of the air in school playgrounds close to busy main roads.[81] Lead in soils persists for a long time and can affect lead levels in vegetables grown in urban allotments and gardens, and especially when grown close to major roads, as often happens in urban agriculture in deprived areas of poorer cities.[82] In the metropolitan area of Caracas, lead pollution problems are severe, lead collecting in traffic tunnels[83] and reaching particularly high levels along major roads. Total Suspended Particles (TSP) levels recorded by the national environmental office, have been as high as 80 µg m^3 and as low 50 µg m^3 in polluted areas. Lead concentrations in day care centres located in areas of high vehicular density were higher than those in areas of low vehicular traffic.[84]

Comparative studies in Oslo, Norway and Madrid, Spain showed that the gradual shift from leaded to unleaded petrol results in an almost proportional reduction in the concentration of lead in dust particles under 100 µm in urban environments.[85] However, the same study gives an important warning about historical legacies in urban pollution: the fact that the highest Pb concentration in the street dust of Oslo is found in the surroundings of a smelter shut down years ago suggests that lead sources other than traffic (i.e. the lead accumulated in the urban soil over the years) may contribute nowadays as much lead to the urban street dust as traffic does.

In Spain, the lead content in the petrol additives has been decreasing over the past years from 0.6 g/l in 1983 to 0.15 g/l in 1991. In 1990 unleaded petrol became available. A concomitant reduction of the urban air lead levels in most Spanish cities was then observed in the years up to 1996.[86] In the urban area of Barcelona a very significant decline in lead concentrations in the urban air has been observed since 1987 when reported concentration was 1.03–1.55 µg m^{-3}, to current 0.18–0.30 µg m^{-3}. In this case, the legislation introduced to eliminate the lead additives in petrol caused a positive effect by diminishing lead concentration in the air and blood and thus protected human health.

Before 1997, industrial emissions of lead to the atmosphere in the UK came within the jurisdiction of HM Alkali and Clean Air Inspectorate which set standards based on the size of a works and the volume of smoke emitted per minute. The concentrations permitted per chimney stack ranged from 0.115 g m^{-3} for stacks emitting less than 200 m^3 of smoke per minute, to 0.0115 for stacks emitting more than 4000 m^3 min^{-1}. In 1976, the average concentration of lead in inspected emissions from UK lead works was 0.011 g m^{-3}.[87]

The former major source of lead released to the atmosphere in the UK from road transport emissions, was reduced steadily from the 1970s. The maximum permitted lead content of petrol was 0.84 g dm^{-3} in 1972, 0.45 g dm^{-3} in 1978 and 0.40 g dm^{-3} in 1981.[88] Ultimately, sales of leaded petrol were banned from January 2000 and road transport only contributed approximately 3 per cent of the 1,100 tonnes of lead emitted to the atmosphere from the UK in 2005.

Lead is one of the eight main air pollutants in the UK's Air Quality Strategy. The air quality standard – which should not be exceeded as annual mean – has been set at 0.25 micrograms per cubic metre (µg^{-1} m^3). The UK legislation controlling lead releases and implementing the EC Directives 76/464 are the Surface Waters (Dangerous Substances) (Classification) Regulations, 1997 (SI 1997/2560). The European legislation relevant to its release is EC Directive 76/464: *Pollution of the aquatic environment by dangerous substances* (plus daughter directives); it is also on the list of 11 substances under review as potential 'priority hazardous substances' under the proposed Water Framework Directive. Its sale and use are covered by EC Directive 76/769 *Restriction on the marketing and use of certain dangerous substances*. The release of lead is also covered by the following three international agreements: the OSPAR Convention for the protection of the marine environment of the North East Atlantic, the UNECE Convention on Long-Range Transboundary Air Pollution and the Basel Convention on the Transboundary Movements of Hazardous Wastes and their Disposal.

In the UK, lead workers are covered by *The Control of Lead at Work Regulations (2000)*. These regulations outline the responsibilities of occupational physicians examining lead workers, either employment medical advisers or doctors appointed by the Health & Safety Executive under the regulations. The blood lead suspension level for workers using inorganic lead has been lowered to 60 µg/100 ml, with suggested maximum intervals between blood lead tests for workers with lower blood lead levels. There are specific guidelines for women 'of reproductive capacity'.[89] Analysis of the trends in lead in petrol and blood levels in 19 countries showed that average population blood lead levels of about 3 µg/dl are widely achievable and strongly indicates that the phase-out of leaded petrol had been a key contributor to decreased population blood lead levels by 1999.[90]

By 2005, following the ending of the sale of petrol with lead additives, concern about lead in the atmosphere had returned to specific locations, such as workplaces and the old buildings in which there was still a risk of lead from paint. Technical changes had removed an air pollution problem, but only after powerful lobbying and pressure on governments.

AIR POLLUTION BY COPPER

Wherever metals were smelted, pollution problems arose. From about 5000 to 3000 BC copper was produced from native copper. Development of means of smelting oxide and carbonate ores, and the appearance of tin–bronze, started the real Bronze Age, when the production of copper increased steadily. Some 500,000 tonnes of copper were produced between 2000 and 700 BC.[91]

Copper production suddenly increased in Roman times, when copper alloys were used increasingly for military and civil purposes, with copper production reaching about 15,000 tonnes a year by AD 10. At this time, half the world production came from the Huelva and Rio Tinto regions of Spain, much of the rest from Cyprus and Central Europe.[92] The total production, in the period between 250 BC and AD 350, was about 5 million tonnes.[93]

Beyond the Roman Empire, South-west Asia and the Far East were important producers. When the Han dynasty (206 BC–AD 220) extended its influence over South-west Asia, copper production in China was about 800 tonnes a year. Around AD 1080 (the northern Sung dynasty), China produced 13,000 tonnes of the world's output of 15,000 tonnes. Thereafter, production suddenly dropped (about 2,000 tonnes a year in the fourteenth century), then began increasing again from the start of the industrial revolution until the present. In Japan, production of copper to make giant Buddhist statues caused widespread environmental pollution from the eighth century.[94]

As in ancient times, modern cities vary in their industrial ecology and emissions to the atmosphere. In their emissions of copper (Cu), as well as in their general energy systems and industrial structure, Stockholm and the New York area represent two extremes when it comes to energy systems and industrial structure. Metal processing characterized the industries of Stockholm while the New York area was a national centre for heavy industry such as copper and petroleum refining as well as the chemical industry. The total per capita emission of Cu was approximately four times larger for the New York area than Stockholm from 1900–1980, largely as a result of major differences in energy systems and industrial structure, since consumption related emissions were approximately of the same magnitude for both cities.[95]

In both urban areas the estimated per capita Cu emissions from fuel combustion and industry have declined but in the case of consumption related emissions the time trends differ. The per capita emissions of Cu from end use in Stockholm are estimated to have increased only slightly from 1910 to the 1950s, thereafter increasing sharply. But in the New York area the consumption related Cu emissions are estimated to have increased from 1900 to the 1940s, but to not increase thereafter. End use was the largest category of Cu emissions in Stockholm during the whole time period studied. In the New York area consumption related emissions became the largest source of Cu emission in the 1950s.

In Chile, emissions from copper smelters are high in sulphur, copper, zinc and arsenic. The levels of arsenic in the vicinity of Chilean smelters are considerably higher than elsewhere in the world.[96] Copper levels in mountain lake sediments close to Santiago, the Chilean capital, show an increase of three to four times the environmental baseline since the onset of the mining activities at the beginning of the last century. However, the results of technological improvements are apparent in a decline in the copper in the uppermost part of the sediments in Laguna el Ocho. The decline in copper follows the installation of dust filters and fume traps in two gas treatment plants built in the smelting and Cu processing line.[97]

PHOTO-CHEMICAL SMOG (GROUND-LEVEL OZONE)

As the 'smoke evil' was finally being overcome in US cities in the middle of the twentieth century, a new, more subtle air pollution problem emerged, photochemical smog. Although completely different from the mixtures of smoke and fog that originally earned the name, when it was first observed in Los Angeles, the contemporary name for urban air pollution stuck to the new problem. Photochemical smog is a mixture of many pollutants, but the principal (and easiest to measure) component is ozone. This chemical, a particularly active form of oxygen found at very low (background) concentrations in all parts of the lower atmosphere, was first discovered in the mid-nineteenth century but remained a scientific curiosity for almost 100 years.

Figure 4.1: Smog forming in the valley at Salt Lake City, Utah, USA
(photo Ian Douglas)

Smog is prevalent in cities in the mid-latitudes that have stable warm air conditions, such as those that prevail in arid and semi-arid regions, such as the south-west of the USA (Figure 4.1). The reactions forming ozone are highly complex and non-linear, and intermediary chemicals, such as peroxy-actyl nitrate (PAN), can be just as harmful to human health as ozone.[98] A good metaphor is that ozone creates a 'sunburn' on lung tissue. In very high concentrations it can cause severe chest pain, breathing difficulties, eye irritation, and impair the normal development of children's lungs. Asthmatics and the elderly can have particular difficulties and discomfort breathing air that has even moderate concentrations of ozone. Ozone can also brown, stunt, and even kill vegetation.

Tropospheric ozone was first noticed as a problem in the early 1940s in Los Angeles when mysterious, noxious clouds began to appear and farmers near highways in the area started to notice mysterious crop damage.[99] Los Angeles presents almost a unique case in that its physical conditions (topography, meteorology, and emissions profile) are highly conducive to the formation of ozone. There are very few natural sources of volatile organic compounds (VOCs) in this semi-arid area, as the incoming winds originate in a marine environment largely devoid of VOC sources. The mountains inland of the city effectively block significant long-range transport. These reasons and the development of a motor vehicle dependent suburban sprawl allowed tropospheric ozone to become a problem in the Los Angeles area nearly two decades before it did anywhere else in the world.[100]

In Los Angeles, air pollution has been an economic disadvantage for local growth coalitions, restricting their ability to attract more growth. This creates a paradox for the local growth coalitions (partnerships of private and public-sector interests that implement strategies to enhance economic development) being largely the result of the growth that provides their members with profits but potentially threatening their past economic gains as well as future investment and economic growth.[101] The first attack of eye irritation in 1942 was assumed to be coming from a synthetic rubber plant near the centre of the city. The attacks disappeared in 1945 when the plant was closed. However, renewed attacks of pollution led to many accusations of those responsible: refineries, chemical factories, open burning, and automobiles, headed the list, none of these explained the almost daily occurrence of 'smog'. Smog, a contraction of smoke and fog, remained a household word even though chemists later established a totally different origin. For many, Southern California had been a haven to escape from the crowded and unsavoury conditions in some of the eastern cities, and when they were confronted with the highly objectionable smog clouds, the reaction was immediate. The public and the press demanded action.[102] In 1945, Los Angeles City passed a 'standard of care' ordinance. This was quickly extended to the whole of Los Angeles, but the county could not enforce its will on the municipalities. The problem was not solved until 1947, when a state bill creating a unified county air pollution control district for the entire area was passed.

Like earlier US efforts to manage local air pollution, the political capital in Los Angeles expended to address automotive air pollution was primarily provided by locally oriented economic elites. Also like earlier pollution control efforts undertaken by such elites, technology was posited as the only appropriate answer to the economic and aesthetic blight of air pollution. Unlike earlier efforts that failed to produce significant reform, the Los Angeles effort to abate air pollution from motor vehicles achieved some success. This was because automotive pollution control technology was relatively inexpensive and could in large part be passed on to the consumer.[103] Five days of particularly heavy smog in Los Angeles in late 1953, called the 'five-day siege of smog', prompted locally oriented economic elites and motor vehicle industries to create a policy-planning organization, the Air Pollution Foundation.[104] In the late 1950s, the Los Angeles automobile industry dropped its longtime position that the automobile was not a major contributor to the formation of smog in Los Angeles. Soon afterwards, in 1960 California enacted legislation requiring the installation of pollution control technology in automobiles.[105]

Since then, California has generally found itself leading the nation in the science and regulation of smog. At first, it proved difficult to detect the cause of the smog. Eventually it was realized it was something to do with petroleum, either from gases from refineries or emissions from motor vehicles. Although

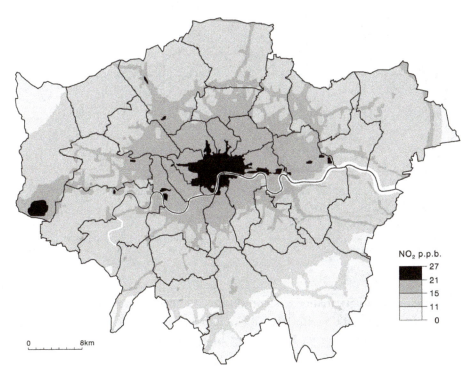

NO₂ p.p.b.

- 27
- 21
- 15
- 11
- 0

0 ⊢——————⊣ 8km

Figure 4.2: Map to indicate typical NO_x concentrations in London, note the node
in the west around London Heathrow Airport and along the North Circular Road
(the arc of 15 to 21 p.p.b. north of the city)
(based on data supplied by London Heathrow Airport)

laboratory experiments in 1952 established how photochemical smog could form, an adequate theory to explain the formation of photochemical smog would not be developed for two decades, after the key role of the hydroxyl radical in atmospheric chemistry was discovered. A complete picture of tropospheric ozone would not emerge until the early 1980s.[106] In general the regulatory approach to the problem has been to impose increasingly stringent regulations on the sources of ozone precursors. As with the case of smoke regulation, this pattern of regulatory solutions (rather than property rights regimes) shows that the framework being used is one of public good. In addition, the smog case illustrates how scientific and engineering progress can affect the governance of a pollution problem, and vice versa.[107]

All cities now show symptoms of photochemical smog, but its intensity depends on the local climate and the frequency of calm sunny days. The intensity of oxides of nitrogen varies considerably across urban areas, usually being highest around the commercial core and along major roads, and at airports, as London shows (Figure 4.2).

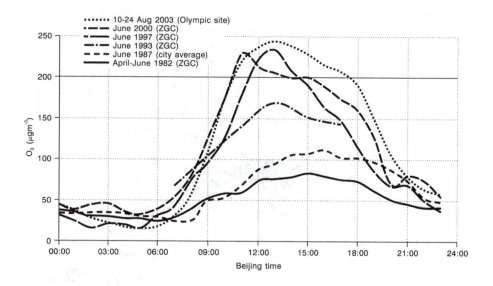

Figure 4.3: Diurnal variations in ambient ozone in Beijing over various periods before 2004, to indicate the levels that might occur at the Olympic Park site (after Shao et al., 2006) (after Pandey, Kumar et al., 2012)

In the rapidly expanding Brisbane metropolis in Australia, major changes in vehicle emission controls were initiated in 1986 and 1997, with a commitment in control technology and fuel quality to match European standards by 2010. In addition, backyard burning in Brisbane was banned in 1986.[108] The outer suburbs ('peri-urban' areas) often experience higher ozone levels due to traffic, industry and biogenic emissions, and sometimes bear the brunt of expectations for high residential amenity. Intensive animal production in response to population growth at the interface between semi-urban and rural areas can add to air pollution levels. Major industries previously sited in forested rural areas near quarries and mines may unintentionally influence atmospheric chemistry. Air quality is thus closely related to the built form and open spaces of urban areas. Particulate levels are not always correlated with the areas of densest population or highest traffic volumes. Indeed, many urban areas in South-east Asia have suffered from haze due to fine particulates created by forest burning during land clearance operations in these equatorial regions.

Ozone remains an issue in many cities, especially those in mid-latitudes that experience long periods of hot stable air conditions. In Beijing, particular efforts were made to reduce air pollution during the 2008 Olympic Games because previous studies had shown that ozone levels at the Olympic site could be above national air quality standards[109] (Figure 4.3).

PARTICULATES

Excess mortality is consistently associated with particulate pollutant levels in cities with differences in air pollution and population characteristics.[110] Motor vehicles also produce fine particles and the polluted air of London continues to threaten its residents' health. Diesel engine emissions can worsen lung function in people with asthma, as the 'real-life' study showed comparing patients who spent two hours on London's busy, bus and taxi crowded Oxford Street compared with those who were in nearby Hyde Park. Diesel engines can generate more than 100 times more particles than petrol engines. The smaller the particle, the deeper it can be inhaled into the lungs and very small particles may even be absorbed into the bloodstream. Oxford Street had three times as many ultrafine particles (less than 0.1 microns in diameter) as Hyde Park. Oxford Street also had more than three times more nitrogen dioxide in the air and six times as much elemental carbon.[111]

In Paris, another trial examined whether airborne particles increased the risk of cardio-vascular disease. A high correlation was found between the state of the tissue that makes up the walls of blood vessels and the amount of suspended particulates in the air. It is possible that as such exposure to particulate pollution increases, it can lead to hardening of the arteries.[112]

PM_{10} levels were extremely high in many crowded Asian cities in the 2000s. The World Health Organization guidelines of 40 µg m³ was exceeded up to fivefold in Indian cities such as Jaipur, Ahmedabad, Bhopal, Delhi, Kanpur and Surat in 2002–3, 24 hourly annual means exceeding 200 µg m³ in a few 2001 cases. However levels in Delhi, Mumbai, Kolkata Chennai and Hyderabad were up to 70 µg m³ lower in 2000–2 than in 1993. This may account for nearly 13,000 fewer cases of premature deaths and fewer cases of respiratory illness in these cities.[113]

Dramatic reduction in airborne particulates can be achieved, as the changes in air quality during the Beijing Olympic Games in 2008 show. In 2001, after Beijing was awarded the hosting of the 2008 Olympics, the city government implemented air pollution control measures including improvements in energy structure, reductions in coal burning emissions from power plants, regulations on vehicular emission standards, closing and moving high-emitting factories, and enforcement of construction dust control. Neighbouring administrative regions also enacted emission control measures to decrease regional transport of air pollutants to Beijing. Temporary measures during the Olympics removed around half of the vehicles (c. 1.5 million) from the city's roads by an odd-even licence car ban and imposed other traffic restrictions for two months.[114]

PM arising from wood burning used for domestic heating may contribute a major proportion of total PM in smaller urban areas in Canada, Australia and New Zealand. In the early 2000s in Christchurch, New Zealand and Launceston, Tasmania, wood smoke PM contributed 90 per cent and 85 per cent of total

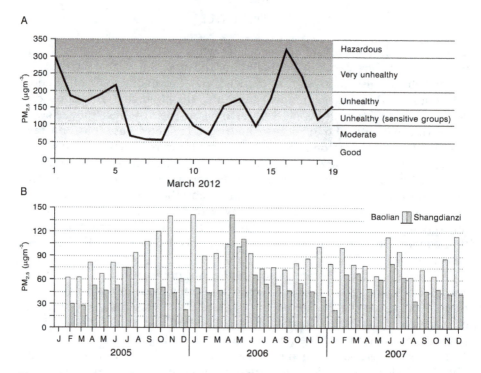

Figure 4.4: Beijing atmospheric fine particulate concentrations (PM$_{2.5}$): (A) Diurnal variations in PM$_{2.5}$ concentrations, as reported by the US Embassy during March 2012, indicating that most daily levels are classified as 'unhealthy' or worse; (B) Beijing Municipality showing average PM$_{2.5}$ concentrations at a rural location, Shangdianzi (SDZ), 100 km to NE of Beijing, and an urban location, Baolian (BL) in the west of the city between the third and fourth ring roads (after Zhao et al., 2009)

PM respectively. Problems with high PM concentrations in Wagga Wagga, New South Wales, came from wildfires, prescribed burning, dust, wood-burning stoves and agricultural emissions.[115] Local residents in many other New South Wales country towns experienced similar wood burning air quality problems after 1990.

Ultrafine particles

Ultrafine particles (UFP), particles less than 0.5 micrometres in diameter, began to attract interest as a factor in urban respiratory disease in the 1990s.[116] Larger concentrations of UFPs in Erfurt, Germany were associated with increased

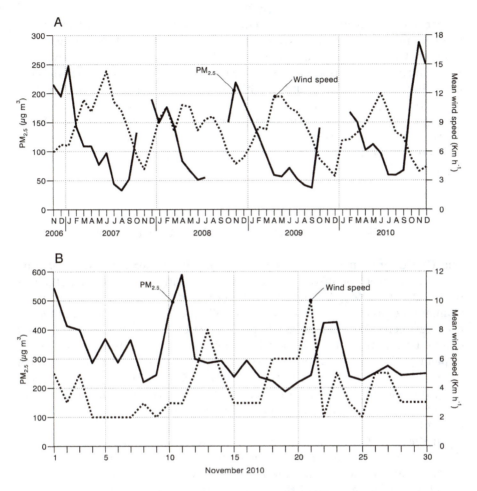

Figure 4.5: Delhi PM$_{2.5}$ concentrations: (A) seasonal variations in relation to wind speed; (B) daily mean concentrations and wind speed (after Pandey, Kumar et al., 2012)

respiratory and cardiovascular mortality four days after exposure with the smallest size fraction (10–30 nm).[117] A multi-centre European study revealed daily hospital admissions for ischemic heart disease to be associated with UFP number concentrations.[118]

By 2012, pollution had become a rallying point for public protest in China. Beijing's environmental bureau bowed to the pressure and began posting hourly readings of PM$_{2.5}$ levels. These levels vary considerably from day-to-day and even within a single day (Figure 4.4) but in January 2012 still occasionally exceeded the 500 maximum value of the air quality index (AQI) used by the US Environment Protection Agency.

Particulate concentrations in Indian city air by 2012 reached similar levels to those found in Beijing. In Lucknow, $PM_{2.5}$, measured at four different locations, ranged between 32.4–67.2 (avg. 45.6 ± 10.9) during summer, 25.6–68.9 (avg. 39.8 ± 4.6) during the monsoon and 99.3–299.3 (avg. 212.4 ± 5.0) during winter.[119] Low wind speeds and clear sky conditions creating an inversion which results in the trapping of aerosols in the lower boundary layer probably account for the higher $PM_{2.5}$ levels in winter. Average monthly surface wind data for Delhi for the last five years (Figure 4.5) indicates that wind speeds over Delhi are relatively low during the months of November and December when high $PM_{2.5}$ levels occur.[120]

IMPROVING URBAN AIR QUALITY THROUGH NATIONAL AND INTERNATIONAL REGULATION

The US Congress passed the 1970, 1977 and 1990 Clean Air Acts enabling the federal government to set air pollution regulations for six key pollutants (CO, NO_2, SO_2, PM_{10}, O_3 and Pb) to be enforced by states and major cities. Combined emissions of these six major pollutants decreased by about 54 per cent between 1980 and 2008, despite increases in population, traffic and energy use. Within the USA, local air pollution control districts worked to implement Federal regulations and to achieve air quality improvements to meet local needs. Under authority of the Health and Safety Code, on 30 December 1947, the Board of Supervisors of Los Angeles County enacted, the first rules and regulations guiding the conduct of the Los Angeles County Air Pollution Control District.

In 1989, the CAA Amendments of 1990 were signed into law by President George H.W. Bush. They required new programmes aimed at curbing urban ozone, rural acid rain, stratospheric ozone, toxic air pollutant emissions and vehicle emissions, and established a new, uniform national permit system.

Since 1977, the South Coast Air Quality Management District (AQMD) has been responsible for air pollution control for all of Orange County and the urban portions of Los Angeles, Riverside and San Bernardino counties. This area of 27,824 km^2 is home to over 16.8 million people, about half the Californian population, is the second most populated urban area in the United States and one of the smoggiest. Since the 1970s, the air quality has improved, despite growth in numbers of people and motor vehicles. By 2012 maximum levels of ozone, one of their worst smog problems, were less than one quarter of those in the 1950s. Nevertheless, air in the South Coast air basin still exceeded the federal health 8-hour standard for ozone on 113 days in 2009. Maximum levels were almost twice as high as the federal standard for clean air (Figure 4.6). It is important to stress, however, that despite the national leadership of the state of California on the issue of air pollution abatement, Los Angeles continues to have some of the worst air quality conditions in the whole country.[121]

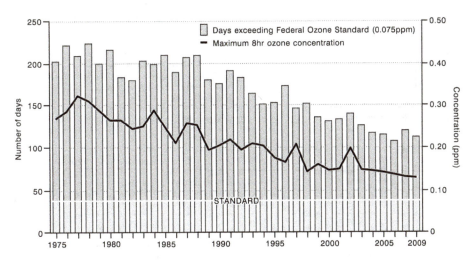

Figure 4.6: South Coast Air basin showing the decline in ozone concentrations, since 1975 and that they remained above the US standard in 2009

Not everything in urban air pollution is concerned with changing patterns of fuels use and technological advances. Problems arising from something as basic as burning wood can lead to local legislation and regulation. Wagga Wagga City Council in Australia took action to reduce the air pollution due to biomass burning mentioned above by listing the Wagga Wagga Local Government Area in the POEO (Clean Air) Regulation 2010, as an area where all open burning is prohibited without approval. This prohibition applies to bonfires, incinerators and fire buckets. Approval can be sought from the council. Wagga Wagga City Council also monitors smoke from wood fuelled heaters through smoky chimney surveys during the cooler months. Households identified as emitting excessive smoke are provided with information on ways of reducing wood smoke emissions.[122]

In Spain much of the progress in environmental protection is being made at the level of the Autonomous Community or municipality rather than at the national level, although this progress is uneven. These have parallels with local authority actions in Manchester, New York and Chicago. However, in Spain, coordination between the national and sub-national levels was weak. Trends up to 2000 and future predictions for the Spanish transport sector show increases in road traffic.[123] A 1981 pollution episode led the Basque government to sponsor the first study of SO_2 and air pollution transport in Spain.[124] Bilbao was well known as having serious pollution problems resulting from being in a deep, incised valley, having many industrial emissions and a close proximity of housing to industrial plants. A similar pollution event in Barcelona several years later resulted in the first epidemiological study of air pollution in Spain, although the pollutant could not be identified.[125]

Table 4.4: Key European air pollution legislation 1970–2000

Date	Name	Objectives
1970	ECF Directive 70/220	Initial EC standards for spark-ignition engines for CO and HC. 'Optional harmonization' adopted. (NO_x added in 1978. All standards tightened through 1987.)
1975	EC Directive 75/716	Initial EC standards for the sulphur content in fuel. (Standards for lead and VOC emissions added subsequently. All standards tightened progressively through 1996.)
1979	UN/ECE Convention on Long-Range Transboundary Air Pollution (LRTAP)	The first international legally binding instrument to deal with problems of air pollution on a broad regional basis. Besides laying down the general principles of international cooperation for air pollution abatement, the Convention sets up an institutional framework bringing together research and policy.
1980	EC Directive 80/779	Initial EC air quality limit values, SO_2 and particles. (Compliance by 1993.)
1988	EC Directive 88/76	Revokes principle of optional harmonization.
1988	EC Directive 88/77 and 88/436	Initial EC standards for diesel engines.
1988	EC Directive 88/609	Large Combustion Plant Directive.
1988	LRTAP NOX Protocol	Freeze NO_x emissions at 1987 levels by 1994. 12 EC nations sign an additional Declaration to reduce emissions 30 per cent by 1998. Establishes Critical Loads concept and calls for further reductions.
1990	EC Directive 90/1290	Established European Environmental Agency (EEA) to collect and provide environmental information to the EU and Member States.
1991	LRTAP VOC Protocol	Reduction of emissions by 30 per cent (Emissions data is sparse and of poor quality, making assessment and enforcement difficult.)
1992	EU Directive 92/72	Requires ozone monitoring and establishes air quality standards for ozone.
1996	EU Directive 96/62	Air Quality Framework Directive sets air quality standards, requires monitoring and notification of the public when standards are not met.
1997	EU COM (97) 88	Community Strategy to Combat Acidification – Recommends continued participation in LRTAP and reductions of SO_2 by 66 per cent and NO_x by 48 per cent in 2010 compared to 1990 baseline values in order to attain 50 per cent gap closure, then further cuts to meet critical loads.
1998	LRTAP Heavy Metals Protocol	Freezes emissions of lead, cadmium, and mercury at 1990 levels, phases out leaded gasoline, establishes stationary-source emission limits.
1998	LRTAP Persistent Organic Pollutants Protocol	Bans or limits the use of 12 chemicals.

Sources: http://ec.europa.eu/environment/air/quality/legislation/existing_leg.htm and related websites

The European Union (EU) has issued a suite of directives that have guided improvements in air quality across the Union (Table 4.4). Some countries already had high standards. Reducing CO_2 emissions from new cars has been a key priority of EU climate change policy. The aim was to limit average CO_2 emissions from new passenger cars sold in the EU to 120 g/km by 2010. The main element in the strategy is an agreement by car producers to limit average CO_2 emissions from new cars to 140 g/km by 2008/2009. This represents a reduction of around 25 per cent compared with the mid-1990s. By the start of 2006, car makers were almost halfway to meeting this target.[126] In addition the Commission requires mandatory labelling of new cars with fuel consumption and emissions data and that governments will base at least 50 per cent of their vehicle registration tax on a vehicle's CO_2 emissions. Some European countries now base all the registration tax on CO_2 emissions, others offer fiscal incentives encouraging people to buy low emission vehicles and a few base the tax on fuel consumption, with a component considering CO_2 emissions.[127]

In the newly industrializing economies of Brazil, India, China, Indonesia and Mexico, severe urban air pollution had led to many innovative regulations and policies to combat the problem. Unprecedented industrial and urban development since 1980, accompanied by a growing population, has increased the amount of environmental damage in Indonesia. The rising levels of air pollution in several large cities stimulated the government to develop a national programme aimed at controlling the quantity of pollutants in the air. However, as in nineteenth-century Chicago, Pittsburgh and Manchester, there was concern about the programme's impact on economic performance and incomes.[128]

Solving the air pollution problem has been a priority of the City of Mexico Metropolitan Environmental Commission, which is integrated with local and federal authorities. Efforts to curb emissions after 1980 were relatively successful. In the 1990s, for instance, the government introduced air quality improvement programmes – PIICA and PROAIRE – that include, among other measures, a rotating one-weekday ban on private car use. On days of high pollution, the ban extends to every second day and some manufacturing activities are curtailed. In addition, car owners must have their vehicles certified every six months. Even though lead, CO and SO_2 levels were reduced and then stabilized, those of other contaminants still exceeded air quality standards in 2010. When PROAIRE concluded in 2000, environmental authorities undertook a longer, ambitious air quality improvement programme: PROAIRE 2002–2010.[129]

For all growing cities in Asia, the dilemma of how to ease traffic congestion and improve the urban environment while improving the mobility of families and encouraging local industry remains. In January, 2008, Tata Motors, India's largest motor vehicle manufacturer announced the 100,000 rupee (US$2,600) Nano car, which at the time was the cheapest new car on the Indian market by far. Immediately critical comments appeared in the press: 'If Tata Motors ... sells all 250,000 of the ultra-cheap cars it is planning to make this year, the congestion and pollution [in New Delhi] will get far worse.'[130]

Since the beginning of economic reform in 1978, many Chinese cities have experienced a period of deteriorating air quality followed more recently by a stabilization, or in some cases, improvement in air pollution levels. Understanding the various economic, political, and institutional forces that guided China down this path is important, both to advance the science of environment and development, and to illuminate future Chinese decision-making on urban air pollution management.[131] China has a unique environmental management system, which is characterized as a top-down administrative system lacking organized and meaningful public involvement. Some agents and forces that have played essential roles in industrialized countries do not exist in China.

On a national basis, China has yet to reach the level of economic development at which environmental degradation will stop increasing with growth. China's investment in environmental protection did not exceed 1 per cent of GDP until 1997.[132] Economic growth has always had higher priority than environmental pollution control issues on China's development agenda.[133]

After 1990, economic growth became one of the most important factors determining local governmental leaders' performance evaluations, which are conducted by upper levels of government and influence their future promotion. Furthermore, local government leaders control the budget, personnel, and more importantly, the appointment and promotion of the director of local environmental authority. The result is that local environmental authorities have not been willing to challenge economic growth openly.[134] Nevertheless, ambient PM levels have declined in most Chinese cities since the late 1980s, partly through the acquisition of a more modern vehicle fleet, which although many, many times larger than before had far lower emissions per vehicle.

China's central authorities took action to control urban air quality at an earlier stage of economic development than has been observed elsewhere. This probably reflects the relatively strong control that the Chinese central government had over local conditions between 1990 and 2005.[135] Elite awareness along with the pursuit of political and social stability has motivated the central government to take action particularly on particulate matter pollution,[136] but also on pollution caused by vehicle emissions, and SO_2/acid rain. However, the allocation of resources to these three problems has been quite different in both quantity and timing. Particulate matter (PM) pollution was the first to get national and local attention, attracting more resources than other contaminants.[137]

Despite the great improvements in many cities, the underlying social and economic conditions in many Asian and African cities, together with long periods of still air and major urban dust domes, make them likely to have the worst air pollution problems and the highest rates of diseases such as bronchitis and asthma. One website listed the following ten cities as having the world's worst pollution in 2012:[138]

1. Ahwaz, Iran
2. Ulan Bator, Mongolia
3. Sanadaj, Iran
4. Ludhiana, India
5. Quetta, Pakistan
6. Kermanshah, Iran
7. Peshawar, Pakistan
8. Gaberone, Botswana
9. Yasouj, Iran
10. Kanpor, India

FISCAL INCENTIVES TO REDUCE URBAN AIR POLLUTION

In 1980, France passed a law introducing a tax on atmospheric pollution. SO_2 emissions began to be taxed in 1985 and NO_x emissions in 1990 (Table 4.5). However, these tax rates were not high enough to encourage active pollution abatement actions.[139] Government action to make the price of petrol without lead (called 'unleaded') more attractive was far more effective in reducing that form of pollution.

The most important application ever made of a market-based instrument for environmental protection is arguably the tradeable permit system in the United States that regulates SO_2 emissions, the primary precursor of acid rain. In a tradeable permit system, the government establishes a cap on total emissions. Quotas (allowances) are then given (or auctioned) to companies totalling no more than the cap. When the goal is to reduce the level of emissions, the cap and quotas can be reduced over time until the goal is reached. A company can release emissions up to the level of its quota. It can reduce emissions below its quota and make a profit by selling the remaining allowances. An older plant, for which reducing emissions would be extremely costly, could emit more than its quota by buying surplus allowances from other companies. To set up a new plant, a company would have to buy surplus allowances.

Such a scheme ensures maximum flexibility while capping total emissions. The emission quotas are mainly temporary permits, not 'rights to pollute'. They can be reduced year by year until air quality has improved to meet national standards. Air quality standards for a cap and trade system should be based on protecting human health and environmental quality. Many argue that cap and trades often turn out to be highly cost effective.[140]

This system, which was established under Title IV of the US Clean Air Act Amendments of 1990, is intended to reduce sulphur dioxide and nitrogen oxide emissions by 10 million tonnes and 2 million tonnes, respectively, from 1980 levels. The first phase of sulphur dioxide emissions reductions was started in 1995, with a second phase of reduction initiated in the year 2000.[141] In 2010 the EPA made a new ruling requiring power plants to reduce their emissions of SO_2 and nitrogen oxides (NO_x) to 71 per cent and 52 per cent of their 2005 levels respectively. Strong public support with ability to regulate standards and to invest in appropriate technology have been important factors in the success of this legislation.

Table 4.5: Key French legislation on air pollution
(largely based on data in Vernier, 1993)

Date of enactment	Purpose	Key attributes
19 December 1917	Control of hazardous industries, pollution, odours	Effectively addressed all sources of pollution
10 March 1948	Use of energy	Regulates type of equipment to be used in building or reconstructing electricity power stations and the consultations that should take place
2 August 1961	Control of pollution and odours	Repealed December 1917 Act; led subsequently to 1973 Ministry charged with nature conservation and environmental protection and to subsequent regulations on atmospheric pollution, combustion of fuels, and particulate emissions, with limits or standards for individual pollutants. Also led to measures to regulate vehicle emissions and the content of petrol and diesel fuels
19 July 1976	New rules for hazardous sites	Fixed levels of particulates admissible in fuel gases; required use of low-sulphur content fuels when meteorological conditions create a pollution hazard; regulations for specific industries such as cement works
1980	Law introducing a tax on atmospheric pollution	Implemented for SO_2 emissions in 1985 and later NO_x, VOC, and hydrochloric acid (HCl). During the 1990s it was claimed that a significant reduction in SO_2, NO_x, and HCl resulted from the tax
1983	Agence pour la Qualite de l'Air (Clean Air Agency) begins operation	Responsibility for monitoring and information of air pollution

Additional rules and regulations were enacted as the need arose. The permit system of the Los Angeles County Air Pollution Control District is one of the most important features of the air pollution control programme. Pollution trading allows a polluter to forego reductions in pollution (or increase pollution) at its own facility in exchange for reducing emissions elsewhere or by purchasing credits which represent someone else's pollution reduction. Pollution trading advocates argue that this approach saves money, promotes innovative technology, and continuously reduces pollution through market incentives.[142] The first major emissions trading programme, adopted in 1976 by the EPA, allowed new stationary sources of air pollution (e.g. industrial plants) to be built in exchange for 'offsets' that reduced air pollution by a greater amount from other sources in the same region. A more controversial trading programme soon followed called 'netting', which used surplus emission reductions at an existing plant to offset increased pollution from expanded operations at the same facility. Then, in 1979, a 'bubble policy' adopted by EPA allowed existing industrial polluters to meet pollution reduction goals in the aggregate through any combination of on-site emissions reductions. In this way, in California, sources that exceed VOC standards for one product can offset excess emissions through over-compliance in other products. California has used a vehicle retirement programme that operates much like a credit system to reduce mobile-source air emissions by removing the oldest and most polluting vehicles from the road.

The Clean Air Act Amendments of 1990 allow states to tax regulated air pollutants to recover administrative costs of state programmes, and allow areas in extreme non-compliance to charge higher rates. Under this structure, the South Coast Air Quality Management District (SCAQMD) in Los Angeles had the highest permit fees in the country.[143] The South Coast Air Quality Management District, which is responsible for controlling emissions across four southern Californian counties, launched a tradeable permit programme in January, 1994, to reduce nitrogen oxide and sulphur dioxide emissions in the Los Angeles area. Cost savings of 42 per cent, amounting to $58 million annually, were predicted. By June 1996, 353 participants in this Regional Clean Air Incentives Market programme, had traded more than 100,000 tonnes of NO_x and SO_2 emissions, at a value of over $10 million.[144]

The Clean Air Act Amendments of 1990 also authorized states and local air districts to develop economic incentives programmes, further paving the way for pollution trading in Los Angeles. Emboldened by national policy developments, an industry coalition called the Regulatory Flexibility Group successfully lobbied the SCAQMD to amend the Air Quality Management Plan to suspend industrial air quality regulations while the details of the market incentives programme were developed. By 2001, the US Environmental Protection Agency was actively involved in 35 pollutant trading projects in 19 different states, from California to Connecticut.

Pollution trading in Los Angeles has led to concentrated toxic air emission hot-spots that have shackled low-income and minority communities with the region's air pollution. However the pollution trading programme in Los Angeles has been criticized, with claims that the city has demonstrated that the more unrestricted an emissions trading programme, the more likely it is that unjust hot-spot impacts, over-allocations, and fraudulent transactions will result.[145] Yet the reforms needed to improve the environmental performance and mitigate the adverse impacts of pollution trading erase the cost savings and regulatory flexibility touted by the advocates of trading.

Europe

The European Commission argues that carbon pricing can provide an incentive for deployment of efficient, low-carbon technologies across Europe. The European Emissions Trading System (ETS) is the central pillar of European climate policy. It is designed to be technology neutral, cost-effective and fully compatible with the internal energy market. It will have to play an increased role. The Commission's 2050 scenarios show that carbon pricing can coexist with instruments designed to achieve particular energy policy objectives, notably research and innovation, promotion of energy efficiency and development of renewables.[146] The objective of the ETS is to contribute to reducing emissions to levels considered 'scientifically necessary' in 'a cost-effective and economically efficient' manner. In 2012, it was thought that the ETS was performing to a certain degree against the first criterion, in leveraging some energy efficiency and fuel switching. However, the overall role of the ETS in emissions reductions is relatively marginal, with other policies (such as renewable and energy efficiency targets) currently playing a more significant role. By 2012, the weakness of the ETS reflected three key issues: 1) a weak and volatile price signal, arising from the current oversupply of permits; 2) more importantly, the lack of a clear and credible post-2020 framework; and 3) a lack of institutional processes and mechanisms to ensure the credible future management of adjustments to the ETS.[147] With the 2012 low price, the ETS was probably not making a fully cost effective contribution to emissions reductions. One of the problems was determining what the cap on emissions should be in any year. A single national government can do this relatively easily, for example, in any given year Australia determined what the cap should be in five years' time. This type of rolling adjustment of the cap gave much more stability to emissions trading in Australia, than the occasional agreements between 27 nation states in the European Commission, where each state is reluctant to give up sovereignty over energy and economic policies. This nationalism and concern for national economic achievement holds back progress towards the even greater goal of cutting greenhouse gas emissions. The unwillingness of some countries to endorse and implement the Kyoto protocol will not only make the air of cities less pleasant, it will lead to greater health, flood and drought risks, and the drowning of sections of many coastal towns and urban settlements.

CONCLUDING COMMENTS ON URBAN AIR QUALITY

The history of urban air pollution is one of decades of protest and campaigning; action after serious incidents or evidence of severe impacts upon public health, development of technologies that shift problems to other localities or other parts of the urban ecosystem and then finding that new technologies have created another type of air pollution. As rapidly as the ability to detect and monitor contaminants increases, the types of emission change and new problems are recognized. The history of urban air pollution is thus one of problem shifting and problem substitution: either altering where the pollution goes, or changing the technology: replacing steam engines and open fires with diesel motors and gas boilers that in turn create new forms of pollution. Until sufficient electricity is generated by non-polluting renewable sources, electric vehicles will not eliminate pollution, merely change its source.

The ecological modernization efforts during the late nineteenth century and through the middle twentieth were not undertaken to develop a more harmonious relationship between capitalism and the environment, or even between capitalism and human health. Instead, such efforts were primarily undertaken to make industrial production and railroad and automotive transportation more congenial to the economic interests of one segment of the capitalist class – local growth coalitions. By taking this into account we can understand why ecological modernization efforts have left many cities with persistently poor air quality.[148] Despite the mobilization of large numbers of people around environmental issues, the air pollution regulatory policies continue to emphasize technology to abate air pollution. Events have moved urban air pollution and greenhouse gas emissions to the centre of world environmental politics. For many people now of retirement age, the industrial smogs associated with coal burning are a thing of their childhood, but the problems of fine particulates (PM_{10} and $PM_{2.5}$) and of volatile organic compounds are new and more difficult to recognize. Sadly, for many in the poorest areas, both the old pollutants and the newer ones are present together. Enforceable emission regulations and fiscal measures, such as taxing vehicle emission levels help to reduce pollutant loads and increase awareness of the links between individual behaviour and consumption and the quality of urban air. By 2012 there appeared to be more concern about fiscal measures and cost-effective actions than about the impact on both human health and food supplies that so concerned women's groups, local politicians and public health reformers in the nineteenth century.

5

Water from the Hills, the Ground, the Sea, and the Roof

Towards Integrated Water Resource Management in Cities

Water management in the Americas may have begun 10,000 years ago. A well 5 m deep and 10 m across at the original ground surface was in use for 2,000 years in what is now the village of San Marcos Necoxtla in the Tehuacán Valley of Mexico.[1] This was probably for domestic supplies. Later wells helped to provide water for irrigating crops but about 1000 BC the first canals in Mexico were built. Primarily for irrigation, the canals would also have supplemented urban supplies from wells and springs. These were large scale hydraulic engineering achievements. The southern Tehuacán Valley had over 1,200 km of canals, feeding a 330 km² irrigated area by 5000 BC. Simple aqueducts carried the canals across valleys and depressions.

Early cities relied on local springs or streams which were regulated to supply fountains in public squares or local precincts. Tunnelled conduits feeding open pools or fountains were notable features of cities in the ancient world. Hezekiah's aqueduct at Jerusalem, feeding the pool of Siloam (c. 725 BC) and the Eupalinian aqueduct, built under the rule of Polycrates, involving a tunnel through Mount Kastro to supply the ancient capital of the Aegean island of Samos with fresh water (c. 530 BC), are well-known examples. Tunnelled aqueducts with manholes at intervals existed at Hecatompylos, an ancient city in west Khurasan, Iran, by 500 BC.

ROMAN WATER SUPPLIES

Rome followed these traditions by building the tunnelled Appian (312 BC, 16.5 km long) and Anio Vetusian (272 BC, over 50 km long) aqueducts. They were

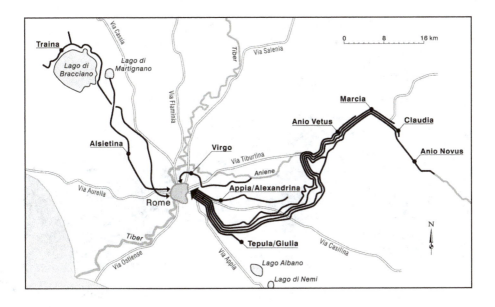

Figure 5.1: The aqueducts of ancient Rome (after Scarre, 1995)

underground mainly for defence considerations. Rome's first overland aqueduct was Aqua Marcia (Figure 5.1) (144 BC, about 90 km long) with 9 km on arches, delivering water at an elevation sufficient to supply the Capitoline, Caelian and Aventine Hills. By AD 97 the nine aqueducts of Rome provided 143 megalitres of water per day within the walls and 75 megalitres outside the walls. In all, ancient Rome had eleven major aqueducts (Figure 5.1), built between 312 BC (*Aqua Appia*) and AD 226 (*Aqua Alexandrina*); the longest (*Anio Novus*) was 95 km long. In imperial times, when the city's population was well over a million, the distribution system was able to provide over one cubic metre of water per day for each inhabitant, more than most people use today. However, despite the large supplies coming into the city, sanitation conditions were primitive in the apartments in the *insulae*, the multi-storey block of small dark dwellings for tenants and sub-tenants. Only the occupants of the ground floors had direct access to the piped supply and connections to drains. Those who lived above them had to fetch water in buckets from fountains in the streets or depend upon notoriously unreliable water carriers. These residents also had to carry their wastes downstairs in buckets to empty them into a pit in the basement or deposit them in nearby cess trenches. There were many instances of wastes simply being hurled from windows into the streets below.[2]

The Roman provinces contain many examples of urban water supply aqueducts, including the Pont du Gard near Nimes in France and the Zaghouan aqueduct (Figure 5.2) supplying Carthage, built by Hadrian in the mid-second century.[3] Almost every significant Roman town in Britain had an engineered

107

Figure 5.2: The Zaghouan Aqueduct near Oued Meliane in Tunisia
(photo Ian Douglas)

water-supply. It went to public baths and, as in Lincoln, to a fountain in the streets. Private individuals could be connected to the public supply on payment of charges. The surplus was channelled into a system of drains.[4] Aqueducts are known to have fed water to Dorchester, Wroxeter, Leicester and Lincoln; others probably existed at least at London, Silchester, Cirencester, Caerwent and Verulamium, towns where evidence of water distribution pipes have been found. The aqueducts supplemented other sources of water, particularly from wells.[5] Thus the Romans practised the conjunctive use of ground and surface water. This could be important in areas where river levels sometimes become low in summer. The aqueduct feeding Dorchester took water from the River Frome at Notton Mill, Maiden Newton, approximately 10 km upstream, and carried it through an 18 km long channel, approximately 15 m wide and 0.7 m deep that followed all the twists and turns of the 90 m contour, falling only 7.6 m between the intake and the west gate of the town.[6]

MEDITERRANEAN WATER SUPPLIES

The Valens Aqueduct or 'Arcade of the Gray Falcon' at Istanbul was started by Constantine and completed in the fourth century AD by Valens. Justinian II had a second tier added; and Mehmet the Conqueror and Sinan had a hand in its restoration and enlargement. The 0.8 km long aqueduct connects the third and fourth hills of Istanbul. Water was conveyed to the Byzantine palaces, city

Figure 5.3: The 13th century aqueduct at Spoleto, Italy, possibly built on Roman foundations (from a drawing by an unknown artist)

cisterns, and then to Topkapi Palace, and the aqueduct helped supply water to the city for over 1,500 years.

Further south in the eastern Mediterranean, the Nabateans built a kingdom that extended from the south of modern Syria to the south of the Sinai Peninsula and the northern Red Sea coast of Arabia around 60 BC. Their water supplies depended on expert hydraulic engineering, using groundwater. While at Petra water from springs and channelled runoff fed more than 200 rock-carved cisterns, at Mada'in Salih, where there is no evidence of surface springs, 130 wells were used and any rainfall was channelled into cisterns cut into sandstone. The stone-lined wells exploited a water table that at the time was 5 metres below the surface.[7]

The Arabs who moved into the Iberian Peninsula constructed infiltration galleries at their military stronghold at what is now Madrid. The Christians extended the galleries after recapturing the town in the eleventh century, calling the subsurface channels 'viaje de agua'.

MEDIAEVAL EUROPEAN WATER SUPPLIES

Mediaeval European city water supplies either used the Roman infrastructure or gradually acquired conduits of their own. The Italian cathedral city of Spoleto has a thirteenth-century aqueduct about 220 m long and 90 m high with pointed arches spanning up to 20 metres (Figure 5.3) At this time, many cities were seeking additional supplies of water. In 1236 a patent was approved for a lead conduit to carry water from the Tyburn Brook to the City of London. By the fourteenth century, Bruges, the great cloth-trading city of Flanders, with a large population for the time (40,000), had developed a system utilizing one large collecting cistern from which water was pumped, using a wheel with buckets on a chain, through underground conduits to public sites. Pipes were laid in Zittau in 1374; and in Wroclaw in 1479, water was pumped from the river and then taken to various parts of the city by pipes, probably made of wood, as was common up until the nineteenth century.[8]

Parisians of the Middle Ages gained their water from wells, the river or springs. On the Left Bank, wells hit groundwater at 4 to 6 metres depth, but they were contaminated.[9] The Belleville aqueduct was repaired in 1457 and with the Pré-Saint-Gervais aqueduct it supplied the city until the seventeenth century.

UK MUNICIPAL WATER SUPPLIES IN THE
SIXTEENTH AND SEVENTEENTH CENTURIES

As late as the fifteenth century, provision of water conduits in London depended on private philanthropy associated with institutions such as hospitals and almshouses. By the late Tudor period these sources were inadequate and a succession of private-enterprise schemes was devised over the next two centuries. In 1581, a great waterwheel was installed under one of the arches of London Bridge to pump water to the city, for cleaning rather than drinking because the tidewater was too saline. More radical was the New River Scheme of 1608–13, by which a channel, effectively a 64 km-long artificial river, brought water from springs in Hertfordshire to a large reservoir in Islington whence it was distributed within the city. Other sources on Hampstead Heath, at the head of the River Fleet, were tapped by the Hampstead Water Company, incorporated in 1692. A series of ponds helped to provide the supply.[10]

In the early sixteenth century a conduit system was established in Manchester through private donations and was maintained by bequests and levies on the inhabitants.[11] The conduit led from a spring to an ornamental wooden building in the market place. It gave rise to the street names Spring Gardens and Fountain Street.[12] The conduit system needed constant repair and in 1570 was said to 'lack water'.[13] Restrictions, in terms of the sizes of container that could be filled started in 1578, followed in 1581 by a ban on drawing water between 2100 and 0600 hours and a lock was fitted to the building. In 1586 the hours of supply were cut to 0600 to 0900 and 1500 to 1800. New sources were sought. A pump was in use in Hanging Ditch in 1602.[14]

Leeds was one of the first towns in Britain to have a piped water supply to houses; this came into operation in 1694. A water wheel pumped water from the River Aire through 1.5 miles of lead pipes to a storage reservoir and then was supplied to the wealthier inhabitants.

In 1695 Derby gained a piped water supply (for those who could afford to be connected) using wooden pipes, thanks to George Sorocold, a talented hydraulic engineer who used a patent wheel which rose and fell without loss of energy with the height of the river. The water was raised by a screw to a tank whence it was piped to a number of public outlets in Derby town centre. The water also drove a device for boring out fresh wooden pipes.[15]

In 1678, George McCartney was paid to lay 1,200 metres of wooden pipe from the Tuck Dam to serve a community of 7,000 people in Belfast, Northern Ireland. The system was fragmented and the operator was unable to collect charges for the water supplied.[16]

EUROPEAN MUNICIPAL WATER SUPPLIES IN THE SIXTEENTH AND SEVENTEENTH CENTURIES

Before 1560 the existing water sources were adequate for the people then living in Madrid, Spain, but when the royal court was moved to the city in 1561, the population grew rapidly, deforestation occurred around the city and many springs dried up. By the end of the sixteenth century, wells had to be deepened and water wheels installed to lift the water.[17]

In 1608, the Samaritaine pump in Paris that lifted 700 m^3 of water from the Seine every day to supply the Louvre and the Tuileries was completed. In 1670, a further 2000 $m^3 day^{-1}$ were being contributed by the pumps of the Notre Dame bridge.[18] The water was distributed by water carriers. Its quality was said to be better than the groundwater, but it was often muddy and it was affected by the debris thrown into the river.

UK URBAN WATER SUPPLY DEVELOPMENT IN THE EIGHTEENTH AND EARLY NINETEENTH CENTURIES

The rapid growth of the West End of London demanded yet another water source, and in 1723 the Chelsea Waterworks Company was founded, which drew water directly from the Thames into a great network of channels. Windmills and horse mills, and after 1750 steam pumps, lifted the water to the slightly higher ground of the West End via reservoirs in Hyde Park and St James's Park. The cuts and channels eventually covered almost 50 ha and pumped nearly 2 megalitres of water per day to the new houses of St James's and Mayfair. Much of Pimlico was turned into a strange suburban fenland, with creeks, sluice gates and footbridges, frequented by water birds and anglers. The intake was exactly where the Grosvenor Road railway bridge now stands and the steam pump was on the site of Victoria Station.[19] Steam pumps assisted the flow of the New River supply after 1760.[20] Pumping houses were added to the Hampstead Heath supply in 1835.[21]

From 1786 onwards, the city of Liverpool negotiated with several private companies, including the 'Town Springs Company' for reliable water supplies. Contracts were signed with two concerns which erected some pumping stations but achieved puny results. Their water supplies were at best intermittent, at worst only available for a few hours per week.[22] Poor people queued for two to three hours to get water. A high incidence of hernia was said to be due to carrying excessive weights of water over long distances.

The Belfast water supply became so unprofitable that in 1791 the recently formed Belfast Charitable Society took over responsibility. Legislation was enacted to allow the levying of water rates and to renovate the system and develop new spring sources. At that time, a water demand of 160 l^{-1} cap^{-1} day^{-1} was said to exist in Belfast.[23]

EUROPEAN URBAN WATER SUPPLY DEVELOPMENT IN THE EIGHTEENTH AND EARLY NINETEENTH CENTURIES

Water shortages in Paris continued. By the late eighteenth century the supply was down to about a litre per person per day. The Périer brothers installed two steam pumps at Chaillot in 1782 which raised water 30 m from the low level of the Seine to supply the Saint-Honoré district. Although the steam engines attracted great attention, the enterprise turned into a financial scandal.[24] In 1785, Paris had 600,000 people, most in great poverty and a life expectancy of 40 years. Overcrowded cemeteries contaminated the underground water supply. An environmental crisis existed and major works were needed to resolve it. The Canal de l'Ourcq built in 1812–15, fed water to many fountains in the city;[25] 150 m^3 hour^{-1} started to be pumped from the Lower Greensand aquifer under Paris in 1841.[26]

Water shortages arose in Madrid also. By the end of the eighteenth century the viajes de agua comprised 70 km of infiltration galleries and only supplied 2,000 to 4,000 m^3 day^{-1}, equivalent to 10 to 20 l^{-1} cap^{-1} day^{-1}. Wells were sunk to seek groundwater, as had been done in Paris, but without success. Eventually thoughts turned to surface sources some distance from the city.

TOWARDS MUNICIPAL WATERWORKS: NINETEENTH-CENTURY MUNICIPAL PUBLIC HEALTH AND WATER WELFARE IN THE UK

The water supplied to London from the Chelsea works was not really fit for human consumption. It was affected by both the tides and by sewage from towns upstream. In 1827, the radical politician Sir Francis Burdett complained to parliament that:

The water taken from the River Thames at Chelsea for the use of the inhabitants of the western part of the Metropolis, being charged with the contents of the great common sewers, the drainings from dunghills and laystalls, the refuse of hospitals and slaughter houses, colour lead and soap works, drug mills and manufactories, and with all sorts of decomposed animal and vegetable substances, rendering the said water offensive and destructive to health, ought no longer to be taken up by any of the water companies from so foul a source.[27]

The debates in parliament led to the 1828 Royal Commission on Metropolitan Water Supply that recommended that the intakes lower down the Thames should be replaced by sources further upstream. Although this was ignored, companies experimented with sand and gravel filters[28] which so improved the water that by 1835 9,090 m^3 day^{-1} were being pumped by the Chelsea Waterworks to 13,000 houses in the West End.[29] This was only a temporary measure, as the growing population was adding to the pollution of the Thames day by day. Cholera outbreaks, especially those in the 1840s, and agitation by people like Edwin Chadwick, eventually led to the 1852 Metropolitan Water Act which required companies to make radical changes in their supplies which resulted in cleaner water, and ultimately a healthier population.[30] The Chelsea Waterworks Company shifted its works to Putney, sold off the Pimlico site to developers, and built a new intake much further upstream at Walton.[31]

The cholera outbreaks of 1849 and 1853–4 provided a good test of the effectiveness of the 1852 Act. John Snow, famous for his mapping that demonstrated the role of the Broad Street pump in Soho as a source of cholera in 1853–4, prepared a further map comparing cholera mortality rates between the customers of two rival companies, the Lambeth Water Company and the Southwark and Vauxhall Water Company during the two outbreaks. In the earlier outbreak, death rates were similar, but in the second, Southwark and Vauxhall had become almost six times more dangerous as a supplier. The difference was due to the Lambeth Company having moved its raw water intake upstream to Thames Ditton above the tidal reach as required by the 1852 Act. The Southwark and Vauxhall Company had yet to take similar action.[32] The Metropolitan Board of Works was established to deal with the increasingly problematic infrastructure issues London was facing. These included foul drainage, streets and bridges and from 1866 fire protection, through responsibility for the newly established London Fire Brigade.

In the west country, Bristol had its first waterworks in 1846; a piped water supply was extended to the rest of the city over the next 20 years. Meanwhile in the Midlands, Derby gained a new waterworks company in 1851, which provided the city with a wholesome supply.[33] Further north, Sheffield began to draw water from the Pennine moors less than 10 km to the west of the city in 1836, initially from the Redmires reservoirs (1836–54) and later from the Rivelin valley (1848).[34] Across the Pennines in 1848, Manchester began to build reservoirs in Longdendale, Derbyshire following the designs of John F. La Trobe Bateman. When completed they were claimed to constitute the largest expanse of artificial water in the world. The three upper reservoirs, Woodhead, Torside

Figure 5.4: Building the Vyrnwy dam in Wales, 1888
(source: http://history.powys.org.uk/images/llanfyllin/damwall.jpg)

and Rhodeswood were to supply water, while the lower Valehouse and Bottoms reservoirs were designed as compensation water resources to release into the River Etherow.[35]

Late eighteenth and early nineteenth-century water supplies for the growing industrial towns and cities of northern England depended largely on earth dams built across the Pennine valleys. For the mill owners in the towns lower down those valleys, the most important use of water was power to turn their machinery. Collectively they had sufficient political power to threaten any bill that might deprive their mills of what the owners regarded as 'ample' water.[36]

Following the techniques used by the canal builders to feed water to the highest parts of their canals, the municipal waterworks engineers built ever higher earth dams across the upland valleys. A disaster was almost inevitable. A warning came in 1852 when a dam at Holmfirth, near Huddersfield, was undermined by leakage, fortunately without catastrophic consequences. The disaster followed in 1864 with the collapse of the 33 m high Dale Dyke Dam, one of a series supplying the city of Sheffield, when it subsided just after it had been completely filled for the first time. Water overtopped the dam and in 20 minutes 80,000 m³ of earth and 800 megalitres of water swept down the valley below killing 250 people.[37] The cause of the collapse is related to the presence of a 10.7 m step in the cut-off trench near the centre of the dam which caused differing resistances in the clay fill, and eventual failure

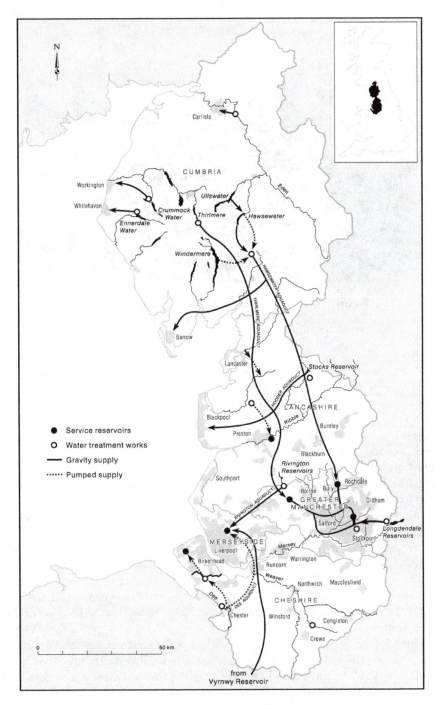

Figure 5.5: The major water supply aqueducts of north-west England
(compiled by the author from various sources)

Figure 5.6: Building the Elan Valley Aqueduct, in Wales
(source: from history.powys.org.uk)

under extreme pressure.[38] The event stimulated a revision of dam engineering practice. Following a construction theory proposed by Professor Rankine of Glasgow University, all later dams were constructed of massive masonry, the first of them being the Vyrnwy dam in Wales built to supply Liverpool with water (Figure 5.4). A drainage system at the base of the dam prevents build-up of water pressure that might otherwise lead to the overturning of the weighty and watertight structure. When completed in 1892, the dam was over 350 metres long and 26 metres high, impounding Europe's then largest reservoir holding nearly 50,000 megalitres of water.[39]

Manchester and Birmingham soon followed Liverpool in developing major dams to tap distant water resources. Manchester's Longdendale supply 29 km east of the city was inadequate by 1885 and thus the Thirlmere dam in the English Lake District, 154 km north of the city was completed in 1894 (Figure 5.5). Meanwhile Birmingham set about building a series of masonry dams in the Elan Valley in Radnorshire, Wales. One of the Elan dams, Craig Coch, is 40 m high. The construction of the 120 km pipeline to Birmingham was also a major engineering feat (Figure 5.6).

The City of Glasgow in Scotland, developed the water resources of Loch Katrine when the Gorbals waterworks became insufficient. An aqueduct to the city involved 30 km of tunnels with a height of 2.75 metres and a roof arch maximum width of 3 metres.

In 1830 the rapidly growing population of Belfast had reached 70,000 and water services were stretched. In 1840 an Act of Parliament established the only elected Water Board in the UK, the Belfast Water Commissioners, who were given powers to levy rates and to acquire water rights. Initially the Commissioners acquired the Woodburn Catchment in Carrickfergus as their first water source outside the city limits. By 1890 they had also gained the Stoneyford and Leatherntown catchments.[40] By 1898 the Belfast supply at 150 l^{-1} cap^{-1} day^{-1} was regarded as ample, but engineers were looking forward to additional supplies from the Mourne Mountains.[41]

EUROPEAN MUNICIPAL WATER SUPPLY DEVELOPMENTS IN THE NINETEENTH CENTURY

From 1800 to 1850, Paris saw the first steps towards the integration of water supplies and sanitation with the construction of the canal de l'Ourcq and the start of an effort to construct a sewer system. The law of 1848 (arrêté ministériel du 21 juin) saw the combining of the Paris Public Works and Highways Department with the Water and Sewerage Department to provide an integrated water and drainage service for the city. Haussman rebuilt the sewer network. The tapping of the principal aquifer supplying Paris by the 548 m deep Grenelle borehole in 1841, when the artesian water level was 126 m above mean sea level, set off a period of rapid exploitation by over 300 wells.[42]

The channels supplying the city of Marseilles with the water of the Durance, by a canal about 97 km long, are among the boldest early nineteenth-century water-supply developments. This canal, begun in 1839, and completed in 1847, is conveyed through three chains of limestone mountains by forty-five tunnels, forming an aggregate length of 13 km, and across numerous valleys by aqueducts; the largest of which, the 80 m high and 392 m long Aqueduct of Roquefeavour, over the ravine of the River Arc, about five miles from Aix, surpasses in size and altitude the ancient Pont du Gard. The immense volume of water, flowing at 11.67 m³ s^{-1}, is carried across by a masonry channel, as in the old Roman aqueducts.

Water shortages in Madrid meant that in 1850 the 220,000 inhabitants only received an average of 7.1 l^{-1} cap^{-1} day^{-1}. Protracted negotiations with private companies failed to deliver a solution that pleased the authorities. Eventually in 1851, a government owned company was created to build a 60 km channel to divert water from the River Lozoya to Madrid.[43] That company, Canal de Isabel II, is still the public company responsible for managing the water distribution in the community of Madrid. The plan was to provide citizens with 90 l^{-1} cap^{-1} day^{-1}, considerably more than in Paris or London at the time.[44]

Although at first the new water supply was more than adequate, even more rapid population growth increased the demand and soon both a second dam on the river and a second storage reservoir in the city were necessary. Although initially it was planned to allow a private company to build the city storage reservoir, this fell through and Canal de Isabel II undertook both new works, reinforcing its position as the Madrid water undertaking. The second dam, the El Villar dam was opened in 1882 and the new urban storage, with three times the capacity of the first, became available in 1879. Nevertheless, with no metering until 1893 and permission for the city council to use as much water as it desired, over-consumption again became a problem as did high levels of turbidity caused by changed flows of the Lozoya River below El Villar. At the end of the century the city faced the need to increase supply, public health issues and a deteriorating infrastructure.

URBAN WATER SUPPLY DEVELOPMENTS
IN THE TWENTIETH CENTURY

By the twentieth century, water supplies were becoming largely municipal undertakings. The criticism of private companies had grown: 'Great popular dissatisfaction resulted from the way in which they held back from participation in the work of development. They were in the business for profit and took as few chances as possible on work which might or might not yield prompt and satisfactory returns. Meanwhile they earned and paid large dividends, and managed their business in the way most satisfactory to themselves and as little as possible with reference to the interests of the public.'[45]

Twentieth-century developments by municipal undertakings in the UK

Parliament and the newly formed London County Council were greatly concerned about future water supplies for London. The council tried to promote a bill to bring water from the Welsh mountains nearly 260 km away. This was defeated and it was decided that London's water should come from the catchments of the rivers Thames and Lea alone.[46] These, together with their underground chalk aquifers, remain the sources of London's water to the present day, although a desalination plant became a possibility in 2005.

The Metropolitan Water Board was founded in 1903 to implement the new supply strategy and to bring the nine private water companies supplying water to London under a single public body. The members of the Board were nominated by the various local authorities within its area of supply. A Royal Commission had reported in 1899 on the need for such controls. Following the re-organization of water management in England and Wales, the Board was abolished in 1974 and control transferred to the Thames Water Authority. Between 1988 and 1993 an 80 km long water ring main (now the Thames Water Ring Main) was laid 40 metres underground in the London clay.[47] The water and sewerage operations of the Thames Water Authority and other agencies were merged in 1989 to form the privatized utility company Thames Water. However, some private companies continue to supply water to the outer suburbs of the London metropolitan region. One of these is Three Valleys Water that was formed in 1994 when Colne Valley, Rickmansworth, and Lee Valley Water companies merged. The company then grew even more in 2000 when it merged with its sister company North Surrey Water to become the UK's largest water only company. It supplies 929 million litres of water per day to approximately 2.9 million customers; 42 per cent from the water supplied comes from rivers and reservoirs and the remaining 58 per cent from boreholes and aquifers.[48]

In the summer of 2000, Thames Water became part of RWE, a large German company that is involved in water supply around the world. RWE sold it to Macquarie, the Australian investment group, for about £8bn. Macquarie then sold it to Veolia Water, a Paris-based multi-national specializing in providing water services. Thames Water itself is now owned by Kemble Water Limited, a consortium led by Macquarie's European Infrastructure Funds. Such is the change in the management of water as a key element of the urban environment.

At the end of the nineteenth century, in the Peak District of Derbyshire, which already supplied the surrounding local towns such as Stockport, Chesterfield, Sheffield and Manchester, an Act of Parliament in 1899 authorized the formation of the Derwent Valley Water Board to provide a joint supply to Sheffield, Derby, Nottingham and Leicester.[49] Developed in three stages, the Howden (1912), Derwent (1916) and Ladybower (1943) reservoirs formed one of the largest schemes in Britain. The Board supplied water to the four cities in the following proportions in 1962: Sheffield 29.7 per cent, Derby 19.3 per cent, Leicester 36.5 per cent and Nottingham 14.5 per cent at the rate of 200 megalitres per day.[50]

Further down the Derwent, Ogston Reservoir was originally created to supply the National Coal Board's Carbonization Plant at Wingerworth but is now run by Severn Trent Water and supplies water for the local area and is used as a holding ground for water for nearby Carsington Reservoir. Designed as the key element in a conjunctive use or 'water compensation' scheme to secure water resources for the East Midlands into the twenty-first century,[51] Carsington was opened in 1992. Water is pumped into Carsington from the River Derwent at times of high rainfall, stored in the reservoir and returned to the Derwent when the river level would otherwise be too low to allow water extraction for treatment (and drinking) further downstream. Additional water can be supplied to the Derwent from Triassic sandstone aquifers near Mansfield, Nottinghamshire. These Derwent valley supplies all became the responsibility of Severn Trent Water following the creation of the Water Authorities in the Act of 1973 and now form a highly integrated, multiple source scheme supplying the cities and towns of the East and West Midlands of England (Figure 5.7). The traditional upland storage reservoirs and direct piped supplies to cities are now coupled with both surface reservoirs and groundwater aquifers. Despite all these measures, Severn Trent Water, like all other water supply operators is now concerned about climate change. In their water supply forward look, the company said: 'There is a potential need for significant new strategic water resource developments to counter the impacts of climate change. However, we recognise that there is considerable uncertainty around the extent of any climate change impact on the supply/demand balance.'[52]

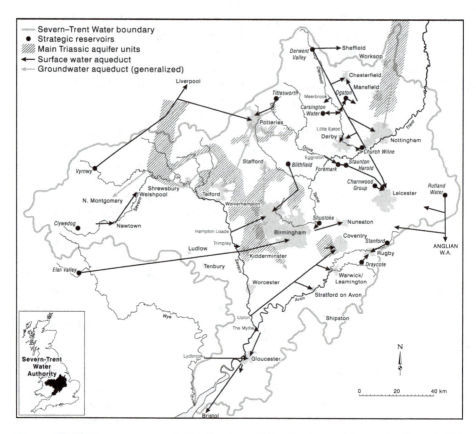

Figure 5.7: Water resources and distribution within the Severn–Trent supply area, UK (after Severn–Trent Water, 2006) (compiled by the author from various sources)

One significant aspect of the use of upland reservoirs was the desire to have tight controls on access to protect the water supplies. These gathering grounds form a significant part of the Peak District National Park (Figure 5.8). There was a long debate about free and open access to the moorlands, partly in competition with the traditional grouse shooting rights and partly in terms of the risk of contamination of the water supplies. Originally many reservoirs were surrounded by tree plantations, on the assumption that they protected water supplies, but in fact they used more water than moorlands and in some cases the forestry operations accelerated erosion that caused continual sedimentation problems in the reservoirs.[53] Over time, access to the moorlands increased and many upland parts of the Peak District now have 'right to roam' access, much to the delight of walkers from the adjacent cities.

Belfast's water supply expanded steadily throughout the twentieth century, initially through additional surface water reservoirs and aqueducts and later through groundwater and conjunctive use schemes. The development of

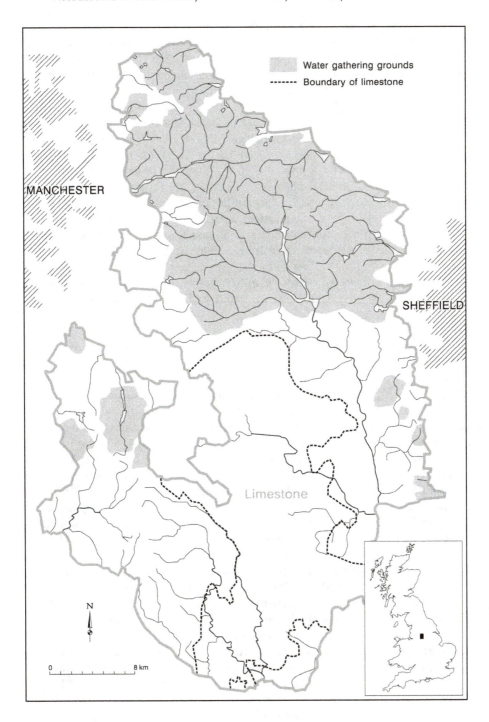

Figure 5.8: The gathering grounds of the Peak District reservoirs in England (after Edwards, 1962) (compiled by the author from various sources)

catchments in the Mourne Mountains began early in the century, but the construction of the Silent Valley Reservoir was delayed by the First World War and not completed until 1932. The Bignian Tunnel that carries water from the Annalong catchment into the Silent Valley reservoir was built in 1953 and the Ben Crom reservoir added further storage in 1957. In the 1960s water began to be abstracted from Lough Neagh.[54] In 1973 what had become the Belfast City and District Water Commissioners and other local suppliers in Northern Ireland were transferred to the Ministry of Development, Water Service. This body later became the Water Executive of the Department of Environment (Northern Ireland).[55] The supply company, Northern Ireland Water, was still government owned in 2011. Lough Neagh is fed in part by the Lagan aquifer, a Sherwood Sandstone formation that underlies that part of Northern Ireland. Increased abstraction from the aquifer began in the 1980s, but concerns were expressed about risks of contamination and seawater intrusions.[56] Nevertheless only 5 per cent of all water used in Northern Ireland in 2011 was drawn from aquifers. Conjunctive use, which recharges aquifers when surface water is abundant and draws water from aquifers when surface reservoirs are low has been developed to help increase the reliability of Belfast's supplies.

European urban water supply developments in the twentieth century

In Paris, the artesian flows from the Lower Greensand aquifer decreased by 1930. The government decided to protect the aquifer by regulations in the Statutory Decree on Groundwater Protection of 1935. A slow-down in drilling followed, only five boreholes were sunk between 1937 and 1965 and the volume of water abstracted fell from 100,000 m^3 day^{-1} to 50,000 m^3 day^{-1} in 1966. Groundwater levels began to rise after 1971, followed by a slower decline after 1980. The 1992 Water Act recognized the interdependence of surface and groundwater, helping to promote conjunctive use of all water sources for Paris.[57]

In 1900 a preliminary plan to upgrade the Madrid supply was approved. A new supply line, the Canal Transversal was approved in 1902, but people were extremely concerned about low flows in the Lozoya in the summers of some years. The new canal was opened in 1911 allowing a maximum flow of 8 m^{-3} s^{-1}. In the meantime a private company, the Hidráulica de Santillana had begun to supply both water and hydroelectricity to a part of northern Madrid. The Canal de Isabel II responded to this by creating another urban storage to the north of the city and began to look at additional sources of surface water.[58]

Spain was one of the first countries in the world to create river basin agencies (*Confederaciones Hidrográficas*) through a 1926 royal decree. The Ebro and Segura river basin agencies were created in the basin in 1926, followed by the Guadalquivir in 1927 and the Eastern Pyrenees in 1929. By 1961 basin agencies had been created throughout the country, integrating the use of water resources. In Madrid, population growth surged after 1950 and new water intakes were required. Additional rivers were dammed and further urban storage was built. By 2005, the Madrid water supply system consisted of 17 reservoirs in the Jarama and Guadarrama basins that supply an urban demand of 500 $Mm^3 y^{-1}$, although the system has other alternative sources, such as groundwater or transfer from the Alberche basin.[59] Persistent droughts can affect reservoir levels during two or three consecutive years. For the southern part of the city, the council aims to provide 250 l^{-1} cap^{-1} day^{-1} and upgraded pumping systems in 2004–6 in order to meet that requirement. Incoming raw water is treated at one of 12 treatment stations with a nominal total capacity to deal with 44.5 $m^3 s^{-1}$ of water from any source of supply. The need to avoid the impacts of worsening droughts with climate change was a major factor in planning future supply improvements.

DEVELOPMENT OF WATER SUPPLIES
FOR AUSTRALIAN TOWNS AND CITIES

The great cities of Australia follow the pattern of reservoir construction in the United Kingdom. Sydney originally developed a small local source in a similar manner to places like Manchester and Leeds. The first supply came from the Tank Stream, so named for the 'tanks' or reservoirs cut into its sides to save water. The stream, which wound its way through the early settlement before emptying into Sydney Harbour at Circular Quay, became severely polluted and was abandoned in 1826. Convict labour, from 1824 to 1837, then developed Busby's Bore, a 4 km tunnel leading from the Lachlan Swamps, (now Centennial Park) and ending in the south-eastern corner of Hyde Park and it remained in service until the 1880s.[60] By 1852 drought and increasing population led to the call for a more permanent water supply for Sydney. A third water source, the Botany Swamps Scheme, began operations in late 1859 but within 20 years, the once copious fresh water supply was depleted. The innovative Upper Nepean Scheme was Sydney's fourth source of water supply. Completed in 1888, the scheme diverted water from the Cataract, Cordeaux, Avon and Nepean rivers to Prospect Reservoir via 64 km of tunnels, canals and aqueducts known collectively as the Upper Canal.

However, the Upper Nepean Scheme bought only temporary relief to Sydney's water supply woes. The drought of 1901–2 brought Sydney perilously close to a complete water famine. After two Royal Commissions into Sydney's water supply, the authorities agreed that a dam be built on the Cataract River. The successive building of the Cataract, Cordeaux, Avon and Nepean dams between 1907 and 1935 greatly improved the Upper Nepean Scheme's capacity (Figure 5.9). However, rainfall is extremely variable in Australia and a wise municipality does not rely on winter rains filling reservoirs every year. Sydney has enough reservoir capacity to meet the rainfall deficits for nine years out of every ten (Table 5.1). But it needed to keep up with population growth and rising per capita water demand.

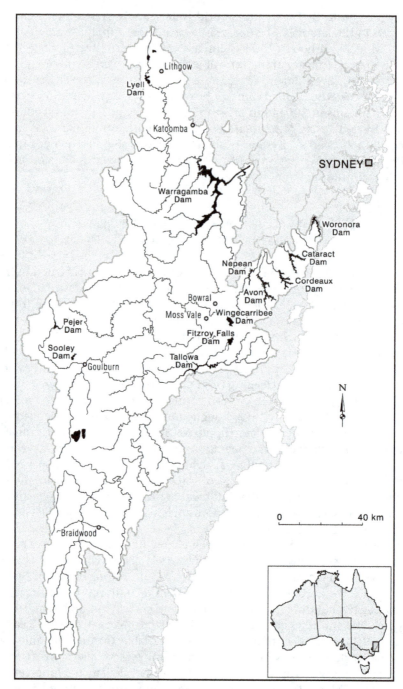

Figure 5.9: The Nepean River catchment, New South Wales,
showing the water supply reservoirs (after Crabb, 1986)
(compiled by the author from various sources)

Table 5.1: Catchments and reservoirs
supplying the Sydney Catchment Authority area

Catchments and Reservoirs	Date completed	Catchment area km²	Available storage capacity in ML
Upper Nepean Catchment			
Cataract	1907	130	94 300
Cordeaux	1926	90	50 600
Avon	1927	140	146 700
Nepean	1935	320	52 000
Unregulated Area		200	
Woronora Catchment			
Woronora	1941	85	71 790
Warragamba Catchment			
Waragamba	1960	9050	1 886 000
Wingecarribee	1974	40	33 500
Shoalhaven Catchment			
Fitzroy Falls	1975	31	10 000
Lake Yarrunga	1977	5750	36 000
Minor storages			14 470
Totals		16 850	2 395 360

In 1977 the large multi-purpose Shoalhaven scheme began to augment Sydney's supplies. The scheme involves three reservoirs, three pumping stations, pressure conduits, tunnels and canals. As is typical of many large post-1950 developments, it is also a multi-purpose pumped storage scheme comprised of the Kangaroo Valley and Bendeela power stations. Water is pumped uphill from Lake Yarrunga into Fitzroy Falls Reservoir via Bendeela Pondage. The water can be released back into Lake Yarrunga to generate power. The scheme can generate up to 240 MW (megawatts). For the water supplies, water is lifted up to the Fitzroy Falls dam, whence it is pumped up to the Wingecarribee dam and then into the Nepean River or into the Warragamba catchment (Figure 5.9). Although agricultural land was lost, the movement of fish along the Shoalhaven disrupted and canoeing and other river recreation restricted, the multipurpose scheme not only added to Sydney's water supplies, but also improved those of towns on the Southern Tablelands, while controlled recreation was allowed on the Fitzroy Falls Reservoir and Lake Yarrunga.[61] In 1977 it was expected that a further large dam, the Welcome Reef Dam, would be constructed in the headwaters of the Shoalhaven River. The reservoir would have covered 150 km² and would have had a capacity of 2,680,000 ML (megalitres), considerably more than the Warragamba Reservoir. However, partly in response to the concerns about environmental and social impacts of the times, the project was not developed and it was officially foreseen that the Welcome Reef resources would not be needed before 2030–40. Nevertheless, the great lowering of water levels in the Sydney reservoirs after the drought of 2002 saw renewed calls from some politicians and engineers for the action on the Welcome Reef dam.

The 2002 decision not to go ahead with the Welcome Reef dam was made in the light of a new responsibility to reduce water demand placed on the Sydney Water Corporation, a statutory state owned corporation, wholly owned by the New South Wales government which has three equal, principal objectives: protecting public health; protecting the environment and being a successful business.

Sydney Water Corporation's (SWC) Operating Licence states that:

Sydney Water must take action to reduce the quantity of water (other than re-use water) it draws from all sources to 329 l^{-1} cap^{-1}day^{-1} by 2010/2011 (being a reduction of 177 l^{-1} cap^{-1}day^{-1} or 35 per cent from the 1990/1991 baseline).[62]

SWC thus has responsibility and leadership of water conservation in Sydney. Already per capita domestic consumption has fallen and projects for recycling water for 'grey water' purposes are meeting approval and the company is aiming to recycle 70 billion litres a year by 2015. A major effort is being made to reduce leaks in Sydney Water's distribution system, but even so additional water was needed in 2006.

In November 2006, the Minister for Planning approved the plans for a desalination plant at Kurnell and the related seawater intake and outlet structures. The plant will use reverse osmosis technology to remove salts and other impurities from seawater to produce drinking water. Water from the desalination plant at Kurnell will be pumped into Sydney's water distribution system through a pipeline from Kurnell, across Botany Bay to Kyeemagh. The desalination plant began operation in January 2010. It operates when surface reservoir levels have fallen to 70 per cent of capacity and continues to operate until they have reached 80 per cent of capacity. The plant is large enough to meet 15 per cent of Sydney's supply, if necessary, but could be enlarged to supply 30 per cent. It relies on renewable energy to power the desalination process.[63] A 67-turbine wind farm at Bungendore in NSW has been purpose-built to generate enough renewable energy to offset the energy use of the plant.

Western Australia's urban water supplies

In April 1891 Sir John Forrest, premier of Western Australia, offered Charles Yelverton O'Connor the position of engineer-in-chief. In reply to his inquiry as to whether his responsibilities would cover railways or harbours or roads, Forrest cabled 'Everything'.

On 16 July 1896, Forrest introduced to his parliament a bill to authorize a loan of £2.5 million to construct a 760 mm diameter pipeline that would carry 23,000 m^{-3} day^{-1} of water 530 km from a dam on the Helena River near

Mundaring Weir to the Mount Charlotte Reservoir in Kalgoorlie for reticulation to various mining centres in the Goldfields. By the end of 1902, as planned, the work was completed for the estimated cost: the great reservoir was ready, the pumps installed, the main laid to Coolgardie and extended another 25 miles (40 km) to Kalgoorlie. The water had completed its carefully regulated flow begun eight months before in the Helena River valley at Mundaring. On 24 January 1903, amid great rejoicing, Forrest turned on the water at Coolgardie and Kalgoorlie. He praised O'Connor, 'the great builder of this work ... to bring happiness and comfort to the people of the goldfields for all time'.

Ten years later, a visitor to the Goldfields commented how the Goldfields scheme had brought water to 30 towns and had 200 km of extensions to agricultural areas and a daily average consumption of 13,640 m^3 of water. Although unprofitable on a strictly actuarial basis, the annual revenues being insufficient to meet operating costs and loan repayments, the gains to the state in other directions would have more than compensated for the deficiency. The state's assets were regarded positively and the visitor thought that under-production and under-population were far greater dangers than borrowing money for such necessary national undertakings.[64]

Two contrasting views on this achievement were expressed about 95 years later. The profits from gold mining made the 1890s tumultuous years in Western Australia. They saw the beginning of responsible government with Forrest as the state's first premier who, with O'Connor's help drove a decade of infrastructure development on a scale perhaps only repeated in the development of the Pilbara iron ore mines and railways after 1970. O'Connor directed the construction of three nation-building engineering achievements: the Fremantle Harbour, the railways and the Coolgardie Goldfields Water Supply. This still operational, engineering masterpiece is now a major heritage and tourism project managed by the National Trust in Western Australia known as 'The Golden Pipeline'.[65]

However another view is more caustic and critical:

The Irish engineer Charles Yelverton O'Connor was the quintessential modern hero—engineer with ambitious designs for Big Projects. After engineering railways in Ireland, New Zealand and Western Australia (where he also designed the Fremantle Harbour) in the 1860s–1890s, O'Connor worked on the Kalgoorlie Goldfields pipeline. Costing two-and-a-half-million pounds sterling for a state population of just 100,000, this 557 km pipeline was a utopian project to dam rivers and catchment areas around Perth and deliver water via a then 'state of the art' system of pipes and pumps to the mining industry and related towns. The Australian Big Water dreaming was articulated at the 1903 opening ceremony by the Premier John Forrest, who declaimed: 'Future generations, I am certain, will think of us and bless us for our farseeing patriotism, and it will be said of us, as Isaiah said of old, "they made a way in the wilderness and rivers in the desert".'[66]

The argument against the big water engineering projects continues by saying that many still imagine Big Water to have a future as grand as its past, as new ideas for heroic water supply projects bubble up, and old ones regularly recycled. Gigantic energy-hungry desalination plants are envisaged for both the dry state of Western Australia and for thirsty New South Wales. These would supply a small percentage of urban water while producing greenhouse emissions that add to the global warming, producing drier climates and water shortages in many parts of Australia.[67] The supporters of this critical view seem to forget that the relative wealth Australian city dwellers enjoy has been totally dependent on big water projects ever since the first gold rushes to Victoria. Cities could not function without large-scale water and sanitation projects and the bold engineers who conceived them, such as O'Connor, should be admired. What had been realized at the start of the twenty-first century was that increasing the water supply is just one part of urban water management, recycling grey water, rainwater harvesting, leakage reduction, metering, appropriate water pricing, and efficient industrial processes and domestic appliances are all part of the array of management tools.

DEVELOPING WATER SUPPLIES FOR NORTH AMERICAN CITIES

Water supplies for California's great cities

Early Spanish settlement in what is now the south-west of the USA established some important aspects of water rights, particularly the 'Plan of Pitic' that the town has authority, on behalf of the community that it represents, over all uses of water.[68] In eighteenth-century Los Angeles, the town council was constantly endeavouring to maintain the potability of the community's drinking water by taking action against anyone dumping rubbish in the town's water channel (the zanja madre) or bathing or washing in it, or allowing drains to discharge into it or building cesspits close to it.[69] This 'pueblo water right' also allowed a community to claim sole use of the water upstream for the benefit of its community. Los Angeles became the most aggressive and successful city in making such a claim, persuading the California courts to grant it exclusive rights to all the runoff from the 1300 km² river basin.[70]

In the early 1860s people in Los Angeles demanded a safe network of covered pipes for their drinking water. Disease, especially the 1863 smallpox epidemic reinforced their demands. In 1868, the Los Angeles City Water Company was given a 30-year supply contract and soon the city began to develop long-term plans for a secure water supply. A five member Board of Water Commissioners was appointed to take control over its water system and rights to all the water of the Los Angeles River Basin. This control of the water soon led to the city growing from 73 to 112 km² by 1900 through annexation of adjacent areas within the basin.[71]

By 1904, the need for additional water resources was recognized. William Mulholland, whose dedication and brilliance took him from labourer to superintendent with the Los Angeles Water Company, knew he would have the foresight to discover other sources. The city which had acquired the water company, hired him to manage it. Mulholland had water meters installed throughout the city and soon produced an operational profit. In 1904 Mulholland knew the Owens Valley could be the future source, but he kept quiet about it for fear speculators would start buying land.[72] The US Reclamation Service decreed that it could not assist the city in developing new water resources unless the project was entirely a municipal one. Lippincott, both the Reclamation Service's supervising engineer and a private consultant gave Los Angeles clearance to acquire more land and water rights. This was achieved in July 1905 and the news became public causing local controversy and a lively municipal election campaign over the expenditure on the Owens Valley scheme (Figure 5.10).[73] By 1913 the first Owens Valley water flowed through the new aqueducts into the San Fernando Valley. The city acquired more neighbouring authorities that wanted to share the water supply, reaching an area of 609 km² by the end of 1915.[74]

Later Los Angeles, in collaboration with 13 other cities and communities, organized as the Metropolitan Water District of Southern California, built the Colorado River aqueduct. The aqueduct's main stem diverts water from the Colorado River at the Parker Dam, carries it across several mountain ranges by pumping, and delivers it to the main terminal, Lake Matthews, 390 km away. The distribution system below Lake Matthews includes a branch to supply San Diego. It takes off from the main stem at 350 km and extends for some 120 km to the San Vicente Reservoir.

The twentieth-century expansion of desert cities in the south-western USA happened in an unusually wet period by comparison with average conditions in the last millennium. The water-supply infrastructure was planned on the basis of rainfall and river flow data for this wet period. Examination of tree-ring climatic records from the basin since 2000 has established past climate variability and now provides a basis for forecasting the changes in water flows that might be introduced by global warming. The outlook for the future water supply from the Colorado is not good. By 2050 the mean flow of the river could be less than the volume of water being abstracted in 2005 to supply the irrigation districts and cities authorized to take water from the river.[75]

In 1999 both Lake Mead and Lake Powell, which was created in 1963 upstream of Lake Mead to ensure that the Upper Basin would have enough water even in drought years to meet its obligation to the Lower Basin, were nearly full with 61,674,093 ML between them. But drought came after 2000 and the seven states with rights to Colorado water had to start discussing how to cope with water shortages.

Cities in the south-western USA began to take action on curbing excessive water use after 2000. Las Vegas prohibited new front lawns, limited the size

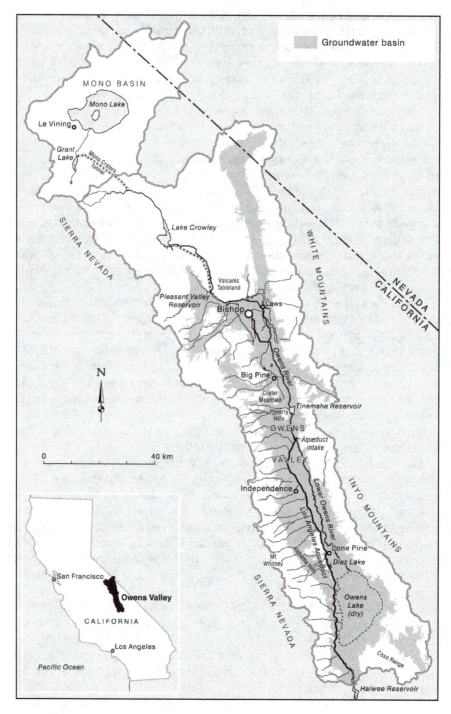

Figure 5.10: The Owens Valley water supply scheme, California
(compiled by the author from various sources)

of back ones, and offered people $21.60 per square metre to replace existing grass with desert plants. Between 2002 and 2006, the Las Vegas metro area managed to reduce its total consumption of water by around 20 per cent, even though its population had increased substantially. Albuquerque also cut down its water use.[76]

In August 2007, El Paso inaugurated a desalination plant so that it could abstract water from a deep, briny aquifer to augment the city's supply. With the cost of desalination falling to $900 per ML, it is still more than the $493 per ML that the Bureau of Reclamation charges small scale users for water drawn from Lake Mead (the irrigation districts pay nothing). One obvious solution for the cities is to buy water from the farmers. In 2003 the Imperial Irrigation District was pressured into selling 247,000 of its 3,700,000 ML of Colorado water to San Diego as part of an overall deal to get California to stop exceeding its allotment. San Diego paid nearly $300 per 1.23 ML for water that the farmers in the Imperial Valley get virtually for free. The US government favours such market mechanisms. At $300 per 1.23 ML, the allocated Imperial Valley water is worth nearly as much as its entire agricultural revenue of around a billion dollars a year.[77]

Further north in California, the Hetchy Hetchy aqueduct designed to carry 1,500 ML day^{-1} from the Sierra Nevada to San Francisco was opened in 1934. The project involved several series of tunnels through coastal mountain ranges. The Mountain Division had over 30 km of tunnels, the Foothills Division another 25 km, while a 40 km tunnel in the Coast Range Division was the longest continuous tunnel in the world when it was built.

Managing residential water demand involves several factors, some of which utilities can control (e.g. price, water restrictions, rebate programmes) and some of which they cannot (e.g. climate and weather, demographic characteristics). During the turbulent 2000–5 drought period at Aurora, Colorado, it was found that: 1) pricing and outdoor water restriction policies interact with each other ensuring that total water savings are not cumulative as if each programme operated independently; 2) the effectiveness of pricing and restrictions policies varies among different classes of customers (i.e., low, middle, and high volume water users) and between pre-drought and drought periods; and 3) real-time information about consumptive use (via the Water Smart Reader) helps customers reach water-use targets.[78] Such information and increasingly intelligent, informed management strategies will be needed in all cities during the rest of the twenty-first century.

US urban water supplies using groundwater: contamination problems

Despite the grand engineering schemes of the great city supplies in the USA, many suburban dwellers depended on groundwater from local wells, especially in relatively low-lying areas, such as Long Island, NY. The rapid suburban development usually saw people relying on septic tanks.

Local authorities found that if they tried to regulate the developers too tightly, for example by requiring the construction of sewer systems before house-building started, the developers simply shifted their investment to another area where the local authority was less demanding. By the 1960s, particularly following the introduction of detergents for washing clothes and dishes, a serious issue of groundwater pollution from septic tanks arose, initially affecting local supplies, but eventually getting into streams, rivers and lakes where it caused eutrophication.[79] Sometimes householders found that water from the tap started to make lather on its own. This was the impact of the detergents that had made their way from the septic tanks to the groundwater aquifer and thence into the pumped local water supply. In one Long Island county alone, 17,000 households were affected, with 27,000 similarly affected in Metropolitan Minneapolis St Paul.[80] Detergent foam became commonplace in lakes and rivers due to the foaming agent, alkyl benzene sulphonate persisting in groundwater for many years and building up in concentration rapidly. The 1972 Federal Water Pollution Control Act called for measures to 'restore and maintain the chemical, physical and biological integrity of the nation's waters'.[81] Further measures for groundwater protection were introduced in 1974. The US government also subsidized suburban sewer constructions, helping to pay for the replacement of septic tanks. By 1977, the majority of the states had enacted regulations about septic tanks.[82]

Chlorinated degreasing solvents had become a national groundwater problem by 1981, the Council on Environmental Quality describing the issue as 'the recent, and seemingly sudden, appearance of toxic organic chemicals in drinking water wells'.[83] Four factors account for the failure of hydrologists, regulators, and industry in mid-twentieth-century California to anticipate and therefore prevent groundwater contamination by these solvents. First, these chemicals were perceived as merely workplace hazards, so that the vapours on the factory floor were the only cause of concern. Second, hydrologists and others did not have the means to sample and analyse the dissolved components of these solvents in groundwater before they reached water-supply wells. Third, there was no guiding scientific paradigm that explained the environmental migration of solvents disposed of following the practices recommended by industrial and insurance associations. Fourth, these three factors interacted in a way that inhibited inquiry – and therefore paradigm creation – by research scientists and engineers who might otherwise have considered the migration and fate of solvents in the subsurface a suitable subject of research.[84]

The first recorded case of groundwater contamination by chlorinated hydrocarbons in the United States appears to have been the release of 2,4-dichlorophenol (an intermediate in the production of the herbicide 2,4-D) from a chemical plant in Alhambra, California, to a sewer in the summer of 1945. The chemical passed through a sewage-treatment plant and was discharged into the San Gabriel River. It then travelled 5 km downriver and seeped into the aquifer supplying the Montebello well field, shutting down eleven municipal wells serving 25,000 people and requiring special treatment for four to five years. The taste and odour that the chemical imparted to the Montebello groundwater indicated its presence, and there is no indication that chemical analysis was attempted to determine its concentration in the aquifer.[85]

In 1979, many towns in Massachusetts, including Bedford, North Reading, and Woburn, found their sole source of water supply contaminated by chlorinated hydrocarbons released by manufacturing plants.[86] In Los Angeles County, California, numerous well fields were identified during 1979–81 as contaminated by solvents released in the San Gabriel and the San Fernando valleys. Releases by the aerospace and electronics industries caused well closures in these valleys affecting more than one million people.[87]

During the 1980s, the Environment Protection Agency (EPA) instigated investigations that detected numerous plumes of dissolved-phase contamination migrating away from industrial facilities and landfills. In a few cases the 'remedial investigation' revealed the presence of pools of solvents in shallow subsurface aquifers. Hydrologists, on the other hand, were not looking for solvent contamination in groundwaters when they first found it in the late 1970s. Remedial action and effective public policy were retarded by the absence of a guiding paradigm until 1988.[88] Water quality management has become an increasing burden for public and privately owned utilities. Regulators are increasingly concerned that standards are met, but the complexity of manufactured chemicals and pharmaceuticals was, in the first decade of the twenty-first century, growing far faster than the ability of the regulators to monitor and detect the new compounds.

WATER SUPPLIES IN ASIAN CITIES

Many colonial cities in Asia developed nineteenth-century water supply schemes based on the classic upland reservoir, gravity transfer by aqueduct, treatment and urban distribution and storage. In the twentieth century such schemes were extended extensively as Mumbai exemplifies (Figure 5.11). Even so they may not be adequate. Often domestic supplies are limited to a few hours a day. Some people buy extra water to store in tanks so that they have a source of water when the public supply is not available. Many sink their own groundwater wells, creating additional problems, such as adding to the subsidence in Bangkok. Others use rainwater harvesting to augment supplies. Water is not yet a limitation on economic growth, but if it becomes more scarce, its price may increase so much that goods become more expensive to produce.

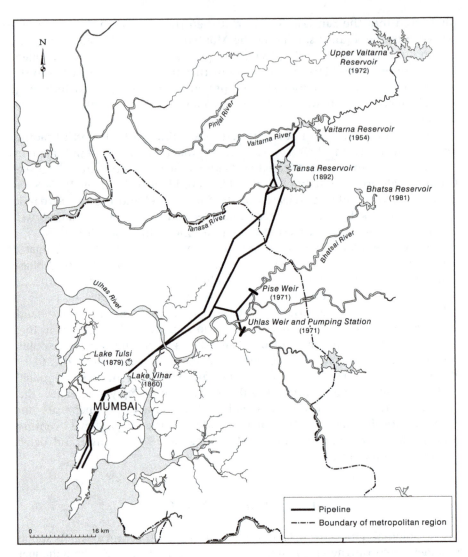

Figure 5.11: Mumbai's water supply schemes, India
(compiled by the author from various sources)

URBAN WATER SUPPLY STRATEGIES
AT THE START OF THE TWENTY-FIRST CENTURY

Cities have two broad sets of strategy to cope with insufficient water: a) those adopted by the state or municipal authorities responsible to the main water supply, whether or not delivery is privatized, and b) those adopted by individuals, households and local communities and, sometimes, by small businesses and petty traders. The former set comprises the seeking of additional and alternative sources of water and measures to conserve water for the city as a whole. The second set are survival and coping mechanisms that range from middle-class people installing private boreholes or water tanks in their properties to the extremely poor scooping up water from roadside pools in Lagos.[89]

Desalinization is rapidly expanding in wealthy countries and those that have large fuel supplies. Kuwait City (Kuwait), for instance, began using desalination in the early 1950s to avoid importing water from Iraq,[90] and is building a new plant that is to produce 227 megalitres (ML) of water per day. While Spain remains the largest user of desalinization, it is widespread in oil-rich Middle Eastern countries, in countries like Israel[91] and Singapore that have few alternative water resources, but also in California, Florida, Australia and now even London, UK. The London plant will use biofuels, including biogas from an adjacent wastewater treatment plant. Pilot projects to use wind or solar energy to power desalinization are underway in Kangaroo Island, Australia (wind)[92] and both Saudi Arabia[93] and Port Augusta, South Australia (solar).[94]

Local renewable groundwater has long been used as the main supply in arid areas and, in conjunction with river water, in large cities on rivers. Hanoi, for example, still relies primarily on groundwater, but now suffers water shortages during the dry season when local wells and irrigation canals run dry.[95] Groundwater use is sustainable if use is less than aquifer recharge. In many arid cities, however, groundwater use far exceeds aquifer recharge, essentially 'mining' groundwater for one-time use. Mexico City has so overused its aquifer that the ground is subsiding 40 cm/year in some regions.[96] Below Beijing the water table has fallen by about one metre a year since 1980.[97] Nairobi experienced a similar rate.[98] Many other fast-growing cities face similar problems, but globally the extent of this groundwater mining by cities is unclear. However, probably a few hundred million urban people are using their local groundwater unsustainably.

When local supplies are inadequate or over-pumped city managers may exploit distant groundwater aquifers. The boldest such scheme is the Great Libyan Man-made River[99] (Figure 5.12) which is taking water over 7,000 years old from aquifers beneath the Sahara desert and carrying it to cities and farms along the Mediterranean coast. Saudi Arabia also relies heavily on deep aquifers, but water levels are declining, for example, the Manjur aquifer level fell 1.8 m per year between 1984 and 1990.[100]

Pipelines from surface water storages are still a favoured response in arid areas close to mountain snow and glacier melt. Long used by the water storages on the Colorado River in the USA that supply the great cities of the south-west, snow and glacier melting is significant for the Indus and Ganges, the Yellow and Yangtze rivers and for parts of the Murray Basin in Australia. China is planning 59 new reservoirs to collect water from shrinking glaciers in its western regions.[101] Even without ice and snow melt, cities, particularly those in Africa, are still building new reservoirs and new pipelines. Nairobi built the Thika Dam, 60 km from the city in the 1990s to double the piped water supply to the city.[102] Lagos is planning a new pipeline from the Oshun River. However, water quality issues

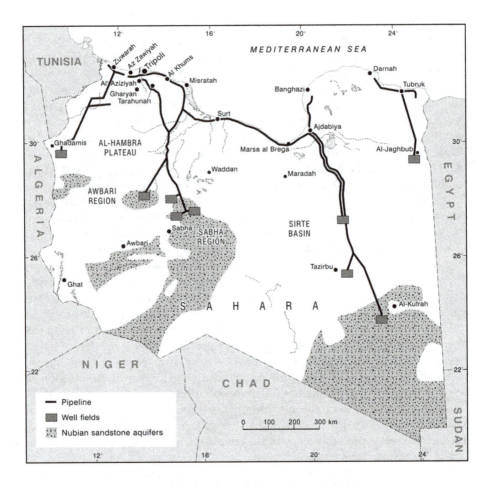

Figure 5.12: The Great Libyan Man-Made River

will arise in the dry season when the flow will be insufficient. Oshun water will have to be mixed with poorer quality water from the Lagos Lagoon giving a pre-treatment water with about 600 mg l[-1] total dissolved solids. Treating this may require a reverse osmosis desalination process.[103]

Interbasin water transfers continue to expand. China is proceeding with a south–north transfer[104] that will ultimately transfer 45 billion m[3] from the Yangtze to farms and cities in the north.[105] Many large Indian cities, including Delhi, Mumbai and Chennai, already rely in part on interbasin water transfers.[106] Such strategies involve reconciling the needs of different communities, but increasingly those of rapidly growing industrial cities outweigh those of poor rural areas.

International water transfer by pipeline is relatively rare. Special cases like Singapore's import from Johor, Malaysia exist, but are often subject to limited term international agreements which cannot easily be extended. Many international rivers link major cities. The River Rhine in Europe provides a model for international river basin management through the International Rhine Commission, the European Directive on the Rhine, and the European Water Framework Directive, but it is a costly system to set up and maintain. The cleaning up of the lower reaches of the Rhine, for example, involved upgrading all municipal sewage treatment works so that effluent reached agreed European standards. Rhine water is now used to recharge aquifers under coastal sand dunes in the Netherlands. By the time the water reaches the aquifer, it is relatively clean.[107]

Re-use of treated water is expanding, usually in conjunction with development of other water supplies. In Orange County California, sewer water is treated by microfiltration, reverse osmosis and ultra-violet light with hydrogen peroxide disinfection before being used to replenish the groundwater aquifer. In the Yarra Valley area, Australia, householders are required either to use recycled water for secondary uses (not drinking) or to have solar water heating or to carry out rainwater harvesting.[108]

Dual water systems exist in places that have, or had, political reasons limiting their access to water, for example both Gibraltar and Hong Kong have a second pipe network distributing sea water for flushing toilets, washing cars and other forms of cleaning.[109] In the Netherlands, houses in several residential developments collected 'grey water' from roofs and other sources,[110] but cases of cross contamination between the grey and the drinking water occurred and such experiments were terminated.[111]

Rainwater harvesting is an ancient technique, but is being adopted more widely in all three categories of city discussed in this book. Legislation requiring all properties above a certain size to harvest rainwater has been passed in Bangalore, Ahmedabad, Chennai, New Delhi, Kanpur, Hyderabad and Mumbai. The Bangalore legislation[112] requires every new house to have a rainwater harvesting system in order to get a drinking water connection. The rainwater is used to recharge boreholes, recharge groundwater by infiltration or for grey water purposes. In the USA, tax incentives encourage rainwater harvesting in Texas and Arizona, while in Santa Fe, New Mexico, and Tuscon, Arizona, all new commercial developments are required to use harvested rainwater for irrigating their lawns and gardens.[113]

Reducing non-accounted for water is an aim of all water supply undertakings. In wealthier cities, the main concern is to reduce leakage from old or damaged water mains and pipes. In Europe, Malta more than halved leakage, while the UK cut leakage by about one-third, between 1995 and 2001.[114] Riyadh was losing 60 per cent of its water through leakage and is reducing it to 20 per cent though measuring the pressure in the system, monitoring flows and attending to the losses so revealed. However, for many fast-growing poor cities, the problem stems in part from the illegal connections of the type found in Lagos, mentioned earlier. When repairs are made and stand pipes installed, the work may be damaged again, by the water vendors whose livelihoods depend on stealing water from the public system.[115] Reducing non-accounted for water in deprived areas of the poorest cities is likely to remain a problem for a long time.

All the above strategies are practised by water suppliers, whether in the public or private sector. Individual households and businesses have long had their own individual boreholes or wells. Today in wealthier cities, an abstraction licence is required before water can be taken from an aquifer, but for decades, drilling a private borehole has been a key strategy to overcome an unreliable public water supply. However, in Delhi, so much groundwater was being abstracted privately, to overcome issues with both quality and quantity of municipal supply, that boring tubewells was practically banned by the Delhi Jal Board, the body that gives borehole approvals.[116] Private boreholes also contribute to water table lowering and land surface subsidence. Excess abstraction in Bangkok has caused subsidence, damaging the foundations of valued historic buildings as well as producing localized flooding because rainwater gets trapped by changes in surface topography.[117]

Local private water selling is widespread in Asia, Africa and Latin America. In poor cities that suffer from both water quality and water delivery issues, a two-tiered system often develops, where richer residents can afford to buy clean water from private vendors while poor residents either endeavour to clean polluted surface waters or buy 'pure' water in plastic bottles or sachets to drink at a high price from local vendors. In Port-Au-Prince (Haiti), the poor might be spending 20 per cent of their income on water; in Onitsha (Nigeria) during the dry season 18 per cent; and in Addis Ababa (Ethiopia) 9 per cent.[118] Poor people who buy sachets of water from local vendors face the risk that it may be of poor quality, cholera outbreaks having been linked to such water.[119] Most households increase storage, with tanks for the middle class and plastic bottles, jerry cans, or stone jars for poorer households,[120] but health risks may arise from deterioration in household storage.[121]

The strategies used by cities vary depending on their financial resources. Excluding rainwater harvesting, in arid climates there is relatively little opportunity for solutions aiming to restore or strengthen natural ecosystem services rather than construct new infrastructure. However, in some cases changes in land management can save water, as in South Africa's Working for Water programme where invasive non-native yet water hungry tree species are removed to increase available water. More commonly, cities simply obtain water from other users, particularly the agricultural sector, effectively changing part of a watershed's land-use from agriculture to a less water-intensive use.[122] For instance, many Colorado farmers have ceased production and sold their water rights to Denver and other cities.[123]

The obvious solution for water quality issues is water treatment, either before discharge by a polluter or before use by urban residents. Many cities are currently unable to afford the tens or hundreds of millions of dollars involved. Most major infrastructure improvements in African cities are usually funded by international aid or loans that pay for building sewers and/or complex water treatment plants. However, numerous other ways to use natural systems have been tried. Wetlands, natural or constructed, help to reduce water pollution. For instance, in Kampaḷa (Uganda) the Nakivubo wetland acts as a filter removing urban wastes from the city before they affect the municipal water intake.[124] More integrated watershed management, even across international borders, can reduce water pollution substantially.

Delivery-challenged cities have few financial resources to deliver water effectively to their residents. However, many such cities are making progress. For example, in 1995 only 74–81 per cent of Dakar's people (Senegal) had access to safe sufficient water, and only 58 per cent of households had a piped connection. Today 98 per cent of the people have access to safe water, and 76 per cent of households have a piped connection. It cost around $290 million to give 1.6 million people new access to safe water, averaging $180/person,[125] relatively little money by the standards of the global economy.

CONCLUSIONS

Water supply has long been seen as a professional engineering task, but water management involves changing people's attitudes and behaviour with respect to water. Adaptive management is often proposed as the most effective way to manage complex water issues. However, social and institutional factors constrain the search for, and integration of, the genuine learning that defines adaptive management. City governments and water utilities have constantly sought to deal with demographic, economic, social and environmental change affecting all aspects of urban water. Many of the most successful improvements have involved new ways of thinking about management, new organizational structures and new implementation processes and tools. Adaptive management encourages scrutiny of prevailing social and organizational norms and this is unlikely to occur without a change in the culture of natural resource management and research. It is likely to be increasingly important in the remainder of the twenty-first century. To succeed, managers, stakeholders and experts will have to work together at the watershed-scale and city-scale to bridge the gaps between theory and practice, and between social and technical understandings of urban water resources and the people their systems serve.[126] While the millennium goal of reliable and safe water supplies and adequate sanitation for all urban people remains unachieved, many cities, large and small, will still face enormous challenges in lowering infant mortality, reducing diarrhoea among children and avoiding cholera. Such a goal cannot be left to private enterprise. Municipal leadership and national government investment is most important in meeting this basic need.

6

Sanitation, Sewage and Mountains of Trash

Wastewater and Garbage in Cities

WASTEWATER

The first urban sanitation systems, as mentioned in Chapter 1, arose in the grid-iron plan cities of the Indus Valley such as Harappa, Mohenjo-Daro and Rakhigarhi. Within these cities, individual homes or groups of homes obtained water from wells. From a room that appears to have been set aside for bathing, wastewater was directed to covered drains, which lined the major streets. Houses opened only to inner courtyards and smaller lanes. The house-building in some villages in the region still resembles in some respects the house-building of the Harappans. Their wastewater systems were far more advanced than any found in contemporary urban sites in the Middle East and even more efficient than those in some areas of Pakistan and India today. The Mesopotamians had similar sewers at roughly the same time, for example at Eshnunna, 80 km north-east of the present Baghdad, where archaeological excavations exposed brick sewers, with laterals connecting to houses.

In the second millennium BC, the Minoan civilization on Crete had a remarkable architectural and hydraulic infrastructure to manage water, stormwater and wastewater sewerage in palaces and cities. Probably wastewater was used to irrigate crops. A room on the ground floor of the residential quarter of the Palace at Knossos was a toilet with a wooden seat and a small flushing conduit, probably the earliest flush toilet in history.[1] Most Minoan baths were connected to independent septic systems outside buildings, a practice indicative of the advanced water resources management and environmental techniques of that period. Rainwater drained from the roof by way of light-wells and was used to flush out sewage from three bathrooms in the East wing of the Palace at Knossos. The plumbing and the sewers of the Minoan cities were carefully planned, with stone-covered, slab-built sewer systems used to carry both

140

wastewater and stormwater found in many cities. The Italian writer Angelo Mosso visited the villa of Hagia Triadha in southern Crete just after 1900 and noticed that all the sewers of the villa functioned perfectly, and was amazed to see stormwater flowing out of sewers, 4,000 years after their construction.[2]

Urban sewer systems occur at several Aegean civilization (*c.* 3400–1200 BC) sites including Thera on Santorini which had a sewer network under the paved streets, directly connected to bathrooms and sanitary facilities, commonly located on the upper floor of houses. The system is similar to the one at Mohenjo-Daro.[3] These technologies were transferred to other Greek settlements around the Mediterranean, notably to Sicily.

Late in the seventh century BC an Etruscan dynasty, the Tarquins, began to transform Rome from a village to a city. The Forum valley was drained by the oldest monument of Roman engineering, the Cloaca Maxima, the great sewer, (Figure 6.1), which still discharges into the Tiber today.[4] Strabo noted that the Romans had paved streets, good water supplies and sewers. Rome also had public toilets from which human wastes were recycled. People deposited their domestic ordure in covered cisterns at the base of stairwells whence it was removed periodically by dung farmers and scavengers. Urine was collected in special jars and used by fullers in working up cloth. The dung farming replenished the soils in farms outside the city with nitrogenous fertilizer. However there may have been more waste than the farms could use because there are reports of open sewers and cess trenches in residential areas that were finally filled in, with their contents in place. It seems that despite the sewers, the Romans failed to deal safely with solid waste, much being deposited in dumps just outside the city.[5]

Mediaeval Paris, despite being the metropolis of Europe and, at least superficially, the focus of refinement in living, had streets that were foul with filth. Montaigne complained that he had difficulty renting lodgings away from the stench of sewage. Parisians poured the contents of their chamber-pots out of their windows, only the lucky escaping being drenched. The poorer classes defecated indiscriminately wherever most convenient. A 1531 law requiring landlords to provide a latrine for every house appears not to have been well enforced. So filthy were the numerous privies in Paris by the time of the French Revolution that people were using the terrace of the Louvre, the Tuileries and the Royal Palace grounds instead. The authorities constructed privies in the latter two places, but people found it easier to use the Louvre where attendants did not bother them.[6]

The methods used to dispose of excrement in mediaeval England were much inferior to the methods developed nearly three thousand years before in Crete. In the castles of the rich and powerful, when there was running water in the moat, garderobes or latrines were sometimes corbelled out over the moat from the face of the exterior wall, so that the dejecta had a fairly clear drop into the moat. If running water was not available, pits or cesspools were constructed to store the excrement received from the floors above through various types of chute.[7]

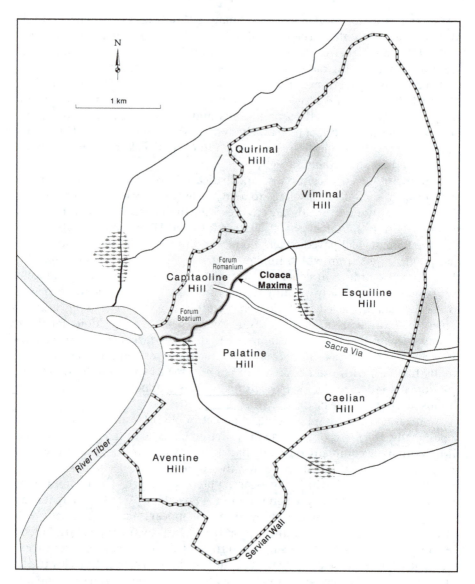

Figure 6.1: Rome in ancient times showing the Cloaca Maxima (after Scarre, 1995)

In overcrowded mediaeval conditions, public latrines, with running water for the clearance of the excrement existed in London before 1290. However there were seldom enough facilities in tenements. For example, in 1579, in Tower Street in the Parish of All Hallows, there were three privies for 85 people. Much excrement was simply thrown into the streets. Occasionally, as in the plague year, 1349, the king ordered city authorities to remove the filth accumulated in the streets.[8] In the fifteenth century, the severe penalties for the pollution of streams established by a Commission on Sewers set up by Henry VI were strictly enforced.[9] Larkey argues that 'The sanitary conditions of 16th century England were much better than we usually have been led to believe.'[10] However, in sixteenth-century Manchester, sanitation was comprised of privies and cess pits. Some privies were built directly over water courses. Barrels of sewage were emptied directly into the River Irwell, supposedly at night.[11]

Certainly, at the onset of the industrial revolution, when migrants moved into British cities in great numbers, conditions were extremely poor for most urban people.

In the nineteenth century the full interdependence of the urban population was recognized. Diseases were no respecters of social differentiation or of wealth. A laundry maid or milkman might introduce typhoid fever to the most exclusive quarters of a city.[12] Poor housing was associated with poverty, malnutrition, crime and disease. Improvements in housing conditions were expected to reduce disease and improve people's health. As discussed in Chapter 2, repeated outbreaks of cholera raised public health concerns in all cities, especially those that had grown rapidly with the expansion of manufacturing.

Typical of these cities was Derby, which grew from 13,000 in 1811 to 32,000 by 1835, but had mounting problems of sewerage, public health, street cleaning and lighting. Derby was controlled by a closed oligarchic hierarchy, mostly high Anglican Tories. However, effective power lay with the Improvement Commissioners established by Act of Parliament for specific tasks and which, in Derby, were usually chaired by the energetic reforming textile magnate William Strutt, with like-minded members such as Thomas and William Evans. The 1835 Municipal Corporations Act ended this cosy administration of Derby by a small elite. The former traditional mayoral families disappeared from the scene. Urban problems beset the local government administration. A report in 1844–5 commented adversely on Derby's high death rate and the confusion arising from the overlapping responsibilities of the Improvement Commissioners and the new corporation. In 1850 the Commissioners gave up their powers to Derby Corporation, and subsequent legislation increased the scope of the corporation's responsibilities.[13]

In the Victorian period the 'miasmatic' theory of disease causation took some strange forms among influential people. In 1844 the physician Neil Arnott (1788–1874) told the Royal Commission for Enquiring into the State of Large Towns and Populous Districts that:

The immediate and chief cause of many of the diseases which impair the bodily and mental health of the people, and bring a considerable proportion prematurely to the grave is the *poison of atmospheric impurity* [his italics] arising from the accumulation in and around their dwellings of the decomposing remnants of the substances used for food and from the impurities given out from their own bodies.[14]

Many others also claimed that fresh air was far more important than clean water, with an emphasis on better housing design and good natural ventilation. All succeeding generations in the next 100 years were taught the value of opening windows and letting the air flow through dwellings.

By the second half of the nineteenth-century efforts to improve housing took various forms. In London, philanthropists like the American merchant, Peabody, and Prince Albert, formed associations to promote better housing for the poor and built experimental working-class homes. From 1851, Lord Shaftesbury led efforts to establish: minimum standards of sanitation; adequate construction and maintenance of workers' houses; and the provision of basic paving, water supplies, open spaces and sewer drainage in new housing developments, which were ultimately imposed by law. Octavia Hill argued that with proper upkeep and supervision of slum quarters, the conditions of worker-occupied properties could be improved to the benefit of both owner and tenant.[15]

The costs of the model housing units promoted by bodies such as the Metropolitan Association for Improving the Dwellings of the Industrial Poor exceeded the levels of rent that poorly paid workers could afford. Eventually model tenements were forced to lower standards. Housing for the poor ensured a basic minimum condition for life, but not a good quality of life.

Joseph Bramah obtained a patent for a modified flush toilet in 1778, and began making water closets and installing them in London houses. Despite problems, they became so acceptable that they were installed at Osborne House, the Isle of Wight home of Queen Victoria by 1841. In 1851 the first modern popular water closets were set up at the Great Exhibition at the Crystal Palace in London, where they became the first modern public toilets. Unfortunately, the rapid uptake of the new flush toilets led to large volumes of water being discharged into antiquated sewers. John Snow, with his knowledge of cholera sources (see Chapter 5), warned of the dangers of contamination that overflows from inadequate sewers might bring. He suggested that the solution was to pipe drinking water from distant sources free from pollution.[16] However, his hypothesis that the occurrence of cholera was associated with polluted water was not accepted in official circles at the time of his death in 1858. When the Houses of Parliament that year were affected by the 'Great Stink' from sewage in the River Thames (see Chapter 7) the minds of legislators became focused on the problems of metropolitan sewage.

Many eminent civil engineers, including Robert Stephenson, Thomas Hawksley and Sir William Cubitt had been consulted on the problem of London's sewage. Eventually, the Metropolitan Board of Works was created in 1855 to take responsibility for the built environment within London's 187 km². Metropolitan improvements 'under the earth and above the earth' were seen as its special function. A contemporary view of the Board was that it was the:

> Appointed physician to the metropolitan organism ... (with) the duty of restoring it to health and promoting its future growth, of giving strength to its muscular, and vitality to its arterial system, roundness to its limbs, and beauty to its face.

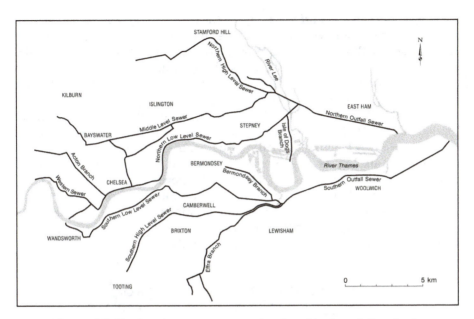

Figure 6.2: The London sewer system developed by Joseph Bazalgette

In 1856 the Board asked Joseph Bazalgette, Chief Engineer to the Board, to report on sewage disposal and urban drainage as soon as possible. His first report recommended the great system of interceptor sewers running parallel with the River Thames (Figure 6.2). Greatly protracted public discussion of this and other schemes followed, involving central government, referees, and the press. As a result of the impact on parliament, Bazalgette was finally allowed to proceed with his plan for the main drainage of London. London's final cholera epidemic, in 1866, in an area not yet protected by Bazalgette's system, helped to ensure that John Snow's hypothesis gained acceptance in official circles.

In 1858, the Board obtained its enabling Act and site work began shortly on the northern mid-level sewer, described by the author as follows:

> The brick-built intercepting sewers were laid to a fall of 2 feet per mile from west to east and it was, therefore, necessary to lift the sewage into the outfall sewers with pumping stations sited in east London ...[17]

The work progressed towards completion, at least on the south side of the river, during the summer of 1864. These interceptor sewers collected the effluent from all the sewers that used to run directly towards the River Thames and carried them to great settlement tanks at what became known as the northern and southern outfalls on the Dagenham Reach of the Thames. Here the liquid effluent was pumped out into the tideway just after high water to prevent it being carried upstream to London, while the solids were loaded on to barges to be dumped in deep water off the mouth of the river. This system prevailed until about 1970 when it was recognized that the dumping of solids was polluting the Thames estuary through the action of the tides.[18] The scheme involved 2,100 km of sewers and 132 km of interceptor sewers which consumed 318 million bricks. Construction coincided with the building of the Thames Embankment, with the northern inceptor sewer beneath it.

The Public Health Act of 1875 became the foundation of all sanitary legislation until 1937. The responsibilities of the Metropolitan Board of Works were taken over by the London County Council in 1889. The Board was always a body appointed by vested interests and it had become subject to much accusation about corruption and abuse of its powers. The London County Council introduced new democratic control and integrated administration of inner London, although the outer suburbs remained under the jurisdiction of the individual county councils of the 'Home Counties'. London's sewers were transferred to the Thames Water Authority in 1989.

RESPONSIBILITIES FOR THE IMPACTS OF
URBAN SEWER OUTFALLS AND URBAN DRAINAGE

Making the polluter pay has long been the policy of environmental legislation, but it is not always clear whose rights prevail in river management: is it the rights of riparian landowners or the rights of users downstream? This question arose when in 1952, the Pride of Derby and Derbyshire Angling Association Ltd, a fishing club that owned a fishery in the River Derwent, in Derbyshire and the Earl of Harrington, who owned land along the river, took the three upstream polluters to court. The waters of the Derwent flowed unpolluted until they reached the Borough of Derby's two sewer outfalls, one discharging stormwater overflow and untreated sewage during flood conditions, and the other releasing inadequately treated effluent from the local sewage treatment works. The river then passed through land owned by British Celanese Ltd, whose effluent polluted and warmed it. Downstream, discharge from the British Electricity Authority's power station further increased the river's temperature. Because the changes in water quality and temperature killed the river's fish and their food supply, the court issued an injunction restraining the defendants from altering the river's quality or temperature or interfering with the plaintiffs' enjoyment of their fishing rights; it then suspended the injunction's operation for two years. The Chancery Division, upon appeal by two of the defendants, confirmed the decision, rejecting the Borough's argument that it had statutory authority to pollute. While the 1901 Derby Corporation Act had established sewage disposal works, it had not authorized pumping untreated sewage into the river. In fact, it had specifically prohibited nuisances:

The sewage disposal works constructed ... shall at all times hereafter be conducted so that the same shall not be a nuisance and in particular the corporation shall not allow any noxious or offensive effluvia to escape therefrom or do or permit or suffer any other act which shall be a nuisance or injurious to the health or reasonable comfort of the inhabitants of Spondon ...[19]

Derby also argued that when it had built its sewage system at the turn of the century it had been sufficient for the local population. Subsequent population growth, a circumstance beyond its control, rendered it inadequate. Lord Justice Denning protested that if local authorities, under the Planning Acts, have control over development in their district, they should be responsible for its consequences:

They know (or ought to know) that the increase in building will cause the existing sewers to overflow, and yet they allow it to go on without enlarging the capacity of the sewerage system. By so doing, they themselves are helping to fill the system beyond its capacity, and are guilty of nuisance.[20]

In this way the courts established the responsibility of the city authorities to ensure that their sewer systems could cope with a growing population and could manage their stormwater overflows.

CHOLERA AND SEWER DEVELOPMENT IN PARIS

A severe outbreak of cholera in Paris in 1892 again showed the impacts of contamination of drinking water by sewage. At that time, maximum contamination of the Seine occurred near St Denis, where there are two islands, and there was a main sewer outfall. Just at this point, some of the very first cases of cholera occurred among the floating population of bargemen. Generally along the urban reaches of the river there was an exceptional frequency of cholera among the occupants of barges moored near sewer outfalls. A correspondent of *The Lancet* at the time found that cholera was chiefly confined to those communes which derived their water-supply from the Seine after it had passed through the city.[21]

Shortly after the cholera epidemic the first of the great wastewater treatment plants in Paris opened at Achères in 1894. By about 1905 85 per cent of the wastewater entering the Seine had been treated. Urban expansion and the two world wars meant that as the total wastewater grew, the proportion treated fell, reaching a low of 18 per cent treated in 1940 and 1944. A great expansion in treatment facilities at Achères and new plants at Noisy-le-Grand, Valenton and Colombes, saw the proportion treated rise to 87 per cent by 1985. From just over 100 million m³ per year in 1890, the wastewater discharge had grown to over 900 million by 1985.

COMBINED AND SEPARATE SEWER SYSTEMS IN THE USA

In the USA, the shift of concern from a combination of industrial waste and sewage waste to a focus primarily on sewage (the waste carried through sewers) was linked to a transition in science from an environmental theory of disease to a germ theory of disease. In 1886 James Olcott in a speech before the Agricultural Board of Connecticut called on his audience and the citizens of Connecticut to 'agitate, agitate' in order to 'cleanse' the state of the 'social evil' of the pollution of 'sewage from families and factories'. He urged them to stop the 'raising of a polluted stream upon any body at the will of ignorant or reckless capitalists'.[22] The post-civil war 'water purity' reformers saw public health reform in terms of political struggle. Their efforts, particularly those for water cleaned of industrial wastes, involved the post-war reformers in a direct confrontation with industrial capitalists. By the early twentieth century, public health advocates abandoned their concern for industrial wastes for a concern over sewage, because the overloading of the nation's water system with sewage waste was causing significant morbidity and mortality.[23]

Melosi divides the history of sanitation services, water supply, sewerage (the physical facilities, such as pipes, lift stations, and treatment and disposal facilities, through which sewage flows) and solid waste collection, in the USA into three time periods: 'The Age of Miasmas: From Colonial Times to 1880', 'The Bacteriological Revolution, 1880–1945', and 'The New Ecology, 1945–2000'. Melosi designates these themes as 'environmental paradigms' that reflect technological choices 'informed by and within the context of the prevailing environmental theory of the day'.[24] For Melosi, in this context, 'environmental theory' appears to mean theories of disease etiology that involve interactions with aspects of the environment: air, water, and land. He examines how the technical choices of city decision makers and engineers have been strongly influenced by prevailing theories of public health; for example, the miasmatic or filth theory of disease and bacteriological theory. His last period, the most recent, on the other hand, is shaped by 'new' ecological theories that do not necessarily correspond to a public health domain alone. Furthermore, this last period includes such phenomena as the infrastructure crisis, the environmental movement, and new pollution concerns that all had considerable influence on sanitary decision-making. He carefully notes the importance of technology transfer from Europe, as well as the successes and failures of these imported technologies.

A key issue that has encouraged wide debate is that of combined versus separate sewers. Combined sewers take both the foul water from premises and the stormwater runoff from roofs and paved surfaces. As indicated in the discussion of the nineteenth-century expansion of flush toilets in Britain, combined sewers, originally mainly stormwater drains, discharge increasing amounts of sewage into the rivers or coastal water bodies to which they drained. Even when interceptor sewers were built, stormwater flows sometimes exceeded

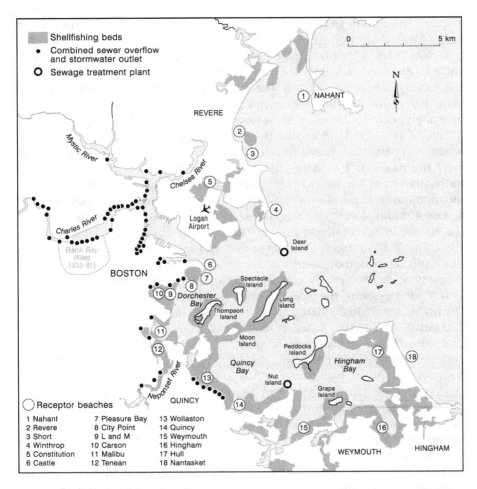

Figure 6.3: Boston Harbor showing sewer outfalls, shellfishing beds and the Nut Island and Deer Island treatment works (based in part on a map in Schaake, 1972)

the capacity of the interceptor and had to overflow into natural water bodies. Throughout the twentieth century, these combined sewer overflows created some of the worst river pollution events in European and North American countries.

By the 1850s in Boston, USA, people were becoming aware that comprehensive planning for urban drainage and sewerage was necessary. Over the next 20 years, Boston undertook a massive landfill and development project for its Back Bay area (Figure 6.3). A major effort was made to have efficient sewers in order to avoid the release of sewage gas and other odours into the air, people still believing that pure air was essential to avoid disease. The sewers were rebuilt so that wastes were discharged into South Bay, rather than into the more stagnant waters of Back Bay.[25] For the next 100 years, Bostonians relied on the three metre tidal range providing enough dilution of wastes each tidal cycle to prevent deoxygenation of the estuary waters.[26] Gradually the need for a comprehensive development plan, especially an integrated sewer system, was urged on the authorities by enlightened engineers.[27] In Boston, a far thinking landscape architect, Robert Morris Copeland argued in favour of careful land use planning and urban infrastructure provision, convinced that careful engineering could meet the needs of a modern city. Although this ran counter to the rugged individualism of the time, by 1889 state legislative approval was given for a metropolitan water and sewer district controlled by the Boston Metropolitan Sewage Commission.[28] The original backbone of Boston's early sewer system the Boston Main Drainage System (BMDS) was constructed from 1877 to 1884. The BMDS intercepted local sewers and carried sewage and stormwater to an offshore disposal point.

In 1919, to oversee the complex Metropolitan Sewerage District (as well as the water system), the Massachusetts Legislature created the Metropolitan District Commission (MDC), now the Department of Conservation and Recreation. The BMDS, however, continued to be owned by the city. Up to this point, wastewater was merely collected and deposited into Boston Harbor. Because of worsening pollution, the MDC constructed primary wastewater treatment plants at Nut Island (1952) and Deer Island (1968) (Figure 6.3). Outlets at Calf Pasture and Moon Island were maintained as a backup for the Deer Island Plant during wet weather. Despite this, combined sewer overflows were still a major problem in the early 1970s. Tides were washing sewage back and forth every tidal cycle, and bacteria were accumulating in the harbour.[29]

Work was carried out at malfunctioning tidal gates and chlorinators were installed at major combined sewer outfalls. In 1977, ownership and operating responsibility for the Boston's sewer system (as well as the water system) was transferred from the city to the newly formed Boston Water and Sewer Commission (BWSC). In 1985, the Massachusetts Legislature transferred the possession, control and operation of the MDC Water and Sewerage Divisions to the newly created Massachusetts Water Resources Authority (MWRA).

BWSC began planning modifications and improvements. In 1988, construction of the New Boston Main Interceptor and the New East Side Interceptor was completed, replacing portions of the original BMDS. In addition, MWRA was also incorporating improvements to the system. Between 1997 and 2000, all wastewater collected by BWSC facilities was conveyed to the MWRA's Deer Island Treatment Facility for secondary treatment whence a 15.3 km outfall tunnel carried treated wastewater out of Boston Harbor to the deep waters of Massachusetts Bay.

SANITATION, SEWAGE AND MOUNTAINS OF TRASH

Seattle: industrial wastes and implications for fish stocks

Seattle had a history of sewer development and subsequent re-organization and major interceptor sewer construction somewhat similar to that of Boston. In 1889 Mayor Robert Moran hired the well-known sanitary engineer, Colonel G.E. Waring to devise a sewerage plan for Seattle. Waring advocated separate sewers emptying into Elliot Bay, but this scheme was too costly for the council. Benezette Williams, from Chicago drew up an alternative combined sewer plan which the city adopted, William's argument being that the coastal waters around Seattle were fully capable of adequately diluting any likely organic waste input. Tunnelling for the northern sewer ran into problems with subsurface water in the diverse glacial sediments beneath the city, whose complexity was not fully appreciated by the engineers of the time.[30] The comprehensive planning goal of the then city engineer, R.H. Thomson, a city with a clean and reliable water supply, a complete sewer system and a street system with less steep gradients than those prevailing over the hummocky glacial terrain, was typical of forward thinking engineers and landscape architects of the time. He pressed on with combined sewers that had outfalls into Puget Sound but also along the Duwamish River that drains into it. In 1898 he began two decades of re-engineering the city, moving millions of tonnes of rock and debris to build sewers and re-grade the streets.[31]

As the city expanded and new suburbs were built a growing number of agencies and local authorities built new sewer lines. The city diverted the last of its 36 raw sewage outfalls from Lake Washington into Puget Sound in 1936, but combined sewer overflows (CSOs) still spilt organic debris into the lake. In 1948, Abel Wolman advocated separate sewer systems, but the Washington State Pollution Control Commission which had been set up in the late 1930s advocated a system of interceptor sewers around Lake Washington. By 1955 there were 21 independent sewer districts representing almost 40 communities, all clustered around Lake Washington, inland from the centre of Seattle city centre, with ten disposal systems built since 1941 all discharging treated or untreated wastewater into the lake. Diffuse pollution from leaking septic tanks, garden and golf course fertilizers and pesticides, and from pet droppings added to the contaminant load of the lake and the Duwamish River.[32] The appearance of blue-green algae in Lake Washington in 1955 provided serious evidence of the lack of oxygen in the lake as a consequence of its high pollutant load. A special State Committee on Aquatic Pollution proposed a Greater Seattle Metro Council to co-ordinate infrastructure in the Seattle urban region. Despite much local opposition, the Metro was established in 1958 and in 1960 produced a 10-year plan for upgrading works. In 1962 it obtained agreement with 15 municipal agencies and sewer districts across King County for the construction of interceptor sewers to carry sewage away from Lake Washington to new treatment plants which would release the treated wastewater into Puget Sound. The work was finally completed in 1982.[33] The clean-up of the lower Duwamish River continued with government designated severely contaminated (Superfund) sites still being treated in 1999. Even then the pollution problems were not over, with polyaromatic hydrocarbons (PAHs) and endocrine disruptors being found in the river.[34] In Puget Sound, wood treatment facilities are a major source of PAHs, since creosote used in wood treatment comprises approximately 85 per cent PAHs.[35]

Significant occurrences of lesions on livers (Hepatic neoplasms) were first found in English sole *(Parophrys vetulus)* from the Duwamish River in 1975. They were much more frequent in fish from estuaries and inlets affected by sewage and industrial activity than in those from more open waters further out in Puget Sound.[36] The distribution of the most affected fish was closely correlated with the highest levels of PAHs in the water and sediments. Shellfish were also affected, a 1999 study showing that tissue concentrations of total PAHs (e.g., fluoranthene, phenanthrene, benzo[a]pyrene), PCBs, DDTs, other pesticides, and selected metals (mercury and lead) were higher in Puget Sound mussels from the urban sites of Eagle Harbor, City Waterway, Seacrest, Four Mile Rock, and Sinclair Inlet than in those from non-urban sites (Oak Bay, Saltwater Park, Coupeville, and Double Bluff).[37]

Flatfish in Puget Sound exposed to chemical contaminants tend to show increases in disease and alterations in growth and reproductive function that may reduce the productivity of fish subpopulations living mainly in contaminated sites. Species such as Puget Sound English sole, which spend critical periods in contaminated near shore sites may be more susceptible to the harmful effects of anti-oestrogenic and other endocrine-disrupting chemicals on gonadal development than species such as winter flounder, which spend a portion of those periods in uncontaminated waters offshore.[38]

Portland, Oregon

The first comprehensive water quality survey of the Willamette River that flows through Portland by Oregon Agricultural College (now Oregon State University) in 1929 measured dissolved oxygen levels during summer low-flow at more than eight parts per million (ppm) for the upper 210 km of river. From Salem to Newberg they were seven ppm, but deteriorated rapidly further downriver. Above Willamette Falls they were five ppm and reached four ppm at Portland Harbor. The survey concluded that dissolved oxygen was less than 0.5 ppm where the Willamette reached the Columbia. When these waste flows reached Portland Harbor, the water quality situation became serious. The municipal wastes of the city, which by 1930 had just over 300,000 inhabitants, flowed untreated into the harbour through 65 separate discharge sewers. Tidal action and backflow from the Columbia kept the wastes generally inside the harbour during the summer low-flow period. The result was a near total absence of dissolved oxygen.[39]

Portland had a particular problem with sewage and water pollution in the Columbia Slough to the north-west of the city centre. In the early twentieth century, millions of litres of Portland's raw sewage were dumped into this slow-moving waterway each month, with additional contaminants coming from 200 industrial sites and a landfill along its banks. Many complaints about the associated smells and debris appeared in the local press from 1935 to 1993. Many NGOs accused the local government of doing nothing about it because many local residents were people of colour. In 1932, the city began to operate a garbage dump on the banks of the Slough. Conditions in the Slough had become so bad by the 1950s that sawmill workers refused to handle logs that had travelled through its waters.[40]

Portland opened a sewage treatment plant in 1951 which alleviated the problem in the Slough somewhat, but seepage from the local landfill and CSOs continued until at least 1993. The North Portland Peninsula became a major industrial zone in which the remaining residents, who were disadvantaged compared to the general population, did not enjoy the environmental improvements elsewhere in the city. Finally in September 1993 the city council voted $125 million to eliminate all CSOs in the Slough using a 5.5 km tunnel to divert contaminated water away from the Slough. Up to that time, the conditions in the Slough were a good example of environmental injustice.

AUSTRALIA: DEALING WITH OCEAN OUTFALLS IN SYDNEY

Early Sydney had many health and sewage disposal problems. Reports of the Sydney City and Suburban Sewerage and Health Board in 1875–6 on houses in the Rocks area close to Sydney Cove noted that only four toilets served almost 100 inhabitants and in some cases cesspits drained directly into street gutters.[41] The city installed a new sewerage system in 1889 but not all the epidemics were controlled because untreated wastes were discharged into Sydney Harbour. By the 1930s the plague and other epidemics that had affected Sydney were largely eliminated, in part as a result of improved sewage, but also because of better general hygiene, diet and health care.

Further improvements began following the 1995 'Cities for the 21st Century' strategy[42] which took an integrative view of planning as an 'all of government' process in which all the relevant agencies had a binding stake in Sydney's development, including water-supply, sewerage, roads and public transport.[43] In 2000, Sydney Water, the statutory state owned corporation, wholly owned by the New South Wales Government, that is the water and sewerage utility for Sydney was collecting, transporting and treating (usually to a primary level) about 1,300 million litres of sewage daily from households and industry. A considerable proportion of the 25,000 km of sewage pipes in Sydney required maintenance and repair. Most of the gravity-fed system led via treatment plants to ocean outfalls. Despite the millions of dollars spent on improvements and upkeep, there remained an ever-present threat of stormwater overflows that would carry sewage into the harbour and on to beaches.[44]

BUENOS AIRES: FROM WORLD CLASS TO
AN URGENT NEED TO EXTEND THE NETWORK

The water and sewerage systems of Buenos Aires could once have been the envy of many capital cities elsewhere: robustly designed and serving over 5 million people, they were the product of a golden age of water engineering in Argentina from 1860 into the 1930s.[45] Obras Sanitarias de la Nacíon (OSN) was established to provide water and sewerage to the Federal Capital (FC) and Greater Buenos Aires (GBA). While in 1991 all the people of the FC had sewer connections only 26 per cent of those in GBA had sewerage. Combined sewers drained the older districts, while newer areas had separate systems. Illegal connections to sewers were a major cause of CSOs: 1.5 million m³ of effluent were discharged every day into the River Plate. Large areas of GBA had only septic tanks and ditches which discharged wastes into local water courses and resulted in both surface and groundwater pollution.

In 1991 the Argentine government took steps to privatize OSN, with Aguas Argentinas, a consortium led by Lyonnaise des Eaux gaining a contract to manage, improve and expand the water supply and sewerage system.[46] This consortium, the world's largest single water supply concession at the time, had a target to connect 1,331,000 people to the water supply and 929,000 to sewers by 1998, but only 630,000 supply and 112,000 sewer connections were made by the due date. Tariffs that were supposed to remain constant for 10 years were raised 45 per cent between 1993 and 2001. Yet, there were claims that privatization had prevented about 375 deaths of young children per year and had had a positive impact on health inequality.[47] The terms of the contract appear to have been arbitrarily altered by the regulator, without consultation with the government. The apparent neglect of sewer improvements, in favour of easier and more profitable water supply connections, as well as increased charges, eroded public confidence in Aguas Argentinas.[48] The consortium's profits were three times those of private water supply and sewerage companies in the UK and one assessment concluded that:

> The private water concession in Buenos Aires has done little that a rejuvenated public sector provider could not have done, and has in fact exacerbated some of the worst socio-economic and environmental problems of the city.[49]

Was the experience of late twentieth-century water and sewerage privatization in Buenos Aires another example of environmental injustice? After privatization, a family living in a newer or more expensive home was being billed using a tariff that was seven times that faced by a family living in an older, poor quality home. However, water and sewer connections cost up to US$1,500 (1996 dollars), far too much for the city's poorest households with average monthly incomes of US$200–$245. The monthly payment installment for connection alone would amount to 18 per cent of such households' incomes.[50]

154

In addition, the water reaching poor households became increasingly contaminated by seepage of wastewater in to aquifers from the growing numbers dependent on septic tanks and cesspits. After 2001, the 'Social Tariff Program' oriented toward households below the poverty line set up by Aguas Argentinas to keep sanitation expenditure below 4 per cent of household income, only reached some 10 per cent of potential targeted beneficiaries. This was clearly counter to the aim of the privatization process to achieve universal service by the end of the concession.[51]

Following the 2002 peso devaluation, Suez (which merged with Lyonnaise des Eaux in 1997) cancelled its Aguas Argentinas contract. When negotiations were completed in September 2005 over 95 per cent of the city's sewerage was still being dumped directly into the River Plate. Disputes between Suez and the Argentine government went to the International Centre for the Settlement of Investment.[52] However, despite all the arguments, the human dimension of this situation is the effect on some 11 million people in Greater Buenos Aires. The business arrangements failed to improve significantly the conditions of the poorest sections of the population, which increased in size dramatically following the 2002 financial crisis. The events recall some of the disasters with water supply companies in industrial cities in the early nineteenth century and remind people of the reason why the UN had a millennium development goal of increasing the numbers of people with safe water and sanitation.

LIVERPOOL'S OUTFALLS AND INTERCEPTOR SEWER DEVELOPMENT

The 1786 Liverpool Improvement Act set aside £175,000 (the equivalent of £13 million at 2010 costs) for improvements in Liverpool's streets and sewerage. The beginnings of a sewer system existed in Liverpool by 1802. In 1816 all Liverpool sewers, with the exceptions of the north and south shore sewers, discharged to the docks and basins along the waterfront. The Liverpool Highways Board laid 80 km of sewers along the city's main roads in 1830–56, but their primary purpose was to carry stormwater.[53] In 1848, John Newlands, the Borough Engineer, proposed a city-wide system and by 1857 there were 130 km of sewers. By the 1950s, many outfalls still released untreated sewage from 450,000 Liverpudlians into the Liverpool shore of the Mersey Estuary[54] (Figure 6.4).

The UK 1951 Rivers Act and 1960 Clean Rivers Act implemented discharge consents containing standards for new discharges. The 1973 Water Act created the North West Water Authority, which set as a focus improvements in sewage disposal. Efforts in the 1970s to improve the river conditions resulted in a 30 per cent reduction in the industrial pollution load. The Mersey Basin Campaign was formed in 1985, with a 25-year programme to improve the water quality and bankside development. By 1987, 40 species of fish could be found in the Mersey basin as sewage treatment improved and the decline of manufacturing industry saw a great decrease in industrial pollution.

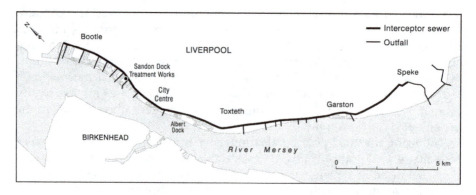

Figure 6.4: Liverpool's interceptor sewer, the former outfalls, which used to discharge untreated effluent into the estuary, and the modern Sandon Dock treatment works

The Mersey Estuary Pollution Alleviation Scheme project created a major interceptor sewer, tunnelled through Liverpool's sandstone bedrock that carried the city's wastewater to a new treatment plant at Sandon Dock that was commissioned in 1991 (Figure 6.4).[55] With later extensions, the once dirty estuary, where tides washed sewage back and forth, became far cleaner and wildlife returned to the salt marshes and sandy islands.

MODERNIZING SEWAGE SYSTEMS

Paris, Boston, Seattle, Sydney, Buenos Aires and Liverpool all saw strong emphasis on public health in the second half of the nineteenth century, but it took another 70 to 100 years for significant improvements in the quality of waters into which combined sewers overflowed to be achieved. Conditions in much of Europe, including the UK, and North America up to the 1970s reflect the 'taken for granted' attitude that was criticized in the UK report on sewage disposal.[56] The 1969 US National Environmental Policy Act and a series of EEC directives on water quality, issued in 1974–8,[57] then began to have an impact. Finally, the European urban wastewater treatment directive (91/271/EEC) which has the objective of protecting the environment from the adverse effects of untreated 'urban wastewater', began to deal with point source pollution (that coming out of factory outlets, pipes or sewers), especially that from combined sewer overflows. The directive establishes minimum requirements for the treatment of significant sewage discharges. Adopted by European Union member states in May 1991, it was transposed into legislation across the UK by the end of January 1995. In this way, the management of sewers and wastewater treatment has become a national, and even international concern, especially on international rivers such as the Rio Grande, Rhine, Danube and Ganges.

Urban sewer management in large urban areas has become the province of public, semi-public or private bodies, but the latter usually require strong regulation by elected governments, be they national, state or provincial. Buenos Aires showed what happens if that regulation is weak or lacks legal authority to punish utility companies that fail to meet standards and comply to the terms of their contracts. Many cities have questioned whether centralized sewage systems are the best solution, particularly in low latitudes where solar energy and biotic activity are high all year. Reed beds used in relatively small scale projects show that pollutants can be converted into plant biomass that can be harvested annually, that can provide wildlife habitat, improving biodiversity in cities and which provide ecosystem services, such as uptake of greenhouse gases.[58] Oxidation ponds and aeration lagoons are widely used for sewage treatment in Malaysia because of their low construction and operation costs.[59] They are simple to operate and maintain but require large land areas. Oxidation ponds may comprise one or more shallow ponds in a series. Natural algal and bacteria growth assists in the sewage treatment and the degree of treatment is weather dependent. They are often used for specific new development areas, avoiding increasing the volumes fed into main sewers leading to large centralized treatment plants.

Concerns have moved from public health to integrated river basin and estuary management and to the use of biological indicators that look at the quality of aquatic ecosystems, rather than specific physical-chemical attributes of water. This concern with ecosystem health runs parallel to new concerns about pharmaceutical chemicals and hydrocarbon compounds, especially PAHs in wastewater and in lakes, rivers and seas. Widespread studies of endocrine disruptors revealed how urban agricultural chemicals and manufacturing have released substances to aquatic food chains that have affected fish that might end up in food markets in towns and cities and thus affect humans.

SOLID WASTE

WASTE DISPOSAL IN ANCIENT TIMES

In Sumerian towns in Mesopotamia around 2500 BC, houses generally had no plumbing, so occupants bathed in the river and most household waste was simply deposited in the alleyways. Municipal workers were employed to keep these communal areas tidy, which for the most part meant spreading a layer of ash and sand over the waste. Over a period of time the accumulated waste, ash, and sand increased the height of the roads, so steps down to the houses on either side were needed.[60]

In North America, the ancient Mayans put their organic waste in dumps and used stones and broken pottery as fill. In the ancient Egyptian city of Heracleopolis, the capital of Lower Egypt in the ninth and tenth dynasties, wastes from the social elite and religious parts of town were collected and dumped, often into the Nile. By 1500 BC, Crete had designated areas for dumping organic wastes. In China around 200 BC, sanitation police oversaw street cleaning and had to remove animal and human carcasses in major cities.[61]

Around 500 BC, the Greeks organized the first municipal waste dumps in Mediterranean civilization. The Council of Athens started to enforce by-laws requiring rag-pickers to dump wastes at least 1.5 km from the walls of the city and banning the throwing of rubbish into the streets.[62]

Rome lacked such tight municipal control, waste was only collected by the authorities after major public events, and otherwise property owners were required, by law, to clean up the streets adjacent to their buildings. While the wealthy employed slaves to do this, and rag-pickers collected recyclable and resaleable garbage and excrement, waste piled up in many areas of the city which by around AD 400 became very unhealthy.[63]

MEDIAEVAL WASTE DISPOSAL

In the United Kingdom the existence of city controls on the burning of rubbish in open dumps can be traced back to the thirteenth century.[64] The English parliament banned waste disposal in public watercourses or ditches in 1388.[65]

Mediaeval Paris gradually acquired regulations dealing with specific nuisances, ranging from restricting the freedom of pigs to run in the streets to insisting that carts that brought goods into the city should take a load of refuse out of the city on their return journey.[66]

WASTE DISPOSAL IN EUROPE BEFORE 1914

Until an urban-industrial culture began to replace Europe's mediaeval agrarian society, refuse problems remained much the same. Pioneering work from the fifteenth to the eighteenth century produced localized improvements, but the major reforms, as in sewerage, began in the nineteenth century.

France

The nineteenth century was marked by an increased reliance on urban raw materials. These alone enabled Paris's newly established industries to expand and to meet demands from its dense and rapidly growing population. Not only was there a large trade in rags (see Chapter 3)[67] but the by-products of abattoirs and other animal wastes were widely used (Figure 6.5).[68] In the 1820s, well before science had understood vegetable nutrition, a hunt for fertilizers had begun in France. The towns and cities were the principal hunting ground, and of them, Paris was the richest source (Chapter 3). Sewage sludge provided an

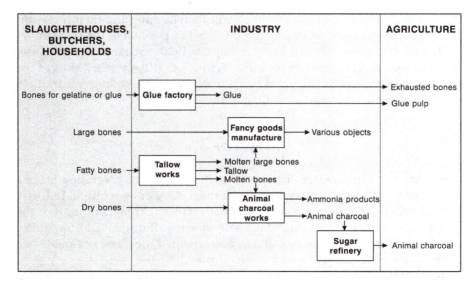

Figure 6.5: Uses of abattoir products in 19th century Paris (after Barles, 2005)

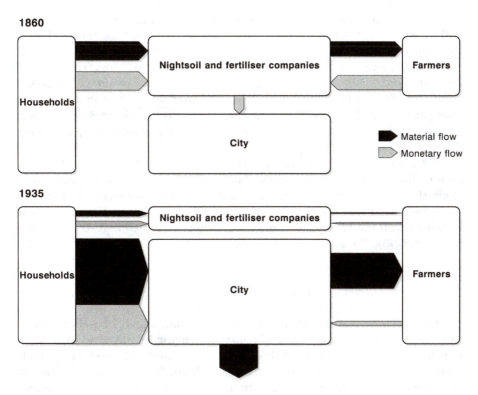

Figure 6.6: Changes in flows of fertilizers and money between farmers and urban households in Paris 1860 to 1935 (after Barles, 2007)

important agricultural resource for the peri-urban farming around nineteenth-century European cities. Sewage sludge fertilized 61 per cent of the farmland in the Departement Seine around Paris, but by the 1920s such use of urban waste in agriculture had become insignificant (Figure 6.6) (Chapter 3).[69] Most of the urban waste that was not recycled in Paris was incinerated; however by 1938 the waste volume was so great that landfilling began.

The United Kingdom

Horses formed a highly significant part of the urban waste recycling process in the late nineteenth century. The use of town dung as agricultural fertilizer constituted one of the means of dealing with refuse. Throughout most of the nineteenth century, for example, the sale of town dung proved a profitable venture for the Corporation of Dundee, and rendered the Carse of Gowrie one of the most fertile fruit-growing areas in Scotland.[70]

In 1898 the City of Manchester had 76,913 pail closets, 22,990 privies, and 13,014 middens, but their numbers were decreasing as the Corporation was providing water closets whenever it carried out alterations to property. About 900 tonnes of faecal matter was collected from the pail closets per week, about half of which was dried and converted into concentrated manure and sold; the remainder was mixed with ashes and rubbish, and disposed of amongst farmers on the Corporation estates at Carrington and Chat Moss. These estates covered about 1,520 ha, and could use about 93,000 t of mixed night-soil annually.[71] Treatment of sewage then yielded over 55,000 t of pressed sludge cake per year. In 1897, 14,233 t, equal to an average of about 39 t day^{-1} was removed by farmers. The balance of 41,875 t was deposited in a tip adjoining the works.[72]

In Britain, Liverpool used two Corporation steamers, the *Alpha* and *Beta*, to dump refuse at sea. Carrying loads of 330 t and 400 t, respectively, the steamers made the 38 km journey to the Irish Sea four times per week. By the turn of the twentieth century, however, there were increasing complaints of refuse washing up on the Welsh coast, and fishermen complained that their trawling nets were being filled with tins and other rubbish.[73]

Incineration in the UK

'Destruction' (cremation or incineration) of municipal household waste embodied the 'refuse revolution'. The first systematic incineration of waste at the municipal level began in Nottingham in 1874.[74] Destructors were large-scale municipal projects that were funded through loans from central government. They were grand technological solutions to the nuisance and public health threat of accumulating waste in urban industrial Britain. Most significantly, destructors marked the shift from a domestic culture of re-use and recycling to technocratic management of waste disposal. From their inception, incinerators were promoted as clean and efficient. By burning rubbish to generate electricity, waste-to-energy incinerator schemes seemed to offer an alternative middle way between re-use and disposal. The destructor embodied 'municipal modernity' because it promised improved public health through efficient management of waste.[75] Manlove, Alliott, and Co. installed refuse destructors at Manchester, Birmingham and Leeds in 1876, when the Fryer destructor was patented. By 1912, there were more than 338 refuse incinerators in Britain and over 80 of them generated electricity for local use. Fire would permit the perfect destruction of 'contagia and virus'. 'There is', preached Goodrich, 'only one method of the final disposition for the whole of the waste, that is the great purifier – fire.'[76] The destructor, as a tool of waste disposal, seemed to possess an unquenchable appetite at a time when Britain confronted the challenges posed by clearly defined waste streams.

Nevertheless, local opposition to destructors highlighted ambiguities surrounding nuisances, public health threats and air pollution in late nineteenth- and early twentieth-century Britain. Technocrats promoted the destructor as the most effective means of neutralizing the public health danger created by decaying rubbish. In the face of threatened legal action, local councils embraced 'purification through fire' as the most efficient way of removing the noisome nuisance of town refuse.[77]

In their efforts to convince people of the benign effects of destructors, nineteenth-century engineers boasted about the close proximity of many of the works to residential homes. T. Codrington noted that the destructor in Whitechapel, London, was located in a densely populated neighbourhood, and that the brickwork of the furnace cells was within a foot of the walls of the adjacent houses. As an impoverished area of the metropolis, Whitechapel was, perhaps, as more modern examples of environmental injustice show, not an altogether surprising location for a destructor.[78]

Torquay's destructor

The introduction of the destructor highlighted tensions between technocratic experts and local residents when municipalities confronted organized waste disposal in the late nineteenth century. Perhaps nowhere is this better illustrated than in Torquay, in Devon, south-west England. Like many of the rapidly expanding urban industrial centres in the Midlands and the North, Torquay opted for the construction of a refuse destructor in the last decade of the nineteenth century. Local opposition resulted in a relatively unique and well-documented investigation into Torquay's destructor. As a borough of moderate size, Torquay provides useful historical insight into waste management. A petition signed by 70 residents of Torquay was submitted to *The Lancet* in 1902. The petitioners were convinced that their health had been 'injuriously affected by the smoke fumes and gases ejected from the [local] refuse destructor'.[79]

Concerned about shortage of landfill sites and the cost of transporting rubbish to more distant locations, after they had exhausted available space at a brickfield clay-pit, the Torquay town council decided that disposal by fire was the only viable option to abate the nuisance caused by the town's accumulating refuse. In keeping with what had become standard practice, three to four years elapsed before Torquay realized its goal of an operational destructor. However, this was not without difficulty. Lord Kelvin, with the assistance of A. Barr, had produced a report in March 1899 that strongly endorsed refuse destructors as virtually smoke-free. The destructor included two multitubular boilers that supplied steam for two engines, which drove a mortar mill, a clinker mill and a dynamo. The latter produced lighting for the works and for the immediate vicinity.

Sanitary engineers contended that Britain led the world in the adoption of destructors because the nation's refuse had a high cinder and ash content and, therefore, a high calorific value.[80] Torquay's had a relatively high organic content and sometimes there was not enough refuse to keep the furnace burning continually. It often had to be shut down for short periods and then restarted. At low temperatures smoke would be emitted.

On 6 November 1900, St Marychurch, Babbacombe and Cockington were amalgamated with Torquay by an Act of Parliament. In February of the following year, the borough council resolved that 'no house refuse be sold or deposited ... in any part of the Borough for tillage purposes but that all such refuse be taken to the Destructor for cremation'. The voracious appetite of the destructor significantly shaped sanitary policy and the geopolitical landscape of the borough.[81]

Perhaps unsurprisingly, the most vocal complaints against the operational destructor did not arise from the poor residents of Upton Valley, but from the residents of the valuable villas on the hills surrounding the destructor. In Torquay, topography had conspired against the usually 'safe' spatial relationship between destructors and social class.

Local opposition to the Torquay destructor gradually petered out. Residents lodged multiple complaints throughout 1902, the year of The Lancet's special investigation, but these subsided in the years that followed. The council firmly believed that technological alterations to the destructor had solved problems with emissions. Undoubtedly, the geographical and demographic expansion of Torquay provided a more generous supply of fuel for the destructor. This, in turn, permitted the council to reduce its reliance on poor-burning organic garden refuse. Just one month after the amalgamation, the council restricted free removal of garden refuse to two loads per house, per annum. In combination with the technological alterations made at the suggestion of G. Davis, these measures probably provided constant high temperatures in the destructor cells, and some mitigation of the smoke nuisance. Decline in opposition, however, also marked the triumph of the refuse revolution.

The decline of incineration in the UK

The political and economic crises engendered by the First World War led to brief rediscoveries of re-use of old materials and equipment, but, in the longer term, the exceptionalism of war failed to translate salvage into enduring peacetime recycling. Incinerators, however, never regained the popularity they enjoyed during the refuse revolution of 1870 to 1914. Whereas there were in excess of 300 incinerators in Britain at the start of the twentieth century, 100 years later, there were just 19. Although displaced by the rise of the 'sanitary landfill' by the 1930s, incinerator technology persisted as a viable alternative.[82]

WASTE DISPOSAL IN THE USA BEFORE 1914

In 1870 there were 1.5 million horses in cities in the USA; by 1900 their number had risen to 3 million.[83] Horses needed feed which became part of a complex ecological system of exchange, the fertility of adjacent rural land often depending on the application of horse and human urban wastes to the soil. Manure from the city was also used for food production on land close by, especially for growing vegetables. Brooklyn (Kings County), Baltimore and Philadelphia all had this sort of relationship with adjacent farming areas. However, the feed supply involved more distant locations as well. Between 1879 and 1909, US hay production rose from 35 Mt to 97 Mt, largely driven by the demand for feed for urban horses. In 1895, New York City used over 400,000 tonnes of hay and Chicago nearly 200,000 tonnes. Urban horse numbers in the USA fell with the advent of motor vehicles, from 3 million in 1910 to 1.7 million in 1920 and less than 1 million in 1930.[84]

In 1885, the first American incinerator opened at Governor's Island, New York, followed in 1886–7 by municipal incinerators at Des Moines, Iowa; Wheeling, West Virginia; and Allegheny, Pennsylvania. The number of incinerators in the USA expanded rapidly in the 1890s, but by 1909, 102 of the 180 built in the previous 15 years had been dismantled or abandoned. Both incomplete combustion and noxious smoke were cited as a cause, but inappropriate, or inadequate, design and high costs, compared with dumping, were also major factors in the closures.[85]

TWENTIETH-CENTURY DEVELOPMENTS
IN WASTE MANAGEMENT IN THE USA

Sanitary landfill

Early trials of sanitary fill at Seattle, New Orleans, and Davenport, Iowa, in the 1910s were little more than land-based dumps. Modern systematic or large-scale disposal practice began in Great Britain in the 1920s under the name 'controlled tipping'. Some progress was made in the 1930s in New York City, San Francisco and Fresno, California. In New York, refuse was placed in deep holes primarily in marshes and then the holes were covered with dirt. In San Francisco, layers of refuse were deposited in tidal marshes to reclaim land, but actual trenches were not dug.

Jean Vincenz (1894–1989), commissioner of public works, city engineer, and manager of utilities in Fresno, California from 1931 to 1941, was the key person in the development of sanitary landfill in the USA. In Fresno, he suggested that the city should not renew the franchise of the Fresno Disposal Company, which operated an incinerator. He thought that the collection and disposal of solid waste should be a municipal undertaking. Having studied the prevailing good practice in Britain, California and New York, he concluded that a true sanitary landfill required components that differed from those used elsewhere, especially systematic construction of refuse cells, a deeper cover of dirt between layers of refuse, and compaction of both the earth cover and the waste. The trenches and the compaction process, along with the daily covering of the fill, were the unique features of the sanitary landfill in Fresno, compaction being the more important of the two.

During the Second World War, under the direction of Jean Vincenz, the US Army Corps of Engineers modernized its solid waste disposal programmes to serve as model landfills for communities of all sizes. Municipalities were slow to adopt this guidance. The California Department of Health Services and several other progressive state health departments established standards for municipal sanitary landfills and vigorously campaigned for the closure of conventional dumps. Nevertheless, after a thorough review of solid waste management practices in the USA, Congress concluded in 1965 that:

> Inefficient and improper methods of disposal of solid waste result in scenic blights, create serious hazards to public health, including pollution of air and water resources, accident hazards, and increase rodent and insect vectors of disease, have an adverse effect on land values, create public nuisances, otherwise interfere with community life and development ... The failure or inability to salvage and re-use such materials economically results in the unnecessary waste and depletion of natural resources.[86]

By the 1970s, solid waste professionals and others began to doubt the adequacy of the sanitary landfill exclusively to serve the future disposal needs of cities. Siting new landfills became problematic in some parts of the country, especially in the north-east. Many communities simply did not set aside land specifically designated for waste disposal facilities. Landfill siting is also a treacherous business because of citizen resistance and increasingly rigid environmental standards. Concerns about the environmental integrity of landfills, especially those without adequate lining or provision for methane gas monitoring, grew.[87] Even so, sanitary

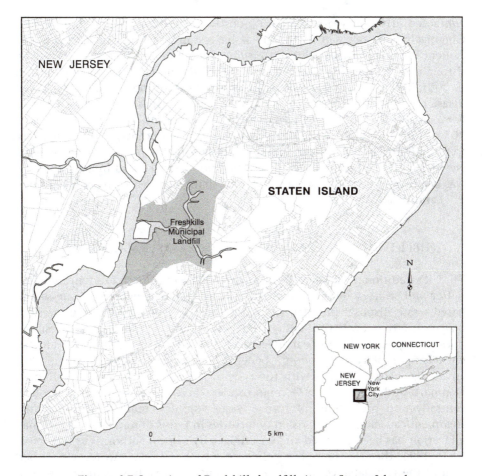

Figure 6.7: Location of Freshkills landfill site on Staten Island

landfill remains possibly the most significant and most widely adopted disposal technology yet developed.

A further development, starting in the late 1950s, involved a rise in private contracting. Firms that provided economies of scale, sophisticated management, and efficient collection absorbed smaller companies and replaced municipal operations. Sharp rises in the costs of disposal as well as a desire to shift labour and operating costs to the private sector also played a role. In the 1980s, private contracting grew rapidly because it was the most cost effective method available. By the last decade of the twentieth century, as new techniques for utilizing recycled materials and controlling waste generation developed, society seemed on its way to a more sustainable balance.

The Freshkills Landfill, Staten Island, New York, opened as a 'temporary landfill' in 1947, this 890 ha site (Figure 6.7) consisted of four sections which contained fifty plus years of landfill, mostly in the form of household waste. Chemicals were released to the air as barges and garbage trucks unloaded; cement crushing trucks released dust into the air; and rain still percolates through waste and into groundwater. Although the landfill officially closed in 2001, later that year it began receiving the ruins of the World Trade Center disaster. Former landfill sites in the New York area are now valuable real estate. For example, in 2008 Waste Management of New Jersey, Inc began to develop 20 ha of the former PJP Landfill Superfund site in Jersey City, NJ on which was to be built an 81,000 m³ distribution centre serving the ports of New York and New Jersey. By 2011, the development had not occurred and in 2012 the city was beginning work to create a recreational park on at least part of the former PJP Landfill site.

PUBLIC OR PRIVATE RESPONSIBILITY FOR WASTE MANAGEMENT

The UK's traditionally decentralized and free-market approach to environmental policy and strategy development with a heavy reliance upon a private-sector based waste disposal industry (virtually 100 per cent for hazardous wastes) has meant that both the ability and willingness to adopt, and invest in, options higher in the waste management hierarchy have been reliant almost entirely upon perceived economic benefits (such as lower liabilities and market advantage). This contrasts with the type of regime seen in the Netherlands, Denmark, and certain of the German Länder where waste disposal is controlled centrally and projections of future waste volumes, required disposal and treatment capacity, and provision of facilities in terms of number and regional allocation has been planned and encouraged by central authorities.[88]

In 1993, the UK's recycling policy set a national target to recycle 50 per cent of the recyclable component of the household waste stream by the year 2000. The EC's Fifth Environment Action Programme on wastes sets a target of municipal solid waste amounts of 300 kg cap⁻¹ yr⁻¹, which is the 1985 average level, exceeded in most member states in 2005, some by significant amounts, 500 kg cap⁻¹ yr⁻¹ being produced in France.[89]

Despite widespread use in many countries (Table 6.1), incinerator facilities and proposals (and also landfills) have faced opposition from local communities in most countries in Europe and North America at least since 1980. While society in general accepts the need for waste to be disposed of in a responsible and environmentally safe manner, many members of local communities amongst whom facilities are to be sited do not wish to accept potential risks and adverse environmental impacts in order to relieve others of their waste problem. Opposition to incinerators is as much a reflection of public opposition to institutional and political arrangements that appear to be directly affecting their lives, as it is to stack plumes, noise, the fear of tragic accidents handling 'toxic' waste, odour, and the general loss of amenity that any major industrial facility imposes upon a local community.[90]

Table 6.1: Proportion of municipal solid waste incinerated in 2005

Country	per cent municipal waste incinerated	Number of Incinerators	per cent of incinerated waste including energy recovery	per cent sewage sludge incinerated
Canada	9	17	7	n/a
USA	16	168	n/a	n/a
Singapore	90++	4		
Japan	75	1900	*	n/a
Sweden	55	23	86	0
Denmark	65	38	*	19
France	42	170	67	20
Netherlands	40	12	72	10
Germany	35	47	n/a	10
Italy	18	94	21	11
Spain	6	22	61	n/a
UK	7	30	33	7

*   most plants in these countries recover energy
++   percentage of non-recyclable waste

In February 2006, the UK government launched a review of its waste strategy with a declaration that it intended to increase its rate of incineration of municipal waste from 9 per cent to 22 per cent. Increased incineration, the government argued, would reduce waste in landfill, and it would produce 'green energy' through waste-to-energy applications. Environmental groups immediately opposed the proposal on the grounds that it would reduce recycling.

Twenty-first-century environmental activists object to the pollution and public health dangers arising from the incineration of rubbish. They, however, operate within a post-1960s environmentalist rubric that weds public health concerns to nature conservation and preservation in a global context. Whereas past discussions assessed the possible benefits arising from waste-to-energy, recent critics of incineration have complained that it detracts from the push for renewable energy sources.[91]

Incineration has to be discussed within the context of an integrated waste management strategy, rather than as a single option. Although landfill is unlikely to lose its prominent role in many countries, closer scrutiny of its long-term environmental impact, increasing concern amongst waste producers to protect their potential liabilities, direct restrictions on the range of acceptable wastes, and requirements for improved engineering control, are already promoting a move to incineration. The latter is technically proven as an effective waste destruction and reduction method. However, to promote incineration as an environmentally sustainable option in the public domain requires a number of actions:

(i) *attention to the operation of integrated systems* where materials (principally metals) are segregated and recovered prior to incineration of the remainder;

(ii) *energy recovery from all plant*, with where necessary the use of economic instruments to promote development;

(iii) *treatment and re-use of the residues*;

(iv) *effective and publicly accountable on-site management and regulatory control*;

(v) *risk assessment* of all proposed and operating plant with public discussion of the results.

Most importantly, the effective management of wastes requires a long-term strategy based on a full understanding of the relative costs and benefits, including long-term environmental impacts, of different options.[92]

SEWAGE SLUDGE

Overall the UK produces some 1.4 million tonnes of sewage sludge annually, some 0.9 million tonnes of which is disposed of on farmland. Much of the remaining sludge is incinerated producing electricity used to power machinery at treatment works or even sold to the grid. For example, Welsh Water's Advanced Digestion plants at Cardiff, Hereford and Port Talbot reduce the company's need to buy electricity by 10 per cent and they cut its gas requirement by 50 per cent. At Didcot sewage works, in addition to generating electricity from burning biogas, treated biomethane gas is fed into the national gas grid. Even so there are ash residues to be dumped at suitable disposal sites, such as that of United Utilities at Frodsham Marsh in the River Mersey estuary, England.

WASTE AND COASTAL RECLAMATION

As indicated above, urban waste was being used for land reclamation in San Francisco in the 1930s. The filling of San Francisco Bay's saltwater marshes continued until the early 1970s with only about 125 km^2 of the original 2,200 km^2 of tidal marsh then remaining.[93]

All waste from the Tokyo area was disposed of on land until 1945. However, since about 1957, the garbage disposal site was located on reclaimed land in

Tokyo Bay. After 1976, almost all the waste was dumped to help reclaim more of Tokyo Bay. In the 1990s the relevant Japanese ministries estimated that waste from the metropolitan area would fill 1 billion m³ of Tokyo Bay within ten years. A scheme was designed to take waste into 600 ha of active reclamation, but the overall projection was that to deal with all the domestic, industrial and construction and demolition waste from the city 2,250 ha of land would have to be reclaimed.[94]

REDUCING THE WASTE STREAM: REDUCE, RE-USE, RECYCLE

Reduction, re-use and recycling of waste essentially involve changing the behaviour of individuals and organizations. Change can be prompted or assisted by legislation; financial incentives or deterrents; and by the provision of opportunities to profit from re-use or to recycle easily. Legislative measures are often directed at specific types of waste. For example, the 1994 European Commission Directive on Packaging Waste[95] aimed to harmonize national measures in order to prevent or reduce the impact of packaging and packaging waste on the environment and has provisions on the prevention of packaging waste, on the re-use of packaging and on the recovery and recycling of packaging waste. A 2004 review clarified the definition of the term 'packaging' and increased the targets for recovery and recycling of packaging waste.

The EU directives have led to major changes in the proportion of waste that is recycled. Data for Ireland show that although waste collection volumes are growing, the amount going to landfill has decreased (Figure 6.8). Facilities to sort waste at source (i.e. at the household, office or business) greatly help to reduce the amount of potentially recyclable material in the average waste bin (Figure 6.9).

Financial incentives

To keep paper and inorganic materials such as metals, glass, and plastics from landfills, a number of cities have found ways to promote recycling and waste-based industries. Drink container refunds are well established. An increase in the refund available for empty beverage containers prompted Californians to achieve a significant jump in recycling in the first half of 2007. More than 16.5 billion of the over 20 billion carbonated and non-carbonated refund-eligible drinks in aluminum, glass, plastic and bi-metal containers bought by Californians were recycled in 2010.

Cities have charged a fee for the collection of unsorted garbage, for example, while picking up at no cost refuse that has been separated for recycling. By adopting 'pay-as-you-throw' systems, at least 11 US cities have boosted recycling rates to the 45–60 per cent range, well above the national average of 27 per cent.[96]

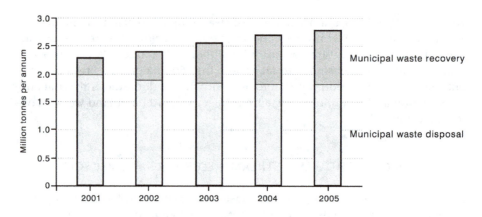

Figure 6.8: Recovery and disposal of municipal waste in Ireland 2001–5

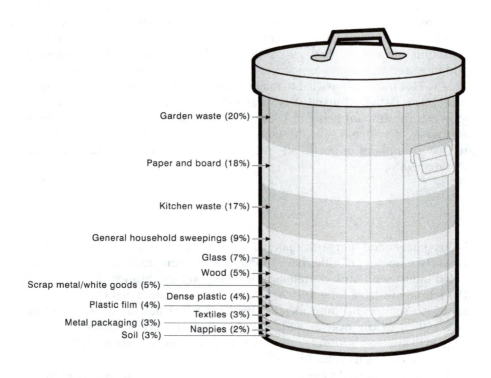

Figure 6.9: Average contents of a domestic waste bin in Ireland in about 2005

Landfill taxes

Landfill Tax is a tax on the disposal of waste. It aims to encourage waste producers to produce less waste, recover more value from waste, for example through recycling or composting and to use more environmentally friendly methods of waste disposal. Landfills in California are subject to fees and taxes levied by cities and counties, as well as by the state. The Integrated Waste Management Act of 1989 authorized a state fee (in 2011 $1.40 per tonne) to fund the activities of the California Integrated Waste Management Board. Many cities and counties collect fees from landfills within their jurisdiction to recover the costs of local solid waste planning and inspection programmes, to operate programmes for the collection and disposal of household hazardous wastes, and to fund some costs of recycling and re-use programmes. In 2011 the Monterey Regional Waste Management District disposal fees for solid waste were $47 per tonne, for food scraps $380 per tonne and for yard waste and wood waste $23 per tonne.

The UK's first environmental tax, the Landfill Tax, was introduced in 1996 by Conservative Secretary of State for the Environment, John Gummer as a key mechanism in enabling the UK to meet its targets set out in the Landfill Directive for the landfilling of biodegradable waste. Originally set at £7 per tonne, it rose every year to £64 per tonne in April 2012 (Table 6.2). Annual tonnages sent to landfill at these costs per tonne were 46,200,000 in 1997–8, rising to over 50,000,000 from 2000 to 2002, and then falling to 24,884,000 in 2010–11. Income from fees trebled while the tonnage landfilled halved.

Some cities have gone a step further toward preventing landfill overflow by involving the industries that create disposable goods or generate waste. In 1997, Tokyo municipal officials looking for new waste disposal options in land-short Japan announced that they would require makers and distributors of plastic bottles to recover and recycle their products. Graz, Austria, has created a labelling programme to spur small- and medium-sized industries to reduce waste: companies receive the city's Ecoprofit label if they reduce solid waste by 30 per cent and hazardous waste by 50 per cent.

RECYCLING

In the past when raw materials were scarce and more difficult to import, industrial waste recycling was much more prevalent in the western industrialized nations which all supported substantial waste paper, waste textile and scrap metal industries. However the early twenty-first century witnessed the substantial globalization of trade and the urban metabolism has to be seen through this inter-continental movement of manufactured goods and scrap materials. In this system items entering the waste stream become 'experienced' resources that can become re-employed in the production of more goods.

171

Table 6.2: United Kingdom landfill tax rates

Date	Standard Rate (£ per tonne)	Lower Rate (£ per tonne)
1996 Oct 01	7	2
1999 Apr 01	10	2
2000 Apr 01	11	2
2001 Apr 01	12	2
2002 Apr 01	13	2
2003 Apr 01	14	2
2004 Apr 01	15	2
2005 Apr 01	18	2
2006 Apr 01	21	2
2007 Apr 01	24	2
2008 Apr 01	32	2.5
2009 Apr 01	40	2.5
2010 Apr 01	48	2.5
2011 Apr 01	56	2.5
2012 Apr 01	64	2.5

The media has given greatest attention to the export of toxic material and e-waste from affluent countries to less developed regions where re-use of waste is much cheaper. In the 1990s, governments in the EU, Japan and some US states set up electronic component waste (e-waste) 'recycling' systems. But many countries did not have the capacity to deal with the sheer quantity of e-waste they generated or with its hazardous nature. Therefore, they began exporting the problem to developing countries where laws to protect workers and the environment are inadequate or not enforced. It is also cheaper to 'recycle' waste in developing countries; the cost of glass-to-glass recycling of computer monitors is ten times greater in the US than in China.

Demand in Asia for e-waste began to grow when scrap yards found they could extract valuable substances, such as copper, iron, silicon, nickel and gold, during the recycling process. A mobile phone, for example, is 19 per cent copper and 8 per cent iron. Between 1995 and 2007, shipments of non-hazardous waste such as paper, plastic and metals from the EU increased dramatically, mostly to Asia, particularly China. The amount of waste paper exported to Asia increased tenfold. For plastics the increase has been a factor of eleven and for metals a factor of five. The shipped waste has also increased within the EU, but at much lower levels. In 2007 as much waste paper was shipped to Asia as was shipped from one EU country to another. The quantity of metals shipped within the EU was larger than the amount shipped to Asia. However, the EU shipped more plastic waste to the Asian market than within the EU. A contributory factor is the low cost of transporting waste to China because the containers used to import goods have to be repatriated and any load is better than none.

In China, e-waste dismantling in Guiyu town has become a major industry, it provides more than 50,000 job opportunities and also saves the material recycled in the process of energy consumption, reducing the possibility of secondary pollution. Re-use of materials from Guiyu occurs in nearby towns and cities. The surrounding area is home to related industries using the reclaimed materials. Recycled plastic is used for artificial flowers, plastic accessories, stationery, gifts and other goods in the city of Shantou. In Chenghai district, electronic components are re-used in toy manufacturing, thus reducing production costs. This type of closed-loop material use along with industrial symbiosis – co-locating or connecting industries so that a waste or co-product from one becomes an input to another – is well established in China and South Korea.

In 2005, more than 15,000 tonnes of used colour television sets were exported from the EU to African countries.[97] In Nigeria, Ghana and Egypt alone about 1,000 TV sets arrived every day. As with used cars and used clothing, the majority of these TV sets are likely to be used again before eventually being scrapped.

SIDE-EFFECTS OF URBAN METABOLISM CHANGES

Internationally, the global trade in waste has had serious side-effects. The export of e-waste to China for disassembly as part of the global circulatory urban metabolism has a wide environmental impact. The air around Guiyu town has far higher levels of pollutants than normally found in urban areas. For example, $PM_{2.5}$ (16.8 ng m^{-3}) particles in air samples collected in Guiyu contained 100 times more organobromine compounds derived from flame retardants in electronic equipment than are usually found in air samples collected elsewhere. Such compounds may be endocrine disruptors and may come from uncontrolled burning of e-waste in the open air.[98]

The illegal traffic of hazardous waste can be more sinister in its impact. In July 2009, 89 containers containing mixed waste were illegally shipped from the United Kingdom to Brazil. The 1,500 tonnes of waste, which were labelled as mixed recyclables, were detected by the Brazilian authorities in three ports. The authorities alleged that the containers held landfill and hazardous waste, including household waste, batteries, used syringes and dirty diapers. The containers were returned to the United Kingdom and the Environment Agency for England and Wales launched an investigation.[99]

GOVERNMENT RECYCLING TARGETS

The EU Landfill Directive states targets for reducing the amount of waste sent to landfill sites in the UK. The targets are:

- by 2010, the waste sent to landfills should be 75 per cent of that sent in 1995;
- by 2013, the waste sent to landfills should be 50 per cent of that sent in 1995;
- by 2015, the waste sent to landfills should be 35 per cent of that sent in 1995.

In order to achieve this directive, 'Waste Strategy 2000' introduced the following targets for waste recovery:

- recover 40 per cent of waste by 2005;
- recover 45 per cent of waste by 2010;
- recover 67 per cent of waste by 2015.

The UK government has also published national recycling targets in 'Waste Strategy 2000':

- 25 per cent of household waste should be recycled or composted by 2005;
- 30 per cent of household waste should be recycled or composted by 2010;
- 33 per cent of household waste should be recycled or composted by 2015.

The recycling target for individual local authorities was 30 per cent by 2005/2006. The government issued a 'Waste Performance and Efficiency Grant' of £260 million to aid local authorities in waste reduction, increased recycling and diversion from landfills.

IMPROVING WASTE MANAGEMENT IN SMALLER TOWNS AND CITIES

Many small towns in countries such as Australia, Canada, and the USA rely on a local town dump, or landfill for the disposal of their solid waste. From 1970 onwards, tighter state or provincial legislation has led to improvements in recycling, but in many small town the landfills have been operating in the same site for decades. The City of Armidale, New South Wales, Australia, a small town of 23,000 people, provides a good example. The council's existing landfill off Long Swamp Road about 4 km to the south-east of the city centre, near the city's eastern boundary, was opened in 1961, but in 2008 had less than 2 years' capacity available.

Echoing the environmental injustice issue in relation to sewage overflows in Portland discussed above, in Armidale, less than a kilometer west of the landfill site, towards the city centre, is an Aboriginal housing settlement, Narwan Village, a former Aboriginal reserve, which is owned by the Armidale Local Aboriginal Land Council. Dust and debris

Table 6.3: Waste collection systems in Armidale and surrounding shires, New South Wales, Australia, 2008 (compiled from information on the Armidale-Dumaresq and Sustainable Armidale websites: http://armidale-new. local-e.nsw.gov.au and http://sustainablearmidale.com.au)

Council	Waste Type	Receptacle and Capacity	Collection Frequency
Armidale Dumaresq	Municipal Solid Waste (household)	140 litre red lidded 'wheelie' bin	Weekly
Armidale Dumaresq	Municipal Solid Waste (Commercial Premises and public spaces)	240 litre bins	Weekly
Armidale Dumaresq	Green waste (garden waste)	240 litre green bins	Fortnightly
Armidale Dumaresq	Recyclables (cartons, metals, plastics and glass)	450x350x300 mm crates (with lid)	Fortnightly
Armidale Dumaresq	Recyclables (clean cardboard and paper)	450x350x300 mm crates (with lid)	Fortnightly
Guyra Shire	Municipal Solid Waste (household)	140 litre bins	Weekly
Guyra Shire	Municipal Solid Waste (public space)	Variable bins throughout the town	Weekly
Guyra Shire	Recyclables	52 litre crates for recyclables	Weekly
Uralla Shire	Municipal Solid Waste (household)	50, 120 or 240 litre bins	Weekly
Uralla Shire	Recyclables	52 litre crates for recyclables	Weekly
Walcha	Municipal Solid Waste (household)	240 litre 'wheelie' bin	Weekly
Walcha	Recyclables	52 litre crates for recyclables	Weekly

from the landfill used to blow over Narwan when the wind was from the east.

Prior to 1993, there was little recycling of waste. The Armidale Hospital collected glass bottles for re-use and glass recycling. In the peri-urban areas around Armidale are 200 or more homes with septic tanks which have to be pumped-out every three to five years to remove accumulated sludge and scum. Formerly this sludge was spread on agricultural land, but changes to environmental and waste legislation in New South Wales prevented this form of disposal of septic tank sludge or grease trap waste. Armidale council adopted a liquid waste strategy in 1996. Two anaerobic ponds and one aerobic pond adjacent to the existing landfill were commissioned in July 1998.

The council's 2003 business plan commits it to waste minimization and developing alternatives to landfilling, with a detailed collection schedule (Table 6.3). It set up a Materials Recycling Facility (MRF) for recyclables adjacent to the landfill in 2003 which incorporates various skips and other disposal points to facilitate hand sorting of various waste materials by residents. 'Skip bins' or other sorting/collection facilities are available for a) general non-recyclable waste, for disposal in landfill; b) metal and metal auto parts; c) general garden waste; d) scrap timber; e) masonry and concrete: f) paper and cardboard, g) plastics; h) glass; i) aluminum and steel cans; and j) old computers. Heavy plastics, car batteries, paints, oils and other chemicals can be placed in various small bins or specific disposal facilities. The facility also includes a 'Resource Recovery Centre', which is a shop where recovered, re-usable 'second hand' goods are offered for sale. Any residual waste not able to be sorted into any of the above categories is classified as putrescible waste that in 2008 was being transferred to the existing landfill. Issues over plans to construct a regional putrescible waste landfill facility off Waterfall Way, approximately 12 km east of Armidale, continued to be debated in mid-2012. Protestors argue that the landfill site is close to the Gara River, which flows into areas of the World Heritage-listed forests. The President of the Gara Valley Environmental Protection Association told the NSW State Planning Commission that the landfill was being built in the wrong place, and argued that the existing site on Long Swamp Road could be extended. He said the proposed new site was located 4 km from the World Heritage-listed site and could have an adverse impact on the environment if the development were to be approved.[100] In the meantime the Armidale council had begun a trial of a household food-waste composting system which would sell the compost to farmers and householders.

ISTANBUL, MOVING FROM DUMPS TO SANITARY LANDFILL AND RECYCLING

Many cities still have open dumps where all kinds of waste are deposited together and where there is little or no attempt to cover the waste on a daily basis. These dumps often have continually burning fires that are extremely hazardous for the people who eke out a living by scavenging materials from the tipped waste. Dump managers in some cities periodically deliberately light fires to reduce the volume of the waste, creating room that extends the life of the dumps. The scavengers may also cause intentional fires since metals are easier to spot and recover among ashes after the fires than among piles of mixed waste.

Scavengers and burning dumps were a major problem in Istanbul until 1995. Before 1953 Istanbul's garbage was dumped into the sea. Then irregular dump areas began to develop in such localities as Levent-Sanayi Mahallesi,

Seyrantepe, and Ümraniye-Mustafa Kemal Mahallesi. These were overrun by informal settlements as the city expanded rapidly, with new dump sites being formed at Habibler, Ümraniye-Hekimbaşi, Yakacik, Aydinli, and other places. Wind blowing over these garbage areas formed dust clouds, which together with toxic gases from the garbage caused local air pollution. Escaping methane caused fires and posed explosion threats. Water from the dumps affected local streams and aquifers. The dumps harboured vermin. Occasionally there were landslides on the garbage 'mountains'. On 28 April 1993, some 350,000 tonnes of garbage at the Ümraniye-Hekimbaşi dump slid 500 m down to the Pinarbaşi settlement burying homes and killing 32 people.

These hazardous conditions ended in January 1995 when the Istanbul Metropolitan Municipality opened two modern controlled landfill sites, at Eyüp-Odayeri, on the European side of the Bosporus, and at Şile-Kömürcüoda on the Asian side. The Odayeri dump site has a daily capacity of 6,100 tonnes receiving garbage coming from the Baruthane, Yenibosna, and Halkali transfer stations. The Asian Kömürcüoda dump site receives garbage from the Hekimbaşi and Aydinli transfer stations with a daily capacity of 2,650 tonnes. Both sites are projected to receive and store garbage for 25 years. A special project to manage medical waste was initiated in 1995. A mechanical-biological waste treatment sorting and composting facility started operation in 1999. The plant has a daily treatment capacity of 1,000 tonnes, which equates to about one sixth of all the municipal solid waste generated on the European side.

AHMEDABAD, INDIA: GAINING ADDED VALUE
FROM WASTE BY USING RECYCLED MATERIALS

In Ahmedabad, Gujarat, in 2006, nearly two-thirds of the solid waste generated at the domestic scale was organic waste and 30 per cent of the inorganic waste was recyclable within the local systems of household separation and rag-picking further down the waste stream. Entrepreneurs in every squatter settlement in the city bought materials collected by rag-pickers. However, rag-pickers were able to improve their income by making new products from waste. Former rag-pickers earned money by manufacturing carrier bags and wedding invitation envelopes from discarded paper and creating useful articles from remnants of cloth. Products made from recycled waste ranged from new roofing materials offering good insulation properties, to ropes twisted from fine gauged plastic bags and new forms of windows using recycled glass and clays. These were being immediately used to improve the slums.

MANILA: GARBAGE OVERLOAD

Early in 1991 as a result of mounting public pressure to improve waste disposal and close the notorious Smokey Mountain, the World Bank-financed 73 ha regional sanitary landfill facility was opened in San Mateo, Rizal. This was followed in 1992 with the opening of the 65 ha Carmona regional sanitary landfill in Cavite, which coincided with the closure of Smokey Mountain. Both facilities were designed and constructed to international standards and represented a major accomplishment for the government. Several large dump sites also operated in the early 1990s, including the Payatas and Catmon dump sites.

In early 1998, heightened public opposition forced the suspension of operations at Carmona, placing more pressure on San Mateo and major dump sites to take additional waste. The impending crisis led to the opening of the Lingunan dump site in Valenzuela, and the stockpiling of waste at Pier 18 in Manila. The Clean Air Act, passed in 1998, effectively stalled plans to build incinerators, further limiting waste disposal options. The forced suspension of operations of the San Mateo sanitary landfill in late 1999 was due to immense public opposition. Within weeks, it brought about a near-catastrophic collapse of the municipal waste system and severe public health risks. Metro Manila was out of options for disposal, and waste went largely uncollected. Uncontrolled dumping at the Payatas dump site produced a catastrophic landslide of waste in July 2000. The tragedy demonstrated the human costs of the crisis. Subsequently, Payatas was temporarily closed, only to reopen later. After 2001, additional controlled dump sites, including the Rodriguez disposal facility in Montalban and the Tanza facility in Navotas, were developed but the crisis persisted, Manila only having two years further landfill capacity in 2003.[101] An attempt to close the Rodriguez facility in 2007 failed, and many other dumps are having their life extended as Manila's waste disposal lurches from one potential crisis to another.

PHNOM PENH: A CLASSIC UNCONTROLLED URBAN WASTE DUMP

In the Cambodian capital waste is collected by a private company and taken to the Stung Mean Chey dumpsite. Material is simply dumped and up to 500 scavengers follow the trucks as they tip their loads seeking anything that can be reclaimed and sold. No formal recycling or re-use of dumped items exists, a bulldozer simply levels the waste.[102] However, a whole informal recycling scavenger community makes a living from the dump, at considerable risk of injury and ill-health. In 2003 about 86 tonnes day^{-1} of material from the dump was recycled, about 9.3 per cent of the total waste generated in the city.[103] Conditions in Cambodia, a legacy of conflicts involving the Khmer Rouge in the last quarter of the twentieth century, mean that there was in 2007 still much child labour in Phnom Penh, including at Stung Mean Chey, where middlemen's premises for buying scavenged waste lined the road to the dump.

After some delays, a new sanitary landfill, the Dorng Kor landfill site, opened in 2009. Initially designed to be the first sanitary landfill in Cambodia, financial and technical staffing difficulties have meant that Dorng Kor landfill is now being operated in a partially sanitary manner as daily soil cover is irregularly performed. Leachate storage ponds were constructed but there is no leachate treatment facility; leachate is pumped from the waste disposal areas into the ponds, and left to evaporate. Waste pickers from Stung Mean Chey moved to the Dorng Kor site under the management of the landfill officer; they all have to register, and must pick up recyclable materials from assigned places.[104]

NAIROBI: WASTE SCAVENGING AND INFORMAL SETTLEMENTS

Municipal waste collection in most cities in developing countries consumes a considerable part of the municipal budget, but is incomplete, inefficient and ineffective in encouraging recycling. In Nairobi, Kenya, much waste goes to large dumps, but in the informal settlements, such as Kibera, large amounts of waste are dumped illegally. Adjacent to Kibera, the Nairobi Dam, commissioned in 1953 as a reservoir of potable water supply, has been heavily contaminated by waste washed downstream during storms by runoff from Kibera. The resulting environmental degradation poses health risks for nearby residents, particularly those from the slums who use contaminated water further downstream to irrigate crops.[105] In Nairobi, many different groups collect recyclable materials such as paper, metal scraps and plastics, for resale (Figure 6.10). Other groups compost organic solid wastes (food wastes), which are sold to urban farmers or landscapers.

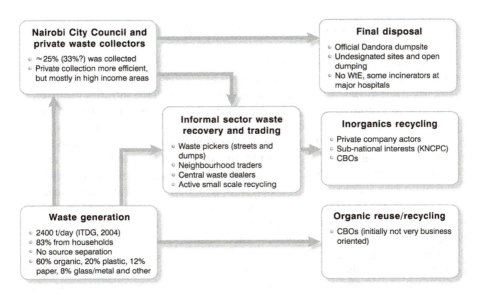

Figure 6.10: The urban waste collection, recycling and disposal system in Nairobi, Kenya

THE PLASTICS PROBLEM IN NIGERIAN WASTE FLOWS

Most municipal solid waste in the Lagos metropolitan area of Nigeria is regularly deposited at open dumpsites such as the Olusosun disposal site in the Kosofe Local Government Area. Originally on the outskirts of the metropolis, the site is now surrounded by residential, commercial and industrial neighbourhoods. The indiscriminately dumped waste includes medical wastes, toxic industrial solid wastes and domestic wastes. The domestic waste may include human and animal faeces that are sources of pathogenic organisms that can affect the waste workers, including scavengers who depend on recyclable materials for their livelihoods. The indiscriminate dumping of inorganic waste materials at the dumpsite leads to continuous pollution by heavy metals. The problem could readily be reduced by sorting solid waste and recycling the inorganic components.[106] Fire periodically breaks out at the dump, generating smoke and contributing to air pollution. Practices at the Olusosun dumpsite do not accord with the best principles of public health and environmental protection. Scavenging plays a vital role in resource recovery/re-use but in the process endangers lives. Scavengers could be incorporated in the formal sector programme for reduced health hazards on workers.[107]

By 2009 a project to extract landfill gas from the Olusosun landfill and to burn it off in a flare was implemented. However, the biogas could be used for electricity generation purposes and thus export power to the local grid. Opportunities are often missed due lack of local government freedom, or willingness, to act.

CONCLUSIONS ON URBAN WASTE

In many wealthy cities the last 30 years have seen a transition from using carrot and stick methods to greater sustainability in the recycling and re-use of used materials, sometimes called 'experienced resources'. The suburbs have up to four different coloured bins or boxes to put out in the street for collection on given days. A visit to the local 'recycling centre' where the dump used to be reveals an array of labelled containers for everything from old television sets to scrap wood and metal. Elsewhere in town, construction and demolition waste is re-used on site or stockpiled at a convenient location to use later. Industrial scrap materials may be used by a neighbouring manufacturer or recycled. Old products get re-manufactured to reduce demands for raw materials. Special wastes and e-wastes are handled carefully to retrieve valuable metals and other components. There is tight control of medical wastes and toxic substances.

Elsewhere, particularly in many Asian, African and Latin American cities, recycling takes a different form, with far less re-usable inorganic material getting into the urban waste stream, because it is collected separately and sold to middlemen. Plastics and organic wastes form the bulk of the problems, and composting is not well developed. In places like Manila and Phnom Penh waste management has many elements found in mediaeval Paris or London. Health risks remain high, and governments struggle to find enough resources to regulate scavenging and children's health and safety.

Melosi has earned the affectionate nickname of the 'garbage historian' contending that the historical roots, complexity, and persistence of solid waste as a problem for cities is often forgotten.[108] Multiple solutions, especially waste reduction and re-use, are beginning to have effect. Landfills, incineration, and recycling are now accompanied by biodigestion of garden waste and food scraps, biogas energy recovery, and composting in dealing with municipal waste. There is no easy, simple solution, and shortage of landfill space has forced many authorities to seek alternatives. However, faced with public anxiety over incineration of any form and general 'not-in-my-back-yard' syndromes, authorities will have to continue to work towards a waste producer pays principle, such as landfill taxes or charges per volume or weight in dustbins (trash cans). Eventually, every piece of unwanted material will have to be seen as an 'experienced resource' looking for a new use. When the price is right, scrap metal becomes so valuable that thieves steal the manhole covers from roadside drains. Thus potentially all residual stuff has a value, even if only as a heating fuel or compost. Taking a global view, those who are wealthy enough throw things away, those who are poor try to find a resale opportunity for any scrap they can lay their hands on.

7

Urban Sounds and Smells

The Noisy, Aromatic City

Managing the modern city for a sustainable future relies considerably on making urban areas more compact, but this introduces the compact city dilemma. Compact cities limit the proliferation of environmental problems; they preserve rural areas and conserve nature, save on energy, and allow an efficient public transport system. But a compact city also produces environmental problems: more noise, external safety risks, odours, and ugliness.[1] Older cities, seeking to maintain their compact footprint, often face problems when they try to redevelop run-down sections of the inner city and turn them into residential areas. National environmental norms in particular, by restricting the locations available for spatial development, seem to contravene the compact city concept.[2]

Although highly noticeable in compact, densely built-up areas, noise and odours are often neglected in accounts of the urban environment, possibly because they are not phenomena that are usually considered in discussions of ecosystems or urban landscapes. However, to people living in cities and towns, they are pervasive aspects of the environment, either a constant background to daily life, or episodic disturbances of their comfort. Throughout urban history, both noises and odours have caused people to complain. Sophocles wrote that Thebes in the fifth century BC was full of varied noises, smells and fragances, from groans to hymns and the stench of wastes to incense[3] and in ancient Rome, the poet, Horace, grumbled about the noise caused by heavy wagons in the streets[4] and Nero passed a law prohibiting the movement of horse-drawn carts during the night because of the noise created by the horses' hooves on the cobbled streets.[5] Nineteen centuries later, Marcel Proust lined his study with cork panels to keep out street noise,[6] while in London, Thomas Carlyle constructed a soundproof room in his Cheyne Walk house in 1853 in order to have the peace and quiet he needed to write his work on Frederick the Great.[7] In sixteenth-century London, the smell of the Stocks Market at the eastern end of Cheapside was so powerful that the congregation in the adjoining church of St Stephen Wallbrook was overcome by the stench of rotting vegetables.[8] In the nineteenth century, the stench from sewage in 'foul burns' (open streams) around Edinburgh's Royal Residence, Holyrood House, grew so vile that Queen Victoria refused to stay there.[9] At the same time, a general medical practitioner in Whitechapel, London, reported that people lived in such deprivation that they had inadequate water to wash their clothes which stank so much that he left the door open when they entered his surgery.[10]

Smells, such as those from a brewery or bakery, can characterize particular parts of a city. In many cases they are also associated with particular noises, such as the smell of aircraft fuel and the takeoff and landing noises around airports. While many find bakery smells an attractive part of urban diversity, other odours, such as the stench of inadequate drains or noxious factory emissions, are a persistent blight on people's lives. This chapter addresses these issues, explaining the steps taken to counteract them through modern urban history.

NOISE

URBAN NOISE, ITS NATURE AND MEASUREMENT

Noise can be defined as an unwanted or undesired sound. Exposure to high noise levels can lead to direct hearing loss and/or hearing impairment. Noise may also reduce life quality, and affect health and physiological well-being.[11] City dwellers have had to cope with unwanted sound, or noise, since the earliest times. In the late nineteenth century, Robert Koch, the great German physician, predicted that 'the day will come when mankind will have to fight noise just as vehemently as cholera and pestilence'.[12] The amount of noise has dramatically expanded since the early stages of the industrial revolution. Today the constant din of urban life affects people's work, causes aural and mental disorders and produces conflicts between neighbours and among restaurant visitors about the levels of noise that city dwellers should be forced to tolerate. 'Sound is no longer produced only by humans and nature, for machines roar everywhere and technologies not only measure sound in a myriad of ways but also produce and emulate sounds, such as video games and movies.'[13]

Noise has two major dimensions: pitch (frequency) and amplitude (intensity). Pitch is measured by the number of sound waves per second passing a given point and is expressed as Hertz (Hz). Amplitude reflects the height or depth of sound waves above or below a median line and is measured in terms of decibels (dB(A)). The logarithmic decibel scale (Table 7.1) ranges from the smallest sound detectable by normal young ears (0 dB(A)) to the threshold of sound pain such as that standing close to a noisy pneumatic drill (above 130 dB(A)).[14]

Table 7.1: Decibel levels
(based on: http://www.gcaudio.com/resources/howtos/loudness.html)

Environmental Noise	
Weakest sound heard	0dB
Whisper Quiet Library at 2 m	30dB
Normal conversation at 1 m	60–65dB
Telephone dial tone	80dB
City Traffic (inside car)	85dB
Train whistle at 160 m, Truck Traffic	90dB
Jackhammer at 16 m	95dB
Subway train at 65 m	95dB
Level at which sustained exposure may result in hearing loss	*90–95dB*
Hand Drill	98dB
Power mower at 1 m	107dB
Snowmobile, Motorcycle	100dB
Power saw at 1 m	110dB
Sandblasting, Loud Rock Concert	115dB
Pain begins	*125dB*
Pneumatic riveter at 1.3 m	125dB
Even short-term exposure can cause permanent damage – Loudest recommended exposure WITH hearing protection	*140dB*
Jet engine at 30 m	140dB
12 Gauge Shotgun Blast	165dB
Death of hearing tissue	180dB
Loudest sound possible	194dB

A single dB(A) measurement says very little about ambient noise. To overcome this ISO 1996/1 recommends measuring percentile levels, $L_{AN,T}$, i.e. that dB(A) level which is exceeded for *N per cent* of a stated time period *T*. Percentile levels reveal maximum and minimum noise levels.[15]

Environmental noise 'pollution' relates to ambient sound levels beyond the comfort levels as caused by traffic, construction, industrial, as well as some recreational activities. It can aggravate serious direct as well as indirect health effects, for example damage to hearing or sleep and later mental disorder, as well as increasing blood pressure. Noise-related increases in blood pressure are consistently seen in children. With regard to ischaemic heart disease there is some evidence in the literature of an increased risk in subjects who live in noisy areas with outdoor noise levels exceeding 65–70 dBA.[16] Noise effects can trigger premature illness and, in extreme cases, death. Night-time effects can differ significantly from daytime impacts. Noise above 45 dBA produces an exponential increase in night-time awakenings (Figure 7.1). Fortunately most cities exhibit a marked lowering of noise levels after midnight with noise rising rapidly after 6 am (Figure 7.2). The 10 percentile level of noise reaches around 75 dBA by about 7 am and remains high until around 4.30 pm in most North American and European cities (Figure 7.3).

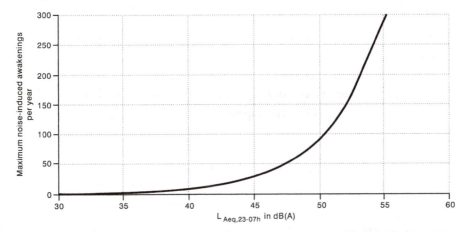

Figure 7.1: Night-time awakenings as a function of noise level
(after Passchier-Vermeer and Passchier, 2000)

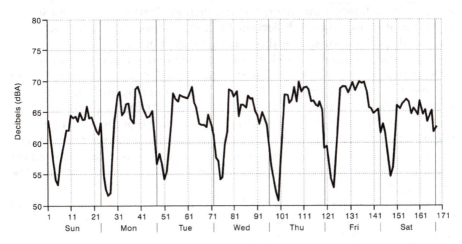

Figure 7.2: Diurnal variations in noise levels, showing the decrease after midnight and lower peak levels over the weekend in Akron, Ohio, USA
(after Harnapp and Noble, 1987)

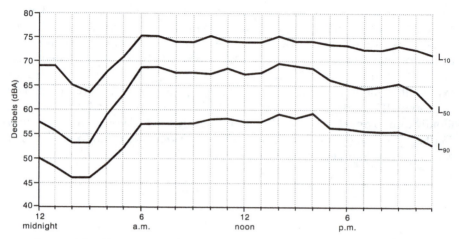

Figure 7.3: Relative frequency of the 10 percentile (L_{10}), mean (L_{50}) and 90 percentile (L_{90}) decibel levels during an average day in a North American city (after Harnapp and Noble, 1987)

MANAGING URBAN NOISE

Noise abatement in the UK

Early nineteenth-century cities were noisy places with a host of street activities. Many complained of the constant disturbance caused by horses and horse drawn vehicles and the noise of competing calls of people selling goods. Such was the din in London that many writers, such as Charles Dickens, constantly alluded to it in their novels.[17] Section 54 of the Metropolitan Police Act 1839 contained specific provision against such sources of noise.[18]

While the middle-class residents of inner London's smartest suburbs such as Kensington and Chelsea welcomed the 1839 Police Act powers, others vehemently criticized them. In 1841, Charles Knight openly supported the street musicians who had been accused of extortion by residents who regularly had paid them to go and play elsewhere. Knight argued that the street musicians ought to be left alone. Two decades later, aristocratic Members of Parliament argued paternalistically on behalf of the working classes that removing all the organ grinders from the streets would deprive the poor of one of their few forms of entertainment.[19]

Generally, the 1839 Police Act failed to stem the increase of street noise in London. Some made drastic adaptations to noise. In part, the campaign against street musicians became seen as a component of the struggle of an emerging professional and intellectual middle class to argue that their intellectual work required a low noise environment. The father of the modern computer, Charles Babbage was a consistent campaigner against street noise. He was frequently followed by critical crowds as he searched for policemen to take organ-grinders into custody.[20] During the Victorian age, street noise became an increasingly severe source of disturbance.[21] Eventually, the MP for Derby, Michael T. Bass, succeeded in 1864 with an 'Act for the Better Regulation of Street Music in the Metropolis' that changed the powers of the police and strengthened the ability of householders to exert their influence on the quality of their immediate urban environment:

> Any householder within the Metropolitan Police District, personally or by his servant, or by any police constable, may require any street musician or street singer to depart from the neighbourhood of the house on account of illness or on account of the interruption of the ordinary occupations or pursuits of any inmate of such house, or for other reasonable or sufficient cause ...[22]

While this was an example of the power of the property owning classes over others, it also had support from health professionals, including Florence Nightingale who argued about the impact of noise on hearing.[23] The concentration on the disturbance of the household was also in part an expression of the growing influence of wealthier women who began to exercise their lobbying power, both within their own homes and in society at large.

Complaints against noise in the UK did not diminish over time, but the causes of noise multiplied and changed. In 1959, John Connell, realizing that there was no authority to turn to with noise complaints, founded the Noise Abatement Society. He described noise as 'the forgotten pollutant' and argued that excessive noise was destructive and harmful to society. Campaigning constantly, he lobbied all the 1959 UK General Election candidates. His energetic promotion of noise abatement was accompanied by practical ideas to solve persistent irritating noise problems. His work led to the introduction of rubber dustbin lids and plastic milk crates. Manufacturers were persuaded that making their products less noisy would be a good selling point. His tactics included waking the then Aviation Minister in the middle of the night to make a point about what is was like to be woken up by loud aircraft noise. He was also enthusiastic about the possible relocation of Heathrow Airport to Foulness Island in the Thames estuary, a move still under discussion over 50 years later.

In 1960 the Noise Abatement Act was added to the UK statute books, with Section 1 of the Act making noise a statutory nuisance for the first time:

> Subject to the provisions of this section, noise or vibration which is a nuisance shall be a statutory nuisance for the purposes of Part III of the Public Health Act 1936.[24]

Noise abatement in Germany

In Germany a whole series of cases about noise occupied the courts in the last quarter of the nineteenth century. They raised the question of how to measure noise levels, an issue that was not resolved until well into the twentieth century. The notion of noise infringing people's rights was demonstrated by an 1884 decision in the Prussian High Court that a printing works' noise could damage the rights of a neighbour. However, no regulatory framework for controlling noise was established at that time.[25]

Germany gradually developed programmes for the detection and regulation of noise pollution. In 1938 a community noise map was produced for Charlottenburg, Berlin, Germany, the first attempt to show the spatial distribution of noise. Since 1951, the city of Dusseldorf has regularly monitored and mapped the occurrence of noise within its boundaries. Dortmund produced one of the most detailed noise maps, based upon readings at 1,449 individual sites.[26] During the early 1970s, the city of Celle introduced integrated traffic planning, producing the first noise map of the city in the mid-1980s.[27] At the same time, the German Federal Government and the Land of Lower Saxony funded noise abatement plans for the cities of Lingen (Ems), Nienberg (Weser) and Celle. Brandenberg was added to the list in 1992. In 1998 regional noise abatement strategies were introduced.[28]

Reaction to noise in France

The first studies of reactions to noise in France in the 1970s showed that approximately 43 per cent of the population was then annoyed by noise. Research in 1986 by Jacques Lambert showed that low income families were four times more exposed to noise than high-income families.[29] A later survey in 1996 found that 40 per cent of the overall French population was annoyed by noise, 43 per cent of the urban population and 56 per cent of those living in central Paris. Noise insulation was the most important factor in house purchase decisions for 47 per cent of people questioned.

In 1979, France had experimental policies for noise abatement in four towns. This successful programme was expanded to 21 more towns in 1982.[30] Although the French town planning code permits noise to be one of the nuisances that are grounds for refusal of a planning application, refusal of a building licence on the basis of noise annoyance alone is extremely rare.[31]

Regulation of noise in the USA

Progress was made in many other countries at this time (Table 7.2). In the US, specific noise control legislation dates back to at least 1852 with the passage of the Peace and Tranquility Ordinance in Boston.[32] In the US, many cities have passed ordinances containing noise provisions, and standards for the measurement of noise intensity and frequency. Individual states have passed laws establishing means for measuring damage to hearing and schedules of compensation that are related to the percentage of hearing damage.[33] A strong argument for replacing the horse with the horseless (electric) carriage in American and British cities in the late 1890s was the alleviation of noise.[34] *Scientific American* warmly welcomed trams and automobiles as harbingers of a new age of urban tranquillity:

> The noise and clatter which makes conversation almost impossible on many streets of New York at the present time will be done away with, for horseless vehicles of all kinds are always noiseless or nearly so.[35]

The American Society for the Suppression of Unnecessary Noise,[36] the most influential American anti-noise organization, was founded in New York in 1906 by Julia Barnett Rice, a physician who dubbed noise 'our most abused sense'.[37] This assault on noise was seen by Smilor[38] as an integral component of the late nineteenth-century environmental crisis afflicting burgeoning cities, which involved overcrowding, air and water pollution, garbage accumulation, and traffic congestion. The assault on noise occupied a prominent place in the spectrum of reform crusades during the Progressive era alongside the better known anti-smoke leagues and sanitation improvement societies.[39] Remedial measures in New York City included regulation of tugboat whistles, establishment of quiet zones around schools and hospitals, and the replacement of whistle-blowing traffic police by traffic lights. These noise abatement campaigns were modelled on previous smoke abatement crusades, but probably the overall consideration was greater efficiency, excessive noise being a waste of energy.

The issue of ambient noise pollution, the subject of campaigns by the middle classes, received much less attention than that of workplace noise. One of the earliest efforts was that of E.E. Free in 1924 in New York City who revealed scientifically for the first time the extent of urban noise. His pioneering study was instrumental in encouraging the New York City Health Department to establish, in 1929, a Noise Abatement Commission to make detailed noise surveys in various parts of the metropolis and to recommend steps to be taken to reduce noise levels. Concern about community noise did not spread to other cities for a generation, Chicago producing an extensive assessment of noise in 1947–9 under the auspices of the Greater Chicago Noise Reduction Council. What effects these early surveys had on noise reduction is unclear, but they were probably negligible. Nonetheless, the concern was obvious, data gathering ensued, and the way was pointed for later studies and more precise analysis.[40]

In the US, sustained federal interest in noise pollution can be said to date from the Noise Control Act of 1972, but point source noise generation had been an important consideration for governments and individuals for some time previous to that. Both state and federal governments, as well as many labour unions, have, for a long time, recognized the necessity to regulate the exposure of workers to machine noise in factories and other workplaces.[41]

Table 7.2: Noise legislation in Australia, Brazil, China, England, India and the USA (compiled from various government and NGO websites)

Country	Legislation
Australia	Aircraft noise is regulated under the Commonwealth *Air Navigation Act 1920*. Generally civil aircraft operating in Australia must comply with the Airports Act and meet noise standards specified in the *Air Navigation (Aircraft Noise) Regulations 1984 (Cth)*. In the Australian Capital Territory (ACT), noise is regulated by the *Environment Protection Act 1997 (ACT)* and its accompanying *Environment Protection Regulation 2005*. In New South Wales (NSW) under the *Protection of the Environment Operations Act 1997* (POEO Act), local councils can serve various notices on people occupying homes and businesses, requiring them to control offensive noise and advising them what noise levels are acceptable. In South Australia (SA) noise is regulated by the following acts and standards: *Development Act 1993* *Environment Protection Act 1993* *Environment Protection (Noise) Policy 2007* Australian Standard AS 1055–1997 Acoustics – Description and measurement of environmental noise Australian Standard AS 1259–1990 Acoustics – Sound level meters
Brazil	National Environmental Policy (as regulated by Federal Decree No.9/9274/90) 1990 Federal Conama Regulation 001/90 defines nationwide noise emissions criteria
China	Law of the People's Republic of China on Prevention and Control of Pollution From Environmental Noise 1996
England	*Control of Pollution Act 1974* *The Environmental Protection Act 1990* *Noise and Statutory Nuisance Act 1993* *Noise Act 1996* Directive 2002/49/EC relating to the assessment and management of environmental noise: The Environmental Noise Directive (END) *Cleaner Neighbourhoods and Environment Act 2005* The Environmental Noise (England) Regulations 2006 amended in 2008 by The Environmental Noise (England) (Amendment) Regulations 2008 amended in 2009 by The Environmental Noise (England) (Amendment) Regulations 2009 amended in 2010 by The Environmental Noise (England) (Amendment) Regulations 2010
India	The Noise Pollution (Regulation and Control) Rules, 2000
USA	*National Environmental Policy Act* (NEPA) 1969 *Noise Pollution and Abatement Act*, more commonly called the Noise Control Act (NCA), 1972 About half of the US states and hundreds of cities passed substantive noise control laws in the 1970s States continue to make new regulations, e.g. the New York Noise Code (Local Law 113 of 2005) Netherlands (1979), France (1985), Spain (1993), and Denmark (1994) set up similar legislation to that in the USA

The 1972 Noise Control Act (NCA) was the major piece of legislation that established the federal role in noise regulation. It was enacted in a period of newly awakened public concern about the environment when Congress passed a whole series of environmental laws. Some branches of industry were pleased to have federal regulation because they were having difficulty coping with a huge diversity of local regulations enacted by different cities. However, in general, industries have come to prefer federal to local regulations because of their greater ability to influence the former.[42] The industries would then realize scale economies in both production and lobbying costs by being regulated only by the federal government. Thus a combination of pressure from industry with the general pro-environment attitudes of the times led to almost universal support for the NCA and the federal pre-emption clause it contained.[43]

The NCA did not satisfy all environmentalists. Industry lobbied successfully against ambient noise standards, the House of Representatives report saying that ambient standards would be equivalent to the establishment of land use and zoning requirements by the federal government. However, a stronger reason for rejecting ambient standards is that noise, unlike ambient air pollutants, is an extremely localized externality. The bill that finally passed Congress did not meet the expectations of environmentalists: it was 'basically an industry bill under the veneer of an environmental programme'.[44]

The Environmental Protection Agency (EPA) coordinated all federal noise control activities through its Office of Noise Abatement and Control (ONAC). However, in 1981, the administration at that time concluded that noise issues were best handled at the state or local government level. As a result, the EPA phased out the office's funding in 1982 as part of a shift in federal noise control policy to transfer the primary responsibility of regulating noise to state and local governments. Nevertheless, the Noise Control Act of 1972 and the Quiet Communities Act of 1978 were not rescinded by Congress and remain in effect today, although essentially unfunded. This situation certainly appears to have satisfied industries, which have been able to retain federal 'protection' from state and local noise regulations. The closure of the ONAC raised little concern among environmental groups who did not really consider noise as important an issue as air, water or toxic waste pollution.[45]

By 1972 only 59 US municipalities had enacted some type of noise control statute. However, citizen concerns rose and in the next five years another 1008 communities enacted anti-noise legislation. Even so, only about 7 per cent of all cities by then had established regulations on land use, motor vehicles, and construction noise using qualitative or acoustical limits. Furthermore, the lack of enforcement means that noise legislation was often merely 'paper legislation'.

In a community survey in South Florida, garden and lawn equipment noise was identified as the most intrusive by respondents. Intrusive noises interfered with sleep, work and studying.[46] Local governments in south Florida have initiated legislation to reduce noise pollution in residential areas. The

City of Coral Gables enforces strict constraints on community noise levels and Miami Dade County ordinances limit noise levels as well. These ordinances both restrict times when heavy machinery is allowed to operate and constrain noise levels in homes that may annoy neighbours including pets, parties and television and audio decibel levels.[47]

In 2006 New York City overhauled its noise code. The new regulations try to balance the important reputation of New York as a vibrant, world class 'city that never sleeps' with the needs of those who live in, work in or visit the city. Enacted in December 2005, the code took effect in July 2007. It was the first comprehensive overhaul to the city's code in 30 years. The previous code was outdated and did not reflect the changing city landscape or advances in acoustic technology. The new law states that: 'the making, creation or maintenance of excessive and unreasonable and prohibited noises within the city affects and is a menace to public health, comfort, convenience, safety, welfare and the prosperity of the people of the city'. Accordingly, it establishes important rules, guidelines and standards for governing noise in the city.

STEPS TO REDUCE TRAFFIC AND AIRPORT NOISE

Traffic noise is a problem for large numbers of urban people. Motor vehicle noise seems to affect fewer people than aircraft noise, but more than noise from railways (Figure 7.4). Vehicle noise attenuation may be achieved by developing quieter vehicles, particularly in order to conform with EC Directive 70/157/CEE adopted in 1970 and amended in 1977; road traffic management through relocation of traffic away from noise-sensitive areas, speed limitations, cutting down traffic volume, restricting the presence of heavy trucks in cities; road design that includes screening, lower highway elevations; special road surfaces; and land use planning giving due consideration to insulation of dwellings from traffic noise and installation of noise barriers. Garbage trucks constitute another major source of city noise. Quieter vehicles and specified hours of collection are the chief means of minimizing annoyance.

Railway operation noise can be attenuated through development of quieter vehicles, minimization of rail/wheel interaction, resilient track support structures, and construction of tunnels and noise barriers. Even train depots and bridge crossings come under scrutiny. Careful construction policies were developed for new railways in London. During the construction of the Docklands Light Railway through areas of dense housing, acoustic absorbent screens were installed which succeeded in providing the required level of noise reduction. These schemes had to accommodate the requirements of the railway for maintenance (leading to the barriers having to be fully demountable), safe trackside walking routes and easy passenger evacuation from trains. During construction, liaison was developed with the local authority for the control of environmental pollution (primarily noise)

Moorhead

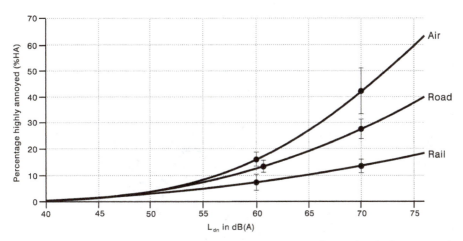

Figure 7.4: Percentage of persons annoyed by noise at different levels for air, road and rail transport (after Passchier-Vermeer and Passchier, 2000)

and hours of working and good relations were fostered with local residents through regular contact.[48]

London's underground railways are notoriously noisy, with average levels reaching 89 dB. One study of four journeys on the Victoria Line found an extreme level of 118 db, the equivalent of a jack hammer or a jet engine taking off in the distance.[49] Noise reduction was one of the objectives of a major renewal programme on the Underground after 2000.

Noise around airports

Airport noise remains a major public concern. Aircraft noise is normally assessed by a combination of factors: the number and timing of aircraft movements; their maximum sound levels; and event duration. Noisy events are readily distinguished from, and exceed by a considerable margin, other more continuous and low-level background noise such as that originating from road traffic. The magnitude and extent of aircraft noise nuisance is typically depicted via a noise-isopleth map, based upon a simulation model which incorporates extensive noise measurement data (Figure 7.5).

Until 1990, the Noise and Number Index (NNI), developed from 1961 studies at Heathrow Airport, London, remained the official index of aircraft noise nuisance in the UK. The NNI at any particular location takes account of the *number* of noisy events and their *peak* or maximum noise levels. Thus, data about aircraft movements and the noise characteristics of aircraft types can be used to estimate the NNI at particular locations. These estimates, in

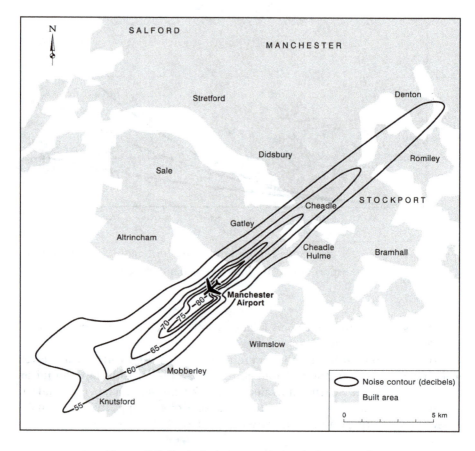

Figure 7.5: Typical airport noise isopleths around
Manchester International Airport, UK

conjunction with actual noise measurements taken each year, contribute to the production of an NNI isopleth map[50] (Figure 7.5).

A major drawback of the NNI scale is its failure to take account of the *duration* of noisy events. This omission is, perhaps, more significant in the current environment of generally quieter aircraft but more frequent aircraft movements, and where technical advances have made continuous noise measurement more feasible. In addition, the requirement to move towards greater uniformity in measures of aircraft noise nuisance at an international level has led to the replacement of NNI by Leq as the standard measure for the UK. Leq measures the total recorded aircraft noise energy in excess of background noise for the duration of an event, and includes all movements throughout 24 hours, although night-time aircraft movements are not weighted more heavily than those occurring during the day. Thus Leq includes relatively less noisy events but de-emphasizes the occasional noisy event in contrast to the NNI index.[51]

Noise around airports has long been a major issue in the urban environment. Much of the concern arises from possible effects on health and human well-being. Chronic exposure to aircraft noise affects school children's learning in two ways:[52] 1) a poorer reading performance, but no association with the other English performance outcomes, spelling, writing, and handwriting; 2) poorer performance on a nationally standardized test of mathematics after adjustment for school type. These results suggest that chronic exposure to aircraft noise is associated with school performance in reading and mathematics in a dose-response function, but that this association is influenced by socioeconomic factors. This association arises because poorer quality schools are more common in socially deprived areas, which are also more likely to be exposed to high levels of aircraft noise. Social deprivation, school quality, and noise exposure are all known to adversely influence school performance.

Airport noise is commonly thought to lower property values, but an economic analysis of the impact of noise from aircraft at Manchester Airport, UK (Figure 7.5), on house prices in Stockport showed that access to and closeness to the airport and its associated transport infrastructure generally outweighed any negative impact on prices, including the cost of higher noise levels.[53]

In the US the planned expansion and re-orientation of Chicago's O'Hare airport required the demolition of several hundred properties. It also changed the airport's flight paths, exposing a new group of households to noise.[54] The impacts led to vociferous opposition to the expansion from nearby residents, who attempted to block the plan in court, despite its approval by the Federal Aviation Administration (FAA). Similarly, in Orange County, California, concerns about noise exposure blocked the construction of a new international airport on a decommissioned military airbase, even with a shortage of airport capacity in the region.[55] At nearby John Wayne Airport, departing flights must practice a steep, high-power climb manoeuvre to gain altitude quickly before passing over the high income community of Newport Beach, and noise concerns in that community continue to limit daily flight volume at the airport.[56] Miami International Airport receives over 1,400 flights daily and has installed a noise monitoring system, a noise barrier, and has rescheduled flight paths to reduce flight noise in residential areas.[57]

Aircraft noise control may include establishment of preferential runways, aircraft noise monitoring, curfews, assignment of flight paths, charging landing fees, and land zoning to ensure that only noise compatible neighbours are located adjacent to the airport. Examining the economics of airport noise regulation, Brueckner and Girvin[58] question whether it is better to apply controls or noise limits by individual aircraft or for the airport as a whole. They conclude that: 1) noise regulation harms airline passengers by raising fares and potentially reducing service quality; 2) cumulative and per-aircraft noise regulation have quite different effects on airline decisions; 3) cumulative regulation appears to be superior from a social-welfare perspective; 4) under realistic sequential airline choice behaviour, the best a planner can do under cumulative regulation is to use an inefficiently tight noise limit that

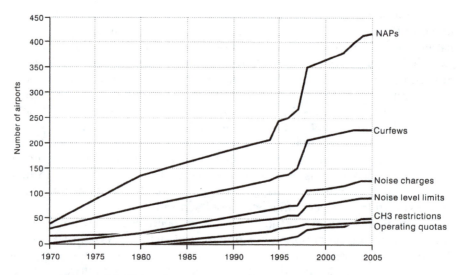

Figure 7.6: Noise abatement procedures at airports 1970–2005
(after Breuckner and Girvin, 2006)

yields lower-than-optimal flight frequency; 5) noise taxation is equivalent to cumulative noise regulation, generating exactly the same airline decisions. They suggest that airport-level regulation may actually be preferable to stringent per-aircraft limits. Regulations grew rapidly after 1995, with curfews on night flights and noise abatement procedures (NAPs) being the preferred controls (Figure 7.6).

CONSTRUCTION, INDUSTRIAL AND RECREATIONAL NOISE

Construction noises also annoy to a great degree, and they are subject in Europe to noise codes of EEC directive 79/113/EE7, which specifies the test procedures for construction machines. This directive was followed by a series of other directives requiring EEC approval for sound emission from construction equipment.[59]

An ever-growing source of urban noise arises from leisure and recreation activities, such as rock concerts, discotheques, 'boom cars' and automobile racing. At present, many of the rules controlling noise in public places are administered at the local city level. As one antidote to urban noises, acoustical insulation of buildings necessarily entails walls, windows, and floors. Among the economic incentives to reduce urban noise level are punitive fines, government support of research on noise attenuating measures, monetary rewards for using quieter equipment, and indemnification of parties affected by noise.[60]

Most noise complaints received by local authorities involve noise between neighbours. For example, in Northern Ireland in 2006, the vast majority of complaints made to district councils (85 per cent) were in relation to noise from domestic premises, such as barking dogs and loud music. Commercial premises and leisure facilities accounted for 6 per cent of all noise complaints, with the main source being pubs and clubs. Only 2 per cent of complaints related to noise from industrial activities.[61] This pattern of reaction is similar to those of Proust and Carlyle when they tried to insulate themselves from noise in their immediate neighbourhoods.

Avoiding the juxtaposition of homes, hospitals and schools to major sources of noise is a key element in urban land use planning. The UK 1994 Planning Policy Guidance (until abolished in 2012) on noise and planning[62] stated:

> It will be hard to reconcile some land uses, such as housing, hospitals or schools, with other activities which generate high levels of noise, but the planning system should ensure that, wherever practicable, noise-sensitive developments are separated from major sources of noise (such as road, rail and air transport and certain types of industrial development). It is equally important that new development involving noisy activities should, if possible, be sited away from noise-sensitive land uses.

The analysis of urban noise problems has been further helped by British Standard BS4142 'Method for rating industrial noise affecting mixed residential and industrial areas' which describes methods for determining, at the outside of a building: a) noise levels from factories, or industrial premises, or fixed installations, or sources of an industrial nature in commercial premises; and b) background noise level. This standard also describes a method for assessing whether the noise referred to is likely to give rise to complaints from people residing in the building.[63]

Noise at work is covered by health and safety regulations, such as those of the UK which provide that:

> Every employer shall reduce the risk of damage to the hearing of his employees from exposure to noise to the lowest level reasonably practicable.[64]

Measures to manage urban noise have improved. Much truck traffic and delivery noise has been reduced by a combination of movement restrictions and good practice. Noise from trains and trams has fallen as improvements have been made to rolling stock and quieter forms of locomotion have been introduced. Aircraft noise has also decreased with improved aero-engines, restrictions on times of take-off and landing, but the sheer expansion of numbers of aircraft in the skies may mean no lessening in the total noise they produce globally. Meanwhile mobile phones and related electronic devices create new forms of noise which can be increasingly annoying in urban areas. Maybe the quiet coaches on trains will one day comprise the whole train, just as non-smoking carriages eventually became the norm!

ODOURS

Lewis Mumford reminded his readers that the mediaeval cities of Europe were closely linked to the countryside, with, despite continuous built frontages to the main streets, large, if narrow gardens and courtyards to the rear of premises, in which trees, vegetables and flowers may be growing. The mediaeval city thus produced a wide array of conflicting odours, from smoky rooms, to the fragrance of flowers and herbs growing in the burghers' gardens. There was the smell of the barnyard in the street, due to the variety of animals housed within the city, a phenomenon which gradually declined through the centuries, save for the presence of horses right through to the early twentieth century.[65]

Although well accustomed to the smells of mediaeval towns, noblemen visiting London in 1306 encountered a new smell, that of acrid smoke from burning coal.[66] In response to their protests, Edward I banned its use (Table 7.3).

Table 7.3: Actions and regulations concerning odours since AD 1300 (compiled from various texts and websites)

Date	Country	Action
1306	UK	King Edward I bans coal burning in London to avoid smell of acrid smoke
1756	Sweden	Linnaeus develops scheme for the classification of odours
1780	UK	Tradesmen in Newgate Street, London afraid to go outdoors because of stench from Newgate Prison
1810	France	Decree to deal with odour nuisances
1827	France	Health report on Paris comments on the smells noticed when approaching the city
1845	USA	Pennsylvania public nuisance legal case recognizes impact of piggery smells on neighbours of a long-standing resident pig farmer
1858	UK	'Big stink' in London caused by sewage pollution of River Thames during hot summer leads to sewer construction
1883	France	Nantes major smell problem from chemical factories: mayor unable to get factories moved away from city
1917	France	December 19 Law on odour problems
1970	Japan	Offensive Odour Control Law, Law No. 91 passed (later amended by Law No. 71 in 1995)
1976	France	July 19 Law on odour problems
1980	Europe	Standards of olfactometry begin to be established in individual countries

Table 7.3 (continued)

1980	Germany	VDI 3881, Parts 1–4, Richtlinien, Olfactometry, Odour Threshold Determination, Fundamentals. Verein Deutsche Ingenieure Verlag, Dusseldorf, Germany (Revised 1989)
1981	France	AFNOR X-43-101, Method of the Measurement of the Odour of a Gaseous Effluent, Bureau de Normalization, Paris, France (Revised 1986)
1986	Germany	Technical Instruction on Air Quality Control specifies methods of assessment of odours
1987	Netherlands	NVN 2820, Provisional Standard: Air Quality. Sensory Odour Measurement using an Olfactometer. Netherlands Normalization Institute, The Netherlands
1988	Netherlands	First National Plan for the Environment or NMP 1 (VROM, 1988) sets specific targets on odours
1989	Netherlands	Inter-laboratory comparison of odour testing standard procedures
1990	Germany	Federal Emission Control Act
1991	New Zealand	Resource Management Act 1991 imposes a duty upon industry to avoid causing 'objectionable' or 'offensive' odours to such an extent that they are likely to have adverse environmental effects
1991	USA	Olfactometry standard ASTM Standard of Practice E679-91 introduced
1995	China	Revised Tianjin emission standard of odour pollutants enacted (DB12/-059-95)
1996	Australia	Victoria State Environment Protection (Scheduled Premises and Exemptions) Regulations state that 'odours offensive to the senses of human beings must not be discharged beyond the boundaries of the premises'
2002	Australia and New Zealand	New standard on odour measurement
2003	Europe	CEN odour testing standard adopted by European Union
2003	UK	British standard for olfactometry introduced (BSEN 13725:2003)
2004	USA	Revised Standard ASTM E679 regarding odour measurement issued
2005	Europe	European Communities (Waste Water Treatment) (Prevention of Odours and Noise) Regulations 2005 (S.I. No. 787 of 2005) contain general binding rules requiring sanitary authorities to ensure that wastewater treatment plants do not cause a nuisance through odours
2008	USA	Colorado Air Quality Control Commission Regulation No. 2 specifies odour control standards for different land uses including residential and commercial
2008	India	Central Pollution Control Board issues Guidelines on Odour Pollution and its Control
2012	Europe	New Odour Emission Capacity VDI guideline 3885/1 to be issued

Nevertheless, coal continued to be used. New bans with 'great fines and ransoms' were imposed. Second offenders would have their furnaces destroyed. The coal smells of the fourteenth century mingled with other odours ranging from those of baking meat to those of boiling glue, from beer brewing to vinegar manufacture, and from decaying vegetables to horse manure.[67] However, these bans were relaxed after 1500 because of the shortage of wood fuel. England came to have the worst quality urban air in the world, but the coal-burning became a major element of the industrial revolution.

By the sixteenth century, in many London churches, including St Paul's, there was the long-lasting smell from graveyards, while many people complained about the smell of other city dwellers in the crowded buildings and narrow alleys.[68] In the 1780s, tradesmen in Newgate Street, London were unable to take the air at their doors for fear of the stench from Newgate Prison[69] (Table 7.3).

Odours in cities have changed over time, yet vary greatly, both in urban areas and between towns and cities in different countries. For many communities a pervasive odour is something they are forced to live with because they cannot afford to move elsewhere. Their situation is likely to become extremely stressful. The way in which people cope with a stressful situation, such as exposure to unwanted odour, is known to influence their sense of well-being and health.[70] Odours from different industries that are of equal concentration can be felt differently by a given observer.[71] People who are accustomed to a particular odour may not be as annoyed by it as someone encountering it for the first time. All these factors make it difficult to decide how to set a quantifiable standard measure of the impact of an odour.

DEVELOPMENTS IN THE CLASSIFICATION AND MEASUREMENT OF ODOURS

Odour has six important dimensions: intensity, frequency, duration, offensiveness, location, and sensitivity of the people affected by it (Table 7.4).[72]

The classification of smells has always been contentious.[73] Linnaeus developed a scheme in 1756 (Table 7.5). Although many other classifications have been suggested subsequently, there is no generally agreed scheme of similarity among odours and of the number of classes among an estimated 400,000 odorous substances.[74]

Although complex schemes of assessment of odours have long existed, many recognize that the sense of smell is shaped by experience, that odours become meaningful through association with other events.[75] Thus, sometimes citizen panels have been used to measure the annoyance due to odours.[76] When such results for different parts of the Rotterdam urban area were compared to instrumental olfactometry measurements, a good correlation was found between the strength of the odour and the level of annoyance the community representatives felt.[77] Overall, there are four key objective measurable parameters for odours, and another four subjective measurable parameters (Table 7.6)

Table 7.4: The six dimensions of odour (after Welchman et al., 2005)

Dimension	Decription
Intensity	How strong a response in an individual/community will the odour invoke?
Frequency	How often over a long time period does the person experience the odour as detectable, recognizable or annoying?
Duration	How long does the odour last within a short time period (i.e. what is the intermittency)?
Offensiveness/ character	How pleasant or unpleasant is the odour to an observer or community (i.e. the hedonic tone of the odour)?
Location	Where was the person when the odour was observed?
The coping ability, or odour sensitivity, of the affected community	Depends on many factors

Table 7.5: Linnaeus' 1756 Odour Classification (after Engen, 1982)

	Class	Example
I	*Aromaticos*	Carnation
II	*Fragantes*	Lily
III	*Ambrosiacos*	Musk
IV	*Alliaceos*	Garlic
V	*Hircinos*	Goat
VI	*Tetros*	Certain Bugs
VII	*Nauseos*	Putrefying flesh

Since 1970 there has been a trend away from using the judgement of an environmental health officer to reliance on quantitative measurements of odour instead. The three broad methods of assessing odours now available are:

1. a physical-chemical method of searching for chemical elements likely to create smells in the atmosphere;
2. a method using an olfactometer and panel of experts in order to determine the presence of an odour and its intensity and the point of emission and in the atmosphere;
3. an inquiry method around a specified site to determine the nuisance experienced by local communities.[78]

Table 7.6: Measurable parameters of perceived odour
(after St. Croix Sensory Inc., 2005)

Parameters	Description
a) Objective	
Odour Concentration	Measured as dilution ratios and reported as detection threshold and recognition thresholds or as dilution-to-threshold (D/T) and sometimes assigned the pseudo-dimension of odour units per cubic metre
Odour Intensity	Reported as equivalent parts per million butanol, using a referencing scale of discrete butanol concentrations
Odour Persistence	Reported as the dose-response function, a relationship of odour concentration and odour intensity
Odour Character Descriptors	What the odour smells like using categorical scales and real exemplars (e.g. fruity – citrus – lemon: from a real lemon)
b) Subjective	
Hedonic Tone	Pleasantness vs. unpleasantness
Annoyance	Interference with comfortable enjoyment of life and property
Objectionable	Causes a person to avoid the odour or causes physiological effects
Strength	Word scales like 'faint to strong'.

Olfactometry has been used throughout the twentieth century in the medical research community. However, results varied because of differences in olfactometer design and operating performance, and in reliability of odour testing methods used. In the 1980s countries in Europe began developing standards of olfactometry. The standards thus created included: France AFNOR X-43-101 (drafted in 1981 and revised in 1986) Germany VDI 3881, Parts 1–4 (drafted in 1980 and revised in 1989) Netherlands NVN 2820 (drafted in 1987 and issued in 1995) (Table 7.3).

Various inter-laboratory studies as well as collaborative projects involving multiple odour testing laboratories in the 80s showed that laboratory results still differed significantly even with these standards in practice. The development of a draft odour testing standard in the Netherlands led to an Inter-Laboratory Comparison study organized in 1989. N-butanol and hydrogen sulphide were used as standard odorants for the study. Through 1990 to 1992 the results of this Dutch Inter-Laboratory study led to the development of strict assessor performance criteria. During the first year, the inter-laboratory repeatability was in the range of factors from 3 to 20. An analysis of the data from this first year showed the majority of variability was between assessors. Individual assessors were repeatable within a factor 3 to 5. The researchers found that the only way to meet agreed upon repeatability criteria was to control the instrument sensor, the human assessors, by selecting assessors who were all similar in sensitivity.[79]

Following developments in The Netherlands, moves have been made towards quantitative odour management based on measurement of emissions, dispersion modelling to define exposure and criteria derived from dose effect studies to define a level where no 'reasonable cause for annoyance' exists. These criteria may be specific to an industry, depending on the offensiveness of the odour. A reliable method for odour concentration measurement is an indispensable tool required for this approach, and such a method is now available in the European standard EN13725:2003 (Table 7.7).[80] This standard defines the European Reference Odour Mass (EROM), or a mass that is just detectable when evaporated into 1 m^3 of neutral gas, as equivalent to 123 µg n-butanol. This rigorously tested measure has made a marked improvement in the performance of olfactometry, which has been verified by blind inter-laboratory tests. These developments were driven by a regulatory demand.[81]

During the 1990s odour laboratories in Europe, North America, and Australia worked together to produce a common standard for odour testing and is now designated EN13725:2003.[82] The Odour Index (Table 7.8) is a standardized way to display and to report odour concentration values for policy and decision makers. It is a logarithmic scale similar in use to the Richter and Moment Magnitude earthquake scales and the Decibel sound scale. The odour index value is dimensionless and universally defined as:

Odour Index = 10 Log_{10} (odour concentration).

Table 7.7: Key international standards for determining odours
(compiled from websites)

ASTM E679-04	Determination of Odour and Taste Threshold by a Forced-Choice Ascending Concentration Series Method of Limits. (United States)
EN 13725:2003	European Standard on Determination of Odour Concentration by Dynamic Olfactometry. (European Community)
NVN2820	Provisional Standard: Air Quality. Sensory Odour Measurement using an Olfactometer. (Netherlands)
VDI 3881	Olfactometry: Odour Threshold Determination. (Germany)

Table 7.8: The Odour Index: Odour Index Examples
(after McGinley and McGinley, 2006)

Odour Index Values	Log Value	Odour Units or D/T	Example of Odour Source or Odour Situation
60.0	6.00	1,000,000	Rendering plant uncontrolled exhaust
50.0	5.00	100,000	Venting anaerobic digester gases
40.0	4.00	10,000	Sludge centrifuge vent
30.0	3.00	1,000	Primary clarifier weir cover exhaust
27.0	2.70	500	Dewatering building exhaust
24.8	2.48	300	Biofilter exhaust
20.0	2.00	100	Multistage scrubber exhaust
17.0	1.70	50	Carbon filter exhaust
14.8	1.48	30	Ambient odour adjacent to biosolids land application
11.8	1.18	15	Ambient odour adjacent to aeration basin
10.0	1.00	10	Design value sometimes used in odour modelling
8.5	0.85	7	Ambient odour level sometimes considered a nuisance
7.0	0.70	5	Design value sometimes used in odour modelling
6.0	0.60	4	Ambient odour level common in a city
3.0	0.30	2	Ambient odour level usually considered 'just noticeable'
0 0	0.00	1	Ambient air in a community with 'no odour' noticeable

DEALING WITH URBAN ODOURS IN THE
NINETEENTH AND TWENTIETH CENTURIES

Actions in Europe

All European cities had a mixture of smells that combined to develop a strong odour perceptible by travellers approaching the city. Much of this was due to the urban dependence on animals not only for local and inter-urban transport, but to supply a whole variety of products from fresh milk to leather. Many manufacturing processes depended on animal products, or the reprocessing of wastes from such manufactures within the city. To this must be added the nitrogen economy of the city that depended on the export of human and animal wastes to fertilize peri-urban vegetable gardens and the farms beyond to grow the crops and animal feed needed by the urban residents. Other wastes were released into local streams, such as the Fleet in London and the Bièvre in Paris, which in turn fed into major rivers such as the Thames and Seine.

how did they clean up the smell of the river thames?

The public health campaigner, Parent-Duchâtelet surveyed the Parisian sewers in 1824 and described their odours in terms of a series of specific smells such as 'insipid' (*l'odeur fade*) and putrid (*l'odeur putride*).[83] Thus in 1827, a report on health conditions in Paris commented that 'the sense of smell gives notice that you are approaching the first city in the world, before your eyes could see the tips of the monuments'.[84]

In the early nineteenth-century industrial cities of England, residents usually found it difficult to avoid the stench of industrial refuse and of open sewers. Poor children played among garbage and privy middens.[85]

In 1858, the polluted River Thames in London had become so odorous that it was known as the Great Stink (Table 7.3). That year the smell was so bad in the summer that the sittings at the House of Commons had to be abandoned. By the middle of the nineteenth century, the rise in sewage carried into the Thames via the Fleet River killed off all the fish, and consequently all the birds that lived off them. It was actually not disease, but rather the smell of the polluted Thames River, that caused the UK parliament to decide to allow the construction of the main London sewers, creating a bypass along the Thames to the sea. At that time, the curtains and wall hangings of the Houses of Parliament were treated with 'chloride of lime' to combat the odours.[86]

The many odour problems associated with the growth of European cities were addressed by a variety of regulations for many hundreds of years. In France, the decree of 14 October, 1810 enabled these nuisance problems to be dealt with. The decree was updated by the law of 19 December, 1917. The law of 19 July, 1976 produced further changes through the registration of sites operated or kept by all persons, physical or moral, public or private, that are likely to create a health hazard or inconvenience for the community, in order to protect the environment.[87]

The French 1810 law, like Edward I's decree against smoke in London, failed to stop some activities essential for urban manufacture and consumption. In July 1883, Nantes, in the River Loire in western France, experienced a strong foul smell, far more intense than the odours that people had complained about before. The smells came from a cluster of factories on the island of Prairie-aux-Ducs in the River Loire. These chemical factories processed a variety of animal products and wastes as well as manufacturing fertilizer from guano and seaweed, treating sewage and producing ammonium sulphate. The first factory had been set up in 1836 and by 1883 there were 28. Although there were complaints about the odours as early as the 1830s, the departmental government (the prefecture) did not give them official licences, as required by the 1810 law, but said it would close them if it became absolutely essential to do so.[88] However, even after the events of 1883, when the mayor of Nantes tried to persuade the prefecture to move the factories away from the island, the move did not occur, the mayors of neighbouring communes did not want them (Table 7.3). The Conseil d'Hygiène appointed to look into the nuisance caused by the smells repeatedly insisted that its task was to advise where factories *should not be located*, not where they *should*.[89]

Coping with odours in the USA

Between 1840 and 1860, the complaints about industrial odours that the US courts dealt with in terms of nuisance were essentially those of the 'traditional' industries associated with processing agricultural products, the breweries and distilleries, slaughterhouses, bone-boiling and fat-melting establishments, soap-and candle-making concerns and tanneries. The foul smells that led American citizens to regard them as material nuisances resulted from the decay of animal urine, manure, offal, blood, spent distillery grains, the foul smoke and vapours emitted into the air when bones, fats, and offal were boiled, melted, or otherwise processed into soap, neat's-foot oil, glue, and other products, and the odiferous chemicals used to tan animal hides into leather.[90] The outward migration of urban residents into peripheral areas occupied by nuisance industries stimulated many of the court cases. Sometimes businesses that had been operating for 30 years or more, long before the new residential areas were built, were forced, by the courts, to close. An 1845 a Pennsylvanian public nuisance case pitted a defendant who had been in business in a relatively remote location for over 30 years against newcomers to the area. The state accused him of allowing stenches and filth from the hundreds of pigs he kept to consume his distillery wastes to foul the air and the water of the Schuylkill River. Nevertheless, despite the defendant's protestations that his was a long-established business, the Pennsylvania Supreme Court declared that people had a right to live in and travel through neighbourhoods where their noses would not be assaulted by terrible smells that might carry disease, even death[91] (Table 7.3).

Mid-nineteenth-century American judges did not oppose modern industries powered by steam engines as strongly as they argued that the foul smells from animal processing factories were a public nuisance. Their decisions contributed to the development of the zoning of industry and residential developments, with the recognition that industrial clusters of noisy and smoky factories might be permitted in areas close to railway yards and canals. Perhaps because they were impressed by new technology, the courts initially tended to treat emissions from gasworks differently from traditional nuisance businesses. However a consensus soon developed, in Britain and in the US, that awful smells, smoke, and water pollution caused by the conversion of coal, pitch, and other substances into manufactured gas needed to be treated like any other stench or fume emitting process.[92] Particular concern arose over odours from slaughterhouses. Such worries persisted into the late twentieth century when legislation on odour limits was directed towards slaughterhouses.

In the United States and throughout Europe in the 1970s and 1980s there was a significant increase in public concern for odours from industrial, agricultural, and wastewater treatment facilities. By the 1990s, the proliferation of large scale animal confinement facilities (i.e. feedlots) throughout the United States, as well as the general trend of urban sprawl moving people closer to

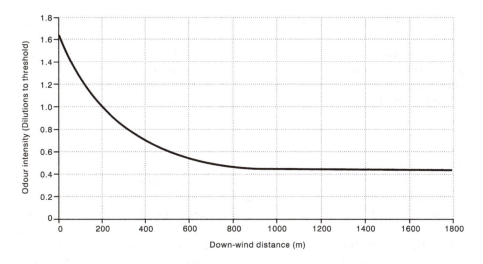

Figure 7.7: Odour decrease downwind of an Oklahoma, USA feedlot
(after Miner, 1997)

odorous industrial facilities, wastewater treatment facilities, and agricultural facilities, created a resurgence in funding for odour related research. Odours from feedlots have strong impacts up to a kilometre downwind of the facility (Figure 7.7). During this time, governments in many European countries implemented standards and regulations for odours. Many of the regulations required the measurement of odours through olfactometry, either to prove compliance or to measure and monitor odours.

A typical US local air quality and odour control programme, for example that of Tulare County, California, requires that new dairy facilities not lie within the windshed area of any incorporated or unincorporated community. The windshed area is defined as one mile upwind or one-half mile downwind from the urban boundary, or within 1,000 feet of a public park boundary, or within 2,640 feet of a group of 10 or more dwellings.[93]

Odours from sewage treatment plants

One particular target for odour regulation has long been sewage treatment works. The problem of smells from these treatment plants causes emotive protests from the general public, especially on hot days from those living downwind of the installations. Persistent odours, such as those arising from proximity to a sewage treatment affect property values, lowering them by 10 per cent or more in relation to those identical dwellings further away.[94]

The treatment works for the town of Hyères, France, suffered odour problems due to hydrogen sulphide (H_2S) for over 20 years.[95] Eventually, in 1986, the odour was reduced by hydraulic solutions that involved replacing a single large diameter delivery pipe by two smaller diameter pipes along which the water would flow more rapidly. The flow rate would be kept up by an intermediate pumping station between the town and the treatment plant. However, 20 years later both the sewage works and the sewer network feeding to it were being extended and upgraded to cope with the increased housing and a continuing problem of odours in the sewers.

Urban odours are not always caused by present-day activities. Legacies from older sewer systems may persist for more than 100 years. In Greater Manchester, the Ship Canal had a large turning basin at its inland terminus which acted as a retarding reach for the waters of the River Irwell. From the opening of the canal in 1894 until the redevelopment of the redundant docks as a residential, commercial and leisure area one hundred years later, the river deposited the solids it carried during storms, including those from combined sewer overflows on the floor of the basin. Over time a 2 m thick layer of organic sediment built up. On warm summer days, oxygen levels in the canal basin became extremely low and gases such as methane and hydrogen sulphide were produced and blocks of organic debris rose to the surface. The smell of hydrogen sulphide greatly detracted from the aesthetic value of the area. With prestigious public buildings, commercial and residential complexes in use (Figure 7.8), these immediate environmental and aesthetic problems could not be allowed to continue, even in the short-term. The regeneration project partners initiated a scheme to pump liquid oxygen at a rate of up to 15 tonnes per day into the worst polluted area of the canal to prevent the odours developing.[96] This brought life back to the canal, the increasing biodiversity enabling fish such as roach and perch to start spawning again, the rate of growth of fish populations, particularly of roach, being amongst the highest found anywhere in England at the time.

Problems in tropical cities

Whilst the odour emanating from plants in temperate countries is bad enough, in hot humid climates it can become unbearable. The Upper Manyane catchment area in Zimbabwe contains the capital city, Harare, and Chitungwiza, in which most of the capital's labour force lives. The lake in the catchment became eutrophic due to high nitrogen and phosphorous discharges in urban waste and sewage overflows, with loss of dissolved oxygen and release of odorous gases. The urban water supplies have become more difficult to treat, but the continuing release of sewage is aggravating the odour problems.[97]

Where resources are available in the tropics, these odour problems can be controlled. At the Ulu Pandan sewage treatment works in Singapore, for example, a series of scrubbers are used to neutralize odours before any effluent leaves the totally enclosed plant. The systems are designed to assure the required pH of the effluent and to reduce odorous emissions. They have to be able to handle the corrosive chemicals used in the neutralization process and to be able to

Figure 7.8: The former turning basin on the Manchester Ship Canal at Salford Docks where the risk of odours had to be reduced by feeding oxygen into the water during hot periods (photo Ian Douglas)

recirculate the neutralizing chemicals, such as sodium hypochlorite (NaOCl) and sodium hydroxide (NaOH).[98] Singapore has also experimented with a new biotrickling filter technology that showed, over three years of operation, an extremely cost-effective biological way of treating sewage odour.[99]

CONCLUSION

Legislation and regulation has generally proved effective in dealing with the worst odours. As legislation and control of atmospheric pollution regulations become more far-reaching, and when urban development encroaches closer to sewage works, increasing pressure will force effluent plant owners to implement means to reduce gaseous as well as liquid pollutants.[100] International standards can be fed back successfully to regional and local governments. Soon after 2000, a new Australian and New Zealand standard on odour measurement led to the review of odour regulation in most Australian states (Table 7.3). In New South Wales the regulator drafted an odour impact assessment policy for point source emissions, based on the new odour measurement standard and defining regulatory dispersion modelling procedures.[101]

In dealing with both noise and odours, the same combination of legislation and technical innovation has been used as with other issues, such as water quality and emissions to the atmosphere. Essentially there has been pressure from affected, but articulate, social groups and campaigners, as well as recognition by utilities and factory owners that they have a responsibility to find solutions. In many cases there has to be a continuing search for new solutions as new substances enter waste streams and as new manufacturing processes are introduced. Legislation is sometimes only triggered when parliamentarians themselves are affected, as happened with the 'Great Stink' from the River Thames in 1858.

Noise and odours in public spaces are often controlled by unidentified operators, particularly those deciding upon background music. More easily identified are those who contribute to the smells of spice markets, the neighbourhood fish and chip shop, or the harbourside fish market. Yet in crowded, compact cities, it will become increasingly difficult to avoid higher noise levels unless there are restrictions on the freedom to use motor vehicles, play music and keep pet animals. Avoiding the selfish creation of noise will have to become a mark of a good citizen. Individual responsibility will be increasingly important.

8

Cities and a Dynamic Earth

Urban Changes to the Land Surface and Responses to Geophysical Hazards

The role of human beings as agents of geologic and geomorphic change is nowhere more marked than it is in urban areas. People constantly alter the landforms in urban areas, digging foundations, filling quarries with waste, levelling playing fields, building barrier mounds along highways and constructing flood defences, harbours and wharves. The vast quantities of materials brought into cities gradually raise the level of the ground, to the extent that many old buildings now have their entrances a metre or more below the modern street level. If a development contractor drills a borehole to investigate foundation conditions, the layers of material found usually show a variety of 'made ground', rubble, fill material, and remains of human food and other consumption, overlying any natural soil or rock. Even urban gardens and parks often have such an anthropogenic stratigraphy beneath them. The processes and forms involved in urban activity as an earth surface process are the subject of urban geomorphology.

Urban geomorphology examines the geomorphic constraints on urban development and the suitability of different landforms for specific urban uses; the impacts of urban activities on earth surface processes, especially during construction; the landforms created by urbanization, including land reclamation and waste disposal; and the geomorphic consequences of the extractive industries in and around urban areas. The diversity of urban substrates (Table 8.1) is a consequence of their geomorphic history, the ways in which past environmental changes, including climatic and sea level changes have affected the form of land and the types of surface materials. These substrates are a record of the environmental history of towns and cities. Now termed the 'sediments of the anthropocene', they record some of the dynamics of urban growth.

Table 8.1: Urban substrates comprising artificial ground due to human activity
(after Rosenbaum et al., 2003)

Substrate	Definition
Made ground	Areas where the ground is known to have been artificially deposited on the former, natural ground surface: engineered fill such as road, rail, reservoir and screening embankments; flood defences; spoil (waste) heaps; coastal reclamation fill; offshore dumping grounds; constructional fill (landraise)
Worked ground	Areas where the ground is known to have been artificially cut away (excavated): quarries, pits, rail and road cuttings, cut away landscaping, dredged channels
Infilled ground	Areas where the ground has been cut away (excavated) and then had artificial ground (fill) deposited: partly or wholly back-filled workings such as pits, quarries, opencast sites; landfill sites (except sites where material is dumped or spread over the natural ground surface, as for landraise)
Landscaped ground	Areas where the original ground surface has been extensively remodelled, but where it is impractical or impossible to separately delineate areas of worked (excavated) ground and made ground
Disturbed ground	Areas of surface and near-surface mineral workings where ill-defined excavations, areas of man-induced subsidence caused by the workings and spoil are complexly associated with each other, for example, collapsed bell pits and shallow mine workings

These basic categories can be subdivided by topographical or landform and also in terms of the material of which they are composed. Often one phase of land surface remodelling is superimposed upon another.

Urban settlements are also vulnerable to a range of geophysical hazards, some entirely natural, but others are sometimes induced, or aggravated in their impact, by the nature of urban development. This chapter begins by considering earthquakes, volcanoes, landslides and subsidence. It then investigates how the relationships between cities and rivers have changed through time, considering flooding, storm surges, and river restoration.

EARTHQUAKES AND URBAN AREAS

Throughout human history, settlements have been shaken and damaged by earthquakes, some highly localized, but others being extensive and having associated tsunamis that damaged urban areas far away across seas and oceans. Earthquakes, like hurricanes and storms can have impacts over large areas. Their primary impacts are through ground shaking, surface fault rupture, and uplift or subsidence. Secondary effects arise through the triggering of liquefaction, landslides and water waves such as tsunamis and seiches (standing waves in lakes or seas). The extent of damages, injuries and fatalities depends not only on the magnitude of the earthquake but on where it occurs, the terrain in which it occurs and the socio-economic conditions of the affected communities. Coastal cities are particularly vulnerable to earthquake damage because they are exposed to all the primary effects and to tsunamis. Many ancient port cities, such as Helike, Appollonia and Seleucia Pieria (Table 8.2) are now below sea level.

Historically, large numbers of people, particularly as a proportion of the total population at the time, died from the consequences of earthquakes, but, caution has to be employed in using the estimated totals. Without modern communications and medical facilities, people with severe injuries died in the aftermath of earthquakes. For example, in 526, more than 200,000 people died at Antioch and in adjacent towns when a large earthquake struck.[1] The nearby port of Seleucia Pieria was lifted up 0.7–0.8 m and the subsequent silting up of the harbour left it unusable.[2]

Really large earthquakes can cause ocean and continent-wide damage. On the morning of 1 November 1755, Lisbon was shaken to its foundations by the great earthquake and the after-shocks, disastrous fires and tsunami that followed. The giant tsunami wave affected the coasts of north-west Europe, eastern North America, the Caribbean and Morocco.[3] The earthquake tremors caused damage to Oporto and other Portuguese towns, but also affected Cadiz, Spain, and Tetuan, Tangiers, Fez and Marrakesh in Morocco.[4] Buildings in Lisbon were completely destroyed, the fires raging for five days. Much of the literary, artistic and cultural heritage housed in the city was lost. This single geophysical event had a lasting impact on the Portuguese psyche and ramifications throughout Europe, Kaplan arguing that it struck at the Enlightenment concept of the benevolence of nature (much as the atomic bomb in a later age would end any idea of the benevolence of science).[5]

Urban authorities and national governments in seismically active areas have increasingly taken measures to improve both earthquake preparedness and earthquake resilience in their communities. Preparedness includes regular drills so that people know exactly what to do and where to go when an earthquake warning occurs as well as the provision of earthquake shelters. Resilience comes by making urban structures capable of withstanding ground shaking and other earthquake phenomena. The establishment, implementation and enforcement of appropriate building codes for all structures, from bridges and tunnels to houses and apartment buildings are a key part of this effort. During the twentieth century, building regulations were gradually tightened, Japan often taking the lead particularly after the 1923 Tokyo earthquake (Table 8.3). Building codes were established in high earthquake risk areas such as California, Japan and New Zealand before 1940. During the 1970s, earthquake hazard reduction began with legislation requiring the identification of seismic-hazard zones, preparation of appropriate hazard maps and restrictions on urban development near or over traces of faults. Increasingly sophisticated international linked arrays of seismic instruments now provide real-time information on earthquakes and tremors.

Table 8.2: Major earthquakes affecting urban areas[6]

Date	Country modern territory	Urban areas affected	Magnitude moment magnitude scale	Fatalities
373 BC	Greece	Helike	Not known	Not known
148 BC	Turkey	Antioch devastated by earthquake	Not known	Not known
AD 37	Turkey	Antioch hit by earthquake	Not known	Not known
AD 115	Turkey	Antioch devastated by earthquake	Not known	Not known
365 (21 July)	Greece Libya Egypt	Nearly all towns in Crete; many nearby; Appollonia, sank below sea level; Alexandria, Egypt wrecked	8.5	Not known (but 50,000 in Alexandria)
526 (20 May)	Turkey	Antioch	Not known	250,000
856 (22 Dec)	Iran	Damghan	Not known	200,000
893 (23 Mar)	Iran	Ardabil	Not known	150,000
1138 (9 Aug)	Syria	Aleppo	Not known	230,000
1531 (26 Jan)	Portugal	Lisbon	6.9	30,000
1556 (23 Jan)	China	Huaxian, Weinan & Huayin, Shaanxi, China (and many other towns)	7.9	830,000
1737 (11 Oct)	India	Kolkata	Not known	300,000
1755 (1 Nov)	Portugal	Lisbon	8.5	70,000
1819 (16 Jun)	India	Rann of Kutch Earthquake: towns of Kothari, Mothora, Naliya and Vinjan suffered serious damage	8.2	1,543
1906 (18 Apr)	USA	San Francisco, CA	7.9	2,500
1908 (28 Dec)	Italy	Messina: severe damage across Calabria and Sicily	7.2	72,000
1915 (13 Jan)	Italy	Severe damage in the Avezzano-Pescina area	7.0	32,610
1920 (16 Dec)	China	Haiyuan County experienced total destruction; cities such as Lanzhou, Longde and Huining, suffered serious damage	7.8	200,000
1923 (01 Sep)	Japan	Tokyo experienced extreme damage and suffered fires and a tsunami	7.9	143,000

Table 8.2 (continued)

Date	Country modern territory	Urban areas affected	Magnitude moment magnitude scale	Fatalities
1927 (22 May)	China	Gulang, Gansu: damage occurred from Lanzhou through Minqin and Yongchang to Jinta	7.6	40,900
1939 (27 Dec)	Turkey	Erzincan: damage extensive from Turcan to Amasya	8.0	23,000
1948 (05 Oct)	Turkmenistan	Ashgabat suffered extreme damage	7.3	110,000
1960 (22 May)	Chile	Valdivia and Puerto Octay	9.5	5,700
1964 (27 Mar)	USA	Anchorage, Kenai. Kodiak, Seward, Valdez and others, Alaska	9.2	131
1970 (31 May)	Peru	Casma, Chimbote, and Yungay (landslide killed many)	7.9	66,000
1976 (4 Feb)	Guatemala	Guatemala City	7.5	23,000
1976 (27 Jul)	Tangshan	Tangshan	7.7	650,000
1985 (19 Sep)	Mexico	Mexico City	8.1	10,000
1988 (17 Dec)	Armenia	Spitak	6.9	25,000
1990 (10 Jun)	Iran	Rudbar, Manjil and Lushan	7.4	40,000
1990 (16 Jul)	Philippines	Baguio, Cabanatuan City, Dagupan City	7.8	1,621
1999 (21 Sep)	Taiwan	Tainan	7.6	2,400
2001 (26 Jan)	India	Bujh, Bhachau, Anjar and Ahmedabad, Gujarat	7.7	12,290
2004 (26 Dec)	Indonesia	Bandar Acheh; the tsunami affected many Indian ocean cities	9.1	227,898
2005 (08 Oct)	Pakistan	Muzaffarabad and Uri severely affected	7.6	86,000
2008 (12 May)	China	Chengdu-Lixian-Guangyuan area severely affected, over 5 million buildings collapsed	7.9	87,587
2010 (12 Jan)	Haiti	Port-au-Prince	7.0	316,000
2010 (04 Sep)	New Zealand	Canterbury	7.1	1
2011 (18 Jan)	Pakistan	Dalbandin, Baluchistan	7.2	2
2011 (22 Feb)	New Zealand	Canterbury (aftershock)	6.3	185
2011 (11 Mar)	Japan	Hachinohe, Sendai, Ishinomaki and Onahama, Tōhoku, (and tsunami)	9.0	15,828

Table 8.3: Progress in the management of urban earthquake risk

Date	Country modern territory	Action
132	China	First instruments to measure occurrence and location of earthquakes
1880	Japan	Development of pendulum seismometers began
1891	Japan	Government earthquake investigation committee
1919	Japan	Urban Building Standards Act
1924	Japan	Revision of Law Enforcement Regulations: inclusion of seismic design standards
1925	Japan	Earthquake Research Institute at Tokyo University founded
1933	USA	California Field Act requires seismic design for school buildings
1935	India	S L Kumar develops earthquake resistant construction
1935	New Zealand	Design standards for buildings in earthquakes were first introduced
1946	USA	Seismic Sea Wave Warning System set up
1954	China	Modern earthquake engineering started at Harbin
1960	China	Earthquake research facilities established
1961	Japan	Disaster Countermeasures Basic Act to ensure comprehensive disaster management
1971	Japan	Emergency Revision of Building Standard Law reduced the spacing of steel ties in concrete columns to 100 mm
1971	USA	Serious earthquake forecasting research began
1972	USA	California Legislature passed landmark law requiring identification of seismic-hazard zones along faults
1972	USA	California's Alquist-Priolo Special Studies Zones Act restricts development near or over surface traces of faults
1975	China	City of Haicheng evacuated before large earthquake
1977	USA	Earthquake Hazards Reduction Act
1990	USA	National Earthquake Hazards Reduction Program Reauthorization Act
1990	USA	National Affordable Housing Act requires seismic risk assessment for all properties assisted under HUD programmes
1990	USA	California Seismic Hazards Mapping Act
1991	Iran	Islamic Consultative Assembly sets up National Committee for Natural Disaster Reduction (NCNDR)
1994	Ecuador	Quito creates disaster prevention and response unit under its planning department

Table 8.3 (continued)

1995	Japan	Act for Promotion of Earthquake Proof Retrofitting of Buildings
2002	India	Urban Earthquake Vulnerability Reduction Project with UNDP (until 2008)
2004	USA	Further amendment of 1977 Earthquake Hazards Act
2004	New Zealand	Building Act requires local authorities to develop policies on earthquake-prone buildings in their area by 30 May 2006
2005	Canada	National Building Code contains details of ground motions for seismic design
2009	Nepal	National Strategy for Disaster Risk Management approved

Some earthquakes have been predicted, usually by observing animal behaviour, as at Haicheng, China in 1975 (Table 8.3), sufficiently early to allow rapid evacuation from high risk zones. Tsunami warnings can be issued and the times of travel of waves across oceans can be predicted, but unless warnings reach the communities at risk, and unless people in those towns and cities have somewhere to go and know what to do, fatalities and injuries can be as high as in earlier centuries. Sadly, such was the case in many Indian Ocean areas after the 2004 Bandar Acheh event, in Port-au-Prince in January 2010 and in north-eastern Honshu, Japan in 2011.

VOLCANOES AND URBAN AREAS

Volcanoes differ from other landforms because they are built up of liquid ejected from deep below the earth's crust that cools to form new rock. Many volcanic rocks contain minerals that break down to provide some of the world's most fertile soils. Thus some of the densest rural populations, and the market towns and business centres they support, are found close to the slopes of volcanoes, for example on Java, Indonesia, on Sicily near Mt Etna and around the Rift Valley volcanoes of Africa, such as Nyiragongo. Many cities, particularly Catania in Sicily, have a long history of recovery from successive volcanic disasters (Table 8.4). Many more have to have high preparedness for emergency evacuation if an eruption occurs.

A volcano consists of a magma chamber, chimney, cone and crater. It may have secondary feeders, with secondary craters. Volcanoes have different shapes, sizes, and activities, depending on the viscosity of the lava feeding them. Shield volcanoes, such as Mauna Kea and Mauna on Hawaii, have low silica, low viscosity, hot basaltic lavas that pour out of fissures and flow down the sides of the volcano. Stratovolcanoes, like Vesuvius, Mt Fuji, Soufrière and Pelée have high silica magmas and consist of alternating layers of lavas and pyroclastics (igneous rock fragments thrown out by volcanoes).

Table 8.4: Major volcanic eruptions affecting urban areas

Date	Volcano	Country modern territory	Urban areas affected	Fatalities
1450 BC	Santorini	Greece	Minoan City of Akrotiri buried by lava and ash	n/a
1226 BC	Etna	Italy	Small coastal settlements	n/a
477 BC	Etna	Italy	Catania all but destroyed	n/a
396 BC	Etna	Italy	Naxos devastated	n/a
122 BC	Etna	Italy	Catania severely damaged	n/a
AD 79 (24 Aug)	Vesuvius	Italy	Herculaneum, Pompeii, Stabiae destroyed	>50,000
AD 1169	Etna	Italy	Catania buildings collapsed	15,000
1224	Etna	Italy	Ognina partly buried by lava	n/a
1631	Vesuvius	Italy	Resina, Torre dell' Annunziata, Torre del Greco and Portici destroyed	18,000
1669	Etna	Italy	Catania, Nicolosi, Belpasso, and 50 other towns destroyed in multi-vent eruption	20,000 to 100,000
1766	Mayon	Philippines	Malinao destroyed	2,000
1783	Asamayama	Japan	Nuées ardentes fell on 48 villages	5,000
1793–4	Vesuvius	Italy	Torre del Greco	n/a
1814 (1 Feb)	Mayon	Philippines	Cagsuaga, Badiao and 2 other towns destroyed	2,200
1815 (5 Apr)	Tamboro	Indonesia	Tomboro, Tempo and Pekate destroyed; later deaths through crop damage starvation	70,000 to 129,000
1883 (27 Aug)	Krakatoa	Indonesia	Created tsunami that swept across Indian Ocean damaging many port cities and towns	>30,000
1897 (23 Jun)	Mayon	Philippines	Tobaco, San Roque, Misericordia destroyed	400
1902 (6 May)	Soufrière	St Vincent	6 towns destroyed	>3,000

Table 8.4 (continued)

1902 (8 May)	Pelée	Martinique	St Pierre destroyed	30,000
1911 (30 Jan)	Taal	Philippines	Guilot, San Jose destroyed; panic in Manila	1,335
1917	Boqueron	El Salvador	San Salvador virtually wiped out	450
1928	Etna	Italy	Mascati and Nunziata destroyed	n/a
1951	Lamington	Papua New Guinea	Settlements destroyed	6,000
1963	Agung	Indonesia	Sebudi, Sebih and Sorgah on Bali buried by ash	1,500
1985 (Nov)	Nevado del Ruiz	Colombia	Eruption triggered mudslides that killed thousands	25,000
1986 (21 Aug)	Lake Nyos	Cameroon	Release of cold carbon dioxide gas	1,700
1997 (25 Jun)	Soufrière Hills	Montserrat	Plymouth 80 per cent destroyed; 4,000 evacuated	19
2002 (Jan)	Nyiragongo	D.R. Congo	Goma damaged, 400,000 evacuated, gas killed 17	17
2010 (14 Apr)	Eyjafjallajokull	Iceland	Town evacuated, ash causes suspension of north Atlantic and European aircraft flights	n/a

As magma cools, water vapour is compressed until blasts create ducts through the magma allowing gases and pyroclastics to escape and form a huge debris cloud. In some cases, the gases themselves are deadly, as when Lake Nyos in Cameroon exploded in 1986 (Table 8.4). In other instances fine ash may be carried into the atmosphere, as when Eyjafjallajokull erupted in 2010 (Table 8.4). Volcanoes like Merapi in Indonesia release pyroclastics and water then moves over the ground into river channels as lahars, flows of hot mud and rock, which carry everything in front of them as they sweep down-valley. Coastal or island volcanoes, such as Krakatoa, may produce tsunamis as well as ash, so affecting urban areas across the seas and also crop yields from distant fields. Thus the impacts of volcanoes on urban areas are complex in both their nature and their spatial relationships. Many cities, such as Naples in Italy or Yogyakarta in Indonesia, are so close to volcanoes that they have to have evacuation plans and exercises in order to be constantly ready for a severe eruption.

Table 8.5: Progress in the management of urban volcanic damage risk

Date	Country *modern territory*	Action
1669	Italy	Pappalardo attempts to divert Etna lava flow away from Catania
1912	Japan	Mukaiyama Observatory established at Tohoku University
1912	USA	Hawaiian Volcano Observatory established
1924	Indonesia	Seismic monitoring begins at Mt Merapi
1928	Japan	Aso Volcanological Laboratory, Kyoto University, established
1935	Hawaii, USA	Jaggar bombs lava flow to spread it laterally
1958	China	Heilongjiang Wudalianchi Volcanic Monitoring Observatory established
1967	Japan	Former Mukaiyama Observatory became Aobayama Seismological Observatory
1977	Japan	Mobile Observation Party for Volcanic Activities attached to Aobayama
1979	Japan	Regional volcanic observation network around volcanoes of Iwate, Akita-Komagatake, Akita-Yakeyama, Chokai, Zao, Azuma, Adatara and Bandai started
1986	Colombia	Observatorio Vulcanológico y Sismológico de Manizales established
1988	Alaska, USA	Alaska Volcano Observatory established
1988	Cameroon	Antenne de Recherches Géophysiques et Volcanologiques (ARGV) set up at Ekona
1988	Comores	Karthala Volcanological Observatory established
1990	Canada	Interagency Volcanic Event Notification Plan begins
1996	Alaska, USA	Seismic monitoring network expansion begins
2000	Democratic Republic of the Congo	Goma Volcano Observatory set up
2001	El Salvador	Seismic-volcanic monitoring programme starts
2004	Canary Islands, Spain	Monitoring of seismicity associated with volcanic systems on Tenerife Island begins

The diversity of volcanic activity and the irregularity of volcanic eruptions mean that preparations for disasters have to rely on knowledge of each individual volcano and on monitoring its seismic activity, the chemistry of its gases, changes in shape and in the temperature of crater lakes, fumaroles and hot springs, and local shifts in gravity and magnetism. Most countries with active volcanoes have established volcano observatories either for specific volcanoes or, more commonly for groups of volcanoes, such as those of the Canary Islands (Table 8.5) or the Cascade volcanoes of the Pacific Northwest of the coterminous USA. Many of the observatories listed in Table 8.5 were established after major disasters, such as that in Colombia after Nevado del Ruiz erupted in 1985. Arrays of instruments around individual volcanoes allow detection of renewed volcanic activity permitting evacuation plans to be put into action when that activity exceeds a certain threshold. Nevertheless, despite instrumentation, it is often only when an eruption has started that volcanologists can get an idea of where the lava, ash cloud and lahars may go. Urban deaths from eruptions (Table 8.4) are generally far less than from earthquakes, because there is usually time to evacuate. However those from gas clouds and extensive fine ash falls may be larger, because of their rapid release to high altitudes and fast spread downwind away from the eruption.

Physical defences against volcanoes, such as walls to deflect lava flows, have been put in place in some instances and sometimes they have been effective. Diversion of lava by breaching the edges of flows and by bombing the flow has been effective (Table 8.5) but there has to be suitable terrain for the flow to go to; otherwise it might damage neighbouring settlements. Warning systems and exclusion measures are the most effective ways of protecting human life, even if it means abandoning some settlements. However, many cities close to volcanoes are still growing. Goma, Democratic Republic of the Congo, sits on the shore of Lake Kivu, and grew from 50,000 to one million population in 20 years after 1990. Largely peopled by refugees from civil wars and conflicts, it is under constant threat from Nyiragongo's lava, which destroyed parts of the city in 2002 (Table 8.4), and also from the release of carbon dioxide and methane from the depths of Lake Kivu, should volcanic activity cause its release. As usual, vulnerability is highest in the poorest cities.[7]

LANDSLIDES AND SLOPES

Many parts of the world, particularly areas subject to earthquakes and volcanoes, have long experienced sequences of landslides, particularly those where recently formed volcanic deposits are still unstable, as in parts of Italy. In Naples 'unnatural' catastrophes have followed one after the other at an unrelenting pace since 1950 and since 1980 have seemed to cause more suffering and death than previously.[8] From 1997 to 1999, a huge number of slides, often turning into extremely rapid debris-earth flows, repeatedly affected the late Quaternary volcanoclastic deposits mantling the carbonate slopes of the Campania region, Italy. The Sorrento Peninsula was the epicentre of the 1997 regional slope instability crisis. The hundred or so shallow mass movements during January 1997 were the latest episode in a long series of slope failure events dating back to the mid-eighteenth century. On 10 January 1997, at about 8:15 pm, a rainfall-induced debris slide and debris flow occurred at Pozzano (province of Naples), mainly affecting the AD 79 pyroclastic products.

Table 8.6: Major landslides affecting urban areas

Date	Country modern territory	Location	Urban areas affected	Fatalities
1618 (4 Sep)	Italy	Chiavenna	Massive mountain landslide buried 2 towns	2,427
1806 (2 Sep)	Switzerland	Goldau Valley	Failure of mountainside led to rock and debris avalanche destroying 4 villages	800
1881	Switzerland	Elm	Unregulated slate quarrying led to failure of mountainside and burying of village	150
1903 (29 Apr)	Canada	Frank, Alberta	Turtle Mountain collapse; 90 million tonnes of limestone slid down the mountainside	>70
1920 (16 Dec)	China	Gansu	Landslides in loess (fine sandy clay) destroyed most of Swen Family Gap town	5,000
1920 (16 Dec)	China	Haiyuan County, Ningxia,	Loess flows and landslides over an area of 50,000 km². Failures in loess caused extreme fissuring, landslide dams, and buried villages	>100,000
1933	China	Diexi, Mao County, Sichuan	Landslide that struck Diexi town then blocked the Min River. When it broke, the flood caused 2,500 deaths	3,100
1938 (2 Mar)	USA	Los Angeles	Widespread landslides in hills	200
1939	Japan	Kobe	Rain-induced landslides damaged 100,000 homes	461
1939	Japan	Kure	Rain-induced landslides damaged homes	1,154
1943 (13 Dec)	Peru	Huaraz, Ancash	Landslide formed a temporary dam on the Rio Santa, two days later it failed and flooded the valley below	5,000
1949 (10 July)	Tajikistan	Khait, Gharm Oblast,	Triggered by the 1949 Khait earthquake, largest of several landslides	4,000
1958	Japan	Tokyo	Typhoon rains produced over 1,000 landslides	61
1959 (29 Oct)	Mexico	Minatitlan	Heavy rains caused landslides in a dozen towns along Pacific coast	2,000

Table 8.6 (continued)

Date	Country modern territory	Location	Urban areas affected	Fatalities
1961	Belgium	Jupille	Fly-ash and slag heap buried village	20
1961 (11 Dec)	Peru	Yungay	Millions of tonnes of snow, rocks, mud and debris tumbled down the extinct volcano of Huascaran and buried town	4,000
1964 (18 Jul)	Japan	Shimane and Totton Prefectures, Honshu	Heavy rains after minor earthquake produced landslides, destroyed villages	233
1966 (11–13 Jan)	Brazil	Rio de Janeiro	Torrential rains caused widespread landslides in illegal 'favela settlements'	239
1966 (21 Oct)	Wales, UK	Aberfan	Huge coal mine waste tip slid into village burying school and houses	145
1967 (17–20 Feb)	Brazil	Rio de Janeiro	Rain again caused landslides in favelas but also put power plants out of action	224
1969 (18 Jan)	USA	Los Angeles	Widespread landsliding in San Gabriel and Santa Monica mountain hillsides	95
1972 (18 Jun)	China	Hong Kong	Hillslope failure after construction work downslope toppled apartment building	67
1972 (19 Aug)	Korea (South)	Seoul	15 landslides after 450 mm of rain in Seoul made 127,000 homeless	180
1993 (11 Dec)	Malaysia	Ulu Klang	Poor water diversion pipes led to soil liquefaction and apartment block collapsed	48
2000 (10 Jul)	Philippines	Manila	Typhoon rains caused major landslide at 'Promised Land' garbage dump at Payatas	>200
2006 (31 May)	Malaysia	Kampung Pasir	Landslide due to failure of retaining wall on a cut slope	11
2008 (6 Dec)	Malaysia	Bukit Antarabangsa	Another landslide 1.3 km from the 1993 Ulu Klang slide: instability in cut slopes	
2011 (21 May)	Malaysia	Ulu Langat	Landslide in heavy rains buries orphanage	21

Table 8.7: Progress in the management of urban landslide risk

Date	Country	Action
1975	USA	National Landslide Hazards Program (LHP) started
1977	China (Hong Kong)	Geotechnical Engineering Office (GEO) (formerly the Geotechnical Control Office) set up to tackle slope safety problems following a number of disastrous landslides in the 1970s
1983	USA	California Landslide Hazard Mapping Act
1985	St Lucia	Landslide hazard map produced for whole country
1991	Portugal	Law No. 113.91 29AGO, Civil Protection Basic Law (prevention: delineate risk areas)
1992	China (Hong Kong)	GEO began public education programme on slope safety to encourage private owners to take responsibility for the safety of their slopes
1992	St Lucia	Landslide Hazard Map revised
1995	China (Hong Kong)	A five-year accelerated LPM Programme introduced as a result of the 1994 Kwun Lung Lau failure
1995	France	Loi 'barnier' du 2 février: plans de prévention des risques naturels prévisible (risk mapping)
1995	Sweden	Commission of Slope Stability of the Royal Swedish Academy of Engineering Science (risk mapping)
1996	UK	Planning Policy Guidance 14: Development on Unstable Land – Annex 1: Landslides and Planning issued
1997	China (Hong Kong)	GEO introduced a systematic landslide investigation programme
1997	Switzerland	Government guidance on how hazards caused by ground movement can be incorporated into the land use planning framework
1997	USA	Following disastrous landslides, City of Seattle establishes policy on landslide mitigation
1998	Italy	Law No. 267/1998 (Statements of decree 180) flood and landslide hazard assessment
1998	Spain	Ley Basica Estatal 6/1998 (Ley sobre regimen del suelo y valoraciones) (land use planning; hazard mapping)
1998	USA	FEMA establishes hazard mitigation programme 'Project Impact'
2000	Poland	Law 18 April Law on Natural Disaster 2 (delineate unstable areas – susceptibility mapping)
2003	Greece	Regulation No. ΔMEO/γ/o/285/ Directives about Road Work Studies (risk mapping)
2008	Canada	British Columbia issues Guidelines for Landslide Assessment for proposed Residential Developments
2008	Sri Lanka	Reissues 'Guidelines for Construction in landslide prone areas'
2008	St Lucia	Landslide Response Plan issued

Following a J-shaped path, the landslide destroyed a private house and invaded the adjacent highway. Four people died, 22 were injured and the highway was closed for about two months. There was less than 200 mm of rainfall in the 72 hour period prior to the landslide, although intense precipitation had occurred during a preceding 4-month period. Nevertheless, the soils became wet creating pressures in the pores between soil particles that eventually caused the slopes to fail. The characteristics of these pyroclastic soils were the key to this particular event.[9] While some landslides are clearly associated with rainfall intensity and duration when the slope materials are at field capacity,[10] in others, the pattern of water movement into the soils and near surface materials, and the internal pressures it creates, are all-important. If urban construction has altered, or constrained, the routes water takes through the soil on slopes, the landslide risk may be increased.

In the deeply weathered rocks of parts of the humid tropics, landsliding is a frequent problem in residential areas of rapidly expanding towns and cities. Following the 1972 landslide (Table 8.6), Hong Kong developed a tight policy to prevent further disasters, establishing its Geotechnical Control Office in 1977 (Table 8.7) and developing both a system for making sure that development was allocated to the appropriate type of land and good engineering design and slope maintenance policies and practices to ensure that modified, engineered slopes would not fail in future. However, other cities in similar terrain subject to high rainfalls have not always implemented such successful policies.

The Ulu Klang area on the periphery of Kuala Lumpur, Malaysia has steep hillsides that are much sought after as desirable residential areas, however they have a history of landslides due to the way the slopes are cut and filled to create large steps on which housing, including multi-storey apartment buildings, is constructed. The first tragic event was the Highland Tower landslide in 1993 when the collapse of a 16 storey block caused 48 deaths (Table 8.6). A second disaster, a short distance away in 2002 destroyed a two storey house, and a third in 2006 at Kampung Pasir damaged three blocks of terraced houses. A fourth in 2008 at Bukit Antarabangsa (Table 8.6) overcame three houses. The design of the subdivisions on which these landslides occurred was inappropriate. Cutting into the weathered rock disturbs the natural movement of water and when retaining walls are used to stabilize the risers of the cut steps, water accumulates behind them during heavy rain, building up an increasing pressure which may cause them to fail.

In addition to landslides caused by human disturbance of natural slopes, there can be major landslides as a result of quarrying, mining or the dumping of waste. The 1881 disaster at Elm, Switzerland (Table 8.6) resulted from unregulated quarrying. The 1966 Aberfan tragedy (Table 8.6) was caused by coal mine waste. Several garbage dumps in the Philippines that are home to dozens of rubbish scavenger families have suffered major landslides that killed people, including Manila's 'Promised Land' dump (Table 8.6) and Baguio's Irisan dump in August 2011. Since 2000, other dump landslides causing more than 10 fatalities have occurred in Chongqing and Shanguio City, China;

Table 8.8: Types of landslide map produced by the
California Geological Survey (after Brabb et al., 1972)

Map Type	Description
Landslide-inventory maps	The most basic landslide maps, portray the location of prior failure. Because one clue to the location of future landsliding is the distribution of past movement, maps that show existing landslides are helpful in predicting the hazard. Inventory maps do not necessarily distinguish fresh movements, but in any one year some of the mapped slides – or more frequently, portions of them – may become active. A landslide inventory reveals the extent of past movement and thus the probable locus of some future activity within those landslides, but it does not indicate the likelihood of failure for the much larger area between mapped landslides. For this hazard, risk or zone maps are required.
Landslide-hazard maps 1) Landslide-susceptibility maps	Describe an unstable condition arising from the presence or likely future occurrence of slope failure: the relative likelihood of future landsliding based solely on the intrinsic properties of a locale or site. Prior failure (from a landslide inventory), rock or soil strength, and steepness of slope are the three site factors that most determine susceptibility.
Landslide-hazard maps 2) Landslide-potential maps	Describe an unstable condition arising from the presence or likely future occurrence of slope failure: the likelihood of landsliding (susceptibility) jointly with the occurrence of a triggering event (opportunity). Potential commonly is based on the three factors determining susceptibility plus an estimate or measure of the probability (likelihood of occurrence) of a triggering event such as earthquake or excessive rainfall.
Landslide-risk maps	Describe landslide potential jointly with the expected losses to life and property if a failure was to occur. The potential for landslide damage to a road system, for example, can be evaluated by considering the exposure of the roads to different levels of landslide hazard and the vulnerability of the roads to consequent damage. Similarly, the risk of excessive sedimentation in streams and other ecological damage can be evaluated by considering the landslide hazard jointly with the properties of streams and their sensitivity.
Landslide-zone maps	Depict areas with a higher probability of landsliding, within which specific actions are mandated by California law prior to any development. These maps typically are binary in nature (a given site is either in or out of the zone) and are designed for use as planning tools by non-geoscientists. Zone maps may be derived from landslide potential or susceptibility, but some have been based simply on slope gradient or landslide-inventory maps.

Padang and Bandung, Indonesia; Medellin, Colombia; and Guatemala City. Most garbage landslide events may go unreported, given the locations and the people involved.

As with other geophysical hazards, mapping of where past landslides occurred and where the terrain may be susceptible to landslides is important. Such information helps in deciding what types of building can be permitted on a particular parcel of land (Table 8.8). The 1972 landslide susceptibility map of San Mateo County, California[11] divides the county area, immediately south of San Francisco city centre, into seven categories of susceptibility to landsliding. Even though most of the areas already built up at the time were moderately stable, landslides in the 1968–9 winter cost almost US$3.6 million.[12] In the 1980s the UK government completed a national landslides database which contains details of 8,835 landslides recorded in the published literature and these are shown on county maps at 1:250,000 scale together with interpreted 'possible areas of extensive ancient landsliding'. The British Geological Survey now can supply information on landslide hazards around any given location through its National Landslides Database. With the development of geographical information systems, much more sophisticated data on landslide risks has become available[13] as well as detailed susceptibility maps.[14]

SUBSIDENCE

The term 'subsidence' describes human-induced lowering of the ground surface, due to abstraction of groundwater, oil and gas, removal of salt, coal and other minerals, and pumping of water from mines. Roofing and paving of the land surface can result in less replenishment of groundwater by infiltration, further lowering groundwater levels. Losses to urban areas caused by subsidence can be high, those for Tianjin, China being estimated at US$18.03 billion up to 2007.[15]

In 1827 nearly a hectare of land suddenly sank close to Wagstadt, in Silesia,[16] probably as a result of the collapse of mineshafts far below the surface. Such subsidence has occurred increasingly frequently in many mining areas, and may be caused by the extraction of mineral matter or by the removal of liquids. In many places it has restricted the growth of towns and often creates depressions on the land surface that fill with water to become lakes. In many places these water bodies can be turned into assets providing ecosystem services for urban communities.

For many cities, however, natural subsidence is a persistent and expensive problem. In the middle of the sixteenth century, Angiolo Eremitano argued that Venice was sinking about 30 cm every century.[17] In 1731, Eustache Manfredi claimed that subsidence was affecting buildings in Ravenna[18] (Table 8.9). Most, if not all, of the subsidence was geologic subsidence due to the continual addition of sediment to the delta of the River Po. However during the twentieth century pumping of groundwater from the delta's alluvial aquifers became a major factor (Figure 8.1). Groundwater withdrawal began in the 1930s reaching a peak between 1950 and 1970. A maximum subsidence rate of 17 mm/yr was recorded in the year 1968–9 in the Venice industrial zone. Pumping has now ceased and a rebound of up to 2 cm occurred in the historical city by 1975. However rising levels mean that overall Venice effectively suffered a lowering of 23 cm in the twentieth century.[19]

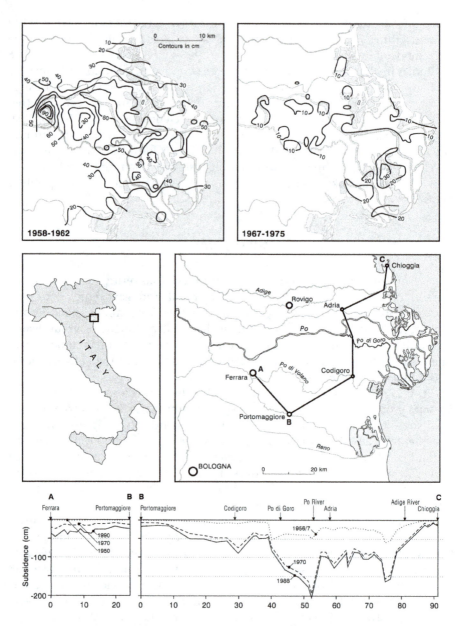

Figure 8.1: Subsidence in the Po Valley of Italy (after Douglas, 2004). The two uppermost diagrams show isopleths of surface lowering (in centimetres) between 1958 and 1962 when extensive pumping occurred and between 1967 and 1975 after methaniferous water extraction ceased (after Caputo et al., 1970 and Bondesan and Simeoni, 1983). The two lowest diagrams show the amount of subsidence in the second half of the twentieth century (after Bondesan et al., 2000) along the transect A-B-C shown of the centre right map of the Po Delta.

Table 8.9: Major subsidence events affecting urban areas

Date	Location	Urban areas affected	Fatalities
1533	UK	Subsidence in salt field at Combermere Abbey near Whitchurch	n/a
1659	UK	Subsidence at Bilkely near Cholmondeley Castle, Cheshire salt field	n/a
1731	Italy	Subsidence affecting buildings in Ravenna	n/a
1879	USA	Catastrophic sinkhole develops over salt beds in Meade County, Kansas	n/a
1920	China	Land subsidence first noted in Shanghai	n/a
1937 (22 Sep)	USA	Potwin, Butler County, Kansas, sudden sinkhole development	n/a
1962 (Dec)	South Africa	Crusher plant building and workers fall down sinkhole on the West Driefontein Mine	29
1974 (Oct)	USA	90 m diameter sinkhole undermines railroad tracks at Hutchinson, Kansas	n/a
1992	Belarus	Entire machine factory lost in sinkhole in gypsum karst	n/a
1998 (17 Jul)	Austria	Lassing Talc Mine subsidence destroyed many houses	9
2006 (21 Apr)	USA	Sinkhole opens beneath house built over old gold mine near Sacramento	1
2007 (23 Feb)	Guatemala	100 m deep sinkhole swallowed about a dozen homes in Guatemala City	3
2010 (12 May)	Canada	165 m long sinkhole at Saint-Jude swallows house and inhabitants	4
2010 (1 Jun)	Guatemala	60 m deep sinkhole swallowed clothing factory in Guatemala City	0
2010 (28 Dec)	South Africa	Sinkholes appear at Bapsfontein near Pretoria; officials want to relocate 3,000 people	0
2011	India	50 houses collapsed following subsidence at Jamuria, Raniganj area, West Bengal, where rampant illegal and unscientific coal mining occurred	5

Table 8.10: Progress in the management of urban subsidence risk

Date	Country	Action
1763	UK	Lease for coal mine near Barlow, Derbyshire required that any subsidence caused by operations should be paid for and put right
1822	Belgium	Systematic study of mine subsidence started because of surface damage to structures
1860	UK	Solution subsidence in gypsum at Ripon, Yorkshire first recorded
1871	Belgium	Subsidence-induced fault reactivation studied in Liège coalfield by Dumont
1908	USA	Illinois State Geological Survey began documenting coal mine subsidence
1916	USA	Relationship between sinkhole formation and pumping first noticed in Alabama
1918	USA	Subsidence due to oil extraction became apparent near Galveston, Texas
1935	USA	Subsidence due to groundwater extraction noticed in Las Vegas
1940	USA	Subsidence first noticed at Wilmington oil field, California
1948	USA	Subsidence first detected in Arizona near Eloy in the lower Santa Cruz basin
1952	UK	Cheshire Brine Pumping (Compensation for Subsidence) Act deals with effects of salt mining
1954	Mexico	Water pumping banned in Mexico city centre and wells moved to north and east of basin
1957	UK	Coal Mining Subsidence Act: repairs to buildings affected by subsidence
1965	UK	National Coal Board publishes Subsidence Engineer's Handbook
1966	USA	Pennsylvania Bituminous Mine Subsidence and Land Conservation Act protects homes, public buildings and cemeteries
1970	UK	Court case over substantial subsidence damage caused the cessation of wild brine extraction from beneath Stafford
1975	USA	Texas Legislature passed a law creating the Harris-Galveston Coastal Subsidence District, the first district of its kind in the United States
1977	USA	Federal Public Law 95-87, the Surface Mining Control and Reclamation Act (SMCRA) starts regulation of mining subsidence
1979	USA	Illinois Mine Subsidence Insurance Act created subsidence insurance as part of a homeowner's policy
1983	USA	Illinois enacts permanent rules to fulfil the federal SMCRA
1985	USA	Illinois Mine Subsidence Research Program established
1991	UK	Coal mining subsidence Act includes provisions concerning new buildings in areas of subsidence risk
2002	UK	Planning Policy Guidance Note 14 Development on unstable land Annex 2: Subsidence and Planning issued
2010	South Africa	National sinkhole database being established

In 1846, residents of Mexico City discovered the artesian aquifer beneath the city. As water was withdrawn, subsidence began, being first noticed in 1891 in the old part of the city but not studied until 1925. By 1939 total subsidence nowhere exceeded 1.5 m. In 1948 it was proved that groundwater withdrawal was causing the subsidence. By 1970 places in the city centre were more than 7 m below the original ground level. The banning of pumping in the city centre in 1954 (Table 8.10) helped to slow the rate of lowering, but new wells elsewhere added to the overall area of subsiding ground in the basin. By 2008, the fastest subsidence rates of 300 mm per year were occurring in the eastern part of the city.[20]

Particularly severe subsidence has occurred under Bangkok, Thailand as water abstraction increased rapidly after 1970 as the city grew, rising from 700,000 m³ per day in 1974 to about 1,200,000 m³ per day in 1980. After a pause in increase from 1983 to 1993, the pumping rose again to 2,400,000 m³ per day in 1999. The removal of water resulted in a maximum subsidence of 1.6 m in the period 1933–87, with a further 0.3 m of lowering by 1997.[21]

In Texas, California, and Arizona, mining of groundwater has caused extensive subsidence. Damages in Texas are largely due to reactivation of faults and submergence. In Arizona, damages are mostly due to differential subsidence and fissuring. The legal approaches to abating subsidence vary in the different states. A key issue is the contrast between an owner's legal right to pump as much water as can be 'captured' from a piece of land and the conflicting right to be able to have lateral support for a piece of land against any possible subsidence due to pumping. One judgment in a class suit against a business pumping groundwater for sale, the landmark Friendswood decision of 1978, led to a decision by the Texas Supreme Court that the plaintiff's demand for lateral support for their land was reasonable and that the old 'right of capture' had to be moderated. Other steps to reduce removal of subsurface liquids in order to avoid subsidence include conservation measures by California water districts, and minor provisions of the 1980 Arizona Ground Water Management Act.[22]

Subsidence over petroleum extraction zones, first described over an oilfield near Houston, Texas (Table 8.10), can cause significant damage to extraction infrastructure itself, including expensive well failures. Parts of Long Beach, California, suffered up to 0.75 m yr¹ land subsidence as a result of oil extraction.[23] Alarmed by this subsidence the City of Los Angeles introduced regulations to ensure that further oilfield development would not cause subsidence. Thus, in the case of the Beverley Hills (East) field 1200 m beneath one of the most densely populated portions of Los Angeles, subsidence has been avoided by injecting water into the voids created by oil removal.[24] The problems of the Wilmington oilfield at Long Beach were also stabilized by injecting water, with a careful programme of monitoring to control the pressure within cavities.

In Cheshire, England, where salt has been mined since pre-Roman times, the effects of solution subsidence on the topography and on structures have been spectacular (Table 8.9). Early mining left pillars to support the surface.

Groundwater eventually dissolved the pillars and the ground above collapsed creating crater-like depressions 10 to 200 m in diameter, and linear hollows over 200 m wide and 8 km long in the surface. In the town of Northwich, very few pre-1900 buildings survived the subsidence damage. Natural brine pumping was phased out in the 1970s, and most modern salt production is by controlled solution mining which causes few problems. Mature cavities are maintained in a stable condition by flooding with saturated brine.[25] However, there remain many areas of Cheshire where development is restricted and railway tracks have to be adjusted to compensate for continuing slight subsidence.

Not all urban subsidence problems arise from extraction of liquids or mining; some are the result of building in inappropriate places, particularly on ground containing natural voids such as caves. Soluble rocks such as limestone, chalk and gypsum can all develop voids and experience solution subsidence. Where such rocks are overlain by clays and sands, the solution phenomena may not be apparent at the surface, their existence only becoming known when a heavy building collapses into the buried void. Around Ripon, England (Table 8.9), where beds of gypsum are overlain by carbonate rock, sandstones and glacial deposits, a 6 km² area suffers a large collapse about once every three years. For decades, many buildings have been damaged by the collapse of caves in the buried gypsum.[26] In the Dserzinsk region of Belarus about four new sinkholes develop every year in gypsum karst, including some induced by construction activities. An entire machine factory fell into a sinkhole in 1992 (Table 8.9). When it was built, four adjacent sinkholes were filled and the factory had at least four failures before the 1992 event.[27] This is an example of a cause of many subsidence problems that have beset urban areas in the past. Old workings have been filled, old quarries and sand pits have been used as rubbish dumps, old mine shafts have been blocked off. Decades later, houses are built on these sites, and the new residents are unaware of what lies beneath the floors, until heavy rains, earth tremors or floodwaters dislodge the fill material and a sinkhole appears.

Sinkholes are particularly common in parts of South Africa, mainly over mining areas and in urban areas above the limestone of Florida. Since 1954, more than 3,100 sinkholes have been entered into the Subsidence Incidence Database kept by the Florida Geological Survey. The South African Geological Survey started a national sinkhole database in 2010 (Table 8.10).

Subsidence is a major problem in some South-east Asian lowlands where alluvial plains overlie cavernous limestone. The buried karst now poses serious problems for civil engineering works. New high-rise buildings require deeper foundations than the low-rise buildings that sufficed until the 1970s. In Kuala Lumpur, Malaysia, the low-rise structures had their foundations on the stiff clay layer within the alluvium. Taller, multi-storey structures require piling into the underlying limestone, as was done for the Petronas twin towers.[28] Analogous karst terrain in north Vietnam and southern China has a range of engineering problems that require careful geophysical investigation before any urban construction work to avoid any future subsidence.

The effects of subsidence can be avoided by not developing in areas at most risk and controlled by incorporating appropriate preventive or precautionary measures in the design of new buildings or structures or modifying existing developments. The UK Planning Guidance notes that all these responses have their place, but controls on proposed development and land use through the Building Regulations and the planning system are the most effective means of minimizing the effects of subsidence on new urban development.[29] A prospective developer or property purchaser can now buy a British Geological Survey Natural Ground Stability Report that briefly describes any natural ground stability hazards if they are present, including swelling clays, ground dissolution, running sand, collapsible or compressible ground that would help those investigating possible subsidence. Many countries have similar hazard information, but developers and planners do not always know to consult it.

CITIES AND RIVERS

Cities were often built on rivers for both water supplies and navigation, and often also originally for defence. Many great cities are prominently sited on major rivers, such as Paris on the Seine, London on the Thames, Bangkok on the Chao Phyra and Chongqing on the Yangtze. Their relationship with these major rivers is one of tension between the advantages of the riverine location and the problems associated with flooding and pollution. All four of the cities named above have major flood defences and histories of past severe flooding. They have had to cope with major pollution episodes and in some cases still suffer from sewer overflows and waste discharges.

Flooding in urban areas can be grouped into four major types: 1) regional floods on major rivers produced by major weather systems, including tropical cyclones (typhoons or hurricanes), as well large slow moving extra-tropical depressions; 2) major floods caused by rapid snowmelt, usually as a result of warm rains falling on a mountain snow-pack in spring; 3) local sewer overflows and surface flooding, known as pluvial flooding, that does not involve defined streams; 4) flooding on small totally urbanized streams. Coastal, deltaic and estuarine cities also face problems of flooding from storm surges and tsunamis.

In addition to their relationships with major rivers, cities also have complex issues related to their small streams and brooks, now often buried deep beneath their streets. Originally sources of fresh water for the early city dwellers, these small rivers soon became urban drains and repositories for rubbish, a situation that frequently still prevails globally, even in affluent European societies (Figure 8.2). As cities have developed, these buried streams have often been connected to the sewer or the stormwater drainage network and today contribute to problems of stormwater and combined sewer overflows. In extreme cases, they have collapsed and caused local subsidence. To examine the environmental history of cities and rivers, the impacts of urban growth on major rivers and

233

Figure 8.2: Supermarket trolley and other materials partially blocking
a culvert carrying a tributary of the River Roch, Rochdale,
Greater Manchester, December 2007 (photo Ian Douglas)

of rivers on the history of cities will be discussed first, followed by a closer
examination of the buried rivers and small urban streams.

CITIES AND MAJOR RIVERS: REGIONAL FLOODS

The Tigris–Euphrates Valley

The very foundations of civilization are associated with managing rivers and
using their waters for irrigation as early as 6000 BC in Mesopotamia. Channels
were dug to divert water from the rivers to grow crops, but occasionally the
rivers would burst their banks and spill out across the flood plain, locally
changing their courses. This process, known as avulsion, happens naturally
but has had a major impact along the Tigris and Euphrates rivers.

The role of avulsion in the evolution of civilization in lower Mesopotamia is
widely recognized. Ancient settlements are closely associated with abandoned
courses of the Euphrates and Tigris rivers. Urban settlements emerged and were

sustained on the avulsion belts of these rivers. Multiple channel networks and avulsion belts created large, naturally irrigated areas, fostering the efficient agriculture needed to sustain dense rural and urban settlements. After channel networks were abandoned during delta evolution, large-scale canal construction was required to sustain settlements but still could not prevent their decline.[30]

In ancient Mesopotamia, the Euphrates flowed past the city of Kish. As long as it remained the centre of a well-watered agricultural area, Kish had a singularly favoured site. However, during the third millennium BC, the Euphrates channel shifted away from Kish and Babylon, only a few kilometres to the west, beside the new channel, succeeded the old city. The Euphrates also ran west of Ur, reaching open water near Eridu. Around 1730 BC, the river was diverted so that it passed by Ur. These cities depended on the support from the irrigated agricultural hinterland. Their survival depended on having the means to cope with the floods on the Tigris and Euphrates.

The Tigris, swollen by the melting snows of the northern and eastern hills, floods at the end of March or the beginning of April, and an overflow of its banks can do great damage to the surrounding country near Baghdad and further south. The Euphrates usually floods at about the time the water levels in the Tigris are beginning to fall. In this case, the damage is not due so much to the velocity of the waters but to the deposition of salt on the land surface by retreating floodwaters. Good drainage to flush that salt out of the fields is needed before irrigation can begin.

The problem was in part solved by avoiding flooding. Canal systems large enough to carry the maximum expected flood overflows were devised and carried out sometimes by diverting the course of the Euphrates just north of Babylon. The rise and fall of towns was closely associated with the opening up and silting up of canals. The siltation, which eventually would raise the canal bed high above the surrounding plain, could only be avoided by annual cleaning for which landowners and townships had to be made responsible. Strong administrations, such as the Hammurabi, could ensure that the canals were well maintained. However, disruptions, such as invasions from neighbouring territories, would prevent regular maintenance of the canals. The resulting siltation and blocking of the canals meant that much agricultural land reverted to marsh. Although cities such as Ur were accessible from the sea, river-borne silt helped to block channels in the delta and assisted the gradual seaward advance of the shoreline. Thus, after the time of the third dynasty of Ur, seagoing vessels were unable to reach the city.

Around 3200–3000 BC, major flooding occurred. It is arguable whether the disaster was people-made, since rivers in the flood plains continually suffered avulsion and channel migration. Changing sea levels had impacts on river courses upstream, but human activity may have tipped the balance. A more or less abrupt change in the main course of the Euphrates occurred. Those who controlled ample supplies of water found that there was no longer enough to support their people and this led to the disintegration of southern Mesopotamian culture and a new pattern of urban settlements emerged.

The picture that slowly emerges over the centuries is one of local centres competing for access to water and irrigable land. Many argue that the most efficient way of using water is management by small-scale, locally organized operations. Such systems emerged repeatedly through the centuries in Mesopotamia after more grandiose irrigation schemes were buried under accretions of salt and silt.[31]

Nineveh, about 640 km north of modern Baghdad, became a royal city with the revival of Assyrian power in 1000 BC. Straddling the River Khasr on the east bank of the Tigris, Nineveh contained public squares and parks, wide boulevards, a botanical garden, and a zoo. The oldest known aqueduct brought water from hills nearly 50 km away to irrigate exotic plants and trees in the parks and gardens. At the height of its power, the city and its suburbs extended almost 50 km along the Khasr riverbanks.[32]

Nebuchadnezzar II, who reigned from 605 to 563 BC, restored many of the canals and much of the urban infrastructure of towns and cities in Babylonia. He built a new canal linking the Euphrates to the Tigris. However, he is most remembered for the rebuilding of Babylon itself, including new temples and palaces. His architects were also responsible for one of the world's greatest architectural masterpieces: the Hanging Gardens of Babylon. The gardens consisted of a series of irrigated terraces a hundred or more metres high planted with a great variety of trees. Water had to be raised from the Euphrates to a pool or reservoir on the highest terrace and then fed to the gardens below.[33]

Throughout later history, the Euphrates and Tigris have sometimes caused major problems for Iraq's cities. The waters of the Tigris and Euphrates are essential to the life of the country, but they may also threaten it. The rivers are at their lowest level in September and October and at flood in March, April and May when they may carry 40 times more water than at low mark. Moreover, one season's flood may be ten or more times as great as that in another year. In 1954, for example, Baghdad was seriously threatened, and dikes protecting it were nearly topped by the flooding Tigris.

The Indus Valley

In the Early Holocene (~ 10,000–7,000 years BP) warmer and wetter conditions in north-western South Asia allowed the Indus River to flow at full strength,[34] favouring expansion of mainly monsoon rain-fed agriculture based on wheat and barley production and supported by the domestication of cattle, sheep and goats (Table 8.11). By the third millennium BC the Harappan civilization had developed (see Chapter 1) achieving its main 'mature' phase from about 2600 to 1900 BC. The core region of the civilization was based along the Indus river valley, which has shifted its course since that time, and another river course, the paleo-Ghaggar-Hakra, the valley of which ran

Table 8.11: Summary of the relationship between climate, river channel change, agriculture and urban settlements in the Indus Valley (based in part on Gupta, et al., 2006)

Climate in the Indian subcontinent (years BP)	Agriculture	Population response
4000–3500 Intensification of dry phase, weakening of south-west monsoon, widespread droughts	Mixed agriculture, both *rabi* (winter) as well as *kharif* (rainy season) crops were grown; kharif crops include maze, millet, rice and a variety of lentils. This more diversified and extensive agriculture provided strategic risk buffering for smaller, local groups.	Indus people migrated to the east towards Ganga (Ganges) plain, fall of Indus civilization. De-urbanization starting 4200–4000 BP (Madella and Fuller, 2006).
7000–4000 Transitional phase with moderate rainfall, south-west monsoon shows step-wise weakening	Wheat and barley were main crops with a shift towards kharif crops.	Rise of Harappan civilization about 5500–5000 cal yrs BP in the face of a prolonged trend towards declining rainfall (Madella and Fuller, 2006), people start migrating to newer areas; traces of human settlement in Thar deserts as early as about 4800 BP.
10,000–7000 Humid phase, strongest south-west monsoon, major rivers like Indus in their full splendour	Winter crops like wheat and barley were main crops grown in Indus region. The higher precipitation would have increased flood levels in the river system and allowed more extensive cultivation on receding floods (Madella and Fuller, 2006).	Traces of first human settlement about 9000 BP in the Indus region near Mehrgarh (now in Pakistan).

parallel to the Indus at least during the Early to Mid-Holocene (Figure 8.3). During the period of the urban civilization it may have been more of a seasonal watercourse in places, but was nevertheless an important focus of settlement and agricultural production. Changes in river regimes and channel morphology greatly influenced cultural and urban development in the Indus Valley at this time.[35]

The original cities and many of the towns seemed to have been built right upon the shores of the river. The Indus, however, is destructive and unpredictable in its floods, and the cities were frequently levelled by the forces of nature. Mohenjo-Daro in the south, where the flooding can be fairly brutal, was rebuilt six times that we know about; Harappa in the north was rebuilt five times.

The massive citadels of Indus cities, which protected the Harappans from floods and attackers, were larger than most Mesopotamian ziggurats

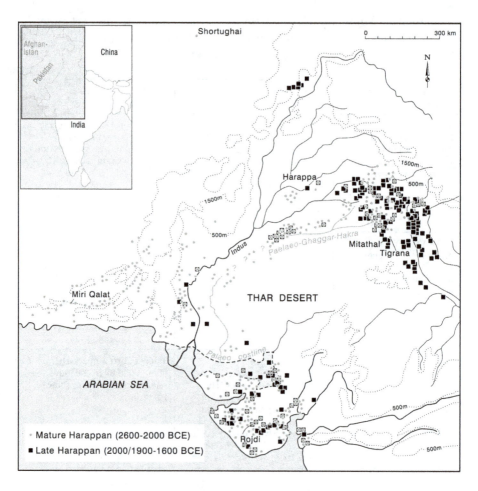

Figure 8.3: The Indus Valley, showing cities, other settlements and former river courses in Harappan times and the paleo-Ghaggar-Hakra, the valley of which ran parallel to the Indus at least during the Early to Mid-Holocene
(after Madella and Fuller, 2006)

and may have been deliberately built to divert floodwaters. Flat-bottomed boats used the rivers to carry goods and to connect to an extensive maritime trade. Instead of building canals, Indus civilization people may have built water diversion schemes, which – like terrace agriculture – can be elaborated by generations of small-scale labour investments. It should be noted that only the easternmost section of the Indus civilization people could build their lives around the monsoon, a weather pattern in which the bulk of a year's rainfall occurs in a four-month period; others had to depend on the seasonal flooding of rivers caused by snowmelt at high elevations.

Around 1800 BC, signs of a gradual decline began to emerge. The possible natural reasons for this are climate change and river regime and channel changes: tectonic events over the last 5 million years have redirected rivers in the Punjab that once flowed into the Ganges into the Indus, which is geologically the oldest river system in southern Asia.[36] These tectonic events, such as the Gujarat earthquake in 2002, that still affect parts of the region, will, over the millennia of human occupance, have contributed to changes in river courses and river regimes. For example, tectonic uplift may have contributed to the capture of the Ghaggar-Hakra headwaters by the Yamuna watershed and led to gradual desiccation during the Holocene, which was well underway by the period of the Harappan civilization (Figure 8.3). The final desiccation of some of these channels may have had major repercussions for the Harappan civilization and is considered a major factor in the de-centralization and de-urbanization of the late Harappan period.[37]

Significant climatic changes in the south Asian monsoon system occurred throughout the Holocene. The largest change happened around 2200 BC, which is about the time of the end of urban Harappan civilization in the Indus Valley. Geologic evidence suggests a reduction in Indus river discharge at that time. Consequently, sustained drought may have initiated the archaeologically recorded interval of south-eastward retreat of Harappan settlements and cultural activity.[38] Supporting evidence comes from lake sediments in south-eastern Arabia that indicate dry conditions around 2000 BC.[39]

Since independence in 1947, floods in the Indus River Basin in Pakistan have claimed more than 7,000 lives and caused massive infrastructure and crop losses. However less attention has been paid to flood damage reduction than to developing irrigation and hydropower. The underlying problem, and future aim, for flood policy will have to be to give greater attention to mitigating social vulnerability to flood hazards in the basin.[40] In the major Indus flood of 2010, embankments were breached to remove the pressure of floodwater on the Kotri Barrage, the last barrage over the Indus River and to save the cities of Hyderabad and Kotri. This led to flooding of low lying small cities such as Sajawal and Thatta and to a massive influx of people from flooded areas into Karachi.[41] In this way rural and urban lives were as intimately linked in the face of environmental hazards in the twenty-first century as they were four or five millennia before.

The Yangtze River

Urban development within the Yangtze basin has been threatened by flood hazards throughout history. The great cities of Chongqing, Wuhan, Nanjing and Shanghai and the major urban centres of Yichang, Shashi, Changsha,

Huangshi, Jiujiang, Anqing, Suzhou, Wuxi and Changzhou all lie along the river. During the Ming and Qing Dynasties (AD 1368–1911) 54 severe floods occurred in the middle basin of the Yangtze.[42] In the twentieth century, 18 severe floods, particularly those in 1905, 1931, 1954 and 1988 caused many deaths and much damage to cities. Over the years, flood defences and disaster management have greatly improved, so that deaths in 1998 (1,320) were many fewer than in 1954 (33,169) and 1931 (145,000). The cities generally have flood defences built to withstand a 1 in 100 year flood. Prolonged immersion in floodwater weakens many of the earth defences, but properly constructed concrete retaining walls generally function well. In 1998, breaches were quickly repaired because of the effective emergency actions and the involvement of the Chinese army.

All the streams flowing into the Yangtze may carry more flood runoff than before, from a given depth of rain, because deforestation and land development in the upper and middle basins has increased. Reservoirs, including the Three Gorge Dam retain some floodwater, but much water from tributaries enters the river below the big dam. Thus the cities have to cope not only with the increased surface water within their much expanded built-up area, but also with the loss of much of the traditional flood storage in lakes along the river due to land reclamation and an increased rural population. Far less water could be released from the river in 1998 than in 1994.[43] As on other major rivers, cities along the Yangtze cope with many floods, but episodically improve both their emergency flood response and their strategic engineered defences.

Flood impacts on cities on the Elbe and Rhine in Europe

Despite centuries of experience and long-established flood defences, extreme events will always risk exceeding the natural, designed capacities of river channels. One such event was an intense weather system that brought heavy rain over the Elbe catchment in Europe in August 2002. Rainfalls, typified by observations of 312 mm in 24 h and 406 mm in 72 h at Zinnwald-Georgenfeld, Germany, caused an extreme flood event, with a return period of 150–200 years, at the River Elbe at the Dresden gauge, where the river level at Dresden rose to a new record height, exceeding the peak of 1845.[44] In Germany, the estimated costs were at least €9.2 billion, and 19 people were killed. People were not expecting such a big flood. Only 11 per cent had adapted their houses to cope with floods, 9 per cent had installed their heating and other utilities on higher floors, 7 per cent had water barriers available and only 6 per cent had a flood adapted building structure, e.g. had an especially stable building foundation, or waterproof sealed cellar walls. Just 50 per cent of the households were insured against flood losses.[45] The flood motivated many people to implement private risk reduction measures, with 42 per cent of the households taking precautionary measures after the event. On the river basin scale, new projects examining the impacts of land-use change for storm runoff were implemented, working within the concepts that underlie the European Water Framework Directive.

The River Rhine experienced major historical floods in 840, 1152, 1172, 1260, and the catastrophic 'St Elisabeth's flood' in 1421 and major modern floods in 1993 and 1995. Flood prevention and navigation requirements have heavily influenced the characteristics of the Rhine. Prior to the nineteenth century, upstream of Worms the Rhine was a multi-channel braided river system and below the city it was meandering.[46] However in order to reduce flooding, the Upper Rhine was canalized between 1817 and 1890.[47] Later and up to 1955, to improve navigation, engineers straightened and embanked the main branch. The works enabled floodwaters to pass downstream much more rapidly.[48] This probably contributed, in the 1993 flood, to the way the peak flows in the Rhine and the Moselle came together almost simultaneously. The resulting peak downstream at Cologne was so high and prolonged that the mobile wall erected to protect the old city was overtopped for about 70 hours.[49] Facing the severe damages caused by the floods of 1993 and 1995, the Ministers of the Environment of France, Germany, Belgium, Luxembourg and the Netherlands (with the agreement of Switzerland) declared on 4 February 1995 in Arles that they deemed it necessary to reduce flood-related risks as rapidly as possible. The Flood Action Plan of the International Commission for the Protection of the Rhine (IKSR) has the overall objective of reducing flooding for the benefit of the whole Rhine basin. Such integrated river basin management of the large rivers of Europe shows that cities can no longer just consider the safety of their own inhabitants but have to ensure that they work with other urban areas and with rural authorities so that the whole river basin functions effectively.

The Mississippi River; cities and embankments

Many ancient towns adapted to potential dangers from rivers by constructing mounds so that buildings were above annual flood levels. The ancient Egyptians did so in the Nile Delta.[50] However, the French colonists in Louisiana did not build their settlements on mounds, they merely built raised walls, or levees, round their towns to keep floodwaters out, as around New Orleans in the 1700s. Levees were also seen as the solution when Americans built Sacramento in California and Cairo at the confluence of the Ohio and Mississippi.[51] The Mississippi has experienced many floods, among the worst being those of 1874, 1882, 1890, 1912, 1927, 1993 and 2008. Breaches of the Mississippi embankment levees occurred frequently in the nineteenth century,[52] with Memphis, Shreveport, Vicksburg and New Orleans being badly affected by levee breaches in 1890. Cairo and cities further downstream were affected in 1912 and 1927, but Hurricane Katrina in 2005 caused the most damaging breaches for New Orleans.[53] Many towns and cities along the river have suffered repeatedly, financial losses increasing through time as, with the construction of levees, development has spread in the area protected by the levee. However, the levee is designed to withstand a particular magnitude of flood, such as that likely to occur on average once in 100 years. When a rare event occurs, such as the 1993 flood, the levee is overtopped and severe damage occurs. After 2008, emphasis, similar to that in Europe, was beginning to be placed on the functioning of the whole river basin and on designating where floodwaters could be directed by opening levees. Nearly all the affected towns and cities have relied on increasing protection and flood insurance, although in the floods of the 1990s, only 10 per cent of the residents of flooded areas had insurance.[54] Occasionally moving a town elsewhere has been tried. One of the most celebrated moves was that of the small community of Valmeyer, Illinois (about 900 inhabitants) that relocated on to a bluff 3.5 km away during the decade following its devastation by the 1993 Mississippi flood, the worst of a series of inundations its people had endured since 1910. Twenty-two government agencies spent around $28 million in creating the new settlement. In the process, they encouraged the people of Valmeyer to incorporate several sustainable design elements into their new town, including energy-efficient construction and passive solar technology.[55]

Snowmelt flooding and cities

Warm rain falling on snow has contributed to several major floods affecting European cities. Melting snow and frozen soil in the higher uplands contributed to the severe flooding on the River Rhine in Germany in January 1995 when Koblenz, at the confluence of the Rhine and Mosel suffered badly and in Cologne, the ancient city centre and some low-lying suburbs were flooded.[56] In 1999 melting of extensive snow cover in the high Alps and heavy rainfall produced flood peaks at the Rhine river level gauges at Basel and Maxau high enough to activate flood retention facilities along the Upper Rhine, avoiding floods in urban areas further downstream.[57]

More severe snowmelt related flooding occurs in Alpine valleys where high volumes of warm rainfall can cause extremely rapid snowmelt, creating disasters like those that affected the Guil valley in the French Alps in 1957, when whole villages on old alluvial fans were destroyed.

Large snow packs can accumulate rapidly in the north-eastern USA. Rapid melting of these large volumes of snow contributes to the flash flood hazard in many parts of the Appalachians, for example in south-west Virginia where a rural region is dotted with small towns and cities and which has two metropolitan cities, Roanoke to the east and Bristol to the west. The 19–22 January 1996 flood there, produced by the rapid melting of 1 to 1.4 m of snow that had fallen over the previous two weeks was termed 'The Great Melt Down'.[58] In the Baltimore–Washington area, on 18 January 1996, there was an extremely rapid thaw brought on by temperatures of 15–18°C along with high dew point temperatures and heavy rain. The sudden snowmelt caused the Potomac River to rise close to levels not seen since flooding caused by Tropical Storm Agnes in 1972. Many small streams and creeks flooded after the rain and the extremely rapid snowmelt, affecting many smaller settlements.

In the Pacific Northwest of Canada and the USA the large river basins produce snowmelt floods that last for days or even weeks, but which are predictable. However, rainfall events produce flashier, less predictable floods, either from intense rainstorms or from rain-on-snow events.[59] For example, the major floods of 1948 in the Fraser and Columbia basins resulted from spring snowmelt. Snow continued to accumulate in the basins until mid-May due to cool weather. A sudden change to very warm weather over large parts of British Columbia led to high snowmelt rates which produced floods along many rivers. On the other hand, local flooding in Vancouver and surrounding areas in late December 2008 and early January 2009 was the result of warm rain falling on accumulated snow in the city streets.

Storm surges and tsunamis

Storm surges are created by changes in atmospheric pressure and associated wind stress. They are particularly severe in shallow seas where strong onshore winds associated with low pressure systems can drive seawater against the coast, creating a surge.[60] When the surge combines with a high tide, an additional 2–3 m can be added to the high water level, potentially overtopping natural defences such as coastal dunes, or sea walls and tidal barriers. Analysis of surges in the Osaka area of Japan[61] shows that the average interval between storm surge disasters in the area is 150 years, close to the recurrence interval for the 1934 Moroto typhoon that produced a surge of almost 3 m. The typhoon and storm surge destroyed schools, houses and factories, decimating the great Osaka cotton industry. During the preceding decades much land has been reclaimed from the sea and the built-up area had expanded greatly. After 1934 a typhoon warning system was developed and 1,323 ha of embankments were built in low-lying areas. This combination proved to be highly effective in reducing storm surge damage. After 1945 old dikes damaged by the Second World War bombing and by land subsidence were rebuilt. Further work started after another storm surge in 1950 with the building of 250 km of embankments along the rivers flowing through the city and the construction of large tidal barrier gates. When the Daini Muroto storm surge and typhoon struck in 1961, over 100,000 people were already taking refuge in public buildings and there were no human casualties, with the only property damage being due to water overtopping the dikes.[62]

Similar storm surge problems have arisen from hurricanes tracking northwards along the east coast of North America. In late August, 1954,

Hurricane Carol produced a storm surge that affected towns and cities from Long Island to Maine, causing havoc in small recreational harbours such as New Bedford, Marblehead, Narragansett Bay, Martha's Vineyard and Nantucket. Four previous hurricanes in 1635, 1638, 1815 and 1938 produced storm surges of over 3 m height in southern Rhode Island.[63]

Tropical storms are not the only forms of low pressure weather systems causing storm surges. Deep temperate latitude depressions have produced a series of events that have affected cities on the coasts of western Europe. On 1 February 1953 winds and low pressure caused a surge in the southern North Sea. In the Netherlands, 50 dikes broke simultaneously and waters flooded 133 towns and villages. Belgium and Britain were also affected. The Thames Barrier was constructed a few kilometres downstream of the City of London a few years later, but by 2011 there was another proposal for a bigger barrage further down the estuary.[64] Many of the reinforcements and extensions to the line of flood defence put in place in the UK after 1953 will approach the end of their design life before 2020.[65]

Coastal protection in the Netherlands has a long history. A key philosophy was set out by Andries Vierlingh (1507–79) who was engaged in a range of hydraulic engineering activities: river works, polders, sea defence and the closing of dike breaches that resulted from storm surges. Vierlingh argued for working with nature, using the natural coastal dunes as the main element to protect low-lying areas, with engineers augmenting the sand supply to beaches and reinforcing natural processes.[66] This philosophy was largely maintained until the 1953 disaster, after which a hard engineering solution, the Delta Plan, saw the mouths of the distributary channels of the rivers Rhine and Mass endiked with huge walls. In the Netherlands, the safety level against coastal flooding is now defined in law as designing flood protection works for the probability of one storm-surge event in 10,000 years for the provinces of Holland, and 1 in 4,000 years for Zeeland, Friesland and Groningen. While the Dutch, with so much of their densely populated urban areas lying below sea level, have emphasized keeping the water out, American policies were more oriented at flood hazard mitigation. Warning systems and evacuation programmes aimed to get people out of harm's way. Some states and the federal government established coastal regulations, including the National Flood Insurance Program. The different emphasis reflects differing cultural attitudes to the role of the state, the Dutch being willing for the government to spend much more on keeping the water out, perhaps because so many of them are aware of the risk of living below sea level.

Tsunamis are long period, long wavelength, low amplitude surface waves produced by submarine or coastal earthquakes. A tsunami 200 km long and 0.25 m high delivers 50,000 tonnes of seawater per metre of coastline. While any coastline can be affected, those of the Pacific and Indian Oceans are particularly vulnerable, Japan being one of the Pacific Rim countries most often experiencing tsunamis (Table 8.12). Virtually every part of the

Table 8.12: Tsunamis affecting Japanese towns and cities

Date	Urban areas affected	Deaths (if known)
684	Haluho	
869	**Sendai**	1,000
887	Ninna Nankai	
1293	**Kamakura**	
1361	Setsu, **Awa**, Yukimoto,	1,000s
1498	Meio Nankai, **Wakayama** port	
1500	Totono	
1605	Keicho Nankai, Shishikui, **Awa**, Kannoura	5,000
1614	Takata, Etigo	
1677	Miyako, Rikuchu, Tsugara, Namba	
1698	Seikaido-Nankaido	
1703	Sagami, **Awa**, Kazusa, Oshima, Musasi	5,233
1707	Tosa, **Osaka**	
1737	**Kamaishi**	1,000s
1741	Sapporo	1,474
1792	Shimbara	
1854	Nankai, Tokai, Kyushu, **Wakayama**, Tokaido, Shikoku, **Osaka**	1,443
1855	Tokyo	4,500+
1896	Meiji Sanriku: **Kamaishi**	28,000
1923	Yokohama, Enoshima, **Kamakura**, Chigasaki	2,144
1933	Taro, Yoshihama, Ofunato, Akazaki	3,064
1944	Towns from Choshi to Tosashimizu	1,223
1946	Kushimoto and Kainan	2,000
1964	**Niigata** City	
1983	Akita, Sakata, Noshiro	104
1993	Kushiro, Hokkaido	
2007	**Niigata**	
2011	Soma, **Sendai**, Ishinomaki	25,000

Note: Places mentioned more than once are highlighted in bold type

Japanese coastline has been affected by tsunamis on several occasions, many towns appearing more than once in Table 8.12. Building sea defences and encasing their steep, gravel-laden rivers between concrete walls have been key tasks for Japanese coastal engineers. As the 2011 earthquake off north-eastern Honshu showed,[67] extreme events still put thousands of people at risk from the biggest tsunamis.

Small fully urbanized rivers and streams

Greater Manchester, UK and the surrounding towns occupy most of the upper part of the River Mersey basin. The steep headwater streams rise on the peat covered moorlands of the Pennines, but in the eighteenth century their water power was harnessed to power machinery in cotton mills and urban settlement spread up the deeply incised valleys. Shorter streams on the plain to the west of the Pennines are now all fully urbanized. During the nineteenth century increasing industrialization led to many mills, works and factories directly discharging waste, including ashes and cinders, into tributaries of the Mersey. Notable cases were in the upper reaches of the Irwell where, before 1870, half the capacity of the channel was lost by dumped coal waste, furnace residues and cinders from domestic fireplaces. The silt in the river below Salford built up so much that whereas vessels of 1.5 m draught reached the wharves in 1840, by 1860 vessels of 1 m draught had difficulties, and at the lowest flows no vessels could pass.[68] Around 1870, Salford township took upstream townships to court for dumping ashes and debris in the river and causing this problem. Reduced channel capacity led to frequent flooding and to many flood alleviation proposals, including a tunnel to divert water from above the city centre of Manchester, beneath a ridge to a point 1.5 km below the city.[69] Although the tunnel was not built, the channel was straightened decades later following a major flood in 1926. After another flood in 1980, flood storage basins were eventually constructed in the meander belt upstream of Salford.

The cinders and debris in the Irwell at Salford form one illustration of the problems of sediment in urban rivers. Mining often creates similar problems. Hydraulic mining was invented in the mountains of the Yuba River Basin, California, USA in 1853 and produced vast amounts of sediment through the 1870s which caused rapid aggradation and exacerbated the pre-existing flooding affecting the city of Sacramento and many smaller towns. The building of levees for flood protection has a long and complex history, involving court cases, state and federal intervention, including the setting up of the California Debris Commission[70] (Table 8.13). Even without sedimentation, floods were not contained within channels, but were largely conveyed through a system of lowland basins. In the early twentieth century, an innovative channel bypass system was

Table 8.13: Progress in the management of
urban soil erosion and sedimentation risk

Date	Country	Action
1870	UK	Royal Commission on Pollution of Rivers
1893	USA	California Debris Commission created by Congress in 1893 to facilitate navigation and flood control
1899	USA	Section 10 – Rivers and Harbors Act: regulates 'all work or structures' placed in or affecting the navigational waters of the US and sediment discharge to such waters
1968	USA	Soil Conservation Service issues 'Standards and Specification for Soil Erosion and Sediment Control in Urbanizing Areas'
1977	USA	Clean Water Act: reduces discharge of pollutants into lakes, rivers, streams and wetlands
1980	Australia	NSW urban soil capability scheme for urban and associated land uses
1987	Australia	NSW Total Catchment Management Policy ensures land is used within its capability
1995	Malaysia	Soil Erosion Guidelines issued by Department of the Environment include urban erosion control
1996	Australia	Soil Erosion and Sediment Control, Engineering Guidelines for Queensland Construction Sites published by Institution of Engineers, Australia
2000	Europe	Water Framework Directive adopted: regulates pollutants, including sediment, entering rivers
2003	Australia	'Best Practice Erosion and Sediment Control' published
2005	USA	Updated 'NY Standards and Specification for Erosion and Sediment Control' issued
2010	Malaysia	New Guidelines for Erosion and Sediment Control in Malaysia issued

adopted that emulates the natural system by routing excess flood waters over a series of weirs and through broad, channelized bypasses that cross the basins.

Similar problems arose through hydraulic tin mining in Malaysia, where the Selangor River was so affected by mining debris that the town of Kuala Kubu had to be rebuilt on a new site on the valley side away from the river. In the late twentieth century, the environmental effects of urban growth in the Kuala Lumpur and Pulau Pinang areas included severe urban soil erosion with areas undergoing construction usually experiencing sediment yields two to three orders of magnitude greater than those under natural forest. The eroded sediment builds up in stream channels passing through cities, reducing their channel capacity and thus increasing the frequency of flooding. Federal government legislation enabling local authorities to exert greater control over the layout and management of construction sites, and an urban drainage design standards and procedures manual for mainland Malaysian conditions (Table 8.13) appear to have encouraged developers in the Federal Territory of Kuala Lumpur to take a more responsible approach to building site layout and management.[71]

In New South Wales, Australia, in the 1970s, the expanding town of Bathurst began to experience more flooding than usual as soil was eroded from construction sites upstream of the town. Sediment reduced the capacity of the river channel through the town and gullies eroded in the bare areas of new subdivisions carried stormwater into the river rapidly.[72] The city council asked the New South Wales Soil Conservation Service to help. A revised plan for street layouts and grassed waterways was adopted and the Soil Conservation Service began an urban soil conservation programme (Table 8.13). The Soil Conservation Service developed guidelines for reducing urban erosion and sedimentation similar to those used in the USA.[73] These came to be re-developed 25 years later for the design of sustainable urban drainage systems. All follow the principle of slowing down surface runoff, reducing peak water and sediment flows by using vegetation to reduce velocities and allow sediment to be trapped and water to infiltrate into the ground.

The buried rivers of cities

Just north-west of the city of London, Hampstead Heath was the source of the Holebourne, which just above its junction with the Thames was known as the River Fleet.[74] On the Heath it was diverted into a series of ponds from the sixteenth century onwards for 'drawing the springs about Hampstead Heath into one head' in order to improve the water supply of the city and to maintain the flow of the river.[75] By that time, however, the lower reaches of the Fleet in the City of London were already receiving discharges from tanneries and wastes from local enterprises. In 1598, John Stow wrote that the Fleet was 'impassable for boats, by reason of the many encroachments thereon made, by the throwing of offal and other garbage by butchers, sauce men and others and by the reason of the many houses of office standing over upon it'.[76] Gradually the Fleet became covered, starting close to its confluence with the Thames and working upstream towards Hampstead Heath. In 1733, the stretch from Fleet Bridge to Holborn (Holebourne) Bridge was covered. In 1739 the Stacks Market, demolished to build the Mansion House, was rebuilt over the Fleet. When the Regent's Canal was built in 1812, the Fleet was covered further north to Camden Town and during the nineteenth century the remainder upstream to the Heath was covered.[77] In the mid-nineteenth century, the Midland Railway company was compelled by the authorities to divert 'the black and foetid torrent' of the Fleet into a huge cast iron conduit under the new St Pancras Station, as well as enclosing its course a little further upstream at Kentish Town.[78]

Sometimes, the burying of rivers was seen as a way of improve the health of a city. In the Middle Ages the navigation on the River Senne in Brussels was the main way in which goods were brought into the city.[79] However, heavy rains often caused floods in the lowest parts of the city. Over the centuries, the river grew more and more polluted and it was thought that when the river flooded, its contaminated water caused disease. In 1867, the Mayor of Brussels, Jules Anspach, used the outbreak of an epidemic of cholera as an opportunity for urban redevelopment. Anspach convinced the city council that covering the River Senne would make the city more salubrious. Furthermore, covering the river would create land on which a network of rectilinear, Parisian-style boulevards could be constructed. Anspach realized this ambitious project by expropriating the properties that lined the river.[80] The underground Senne was further diverted for Metro construction in the 1950s and in the 1970s the pré-métro (underground tramway line) was built along the former bed of the Senne.

Deculverting ('daylighting') buried rivers and streams

The idea of covering a polluted river was adopted by councillors in Rochdale, Greater Manchester, UK at the beginning of the twentieth century. Between 1904 and 1926 successive sections of the River Roch in the town centre were covered by ferro-concrete arches. By 1994 severe deterioration of much of the concrete led to many repairs of the 'widest bridge', the buried section of the river. In 1995–7, much repair work was undertaken. However, in the town's 2010 strategy for regeneration, the council emphasizes the role of water spaces in the city and proposes the deculverting of the Roch and the creation of an attractive water feature in the town centre.

One of the best known examples of deculverting, or daylighting, is the Cheonggyecheon River restoration project in the centre of Seoul, South Korea.[81] An elevated highway was demolished and the river opened up with pedestrian access and tree planting. The project's overriding goal was to restore the ecological characteristics that used to exist along the open river. It also improved Seoul's landscape, economy and attractiveness to tourists. Many daylighting projects have been undertaken in US cities such as Denver, CO, but these are mainly in suburban areas where there is room to create a vegetated riparian zone. Other examples are the daylighting of Spanish Banks Creek and Thain Creek in Vancouver, Canada and restoration of the River Alt in Merseyside, UK.[82]

In the USA an aquatic ecosystem restoration and protection project has to be able to improve the quality of the environment and be both in the public interest and cost-effective.[83] Culverts can alter local river and wetland habitats by modifying substrate, altering flow, reducing algal and plant growth and dissociating the stream from the surrounding terrestrial environment. Removing may therefore lead to an improvement in aquatic and marginal habitats. The major deculverting scheme on the River Quaggy, in Greenwich, London achieved such outcomes and gained several 'best practice' awards.[84]

Deculverting schemes can deliver multiple benefits, including positive economic, environmental and social impacts. Not all deliver aquatic benefits sufficient for a local nature reserve, as happened on the River Quaggy and not all provide the positive city visitor attractions of the Cheonggyecheon River. However, the relatively sparse evidence available in 2011[85] showed the need to assess every proposal carefully and to integrate river works with other aspects of urban greening and urban regeneration.

CONCLUSION

Urban life requires living within environmental constraints and adapting to changes within those constraints, whether they are due to human action or to extreme natural events. Throughout the history of urban settlement, people have responded to disaster in the following months and years by building defences and making plans for the next emergency. However, as the memory of the disaster fades, settlements expand, often into riskier sites, on unstable slopes, on soils that will shake violently in earthquakes, into potential paths of lava or onto flood plains. Gradually the space for flows of water, snow or lava may be reduced. River channels may be narrowed and also suffer from accumulations of sediment and debris. Generally, actions in one part of an urban area may be increasing risks in another.

Many governments have encouraged the investigation of potential risks by defining flood hazard zones, putting restrictions on the development of flood plains, mapping landslides and classifying slopes according to their suitability for particular types of urban land use. Occasionally however, a change of government may lead to a party in favour of 'small' government, abolishing or relaxing planning regulations and guidance, and thus allowing building in potentially hazardous areas. Other administrations have developed disaster response procedures, warning systems and various types of insurance against hazards. Most of these actions have been prompted by particular tragic events, but the loss of life from the types of hazard described in this chapter has decreased most in affluent cities. Where people live in poverty in informal urban settlements, their vulnerability remains high. Their recovery after disaster is often long-delayed, as the slow reconstruction and regeneration of Port-au-Prince, Haiti shows.

The clear message from earth science for every citizen is 'Know the ground you build on'. People buying or renting property should find out what risks affect the site: Is it on a flood plain? Is there a subsidence or slope failure risk? What was on the site before: am I buying something built on a filled-in quarry or over an ancient mine? The other important element is knowledge of what any construction activity or re-direction of drainage water might do to the stability of the ground and behaviour of excessive rainwater or flood flows. Urban environmental history is full of examples of what has happened in many cities. However, that history is not readily available. Sometimes this is because subtle steps are taken to reduce publicity about risks. Gradually, through production and electronic distribution, flood and earthquake risk maps are becoming more accessible through agency websites. However both climate change and new urban development can alter storm runoff patterns and change stresses on slopes and soils, making projections of flood frequencies and earthquake impacts based upon past events likely to be unreliable.

9

Urban Greenspaces

The Tamed and Wild Nature in Cities

OPEN SPACE IN CITY PLANNING

A modern city has a huge variety of open spaces, from paved squares to remnants of ancient woodland or heath whose basic vegetation has been unchanged for centuries. Urban vegetation colonizes many surfaces, even walls, cracks in paving, roofs, and ill-maintained drains. All urban vegetation provides habitats for other organisms. It also performs critical functions in the urban circulations of energy, water and materials. It uses rainwater, reduces urban warming, provides shade and wind breaks, retards the flow of surface water to rivers and absorbs pollutants. These ecosystem services are becoming more and more important in reducing the impacts of both local and global environmental change and can help cities adapt to climate change. Urban vegetation can introduce a variety of emotions. Some landscapes will attract people, make them feel calm and at ease, help them to reduce stress and produce a feeling of well-being. However, shady trees encroaching on a narrow ill-lit path along which commuters walk in dark evenings, may induce feelings of fear and insecurity. People react to urban nature in different ways and this influences what they do with their private gardens and how they use public open spaces.

The green open spaces range from cemeteries and churchyards to canal banks, reservoirs and patches of derelict land. They include private gardens of all shapes and sizes, city squares, suburban golf courses, sports grounds, lawns around institutional buildings, offices and town halls, railway cuttings and embankments, highway reservations, and derelict land. Particularly important are remnants of the countryside that get surrounded by suburbs yet become treasured accessible open space, such as the urban commons in great cities. Nevertheless, for many people, the urban greenspaces that matter are their own gardens, if they are fortunate enough to possess them, and the public recreation areas, be they parks, river valley reserves, commons, heaths or woodlands.

Reserves, greenways, parks, plazas, squares, and promenades make up a regional to local hierarchy of open-spaces serving a variety of uses: nature conservation; education and community events; active recreation; playgrounds for the youngest; strolling grounds for the oldest; all comprising a set of foci for the community. Only by providing all the elements of this hierarchy can planning authorities ensure that people enjoy the quality of life planning regulations and legislation are intended to promote. Care has to be taken to design the open spaces to meet specific needs, and to avoid them being the odd patch of green that is left over after the developer has finished laying out the houses.[1]

These greenspaces can form networks or wildlife corridors that bring multiple ecosystem services to the people of cities (Figure 9.1). By the early twenty-first century local authorities were being encouraged to map the urban green infrastructure and develop policies for enhancing the integrity of greenspace networks (Figure 9.2). As the benefits of green areas were demonstrated in terms of adaptation to climate change, human physical and mental health, sustainable urban drainage, biodiversity, recreation and visual amenity, national governments tried to engage with professional and civil society organizations to achieve objectives akin to those of the English Green Infrastructure Partnership:[2]

- more Green Infrastructure planned and successfully delivered at the local, citywide and landscape level;
- more green space in England's towns and cities (including street trees, gardens, green roofs, community forests, parks, rivers, canals, wetlands);
- better connected networks of ecological habitats and biodiversity;
- More accessible and connected green space that meets communities' (social, economic and environmental) needs;
- better resilience and adaptation to climate change/flooding;
- better management of green infrastructure over the long term.

The motivations for creating parks and other urban spaces in cities have varied through time and across cultures. Originally parks were largely luxuries for royalty, ruling elites and the wealthy. However people usually had relatively free access to spaces on the fringes of cities. They were also places of entertainment for the masses, exemplified by the circuses of ancient Rome. Ancient cities had agriculture and market gardening both within and just outside the walls, creating productive greenspaces that would have supported populations of insects, birds and mammals. Many ancient gardens also had their own aquatic ecosystems in fish ponds. Nonetheless, there is a persistent theme through urban history of private parks and gardens for the elite and entertainment grounds for the masses. Perhaps this is reflected in the contrast between football stadia visitor attractions, with their megastores, stadium tours and football club museums, and elite, and sometimes exclusive, private golf and country clubs in the modern world.

Figure 9.1: The Water of Leith, Edinburgh, Scotland an urban greenspace wildlife corridor (photo Ian Douglas)

ANCIENT CIVILIZATIONS AND PARKS AND GARDENS

Records from ancient Egypt show that both horticulture and designed enclosed gardens flourished in the Nile Valley in the fourth dynasty. The early Egyptians described trees being transplanted with balls of soil over 4,000 years ago.[3] Ancient Persia and Assyria had great hunting grounds in which there developed an artistic treatment of nature that evolved into the concept of a park. Enclosed gardens also flourished, with the Hanging Gardens of Babylon being the finest example. The Greeks had palace gardens in Mycenaean times, Homer describing the gardens at Alcinous. The philosophers frequented quiet shaded public gardens such as the Lyceum in Athens.

Roman gardens were largely private spaces, flourishing under the inspiration of Lucullus, whose gardens in the Pincian were considered to be among the most elaborate of the imperial properties. Nero (Emperor from AD 54–68) built his Golden House in a 100 ha park, on land compulsorily purchased, extending from the Palatine Hill across the valley to the Esquiline. In the valley was an artificial lake surrounded by features such as pavilions, grottoes, fountains, columns and gazebos. After Nero's death the palace became a public

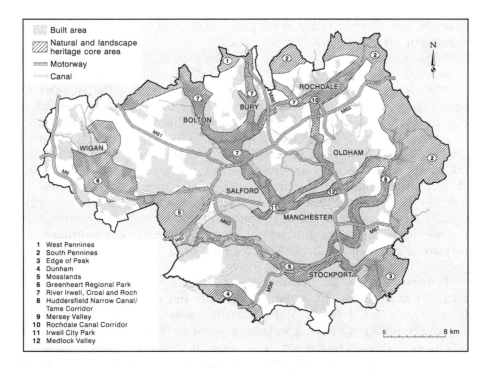

Figure 9.2: The green infrastructure of Greater Manchester
(mapped as natural and landscape heritage core area)

building. It is not clear whether the public then had access to the gardens, but if they did, it would be an early example of the conversion of royal gardens to public open space. However, the Golden House was badly damaged by fire in AD 104.[4]

Subsequently the Baths of Trajan were built over part of its ruins. Trajan also constructed a new Forum, a formal, paved open space, quite different from the gardens of the Golden House. Many private villas in the city had significant gardens,[5] but public open space was more restricted in extent.

Islamic legislation on the preservation of trees and plants was laid down in about AD 600. The Prophet Muhammad declared the uncultivated trees in and around the holy cities of Makkah and Madinah to be protected. Caring for trees was seen as a duty expected of early Muslims.[6] The rise of Islam brought another influence on urban landscape design which saw the development of the concept of the garden as paradise, an oasis with water and cypress in the desert. The design is essentially abstract, but involves a high level of technology to irrigate the plants, provide cooling jets of water, have orchards for shade, and maintain the walls and their decoration. The seventeenth-century Taj Mahal, a far later creation than the fourteenth-century gardens of the Alhambra in

Granada, was made accessible to the public in the will of Shah Jahan, another example of the opening up of royal parks.

In contrast to the abstract formality of the Islamic gardens are the densely vegetated and highly ornamented gardens of the ancient Chinese palaces. Highly contrived and carefully tended, these parks bring the wonders of nature and human skills together. Artificial hills, grottoes and lakes abound in Chinese parks. Romanticism and tradition drive much of the design of parks in Beijing. For example, the Qiong (Jade) Island in Beihai Park is designed after a fairyland believed to be out in the open sea. Beihai Park dates back to the tenth century in the Liao Dynasty when a pleasure palace called Yaoyu (Jade Islet) was built on the site. More structures were built subsequently, but the design centred around the White Dagoba on the Qiong Island, with temples on the southern side of an artificial hill, and halls and pavilions on the northern side.[7] In the thirteenth century, Kubla Khan ordered that trees be planted along all public roads in Beijing, China, to provide shade and to indicate the edges of streets during snow.[8]

Japanese gardens and parks have a unique beauty stemming from attention to combinations of natural elements and compositional harmony. In the Heian Period (AD 795–1185), courtiers sought relief from oppressive summer humidity by having waterfalls, small streams and ponds in their private gardens. Built on the southern side of the house, the garden was often created as a simulation of the Buddhist Garden of Paradise.[9] Modifications to the principles of Japanese design occurred as the ideals of regimes changed over subsequent centuries, but themes of balanced, harmonious design and the sense of peace and tranquillity remained. The tradition of using gardens to modify the household microclimate also persisted. Trees and shrubs are planted in the garden where their natural evapotranspiration process cooled the air. While providing shade, plants allowed breezes to add to the cooling process. A *hishaku* (a wooden cup with a rod) was often used to sprinkle water over leaves, stones and the ground to cool the air by evaporation. Garden ponds added to the evaporative effects, so helping to achieve cooling of the household during the hot and humid Japanese summer.[10]

FOUR TRADITIONS OF PARK DESIGN

From these differing origins four main traditions of park design have impinged on the development of urban open spaces since the expansion of cities was triggered by the industrial revolution at the end of the eighteenth century: the formal park (sometimes called the baroque style);[11] the pleasure grounds and parks for active recreation (sometimes designed according to the romantic ideal of natural arrangements of plants and trees);[12] the Islamic tradition of abstract design; and fourthly, the Chinese and Japanese traditional styles. The concept of the formally laid out park is associated with a royal palace that was later made available to the public, essentially for passive

Figure 9.3: The 'Prehistoric' park at Shenzhen, China (photo Ian Douglas)

recreation. This was often the urban equivalent of the landscaped parks attached to the great European chateaux and country houses. The newer tradition of pleasure grounds and parks for active recreation is often said to be deliberately created to help the workers of the city and their children engage in healthy team games and other sports. These parks paid much more attention to facilities for visitors than to creating harmonious and visually exciting landscapes. Nonetheless, some, such as the Parc Josephat in Brussels, managed to provide both fairly successfully. The third, Islamic tradition involved walled, abstract design gardens, with an emphasis on water and shade. The fourth persists as a continuing tradition of symbolic, highly contrived and managed parks in China and Japan. Even in the burgeoning new Chinese cities, like Shenzhen, parks are being created with traditional landscape elements, often containing artificial hills and caves (Figure 9.3).

The impacts of these four traditions has to be set against a growing awareness of biodiversity and the value of wilderness and the desire to experience 'wild nature' in, or close to, cities. Gradually there emerged a shift away from the more formal parks for passive or active recreation, to quasi-natural areas with urban nature reserves and lighter management regimes. This has produced a great variety of open spaces in urban areas. Even those readily accessible to the public vary greatly in form and function, but often there is an uneven distribution of parks of different types in relation to the social character of different parts of any city. A question that was current throughout the nineteenth century is still relevant: who were the parks really for and who benefited most from the public investment in them?

Today in some sectors of major urban areas, parts of parks and many smaller open spaces have become 'no go' areas because young people with little to do, or the homeless, or drug addicts may congregate in them. As always the uses and users of parks reflect the culture and society of the area in which they are located. However, some of the intentions of the creators of parks, particularly in the nineteenth century involved both social and environmental engineering, the creation of a better society and a better landscape. By the twentieth century planners were setting open space standards and by the twenty-first century they were achieving multiple uses from urban greenspace, especially in the context of protecting biodiversity and adapting to climate change.

An alternative approach to understanding the motivations behind the creation and design of urban parks and greenspaces is to look at them in terms of culture and national ideals. To a certain extent, the Chinese, Japanese and Islamic traditions can be seen in this context, but a detailed look at three Baltic cities suggests more subtle contrasts.[13] Helsinki was planned to have open spaces as much to imitate other cities such as Paris, whereas Stockholm's open space was influenced by nascent environmental movements and the spread of the city over an archipelago. St Petersburg's growth was the more erratic climbing steeply during the early twentieth century and then dropping after losing its status as a capital and because of the Second World War.

The provision of open space in St Petersburg was strongly influenced by ideology, especially that of Howard's *garden cities* until it was dismissed as utopian and petty bourgeois in the late 1920s.[14] On the other hand, American cities have long retained evidence of the rural lifestyles of the early European settlers who first established them. In 1662, William Penn designed Philadelphia to have five open spaces of 5–10 hectares each.[15] Following the revolution, American cities found a new identity, with an emphasis on incorporating nature in urban design as well as seeing nature as a source of moral virtue. The commission charged with selecting a capital for the state of Mississippi in 1821 recommended that the new capital have every other block filled with native vegetation or be planted with groves of trees. The commission felt that this would provide a more healthy environment and also easier fire control for a city largely built of wood.[16]

THE EVOLUTION OF GREENSPACE IN LONDON

Roman London probably had large spaces of open ground within its walls that were not built-up in the fourth century AD. The areas within the walls were still not wholly built over in the Middle Ages, with orchards and gardens right in the heart of the city. Just outside the city, the general public had the right to hunt wild animals in any unenclosed lands outside the protected royal forests. Chasing animals with dogs and bow in Southwark Woods would have been a typical afternoon's recreation.[17] Slightly further out from the city, Blackheath, in the south-east was a common grazing ground for prehistoric people, a place for temporary military camps and of ceremonial gatherings from 1000 to 1660. The heath was split between the manors of Greenwich and Lewisham, the portion in Greenwich becoming the royal park attached to Greenwich Palace (later to be re-opened to the people) while that in Lewisham remained a common, albeit, in part encroached upon by special developments.[18] In 1871 the management of Blackheath was transferred to the Metropolitan Board of Works, then to the London County Council, and finally to the London Borough of Lewisham. Wandsworth and Wimbledon Commons and Hampstead Heath have similar histories of multiple uses, but also have faced threats of encroachment and of being split by roads and ancient enclosure rights.[19] To the north-east of London, Epping Forest, part of the once huge Waltham Forest, had been a common grazing ground before William the Conqueror made it a royal forest in the eleventh century. The last king to hunt there was Charles II in the late seventeenth century. By 1793, the Land Revenue Commissioners were reporting that the 4,000 ha of common land were highly used for recreation by Londoners from the East End, but also that much sand and gravel was being dug illegally, turf had been removed from many areas, deer were stolen and encroachments and enclosures had occurred. The Corporation of the City of London had common rights over the whole of the forest and challenged all the enclosures that had taken place. Eventually the Corporation bought out all the rights of the lords of the manors around the forest and made Epping Forest available for the free enjoyment of the people of London.[20]

People have long fought to keep open space in their cities. In 1630 people living to the west of the city of London protested that Leicester Fields should not be taken from them to build new houses. A fragment of their success remains, the now paved Leicester Square. A few years later the resident's of Lincoln's Inn protested about proposals to build houses on Lincoln's Inn Fields. The Society of Lincoln's Inn insisted in 1638 that the fields be kept as a public park with walks. Despite their influence as lawyers, the society failed to win that battle, although parts of the fields have survived.[21] Hyde Park in London, a royal park, was opened to the public in 1635.[22] There were also protests, further west of the city, at Charles I's plans to enclose Richmond Park. His action in so doing greatly benefited future generations, Richmond Park now being one of the most remarkable open spaces in modern Greater London.[23]

In addition to these protected fragments of the previous rural landscape, new urban parks with entirely different purposes from the countryside they replaced were created. Henry VIII had St James' Park created from marshy land into a deer park, bowling green and tennis court. Charles II had it converted by Le Notre[24] into a pleasure ground with a canal which was converted into a lake when John Nash reorganized the park in 1827–9. Other parks originated in the late seventeenth century as private residential squares, beginning with a London building boom from 1713 to 1735 when Mayfair west to Hyde Park and north to Oxford Street was laid out in spacious squares and neat terraces. The gardens in places like Berkeley and Grosvenor Squares were laid out in formal beds following the classical (later termed Baroque) tradition. A second boom from 1763 to 1795 saw further development of both Mayfair and Bloomsbury.[25] Access to many of the gardens was (and in some cases still is) restricted. However the formal layouts were transferred to larger parks elsewhere.

At the same time there developed a series of parks for public amusement, or pleasure grounds, which were complete centres of entertainment with taverns and pavilions for eating, drinking, dancing and music. Starting with the Ranelagh Gardens in Chelsea, opened in 1742, with its lake, Chinese Pavilion and rococo rotunda, these pleasure grounds were quite different in purpose from the more formal parks on the nineteenth century.[26] However, Vauxhall Gardens with its Grand Walk and music, restaurants and entertainments stayed open until 1859.[27] In a way it was succeeded by the fun fair at Battersea Park in the twentieth century.

In 1810, Regents Park was custom designed as a public park by John Nash on royal land with upper class residential development around it. In the middle of the park, designed on the scale and in the manner of a large landscape garden, was a botanic garden (1830) established by the Royal Botanic Society and at its northern edge, a zoo (1826) founded by the London Zoological Society.[28] Again this was a park closely linked to the fine terraces of houses for the wealthy built on three sides of the park.

The 1833 UK Select Committee on Public Walks noted that 'during the last half century a very great increase has taken place in the population of large towns ... and little or no provision has been made for Public Walks or Open Spaces, fitted to afford means of exercise or amusement to the middle or humbler classes'.[29] In 1840, 30,000 people living in London's East End petitioned the government for a new park in their area. Four years later work started on the new Victoria Park which was enthusiastically appreciated by the people. It was followed by further large parks at Battersea (1858), Southwark and Finsbury (both opened in 1867), all laid out according to the fashion for formal Victorian parks with sweeping drives, ornamental lakes, bandstands and pavilions.[30]

Through the nineteenth century, concern for urban open space grew. Following the closure of all city burial grounds in London in 1852, there was a move to turn all the graveyards into parks and squares.[31] Octavia Hill, later a key activist in setting up the National Trust for England and Wales, wanted the small graveyards to become 'open-air sitting rooms for the poor'. This enthusiasm led to the founding in 1882 of the Metropolitan Public Gardens Association which protected some 500 churchyards some of which still provide patches of calm in central London. In 1883, Octavia Hill wrote an appeal for funds to buy and preserve as open space the field between Marylebone and Hampstead in London, where the working people of Lisson Grove and Portland Town had been accustomed to stroll. In the 1860s, the Society for the Preservation of Commons in the Neighbourhood of London had helped to secure the preservation of areas such as Wimbledon Common and Epping Forest, several kilometres further from the city centre. Meanwhile, the legal basis for the acquisition and management of open space in London was provided by the Metropolitan Open Spaces Act 1877.[32] By 1904, the provision of open spaces began to become regarded as a duty of local authorities in the UK. The Interdepartmental Committee on Physical Deterioration recommended that in building by-laws, attention should be paid to the preservation of open spaces and also that a duty should be imposed on local authorities of providing and maintaining open spaces in some definite proportion to the density of population.[33] This foreshadowed the development of open space standards that were gradually adopted through the twentieth century. Park provision was good for people and planning authorities and developers were expected to work towards providing adequate urban open spaces as part of the social engineering that saw the design of new social housing estates for people living in dilapidated slums, and garden cities and suburbs for people who could afford to buy their own houses.

Many public parks were created by the acquisition of private parks. For example, in the 1920s, the Rothschild family sold Gunnersbury Park in west London to the local councils on condition that they used it for parkland. The estate was opened as a public park in 1926. The rapid expansion of London in the 1920s and 1930s led to greater attention to open space provision in new estates. Unwin recommended to the Greater London Regional Planning Committee in 1929 that 2.83 ha of open space should be provided per 1,000 population, with a private to public open space ratio of 3:4.[34] Specifically, the provision of playing fields was seen as a means of combating juvenile delinquency. Abercrombie's proposals for the County of London, drawn up in 1943–5 formed the basis for the parks and open spaces in London as seen today. The merits of open space were promoted for recreational use and promotion of healthy lifestyles. The poor distribution and deficiency of open space provision across London persuaded Abercrombie to set open space standards at 1.62 ha per 1,000 population and the development of a 'Parks System'. This was a connected set of spaces forming green wedges leading out to a 'Green Belt' around London. The Green Belt was formed from the countryside around London, safeguarded for weekend recreation and short breaks.[35]

Table 9.1: Categories of open space recognized in the UK Planning system

1. green spaces;
2. parks and gardens, including urban parks and formal gardens;
3. natural and semi-natural urban green spaces, including urban forestry, scrub, grasslands and open and running water;
4. green corridors, including river and canal banks, cycle-ways and rights of way;
5. outdoor sports facilities, including publicly and privately owned sports pitches, school or other institutional sports pitches, golf courses;
6. amenity green space, including informal recreation areas;
7. provision for children and young people, including play areas, skateboard parks, 'hanging out areas' and other informal areas;
8. allotments, including community gardens;
9. cemeteries and churchyards;
10. civic spaces;
11. civic squares; and other hard surfaced areas that have been designed for pedestrians.

London went a long way to providing the needed open space, especially in areas of regeneration and in new estates and the new towns. However, by the 1980s people were complaining of the neglect of public parks. The next 20 years saw a decline in the quality of parks across Britain, including most municipal parks in London. One 1995 report stated that although nationally eight million people visit parks every day, government and local authorities largely ignored their role in social and cultural life and the parks had been in a condition of 'desperate decline' with reduced staff and declining budgets.[36] Nationally efforts were taken to counteract this through new planning guidance and the creation of CABE Space which works with local authorities and other national, regional and local bodies involved with the delivery of parks and public spaces in the public, private and voluntary sector to help them think holistically about the value and benefits of well planned, designed, managed and maintained parks and public spaces (Table 9.1). In London, the Greater London Authority encouraged London boroughs to develop open space strategies through widespread public participation. Many of the boroughs, such as Tower Hamlets[37] and Haringey[38] have produced detailed maps of their open spaces as part of their strategies. The need for a diversity of open spaces is recognized. There may still be an agenda that parks are good for people and the authorities know what to provide. CABE Space says 'The aim is for all children and young people in England to have regular access and opportunity for free, inclusive, local play provision and play space.' But it does also invite people to say what they think via its website.[39]

OPEN SPACE DEVELOPMENTS IN OTHER CITIES

This account of changes in London's open space shows how the nature of open space reflected the state of society and the prevailing cultural influences through the centuries. Similar progress was made in other cities. Squares and crescents were laid out in the spa towns of England, such as Bath (by the brothers Wood in 1730–67) and Cheltenham. The great cities of Europe also underwent major changes in the eighteenth and nineteenth centuries. For many the walls were removed and new parks created around the urban core, as in Amsterdam. After the French Revolution, the great royal parks of Paris, the Champs Elysées, the Tuileries, the Royal Botanic Gardens and the Parc de Monceau, were all open for public use by the early 1800s.[40]

These European ideas were exported to their colonies. Singapore provides an example of how the values of part of the colonial elite became adapted and extended after independence. Large-scale deforestation of the forests of the Malay Peninsula and Singapore Island caused concern and in 1883 the Superintendent of the Singapore Botanic Gardens was commissioned to undertake a survey of the forests of the then Straits Settlements (Penang, Malacca and Singapore). Finding that 93 per cent of Singapore's forests had been cleared he recommended that a forest reservation covering 11 per cent of Singapore's land area be created. In 1884 the Wild Birds Protection Ordinance was passed, followed by the Wild Animals Ordinance in 1904, which was further amended to protect all vertebrates in 1941. However, after the Second World War, the colonial government revoked the forest-reserve status of the protected areas. In 1951, the Nature Reserves Ordinance was enacted, designating five forest reserves as nature reserves: Bukit Timah; Pandan; Kranji; Labrador; and the Central Catchment Area. By 1955 the planning department had incorporated these nature reserves into its master plan for land allocation. The Nature Reserves Ordinance was upgraded into the Nature Reserves Act 1970 and a Nature Reserves Board was established. Later reviews of the master plan saw the downgrading and eventual reduction in areas of some reserves, while Labrador's status was changed to a nature park. Singapore as a growing economically successful new nation had to balance the needs of industry, water supply, infrastructure and housing with conservation of its best natural areas. The 1987 Concept Plan Review led to a re-evaluation of natural areas that took coral reefs and the offshore islands into account and in 1990 the National Parks Act replaced the Nature Reserves Act. The gazetted Nature Reserve Lands now comprise the Central Catchment and the Bukit Timah Nature Reserve.[41]

In North America new cities were being founded and the older colonial cities began to grow rapidly. Washington DC was one of the first planned new cities, with major emphasis on formal open space suitable for the capital of a great republic. The development of the public parks in the expanding cities of Europe and the USA in the nineteenth century evolved out of the Romantic Movement. Parks were created to bring nature into the city to improve the health of the people, by providing space for exercise and relaxation. The value of urban greenspace for human well-being is a persistent theme in the development of parks and natural areas in cities.[42] In 1851, David Thoreau conceived of a fundamental opposition of nature to the city, saying 'In wilderness is the preservation of the World'. This has been interpreted as seeing the great parks of American cities as an opposition to the built environment, particularly the parks designed by Frederick Law Olmsted: Central Park New York (1858); Prospect Park Brooklyn; the Boston Park System; and Fairmount Park, Philadelphia.[43]

Nevertheless, in the USA, the construction of pleasure grounds extended well into the nineteenth century. Pleasure grounds were intended to serve all elements of society. However, in reality they were the domain of the idle classes. In 1890 a newspaper criticized the park commissioners in San Francisco for spending too much for the convenience of vehicles and not enough on the comfort of pedestrians. Park locations were often peripheral and the cost of public transport fares limited park use to special occasions. Park regulations often forbade highly popular activities such as gambling, animal fighting, vaudeville, minstrels and roller skating.[44]

During the nineteenth century, new city planning wisely promoted landscape improvement, along with better housing and sanitation, as a solution to a widespread urban health crisis. By the mid-twentieth century, this planned allocation of open space had created a view of the ideal modern city as being fully integrated with the natural environment, made up of vast conservation areas, continuous waterways, agricultural green belts, recreational trails, frequent parks, and gardens around every building. Urban plans today require adequate provision of open space. However, in practice, this is interpreted in far from ideal ways by developers and some local authorities. In the conventional suburbs of the sprawl around American cities, this relationship with nature is represented by engineered pits surrounded by chain-link fences, exaggerated building setbacks at road frontages, useless buffers of green between compatible land uses, and requirements for trees in parking lots.[45] Such greenspaces are little used, perhaps because they are so configured that they lie between and behind backyards and appear to be private property.

In the USA, in the 1960s, a number of civil engineers and conservation officials started arguing that open space has a functional value as a check against flooding, recognizing that communities could save expenditure on public works by preserving flood plains and wetlands as natural storage areas for floodwaters, which could infiltrate into the ground rather than add to the flow of rivers further down valleys, creating sustainable drainage systems. The conservation arguments went further in saying that open space was necessary to maintain the 'ecological balance', i.e. to sustain the complex community of living things on which human life depends.[46] These ideals were supported by an aesthetic argument that open space brought relief from 'urban ugliness' and the monotony of sprawl, but also because people wanted and needed a chance to enjoy the beauty of nature. Although the latter was not new, it was becoming more widespread, especially as people became more aware of the need to preserve wild places through television and film media.[47]

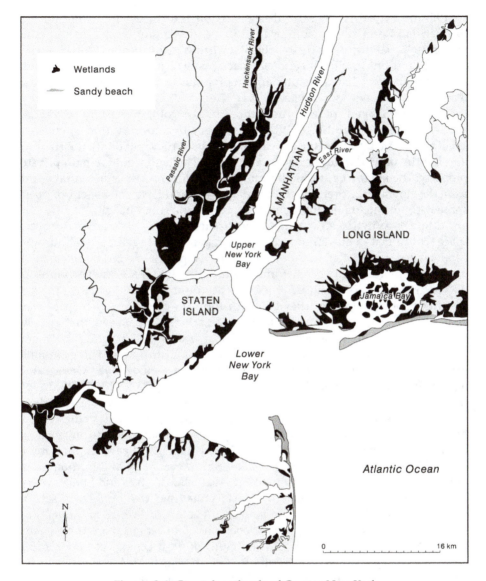

Figure 9.4: Coastal wetlands of Greater New York

Recreation professionals argued for a hierarchy of suburban open spaces from structured playgrounds to natural areas, pointing out that modern suburbs were not meeting those needs. Some went as far as to suggest that more open spaces would mean less crime because access to nature would help ensure the healthy social development of children.

A leading light in the debate about open space was William Whyte whose 1956 book *The Organization Man*[48] was a best-selling social analysis of suburbia.

In 1957 he helped to organize discussions on the threat cities were posing to open land and the exploding metropolis, developing a plea to save the vanishing US countryside. He was the first witness to testify at a 1961 US Senate hearing on a bill to encourage open space preservation. His influential book *The Last Landscape* had a chapter arguing for cluster design of housing areas: 'People have to live somewhere, as it is often said, and if there is to be any hope of having open space in the future, there is going to have to be a more efficient pattern of building.'[49] Whyte also argued for conservation easements. If citizens wanted to preserve a meadow or marsh, they could buy the right to develop the property, but never use that right. The land would remain private property; the landowner would be compensated for the loss of potential profit from development. In return, the community would have the benefit of open space without the financial burden of acquiring the land outright.[50]

Although Whyte's ideas gained much support, the destruction of open space continued. One strand of the campaign that gained ground was support for more regulation of urban development. From it emerged a distinctly environmentalist rhetoric and imagery. In 1965 President Johnson had accused cities of reaching 'out into the countryside, destroying streams and trees and meadows as they go'.[51] For him, the threat to open space was a major justification for anti-pollution legislation. He believed that people should have the right of access to places of beauty and tranquillity, there being a public duty to keep such places clean and unspoilt. These notions were further developed by the Audubon Society in a guidebook, 'Open Land for Urban America', that discussed the functioning of a city in terms of the organic analogy (see Chapter 2), but emphasizing the role of urban greenspaces in that functioning.[52] In the meantime, individual cities saw a host of local campaigns and activities to preserve urban greenspaces, such as Open Space Action Institute in New York and the Open Space Council in St Louis. The *Saturday Evening Post* reported that 'In every city and in thousands of towns and obscure neighbourhoods, there are housewives and homeowners banding together to fight, block by block, sometimes tree by tree, to save a small hill, a tiny brook, a stand of maples.'[53] The opportunities for protecting urban greenspaces are even greater if coastlines and estuaries are considered. Greater New York has large areas of wetlands of great ecological importance, especially for migrating birds (Figure 9.4).

By the late 1960s, the effort to preserve open space and the environmental movement had become intertwined in complex ways. The emergence of a popular ecological consciousness strengthened the conservation argument for open space. A 1970 survey reported that 95 per cent of Americans listed 'green grass and trees around me' as an important part of their physical environment.[54] At the same time, the campaign for open space increased the range of support for the environmentalist cause.[55] One of the first outcomes was a much more vigorous debate about the wisdom of using bulldozers to shape the land so that building could take place on wetlands, hillsides and flood plains.

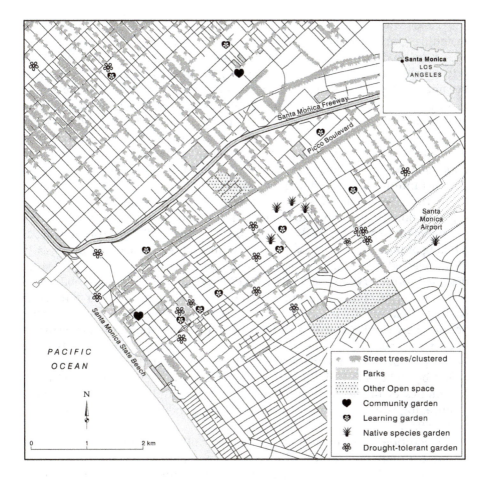

Figure 9.5: Detailed urban greenspace mapping in Santa Monica, California

Despite the debate and arguments, in the 25 years before 1970, the extent of large scale public land in the USA did not increase. Part of the problem was due to policies that failed to stress the need to acquire more land for public recreational use, but probably more serious were the costs of so doing. The increasing sprawl of urban areas raised the price of an acre of suburban land to over $22,000 in 1974. In 1969 the Bureau of Outdoor Recreation reported that an additional $25 billion at that year's expenditure level would be needed to give urban dwellers the same amount of nearby recreation opportunity in 1975 as was available in 1965.[56] The 1962 Outdoor Recreation Resources Review Commission (ORRRC) had recommended the establishment of a fund to be used for the preservation of open space, especially near large metropolitan centres. Authorized by Congress in 1964, the Land Water Conservation Fund paid out $500 million annually in matching grants between 1965 and 1969, but President Nixon reduced the allocation to $300 million for the 1973–4 fiscal year. With suburban land prices rising at 10 to 20 per cent per year, state and local governments became more wary of providing the necessary matching funds to buy more recreational land. Nevertheless, by 2007, 40,000 projects had been funded at sites located in over 98 per cent of the nation's 3,141 counties since 1965. Even so, the 2007 Annual Report revealed a consistent picture across the country of increasing demand for recreation facility development and parkland acquisition funding, with 84 per cent of the states reporting an unmet funding need exceeding 80 per cent.[57]

In the USA, some states tried to preserve open space by setting open space standards requiring that subdividers dedicate a portion of each new development to public recreational use. Landowners challenged this measure as a taking of property.[58] A decision by the California Supreme Court in the early 1970s rejected such a challenge. The developers insisted that a city ordinance designed to preserve for park use 1 ha of land for every 100 new subdivision residents was a taking of property. The ordinance required each subdivider either to dedicate a portion of his tract or to pay a fee. The court held that because new subdivisions led to increased city population and less available open space, the city's measure was a legitimate way to maintain a balance between population and park areas. The court implied that the ordinance would be valid even if the new park were not located near the subdivision.[59] Inventories of urban greenspace are made by many local authorities. Santa Monica, for example, carefully maps street trees and different types of garden (Figure 9.5).

In addition, new disciplines, or sub-disciplines, arose to care for and promote urban greenspaces. In response to a 1967 recommendation of the Citizens Committee on Recreation and Natural Beauty, the Pinchot Institute for Environmental Forestry Studies was set up in the US Forest Service in 1970.[60] The Urban Forestry Act passed by the US Congress in 1972 specifically encouraged the 'establishment of trees and shrubs in urban areas, communities and open spaces'. In 1978 the US Co-operative Forestry Assistance Act expanded the commitment to urban forestry by making funds available for urban and community forest activities. The actual allocations remained of the order of $1.5–3 million annually until the amendment to the Act introduced in the 1990 Farm Bill which raised the funding for urban and community forestry to $25 million in 1993.[61] The definition of urban forestry in the 1978 Act recognizes the importance of individual trees:

Urban forestry means the planning, establishment, protection and management of trees and associated plants, individually, in small groups, or under forest conditions within cities, their suburbs, and towns.[62]

Urban forestry thus has become well established as a profession, yet there are criticisms that the professional managers may be more interested in the biodiversity and nature conservation benefits of urban trees and woodlands, than in their social benefits. In England, people have highly personal interactions with urban trees, even 25-year-old plantations being regarded as providing important natural environments. In this context, urban forests are used for a variety of life events and functions, where the relationship is defined by social parameters and social need, which are derived from the urban populations that they serve. An effective urban forestry strategy has to take into account these dimensions. Some investigations found little evidence of such an understanding among professionals.[63]

A special way of managing land for public benefit arose in Saskatoon, Canada where through tax forfeits, the city held 8,500 building sites in 1945 and there was little developable private land within the city limits.[64] By selling its land holdings in an organized manner, the city used its land holdings to provide a variety of social benefits, helping to avoid incompatible uses of land and associated environmental decay. Precious open space could be preserved for aesthetic and recreational purposes.[65] The city has a strict land use plan and manages a large urban parks and urban forestry section. The result is an orderly, predictable and attractive development.

Dilemmas remain; while people argue for the benefits of open space in cities, some parks and other open spaces remain underused. There are conflicting views as to genuine needs and to the appropriate mechanisms through which inner city recreational needs can best be provided. City and local government officers try desperately to find resources to allocate to parks and natural areas, especially to serve new developments, yet many of their existing parks may be underused or misused.[66]

Community cannot form in the absence of communal space, without places for people to get together to talk (Figure 9.6). Open spaces such as parks and public squares are a key part of this. In the absence of walkable public places – streets, squares, and parks, the public realm – people of diverse ages, races, and beliefs are unlikely to meet and talk.[67] For Duany et al.[68] the key technique for preserving the countryside around cities is the 'Urban Growth Boundary': a line defining the edge of the metropolis, most famously employed in Portland, Oregon. However, while these boundaries have sometimes proved effective, they are rarely long-term solutions – even Portland's growth boundary faces constant legal challenges. A better technique is to designate protected nature reserves, which may be multiple parcels, such as the national parks on the hills outside Barcelona, Spain,[69] or the forests of the Main Range, the quartz ridges[70] and Templer Park[71] on the north-western and northern sides of Kuala Lumpur, or continuous reserves, such as the protected Mata Atlantica Forest around Sao Paulo Brazil[72] (Figure 9.7) or the arc of national parks, from Kuring-Gai Chase in the north, through the Blue Mountains to the Royal National Park in the south around Sydney, Australia.

Figure 9.6: Community greenspace among high-rise apartments in Shenzhen, China (photo Ian Douglas)

URBAN GREENBELTS AND PERI-URBAN BIOSPHERE RESERVES

By the late 1880s, the Garden City movement, led by Ebenezer Howard was advocating cities of 30,000 inhabitants surrounded by an agricultural green belt, separating them from other urban areas. After witnessing ribbon development along arterial roads with the coming of the motor car in the 1920s and 1930s, British planners strongly advocated the notion of planning controls and the declaration of green belts around urban areas. The principle is that a certain area around a metropolis has certain controls against development in place. The green belt became a foundation stone of British planning and has been adopted widely across the world.[73] By 2012, England's 14 Green Belts covered over a tenth (13 per cent) of the land, and provide a breath of fresh air for 45 million people. Altogether, 88 per cent of the population lives in the urban areas within Green Belt boundaries.

Similar policies were adopted in many European countries. Belgium had its Plan Vert in the 1960s. The Netherlands links green and blue (water) spaces in planning, developing an Ecological Main Structure, the Green Heart (Figure 9.8) and Buffer Zones.[74] These areas involve links to the cities through

Figure 9.7: Part of the San Paulo Greenbelt Biosphere Reserve where it is
dissected by the railway to Santos (photo Ian Douglas)

green wedges, particularly in Amsterdam where the 1,000 ha Amsterdamse
Bos Park creates a green wedge between highly developed urban fingers.[75]
Freiburg in Germany also operates a 'green wedge' planning strategy to
link the city centre to the surrounding countryside. Helsinki, Finland, has
a 10 km long central park extending northwards from the city centre to an
old growth forest. Copenhagen, Denmark, has a finger plan strategy where
green wedges alternate with built-up areas, creating a greenspace network
which 90 per cent of its residents can reach within a 15 minute walk.[76]
These Nordic cities, like many others, have had the challenges of involving
citizens in the planning of open spaces, and providing multi-seasonal spaces
for a postmodern citizenry.[77] Essentially, they, like other urban authorities,
have to cater for a variety of attitudes towards, and demands upon, urban
greenspaces.

Zurich, Switzerland, a city of some 500,000 people, has about a quarter
of the urban area in forest and common land managed to provide timber
recreation and athletic facilities, wildlife, agriculture, visual amenity, education
and the benefits of a green belt. The forests produce logs and pulp that
provide an income for the city that meets 55 per cent of the total park costs.[78]

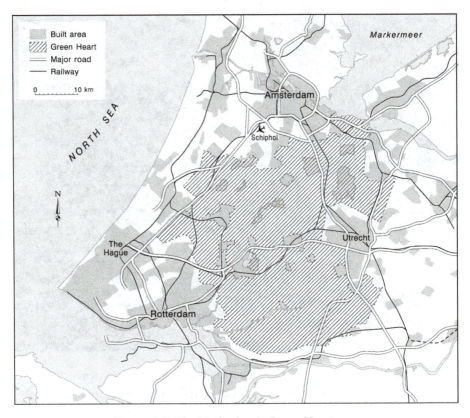

Figure 9.8: The Netherlands Green Heart area

Bringing rural occupations into the city provides many benefits that conventional parks do not. As in ecology parks, there is an important educational aspect. It also brings the city's dependence on the countryside closer to the everyday lives of urban people.

Portland, Oregon, USA began greenspace planning at the regional scale somewhat later than these European cities, but was regarded as having landscape features suitable for the development of an integrated system of parks, nature reserves and scenic boulevards by Olmsted Sr as early as 1903. In 1971 the Columbia Region Association of Governments (CRAG) drew up a plan for a bi-state Urban-Wide Park and Open Space System. It took 17 years for public concern over the loss of local greenspaces to gain enough political momentum for the report to be implemented. Funds were raised through bond issues by Portland Metro to enable the region to acquire over 3,321 ha by June 2002, so providing a green infrastructure with elements of both a greenbelt and a series of green wedges.

Even more striking is the development of urban greenbelts within the Atlantic rainforests of eastern Brazil, around the city of Florianopolis on Santa Catarina Island and on the mainland, around the megacity of São Paulo. In and around Florianopolis, the Biosphere Reserve, which encompasses the greenbelt, is fully incorporated into the urban planning scheme, with participatory processes jointly implementing the Local Agenda 21, the Biosphere Action Plan and the Municipal Master Plan. Within the general Mata Atlântica Rainforest Biosphere Reserve, the forests surrounding the 23 million population of the megacity form the São Paulo City Green Belt Biosphere Reserve. This green belt is formally protected from urban encroachment, but with 30 per cent of the city's population living in informal or illegal housing, unoccupied land adjacent to built-up areas is under constant threat.[79] The designation and the boundaries of the Reserve are contested, but the managers engage actively with local communities living at the forest edge to create understanding and personal involvement, often by employing young people or encouraging them to volunteer in projects using the resources of the forest, while protecting it.

However, planning systems may change and priorities may be altered. In 2011, the UK government announced a new planning framework for England with a presumption in favour of sustainable development that many thought put existing green belts at risk. While the framework pays great attention to the relationship of planning proposals to existing green belts, environmental organizations of all types, including the Council for the Preservation of Rural England renewed vigorous campaigning for the protection of the green belts.

THE IMPACT OF INDUSTRIAL POLLUTION ON URBAN PLANTS AND ANIMALS

Just as the health of people in the early nineteenth-century industrial cities was affected by air pollution, so was ecosystem health in and around the smoke laden urban areas. In 1842 the *Manchester Guardian* newspaper compared Manchester unfavourably with London, noting the flourishing trees and plants of London's squares and parks and the decline of stunted trees in Manchester:

In one of the most open spaces in the interior of Manchester, -namely, the garden of the infirmary, flowering shrubs will not grow at all; and of a long line of trees which were living some years ago, the one or two which alone are left standing are in the last stage of decline and decrepitude; -clearly showing, that in this town the air is vitiated to a far greater extent than in the metropolis.[80]

By the late 1840s, efforts were being made to provide Manchester with parks and playgrounds. In 1846 the first public parks were opened in Manchester and Salford: Philips Park at Bradford, Queens Park at Harpurhey and Peel Park at Salford.[81] Nevertheless, the impact of air pollution remained. A Manchester Corporation special sub-committee reported in 1870 that the air pollution had severely damaged the trees in Philips Park. Park managers made a special effort to find plant species that could withstand the pollution. The displays of flowers in the parks owing everything to the skill of the gardeners in selecting appropriate plants. The Manchester Parks Department established a 20 ha nursery, 15 km south of the city in Cheshire, that supplied plants for the city parks and for display in tubs in Manchester's city squares in an effort to bring greenery to the citizens.[82]

The effects of the smoke spread far beyond the city. At Alderley Edge, 23 km south of Manchester the leaves of trees were 'gradually smirched by the creeping grime from Manchester.[83] Many species of birds were forced out of the urban area by the pollution and the resultant habitat loss. In Peel Park in 1882, only five types of bird were found, of which only the house sparrow and starling were nesting.[84] Insects adapted, with the melanic form of the peppered moth gradually replacing other forms after 1848. By 1895 black peppered moths accounted for 98 per cent of the total peppered moth population.

However, the greenspaces of Britain's great cities remain heavily used. By 1978 it was noted that 'The grassy urban parks, urban commons and riverbanks are great attractions and where in towns there are rivers or lakes or canals to fish and boat in, then except in a few places where bad pollution remains, they are intensively used.'[85]

People can collectively change urban greenspace issues. In Hulme, part of inner city Manchester, there was a celebrated struggle to preserve the 'Birley Tree' when the unpopular post-war multi-storey crescent shaped flats were pulled down. Local residents campaigned.

In 1999 Hulme residents fought a sustained campaign against the local authorities, to protect a much loved Poplar tree known as the 'Birley Tree', located in Birley Fields. During the campaign, local people marched to the Town Hall, brandishing branches of the tree which Council henchmen had lobed off in a previous attack. The Poplar was the oldest tree in Hulme, and was sadly slayed by the authorities on a dark winter night in 1999, breaking the hearts of many local people in the process. After the campaign, the prospective developers pulled out from the site, which six years later remains vacant, as are many of the nearby office blocks that were built on Birley Fields at the time. All that remains is a sombre, steel-scaffold cross as a memorial, but the spirit of the Birley Tree lives on in Friends of Birley Fields. We are protesting against the authority's threat to steal the green, open space, which is the soul of the local community.[86]

After the slaying of the Birley Tree, one local resident built a giant wooden sculpture designed to express how local people felt about those who devastated the precious Birley Fields, with no respect for the local residents. The sculpture represented a set of scales, with the forces of development on one side, outweighing the well-being of the community. The centrepiece of the sculpture was a big finger, pointing at the office of the Moss Side and Hulme regeneration partnership block down the road.

TOWN PLANNING AND URBAN FOOD PRODUCTION

A classic example of an unplanned interaction between pioneer modern town planners and the people can be found in Barcelona. Ilfonson Cerdà's dramatic grid iron extension of the city took more than half a century to develop fully. Begun finally after an edict from Madrid in the 1870s, it was barely complete at the outbreak of the Civil War. Meanwhile, generations of families had used the undeveloped plots for vegetable gardens and recreation. In the shanty towns which grew up on the outskirts of Barcelona before the First World War, the very poor survived by growing their own food.[87]

Such situations find their modern parallels in the expanding cities of Africa and Latin America, where shanty towns occupy much unused land and peri-urban informal agriculture supports thousands of families. Growth of urban populations and an increase in built-up areas raises the total agricultural production in urban areas. From 1980 to 1996, this source of food grew 30–40 per cent.[88] The proportion of urban families engaged in urban agriculture is difficult to determine precisely, with estimates ranging from 15 to 70 per cent,[89] but the importance of urban food production, particularly in the poorest countries is evident from data collected by Smit and colleagues in the 1990s (Table 9.2).

Some of the impacts of peri-urban agriculture can be damaging to the environment. In Harare, Zimbabwe, particular combinations of farming practices, crops and soil characteristics have caused severe soil loss, but changing land management practices and preventing rapid surface runoff could reduce these losses. There are many existing practices that do not cause major soil losses. Only 40 per cent of plots in one survey had severe soil loss; 73 per cent of these losses can be reduced by simple soil conservation techniques such as ridging and furrowing for sweet potatoes and rough-ploughing for maize.[90] A major issue in many African cities is the lack of security of land occupance for most urban and peri-urban cultivators.[91] Tenure regularization on peri-urban land and a policy linking peri-urban agriculture to food security are needed. Peri-urban areas are highly contested places where increasing landlessness is occurring. Tenure reform would be inadequate without land reform. Land tenure issues in peri-urban areas currently involve a clash between traditional and official legal systems. The debate focuses on food production versus urban land use planning. Being both a technical and a political issue peri-urban land tenure planning and regularization requires participation by both central and local government.

Table 9.2: Selected data on the extent of urban agriculture (based on data compiled by The Urban Agriculture Network from various sources, as presented in Smit, 2001, and on other internet sources)

Country	Cities or regions involved	Extent of urban agriculture
AFRICA		
Mali	Bamako	Self-sufficient in horticulture products and some products are shipped outside the metropolitan area for consumption
Uganda	Kampala	70 per cent of poultry needs (meat and eggs) is produced inside the city
Zambia	Lusaka	Subsistence food production accounts for 33 per cent of the total consumption by squatters
ASIA		
China	18 largest cities	In the 1980s, over 90 per cent of vegetable demand and over half of meat and poultry demand in China's 18 largest cities were met through produce grown in urban provinces
Indonesia	Jakarta	Almost 20 per cent of the food consumed by squatters is self-produced
Nepal	Kathmandu	37 per cent of food producers surveyed met their household plant food needs and 11 per cent met their animal food needs
Singapore	Whole city state	80 per cent of the poultry and 25 per cent of the vegetables consumed are produced within the city
EUROPE		
Germany	Whole country	1.4 million allotment gardens in Germany occupy a total of 470 m²
Netherlands	Whole country	240,000 allotments
Romania	Whole country	With new government policies and programmes, from 1992 to 1998, urban production increased from 14 per cent to 26 per cent of all agricultural production
Russia	Moscow	From 20 per cent in 1970 the proportion of Moscow families engaged in food production increased to 65 per cent in 1990. By 2011, urban food production remained important for many Moscow families
UK	Whole country	About 300,000 allotment plots were cultivated in Britain in 1997: since then people's interest in growing food has increased
UK	London	In 2002, 14 per cent of inhabitants already grew some food in their gardens. It is estimated that Londoners could produce up to 232,000 tonnes of fruits and vegetables, or 18 per cent of the conurbation's daily nutritional needs
AMERICAS		
Argentina	Buenos Aires	20 per cent of nutrition needs of the city are produced by part-time farmers
Cuba	Urban areas	From 1992 to 2000, urban food production increased by 300 per cent and children are eating four times as many vegetables as they were in 1982
USA	Metropolitan areas	30 per cent of agricultural products in the country are produced within metropolitan areas

Urban agriculture issues are far from being confined to Africa. In Latin America, cities like Rosario, Argentina, experience high rates of in-migration from rural areas, with 250,000 out of 1.1 million inhabitants in Rosario living in squatter settlements. Several thousand people live by recycling rubbish around some 180 waste dumps on the edge of the city. Urban agriculture is seen as a powerful tool helping the poor squatter families, particularly by helping women to build their self-confidence and self-reliance, by empowering the community and by creating work. Some 4,000 people are involved in food, medicinal plant and urban animal production. Projects emphasize urban agriculture as organic food production, through composting, vermiculture and the production of food, decorative plants, flowers, vegetables, and medicinal and aromatic plants.

In India too, the livelihoods of inhabitants of urban and peri-urban areas are dependent on access to cheap and safe food of high nutritional quality, much of which (particularly the highly perishable vegetable produce) will originate from peri-urban agriculture. Urban fringe farming is dominated by small scale farmers who depend on cultivation for both household food provision and income generation. However, despite evidence from elsewhere in the world, that urban and peri-urban agriculture is crucial for improving food security and livelihoods of the poor, agricultural policies in India have continued to focus strongly on rural areas with a view to achieving self-sufficiency in food production and reducing rural poverty. Despite its multiple benefits for the city and its contribution to global sustainability by reducing the distances over which crops have to be carried, urban and peri-urban agriculture is given insufficient attention and support by most central and local governments.

After the political changes in 1989 in central and eastern Europe, a period of economic crisis started during which urban agriculture functioned as a safety net for people with low incomes and for the increasing number of unemployed, pensioners and disabled people, whose monthly payments were falling in value and who faced rising food prices. Many people, driven by the need to survive, started to use vacant municipal or private land in the inner city and suburban areas (along railroads and motorways, below power lines, and on temporarily idle land).[92] After the turbulent immediate post-communist period in the 1990s, some municipalities discovered the multiple benefits of urban agriculture in addition to food production. Allotment gardening contributes to maintaining urban green areas, management of the peri-urban landscape and biodiversity; provides recreational services to urban tourists, helps to reduce greenhouse gases and creates a use for compost generated from municipal waste.

Several industrialists were reformers in the town-planning sense; both Cadbury and Krupp established workers' houses with gardens.[93] One French example is the Le Phalanstère experiment at Mulhouse designed to allow people to enjoy the health benefits of gardens for recreation and play. In France, socialist deputies encouraged workers' gardens in St Etienne, Valenciennes, Le Puy and

Millau. Frédérick le Play's support for house and gardens for workers was well received. While parks were seen as a top-down activity, gardens and vegetable plots could be very much a 'bottom-up' realization.[94] Allotment gardens became an established feature of early twentieth-century European towns.

Their numbers increased greatly during the Second World War: 1,400,000 allotment gardens provided 10 per cent of all the food produced in the UK and 50 per cent of the national requirement for fruit and vegetables. This was part of the national war effort when much land in both public and private recreation areas, parks and sports grounds was devoted to allotments for growing food. Suburban gardeners dug up parts of their lawns and flower beds to increase their home vegetable plots, many also keeping chickens and putting their food scraps into kerbside pig swill bins for collection and delivery to local pig farms established to provide immediate local sources of meat within the suburbs.

Some of these wartime allotment gardens survived, but their area has greatly declined. In the years since 1980 there has been a resurgence in demand and local authorities are usually unable to supply enough plots. While a German 1994 law 'guarantees the rights of gardeners to their land more irrevocably than at any time in their past history', and Denmark passed a similar tough law in 2001,[95] the allotment gardeners in the UK have no such long-term guarantees to the land they use. While every UK citizen has a right to apply to the local council for one, allotments are normally offered to plot-holders on a renewable one-year lease. The agreement usually sets out how the tenancy can be terminated and the allotment provider has to give 12 months' notice of termination.

In addition to providing food and attractive places in which to relax among trees, shrubs and flowers, urban household gardens are important for biodiversity. Domestic gardens in English small mediaeval towns were often strips of 50 to 100 m in length behind a house built directly on to the street. These gardens were essentially kitchen gardens producing vegetables and fruit for the household. As contacts with other countries expanded during the sixteenth and seventeenth centuries, more lush and exotic crops were grown in these gardens, diversifying the habitat and attracting molluscs, diplopods, insects and rodents in increasing numbers.[96] Plans of English towns, such as Bedford and Chester, in 1801 clearly show these long strips of garden and other areas of cultivation occupying a large part of the town's area.[97]

Private gardens of urban houses should not be neglected as part of urban greening. They occupy more urban greenspace than any other urban land use type. For example, residential areas cover almost half of 'urbanized' Greater Manchester, UK. A large proportion of such areas is devoted to gardens. While in high density residential areas built surfaces (i.e. buildings and other impervious surfaces) cover about two thirds of the area, in medium density areas they occupy only half and just one third in low density areas. Trees cover 26 per cent of low density areas, 13 per cent of medium density areas, and 7 per cent of high density areas.[98] Over the whole of Greater Manchester, there is more land with trees in gardens than in any other land use category.

Of some 24.5 million dwellings in Britain, probably between 15 million and 20 million have gardens.[99] With a retail turnover of over £5 billion a year, the UK gardening industry is a buoyant and growing market. Altogether these gardens occupy some 4,000 km². They offer varied habitats. A detailed investigation in Sheffield revealed that the city had 175,000 domestic gardens covering around 30 km² and containing 25,000 ponds, 50,000 compost heaps and 360,000 trees over 2 m high.[100] They make a significant contribution to all the ecosystem services provided by urban greenspace.

OPEN SPACES FROM OLD INDUSTRIAL LAND

The pattern of using former industrial and mining land to create urban greenspaces began to be established with the spread of cities beyond their mediaeval walls. Thus the gardens of the Tuileries in Paris are situated on the site of former clay pits used to extract materials to make roof tiles ('tuiles').

In the 1970s there was increasing concern about the decline of industrial towns in northern England and the increasing quantity of derelict land in and around them. An organization designed to bring together central and local government, business and the community, called Groundwork, was established in the late 1970s. The Countryside Commission proposed a major experiment to improve the often run-down and derelict physical environment of the urban fringe. Following the 1979 general election, the experiment was named 'Operation Groundwork' and the first Groundwork Trust in St Helens and Knowsley was launched in December 1981. By July 1983 five more Groundwork Trusts had been established in north-west England. The movement then went national and trusts were quickly established in Hertfordshire, East Durham, Leeds and Merthyr Tydfil. The Groundwork Foundation (now Groundwork UK) was set up to co-ordinate expansion and to support the network by building national partnerships and raising new resources. In 1990 at the request of the government Groundwork expanded its work to include inner cities and town centres and began concentrating on supporting people and businesses in deprived neighbourhoods.[101] Improvements to open space became a less central focus of the work.

Reflecting growing public interest in the environment in the UK, there was a phenomenal increase in the number of wildlife reserves acquired in the late 1970s and early 1980s. Education and work in urban areas started to develop fast. In 1992, the Urban Wildlife Partnership was formed to co-ordinate the urban wildlife movement in the UK. In contrast to Groundwork, the Wildlife Trusts worked as a civil society organization to preserve wildlife and maintain and increase biodiversity.

By 2007, Groundwork had helped to change the image and physical appearance of many old industrial areas and had actively engaged in helping the unemployed, disadvantaged and disabled gain new skills and confidence

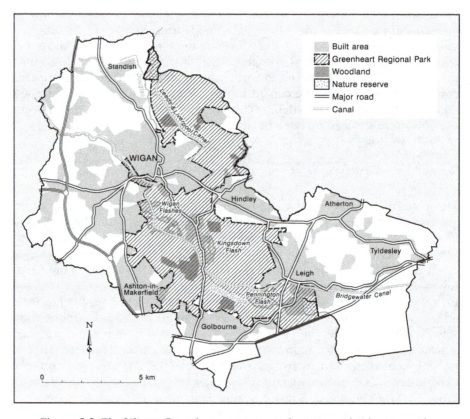

Figure 9.9: The Wigan Greenheart area around mining subsidence ponds (flashes) in Greater Manchester

in a work environment. It aims to be highly participatory and to bring benefits equally for people, to create learning and working opportunities and to help them become more active citizens; to deliver environmental improvements that create cleaner, safer and greener neighbourhoods; and to increase prosperity, by helping businesses and individuals fulfil their potential.

More modern transformations involve the re-use of sand and gravel pits, many now in peri-urban areas. Thus the water parks along the Mersey in Greater Manchester occupy pits created by the extraction of gravel to build the embankment of the M60 motorway. Not far away, at Wigan, lakes caused by mining subsidence have been transformed into nature reserves and recreational areas, contributing to the ambitious Wigan Greenheart project (Figure 9.9). Similar plans are being developed at Huaibei, China where large scale subsidence has also created a suite of lakes (Figure 9.10). Also in Wigan is the Seven Sisters Recreation Area, the sisters being former coal mine waste tips that have been revegetated.

Figure 9.10: Lake formed by mining subsidence at Huaibei, China with new parkland in the foreground and industrial premises in the background (photo Ian Douglas)

A more ambitious gravel pit restoration project is the Penrith Lakes Scheme at Castlereagh in outer Western Sydney, Australia. Conceived in the late 1960s, the Scheme is a quintessential 'hybrid landscape', aiming to rehabilitate 2,000 hectares of open-cut gravel quarries by creating huge artificial lakes and landforms. But its development destroyed a rich palimpsest of earlier farming and Aboriginal landscapes, both of which had also transformed the environment. The rich succession of human use and occupance illustrates the shifting meanings of this environment, the different ways the Aboriginal, rural settler, industrial and urban users of this area knew and shaped this country, and the politics and strategic uses of different types of environmental knowledge.[102]

MANAGEMENT OF URBAN OPEN SPACES

The perceptions of citizens vary greatly, but the normal practice in most cities is to mow grassed areas regularly and to present a highly regulated and controlled environment to the public. Yet mowing regimes can reduce the multiple benefits of public open space, especially in terms of biodiversity.

They can also be expensive. In 1978 the Canadian city of Winnipeg spent almost $2 million on cutting grass along streets and boulevards: for a population of 500,000 in an environment that has a growing season of only 5 months.[103]

In Britain the conventional management policies are being challenged in two major ways, through the planting of wildflowers in open spaces and on traffic roundabouts and through changing mowing regimes. The charity Landlife, based at the National Wildflower Centre in the borough of Knowsley, adjacent to the city of Liverpool, has worked with the borough council to introduce wildflower planting in many different situations, especially on informal open spaces in public housing areas, for example at the Old Rough, Kirby, Merseyside, and on roadside embankments and roundabouts.[104] The Highways Agency continues a policy introduced by the UK Government Department of Transport of reducing mowing on motorway (freeway) verges. Properly managed to succeed naturally, the verges assume the character of wildlife corridors, both within cities and across the countryside. The Agency is also the largest planter of trees in England. The result is a more varied open space network, an increase in plant and animal biodiversity and a visually more pleasing roadside landscape.[105]

ECOLOGICAL PARKS AND URBAN NATURE RESERVES

The second half of the twentieth century saw an important change in thinking about informal recreational open space in urban areas; the natural world took greater significance.[106] The William Curtis Ecological Park created in 1977 was a new form of urban park on a plot of just under a hectare in central London. It aimed to show how vacant and derelict land could be put to use as a centre for research and study of urban ecology for London schools.[107] Over several years a plant cover of many naturalized and native plants was established on 350 truckloads of mixed fill of construction and demolition waste dumped over the hardcore of the original site.

A set of varied environments from a pond to a woodland, a copse to a cornfield has been established. However, this highly successful park was always intended to be temporary and in 1985 it was returned to its owners. The park's creators, the Trust for Urban Ecology now runs Dulwich Upper Wood, a nature reserve, educational facility, research area and a place of recreation, Greenwich Peninsula Ecology Park, a freshwater habitat, set within a massive dockland regeneration project started in 1997; Lavender Pond Nature Park created in 1981 by the London Borough of Southwark to provide a haven for wildlife, an amenity for local residents and an educational resource; and Stave Hill Ecological Park, nature reserve, educational facility, research area and place of recreation.

ACCESS TO URBAN GREENSPACE

Each UK local authority has to set its own open space provision standards that apply to new developments. Thus, for example, at present the level of general open space available to residents (including playing pitches and accessible countryside) varies across Teignbridge. Newton Abbot has 2.95 ha per 1,000 population, whereas Dawlish has only 1.37 ha per 1,000. Developer contributions will be based on an average requirement of 2.2 ha /1,000 (from the audit of current provision) reflecting local need. This figure compares with the National Playing Fields Association (NPFA) recommendation of 2.4 ha per 1,000 population.

This provision is further divided by type of open space:

- for play areas: 1.5 m² per person (with an additional 0.1 ha per 1,000 population for older children)
- active sports facilities: 12 m² per head of population
- parks and gardens, informal open space, natural green space: 8.25 m² per head (This compares with the NPFA recommendation of 10 m² per head)
- allotments: 10 plots of approx 250 m² per 1,000 population
- tennis (all weather – new): 0.25 m² per head
- bowls (new): 1 m² per head
- all weather pitches (upgrade): 2 m² per head.

In the USA, standards were developed by the National Recreation Association which recommended 0.5 ha of playground per 1,000 persons within 400 m of each residence. Recreational playing fields should be within 800 to 1,600 m of each residence at the rate of 0.5 ha per 1,000 population. By the mid-twentieth-century Los Angeles had 0.81 ha of total park space per 1,000 population, Philadelphia 2.02 ha per 1,000, and Seattle 2.63 ha per 1,000.

New standards have now emerged; with the average USA total urban open space provision being 3–7.5 ha per 1,000 population, compared to 6.5 ha per 1,000 in the UK, 2.8 ha per 1,000 in Natal, South Africa[108] and 0.6 ha per 1,000 in Tokyo, Japan (target for 2000).[109]

Natural urban open space has received special attention. In the 1970s how people interpreted, understood and used urban open spaces became important. In the 1980s there was a great expansion of the study of recreation and tourism. The two came together in studies of how people used green publicly accessible areas in towns and cities. Important 'left-over' pockets of land were found to be highly important for children's play and natural areas helped socializing among both young people and adults.[110] Such pockets are often colonized by spontaneous assemblages of plants,[111] yet are seldom included in official open space inventories. One survey of Greenwich, a London borough with one of the largest amounts of open space, found that these small pockets of unrecorded open land were used just as frequently as well-known public open spaces.[112]

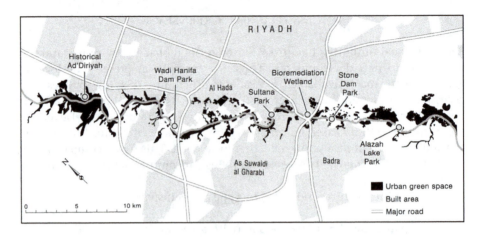

Figure 9.11: Urban greenspaces along the Wadi Hanifa, Riyadh, Saudi Arabia

Close to home, often wild in character, they were an unacknowledged but well-used part of the open space resource.[113]

Recognizing the value for both recreation and nature conservation of the urban wild, the proximity of such natural greenspace to people became asserted to be an extremely valuable part of our children's inheritance. New targets for accessible urban greenspace in urban areas were proposed:

- an urban resident should be able to enter a natural greenspace of at least 2 ha within 0.5 km of their home;
- provision should be made for Local Nature Reserves in every urban area at the minimum level of 1 ha per 1,000 population (equivalent to 10 m^2 for each resident).

Planning Policy Guidance 17 for England and Wales drew attention to the importance of natural and semi-natural urban areas but said that standards should be set locally to suit local conditions and needs. Thus Swansea, Wales, suggests that no one should live more then six minutes walk (300 m) from their nearest natural open space. Perhaps the ideal is to create greenspaces as close as possible to the people who are likely to use them. In Riyadh, Saudi Arabia, the opening up of the flood plain of the Wadi Hanifa that runs through the city has created many new recreation areas (Figure 9.11), similar to the impact of the river valley corridors in Greater Manchester.

CONCLUSIONS

Urban greenspaces are a key element in urban life. They are multifunctional and assist in improving human health and well-being. Well-managed and cared for by local authorities and local communities they can provide everything from adventures and first encounters with small animals for children to peace and relaxation for senior citizens. Increasingly people are recognizing their significance for wildlife and biodiversity and their societal value in terms of human mental and physical health. Their wide range of ecosystem services can help society adapt to climate change, increase food production, grow fuelwood, reduce the urban heat island effect, trap a proportion, albeit small, of air pollutants, provide space for sport and games, even golf, and support a diverse flora and fauna. They can be planned for one purpose, such as sustainable urban drainage, but serve others. Urban food production, even on rooftops and in window boxes is likely to increase. For the poor in many African, Latin American and Asian cities urban farming will continue to be essential to ensure affordable food supplies.

Competition between potential urban greenspace users has always led to conflict, as one person's rubbish dump might be another's source of useful materials and a third's habitat of unusual plants. Over the centuries, gardens have moved from being the private spaces of religious leaders and emperors to often being places accessible to everyone and cherished by the local populace. For all our urban children and grandchildren these are where they make their first encounters with nature. History has shown how inspiring that can be.

10

Urban Sustainability

Cities for Future Generations

For centuries, the majority of the world's urban settlements were sustainable in that they supported their population with food and water from their immediate surroundings and used local materials for their buildings and streets. Only the largest cities, such as ancient Rome depended on food supplies and raw materials from distant regions (see Chapter 3). In the Roman world generally there was a close link between town and country. Other than Rome, the towns of the Roman Empire in Italy were, at most times, largely self-supporting for basic commodities,[1] although the diet of Roman towns in Britain, such as Silchester, contained many Mediterranean foods transported across the empire.[2]

Mediaeval cities, such as Florence, retained this close link with the surrounding countryside, with the terraced vineyards, trim fields protected by windbreaks and grazing animals on the hills supplying a daily flow of fruit and vegetables into the city and a carting out of dung, refuse and woollen wastes from the city to the fields.[3]

In the twentieth century no city could sustain itself by drawing only on the resources within its boundaries. Many still relied considerably on resources from their immediate hinterland. Large Chinese cities, such as Beijing, Shanghai and Chongqing, occupied municipal territories many times the size of the actual urban area and thus had considerable food-producing and raw material supplying land under the control of the municipal council. That was unusual. Even so, in the 1980s, individual towns within those municipal boundaries, such as Beipei in the Chongqing municipality (Figure 10.1), had goods from many parts of China on sale in their markets.

Nevertheless, throughout the twentieth century, dissatisfaction with the ways urban areas were growing promoted many words, and some action, to develop better towns and cities. In the Netherlands, the 1935 Amsterdam Development Plan proposed a network of green belts providing recreational routes linking parks in the various neighbourhoods, districts and suburbs.[4]

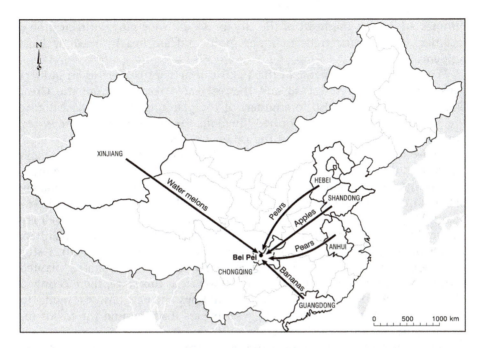

Figure 10.1: Sources of food supplies to the market of Beipei, Chongqing Muncipality, China in 1988

There was a great deal of greenery in residential areas, but much was basically for visual delight rather than use for play and recreational activities. Nevertheless, the plan had a major influence on urban planning throughout Europe and its principles were implemented widely after 1945.

In the USA, moves to establish parks on the edge of urban areas began in the 1930s. The East Bay Regional Park District (EBRPD) in the San Francisco Bay area of California, created in 1934, has long been a leader in urban nature conservation.[5] By 2011 the EBRPD was providing 40,000 ha in 65 parks including over 1,200 miles of trails for hiking, biking, horseback riding and nature study (Figure 10.2). The Park District offers lakes, shorelines, campgrounds, visitor centres, interpretive, educational and recreation programmes, picnic areas, indoor/outdoor rental facilities, and golf courses. It provides areas for intensive activity and areas of nature reserves, foreshores, urban parks and forested hill parks. This variety of parks is a good example of a multifunctional urban greenspace network.

In 1939 the Huron-Clinton Metropolitan Authority was established to allow the counties around the Detroit urban area, Oakland, Wayne, Washtenaw and Macomb, to join in a metropolitan district for the purpose of planning, promoting, developing, owning, maintaining, and operating parks, connecting drives, and/or limited access highways. The parks, located not more than 45 minutes drive from the heart of the city, provide a wide range of recreational facilities, from mature trails to water sports and are heavily used by local residents.[6]

While these developments in the 1930s can perhaps be seen as an indirect consequence of the New Deal and the associated recovery from the Great Depression, they were also forerunners of the planning that emerged during the Second World War in the United Kingdom. Two pictorial magazine issues, one, *Picture Post*, from 1941 and the other, *Life*, from 1970, show how ideas developed over the mid-twentieth century. The *Picture Post* issue contains a plan for Britain, the editorial stating 'We have tried to outline a fairer, pleasanter, happier, more beautiful Britain than our own – but one based fairly and squarely on the Britain we have now.'[7] Using a picture of the Coventry City architect's plan for the rebuilding of Coventry after the Blitz (see Chapter 2), Maxwell Fry argued that within 25 years, the towns and cities of Britain could be replanned, with soot disappearing, great swathes of parkland 'never more than a step round the corner from the homes of the people' and rivers reclaimed, planted with trees and provided with footpaths. However, at this stage, there is only a plea to scrap the old inefficient family car and buy the new post-war model to drive along straight and wide roads, with bypass roads around the towns for heavy traffic.[8]

While modern green infrastructure and accessible urban greenspaces are envisaged by Fry, there is little to warn of the emissions from vehicles. The national vehicle fleet was then far smaller than at the start of the twenty-first century. In 1937 the UK produced 492,000 passenger cars and commercial vehicles; in 2008 it produced 1,650,000. The great concerns in 1941 were to secure full employment, to make the cities cleaner and healthier by getting rid of the smoke and soot, to modernize the housing stock, and to avoid suburban sprawl. Contemporaries were beginning to address the issue of containing sprawl by building satellite towns, such as Letchworth or Welwyn, north of London, UK.[9] Satellite towns would be sited around a central city, but there would be at least eight kilometres of 'genuine agricultural country' between the various satellites and the regional city: 'no park wedge or mere Green Belt will do'.[10] This agricultural land would supply 'protective food', such as milk, to the towns so that really fresh food could be delivered to the households.[11] The emphasis on local links to, and interdependence with, the countryside between towns and cities looks back to the nineteenth-century urban metabolism (see Chapter 2) and forward to ideas of the city in its bioregion.[12]

The 3 August 1970 issue of *Life*, devoted to environmental issues, carries a satirical piece[13] that mentions not only that America's road engineers had by then paved an area as big as the state of West Virginia, but that Congressman W.H. Natcher, through his role as Chairman of the House sub-committee for appropriations for the Federal Capital had continued the building of new highways to carry commuters across the Potomac rather than build underground railways. Motor cars were already being seen as a key factor in the impact of cities on the environment and in the quality of urban life.

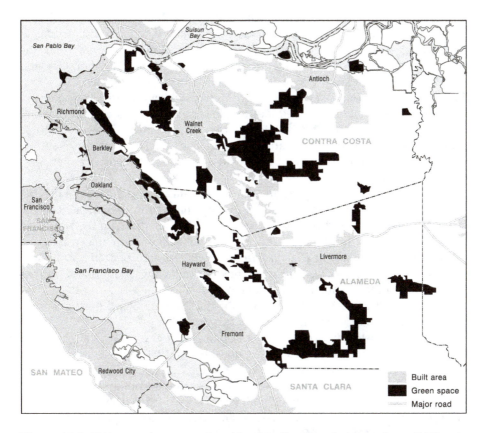

Figure 10.2: Urban greenspace and parkland in East Bay, San Francisco, California

McHarg's work[14] on the integrated planning of development in harmony with nature is given prominence and there is also mention of the notion of limits to growth, presaging the later adoption of the concept of sustainable development.[15] At about the same time, planners, such as Gans, were also beginning to criticize the spate of highway construction since 1945, which encouraged the exodus to suburbia, failed to reduce congestion, and took more customers away from the then declining mass transit systems and central business districts.[16]

At this time too, strong arguments were being made for effective planning of peri-urban greenspace, Nan Fairbrother arguing that we could 'convert our disturbed areas into green urban landscape: stripping out everything decrepit and unused and obsolete, replanning to suit our new needs, installing the new equipment of new land-uses, and then decorating the whole'.[17] When Fairbrother wrote, that transformation was already underway in the UK, for in 1971 work started to reclaim derelict coal mining land in the Rhondda Valley in Wales, where the Dare Valley Country Park was opened in 1973. The 1968 Countryside Act made such parks possible, as sites where people could enjoy the countryside closer to home than the often overcrowded national parks, particularly the Peak District in England and Brecon Beacons in Wales. The first Country Park, opened in March 1969, was the Wirral Way across the Mersey Estuary from Liverpool.[18] It used land along an abandoned railway line beginning in Birkenhead and extending south-westwards towards the Dee Estuary, near Chester. In these moves to re-use old industrial and transport corridor land, we can now see elements of the modern intra-urban and inter-urban greenspace networks coming together.

In 1973, Mabey coined the term 'The unofficial countryside' for the derelict unused land that became colonized by invasive plants in urban areas.[19] At the same time, Lovelock and colleagues developed the Gaia hypothesis.[20] Coupled with the messages from Rachel Carson's *Silent Spring*[21] and many national studies, such as *Australia as Human Setting*,[22] there was a great swell of thinking, both scientific and popular, moving towards reducing the human impact of the environment and making cities better places in which to live. From this developed the notion of living within the limits imposed by the world's resources, which later became known as sustainability.

The term 'sustainable development' had its origin in two key reports: 'The World Conservation Strategy',[23] published in 1980 by the International Union for the Conservation of Nature and Natural Resources (IUCN),[24] and 'Our Common Future'[25] (also known as the Brundtland Report after the chairman of the committee), published seven years later, provided the answer as 'sustainable development' – and thus the concept of sustainable development was born. After 1980, what was being sought in terms of sustainable development was not 'cities that can sustain themselves' but cities (and rural areas) where the inhabitants' development needs are met without imposing unsustainable demands on local or global natural resources and ecosystems.[26]

The issues surrounding sustainable cities were thoroughly discussed in a Friends of the Earth report in 1991[27] that saw sustainable urban development as a new goal, requiring the identification of environmental constraints to human activities in and related to cities and the adoption of methods designed to keep the results of our activities within those constraints. The report emphasized that the city must be treated as a whole, stressing that the influence of urban activities on economic and ecological systems extends far beyond the actual built form of the city. It argued that cities can be made more sustainable. Commitment and participation from all sectors of society would be needed. However, above all, governments needed to recognize that existing urban systems had a high potential for environmental damage and should take immediate precautionary action to establish a framework within which all sectors could contribute to the achievement of sustainable development.[28]

In a world increasingly dominated by cities, the international community began to address urban sustainability at the 1992 Earth Summit in Rio with Agenda 21, which set up the framework for multi-sectoral involvement in progress towards sustainability. Many cities and municipalities established their own Local Agenda 21 committees. Further progress was made at the 1996 UN City Summit in Istanbul. The 100-page Habitat Agenda, signed in Istanbul by 180 nations, states:

> Human settlements shall be planned, developed and improved in a manner that takes full account of sustainable development principles and all their components, as set out in Agenda 21 ... We need to respect the carrying capacity of ecosystems and preservation of opportunities for future generations ... Science and technology have a crucial role in shaping sustainable human settlements and sustaining the ecosystems they depend upon.[29]

On sustainable human settlements, Agenda 21 specified that to make urban life more sustainable, governments should ensure that poor homeless and unemployed people get access to land, credit and low-cost building materials. Such persons should also be able to obtain security of tenure and legal protection against eviction. Informal settlements and urban slums ought to be upgraded to ease the shortage of urban shelter. All urban areas require the basic services of clean water, sanitation and waste collection. Higher income neighbourhoods should pay the full cost of such services. Construction programmes should use local materials, energy-efficient designs, materials that do not harm health and the environment, and labour intensive technologies that employ more people. Agenda 21 also favoured public transport, cycling and walking over motor cars; reductions in air pollution; encouragement of the informal economic sector and small businesses; rural development to reduce migration to cities, prevention of urban sprawl and design of settlements to reduce vulnerability to disasters.[30]

Agenda 21 has no particular emphasis on city size. Perhaps its writers realized that some large urban areas were governed by large unitary authorities, such as the great Chinese cities, or Brisbane in Australia. Many other large urban areas are governed by a multitude of local authorities who may react differently in response to environmental challenges such as those in Agenda 21. In some cases small to medium size cities (usually those of less than one million, but in some areas only those less than 500,000), can act more rapidly than larger authorities in response to promoting sustainability and developing environmental action plans. Certainly Newcastle, Leicester and Brighton in the United Kingdom demonstrated this. Many smaller Chinese cities with enterprising Communist Party secretaries-general and mayors working together have developed innovative eco-city plans. However, in other countries, smaller urban settlements lack the expertise and specialist offices to deal with the challenges set by Agenda 21. Not surprisingly, the uptake of, and efforts to implement Agenda 21 were highly varied in commitment and in impact.

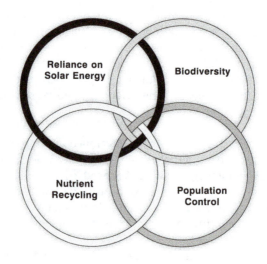

Figure 10.3: Interrelated dimensions of sustainability

Following the promotion of Agenda 21, a worldwide range of activities began. In Europe, the urban agenda was set out in the Green Paper on the Urban Environment.[31] It was then developed through the Aalborg Charter, the Lisbon Declaration, the EU Climate Alliance, the EU Sustainable Cities Project,[32] the EURONET database and several other activities.[33] The EU Sustainable Cities Project (ESC), launched in 1993, was based on a challenging experiment in European networking linking 40 urban environment experts from 15 member states. The network was supported by EURONET, a European research network based at the University of the West of England. The final ESC report in 1996 explores the prospects for sustainability in urban settlements of different scales, from urban regions to small towns, but with a main focus on cities.[34] Sustainable development was seen as a wider concept than environmental protection, having economic, social, health and environmental dimensions, involving notions of equity between present and future generations and the interactions between reliance on solar energy, biodiversity, population control and recycling (Figure 10.3).

One outcome was a EURONET and ICLEI (International Council for Local Environmental Initiatives) Local Sustainability – European Good Practice Information System that involved both web-based and hard copy case studies of actions in individual cities and towns. This database is incorporated into SURBAN, the database on sustainable urban development in Europe available at: http://www.eaue.de/.

Such initiatives are also found at the national level. China has made a particularly strong effort at sustainable city development. China's Agenda 21 is management oriented. It is based on four pillars: a comprehensive strategy and policy of sustainable development, sustainable social development, sustainable economic development, and rational use of resources and environmental

Figure 10.4: Historic city gateway and new apartments face each other across the tree-lined historic canal at Yangzhou, China (photo Bao Long Han)

protection.[35] Different ministries and agencies established demonstration projects, including a system of Ecological Demonstration Districts (ecoprovinces, ecocities and ecovillages) initiated by the State Environmental Protection Agency. The Agency also promulgated a set of eco-city assessment indicators to measure eco-sustainability, including economic productivity, scientific and technological creativity, ecological integrity, governance coordinating ability, social integrity, and external openness.[36] Applying such indicators to the 4.5 million population city of Yangzhou (Figure 10.4), in the Yangtze delta region, in 2000 and again in 2005 showed that, by following an eco-city development path, the city had made progress, rising from seventh to first in Jiangsu Province in terms of the sustainable development indicators.[37]

UN Habitat and UNEP launched the Sustainable Cities Programme (SCP). The environmental planning and management (EPM) approach of the SCP supports the efforts that cities make in developing their environments by improving their environmental information and expertise; their strategies and decision-making; and their implementation of strategies. Improved EPM capacity and policy application processes enable municipal authorities to address priority local environmental issues more thoroughly. On a broader scale, the SCP helps to reduce poverty by more efficient and equitable management of environmental resources and the control of hazards and by promoting employment through improved environmental service delivery. To strengthen local capacities (for EPM), the SCP helps local authorities and their partners to achieve a well-managed urban environment as part of a sustainable urban development process that empowers all city dwellers. Consequently, SCP aims to promote good environmental governance at all levels: local, national, regional and global.

UN Habitat also established the Localizing Agenda 21 Programme which targets secondary cities. Such cities and towns often lack the competencies needed to deal with their evolving environmental problems, and may not be benefiting from international support. By using the participatory EPM process, each town can create a shared vision for its future development. Building on this vision, local authorities can develop sustainable action plans to tackle existing environmental problems.

Table 10.1: Formulae for the calculation of the City Development Index

Index	Formula
Infrastructure	25 x Water connections + 25 x Sewerage + 25 x Electricity + 25 x Telephone
Waste	Wastewater treated x 50 + Formal solid waste disposal x 50
Health	(Life expectancy - 25) x 50/60 + (32 - Child mortality) x 50/31.92
Education	Literacy x 25 + Combined enrolment x 25
Product	(log City Product - 4.61) x 100/5.99
City Development	**(Infrastructure index + Waste index + Education index + Health index + City Product index) / 5**

To gauge urban progress towards greater sustainability, UN Habitat developed the City Development Index (Table 10.1), a measure of average well-being and access to urban services by individuals.[38] The CDI has been cited as an effective index of urban poverty and urban governance. Health, education and infrastructure components are particularly appropriate variables for measuring poverty outcomes in cities. Similarly, infrastructure, waste and city product components are key variables for measuring the effectiveness of governance in cities. The CDI is strongly associated with the city product; other things being similar, a high-income city will have a higher CDI. The CDI correlates well with the national Human Development Index (HDI) (Figure 10.5), but because there is considerable variation between cities in any particular country, it provides a better measure of real city conditions than the national level HDI.[39] Unfortunately, no data more recent than those for 1998 have been provided by UN Habitat.

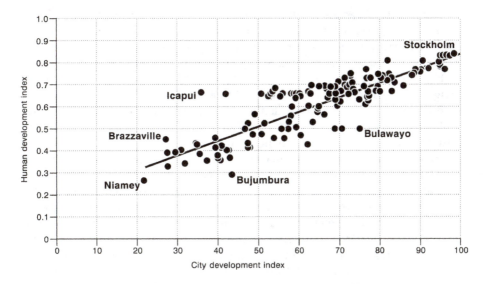

Figure 10.5: Plot of the human development index against the city development index (after World Bank, 2009)

In 2009, the World Bank put forward its 'Urban Development Strategy'.[40] The Urban and Local Government Strategy will help governments at all levels make cities more equitable, efficient, sustainable, and environmentally friendly. The strategy draws on two principles. First, that density, agglomeration, and proximity are fundamental to human advancement, economic productivity, and social equity. Second, that cities need to be well managed and sustainable.[41]

Urban sustainability is a powerful investment that will pay compounding dividends. In a fast-paced and uncertain global economy, cities that adopt an integrated approach are more likely to survive shocks, attract businesses, and manage costs. To promote these urban initiatives in the developing world, 'Eco2 Cities', a new World Bank initiative, aims to help cities achieve greater ecological and economic sustainability by providing a foundation for integrated and sustainable urban development.[42] It is a unified, integrated approach that helps cities plan, design, and manage integrated urban systems. This more holistic framework for decision-making and investment planning incorporates and accounts for life-cycle cost-benefit analysis, the value of all capital assets (manufactured, natural, human, and social), and a broader scope of risk assessments in decision-making. The Eco2 analytical and operational framework can be adapted and customized to the particular needs of a city.

All these programmes and projects beg the question about what was actually achieved in the 20 years after the 1992 Rio summit and Agenda

21. Sustainable cities are viewed in different ways in different parts of the world. While sustainability has been a constant theme since 1992, Local Agenda 21 was the catch-phrase in the remainder of the 1990s, being replaced by eco-city by 2005. As engineers began to realize they had a key role in making towns and cities more sustainable and capable of adapting to climate change, practical solutions such as sustainable urban drainage systems[43] began to be adopted. What might be achieved, if there is the political will, is set out in Peter Head's 2008 Brunel Lecture[44] which shows exactly how energy consumption per household can be reduced by up to 80 per cent, even in the sprawling suburbs of Australia and the USA. To engineers he says that radical change to the infrastructure that supports life on the planet is needed if we are to attain a sustainable future. Strong partnerships between public, private NGO and community groups are needed to make progress. However, engineers with global experience, used to multi-disciplinary team working, will be essential to carry the required changes for sustainability projects forward.[45] While technology is not the only solution, it has always been a key element in the changing environmental history of cities. Facilitating the adoption of new, more sustainable technologies is also part of the process. Changes to building regulations, on such basic matters as insulation and double-glazing, have helped to make homes in many towns and cities more energy efficient, just as taxation of motor vehicles based on CO_2 emissions encourages the purchase of more efficient vehicles; landfill taxes persuade people to recycle used materials; and feed-in tariffs promote the installation of solar photovoltaic panels to generate electricity.

Nevertheless, for many poor urban residents, basic shelter and access to safe, clean water and sanitation remain major issues. In Latin America, the emphasis within urban problem solving was on poverty. The environmental management component of Agenda 21 prompted urban specialists and community activists to recognize that environmental management of the city requires a holistic vision that includes peri-urban agricultural areas in both affluent and poor districts.[46] Good governance was also a major concern. In Peru, people emphasized that changing cities to meet sustainability goals has to be based on management systems that give priority to urban environmental problems caused by different social actors. This in turn mobilizes the people involved to participate at a grassroots level in new institutional settings that integrate and do not exclude.[47] Both clear, consultative leadership and fully participatory processes are needed for sustainable urban development.

In Colombia, in the small (57,000 population) city of Manizales, post-Rio 1992 activities led to a Local Environmental Action Plan (LEAP). The city's Bioplan was integrated with this, giving priorities for bio-tourism, bio-transport, popular environmental education, integrated waste management and a LEAP for one of the poorest areas of the city, Olivares.[48] A comprehensive system of assessment of progress with the plan involved urban observatories in locations regularly used by local communities and a set of indicators which were scrutinized by a technical committee, the municipal government and the territorial planning council. In this way real progress was made and errors were corrected.[49]

In China, eco-city indices have been taken to represent indicators of environmental performance, in terms of greenspace, air pollution, water quality, solid waste and energy sources and efficiency.[50] In Africa, the labels eco-village and eco-city have been given to a variety of projects. The eco-city project in Johannesburg comprised a village in Midrand, one of the most deprived suburbs of Johannesburg, which suffers from a housing shortage. Homes were designed to minimize energy consumption, particularly through the use of solar energy. The project led to a reduction in coal-burning, which had been a major source of pollution and is responsible for causing respiratory illnesses affecting up to 30 per cent of local children.[51]

An ambitious new eco-city and free-trade zone is being developed with Chinese investment on the western shore of Lake Victoria near Goma, in Uganda. The developers claim that 'All developments in this city shall strictly adhere to the principles of sustainable development which can enhance the health and wealth of the people in the zone and its neighbours'.[52] The Sseesamirembe Eco-City is planned to be a sustainable flagship of post-industrial development for Uganda and the entire Sub-Saharan region. The eco-city is believed to be a replicable model low-carbon city that will help the poor to become economically prosperous and will act as a magnet for regional economic development.

In 2009 work began on Kenya's first eco-city: an environmentally, socially, economically and culturally self-sustaining residential settlement in the outskirts of Mombasa. The project included the development of wetlands to harvest, biologically treat, and recycle runoff water for household use, a solar/wind power station, and the planting of 10,000 trees.[53] The buildings are designed to make the best use of the sun, wind and rainfall to supply the energy and water needs of the residents.

These are just some of the examples of eco-city developments that occurred after 2000. From a global survey, Joss compiled a table of eco-city initiatives (Table 10.2), some of which are totally new developments, while others involved retrofitting existing towns and cities.[54] The survey revealed four broad features of the emerging eco-city phenomenon: 1) after the mid-2000s there was a surge of practical eco-city initiatives; 2) the surge was global, with significant initiatives on all continents and increasing activity in international practitioner and research networks; 3) it had a diversity of conceptual approaches, forms, scales, and implementation modes; and 4) it became more embedded in policy-making, with more initiatives and programmes by local, national and international governments, such as the 'eco-budgeting' process adopted by Vaxjo city council; the climate change declaration by Freiburg city council; the English eco-town initiative; eco-city pilot schemes in India and Japan; the European Commission's eco-city project; and the international sustainable cities initiative by the C40 Cities Group and the Clinton Foundation.[55]

Table 10.2: Different types of eco-city initiatives (based in part on data in the 2009 global survey by Joss, 2010)

Country	Location	Description	Country	Location	Description
Abu Dhabi	Masdar	Zero-carbon model sustainable city	Netherlands	Nieuw Terbregge	Renewable energy neighbourhood of Rotterdam
Australia	Sydney	Integrated sustainable development	New Zealand	Waitakere	Community-based sustainable planning
Brazil	Curitiba	Integrated public transport; waste recycling	Norway	Oslo	Public transport and waste reduction policies
Bulgaria	Black Sea Gardens	Five inter-connected car-free resorts	Norway	Trondheim	Renewable energy district
Canada	Toronto	Reduced CO_2 emissions and renewable energy	Philippines	Puerto Princesa	Reforestation programme; electric three-wheelers
Canada	Vancouver	Eco-density, urban greening, sustainability policies	Slovakia	Zilina	EU-funded renewable energy district
China	Changxing, Beijing	Private-sector eco-park	South Africa	Johannesburg Eco-City	Social and environmental sustainability projects
China	Dongtan, Shanghai	Low carbon, low-waste model city	South Korea	Gwang Gyo	High density town with vertical greenspace
China	Mentougou, Beijingu	Revitalized industrial town aiming to be sustainable	South Korea	Incheon Eco-City	350,000 residents sustainable technology centre
China	Rizhao	Residential and renewable energy policies	South Korea	Songdo	75,000 resident green building development
China	Caofeidian, Tangshan	150 km² city built with Swedish expertise	Spain	Zaragoza	Ecociudad Valdesparta sustainable housing

Table 10.2 (continued)

China	Tianjin	Eco-city for 350,000 people with Singapore help	Spain	Logrono Montecorvo	Governmental 600 unit housing and technology centre
China	Wanzhuan	Governmental integrated urban-rural city project	Spain	Tudela	EU-funded renewable energy district
Denmark	Helsingborg	EU-funded retrofit and newbuild energy efficiency	Sweden	Glumslov	Patented sustainable house; recycling system
Denmark	Kalundborg	Industrial ecology in practice: sustainable resource use	Sweden	Gothenburg	Aims to become super sustainable city
Ecuador	Bahia de Caraquez	Resort town rebuilt following natural disasters	Sweden	Hammarby Sjostad	New Stockholm district with recycling model
Ecuador	Loja	Advanced organic waste reycling system	Sweden	Malmo	600 unit housing and technology centre
France	Chalon sur Saone	Neighbourhood model/visitor centre	Sweden	Vaxjo	75 per cent CO_2 emission cut, bio-energy projects
Germany	Erlangen	Pro-bicycle policy; solar power technology	Uganda	Kampala	National park zoning in city: public transport
Germany	Freiburg	Solar city: renewable energy technologies	Uganda	Sseesamirembe	Eco-city free trade zone on Tanzanian border
Germany	Hamburg-Harburg	Creative industrial port redevelopment	UK	London	BedZED low carbon neighbourhood
Germany	Hamm	Government-supported ecological model city	UK	Bicester	One of four 'eco-towns'

Table 10.2 (continued)

Germany	Heidelberg	Energy saving measures cut CO_2 emissions by 35 per cent	UK	Greenwich, London	Millennium village 1,800 sustainable units
Iceland	Reykjavik	Geothermal energy, hydrogen bus fuel	UK	Hanham Hall, Bristol˙	150-unit zero-carbon district
India	Auroville	Community-based sustainable 'future city'	UK	St Davids, Wales	Self-declared first UK carbon-neutral city
India	Kottyam	Pilot for 6 government eco-city initiatives	UK	Thames Gateway	Major redevelopment project with sustainability aims
Ireland	Colnburris, Dublin	15,000 unit suburban development	USA	Aerial Treasure Island	6,600 new homes on former airbase
Italy	Ferrara	Advanced city-wide recycling	USA	Arcosanti	P. Soleri's high density, low resource city
Italy	Segrate, Milan	New 2000 unit sustainable suburb	USA	Bicycle City	Car-free concept
Japan	Tajimi	Renewable energy projects, green roofs	USA	Destiny, Florida	Urban centre in 165 km² private development
Japan	Yokohama	Part of 6-city government CO_2 emission cut project	USA	Ithaca	Ecovillage sustainable housing initiative
Jordan	Amman	Large new city modelled on Masdar	USA	Sonoma Mountain Village	1,900 unit town on derelict industrial site
Kenya	Hacienda Ecocities	Gated development; renewable energy focus	USA	Portland	Public transport network and greenspace strategy

The city is more than a built entity. It reflects the aspirations and hopes of diverse people and cultures. The form, functions, fashions and fascination of a city are expressions of a whole set of moods, habits, customs and lifestyles. Making cities more sustainable involves understanding the interrelations of these elements and ensuring that their diversity is represented in discussions, planning, and actions to improve urban ecology and enhance sustainability. Human relations and individual priorities differ so much that plans drawn up by a narrow elite are unlikely to be readily accepted and may result in rapid degradation of whatever improvements are made. The failure of much high-rise social housing in Britain reflects, at least in part, top-down planning by architects and theorists, as well as poor management isolated from the needs of individuals. The challenge in creating cities for future generations lies in the way our ideas are built on past experience and old technologies. This is particularly the case in profit-driven private developments, which are often over-concerned at getting the maximum number of dwellings on a given piece of land and usually exhibiting an unwillingness to engage in eco-efficiency, energy saving, water harvesting and sustainable urban drainage. All the components of the residential housing system, including the providers of finance and the designers of traffic systems have to think, for the future, about more sustainable ways of living in cities.

The identification and the separation of individual factors and elements driving change and improvement in urban sustainability can over-simplify the complexity of real cities and may generate widely differing interpretations and explanations of what works and what does not. That is why the idealists behind Agenda 21 sought to get all the different sectors of urban society, from business and local government to residents' groups and environmental campaigners to work together. However, in practice, such harmonious collective decision-making is either not completely possible, or involves compromises that ignore problems such as balancing the employment, business and social advantages of an expanding airport against its environmental destruction and noise, health and fossil fuel use implications. Constructing a cultural and durable approach to the sustainable city and sustainable development involves much learning and much listening by all the parties involved and a real willingness to consider many alternatives.

Faith groups also began to take steps to implement more sustainable agendas. Most religions embrace concepts of the wise use of resources and living harmoniously together. In North America, Jewish communities have begun to develop approaches to food ethics, community gardens and management of the land that combine social justice with ecological responsibility and Jewish traditions.[56] Christianity's concern for sustainable community and sustainable development has historical roots in what numerous observers refer to as 'the social question' or 'the modern social problem'. This view embraces the equity and social justice components of sustainability. Care for others and for wise resource use would be demonstrated by adopting Buddhist principles such as removing greed (*lobha*), hatred (*dosa*), and ignorance (*moha*) from our lives and institutions. Such moves would provide a good start along the path to sustainability, including greater equity. The *Qur'an* and the *Hadith* provide the framework for the spiritual and physical welfare of humanity. There are over 500 verses in the *Qur'an* giving Muslims guidance on matters relating to the environment and how to deal with it, and many events in Islamic history that provide models for justice and equity.[57]

Islam has many principles that guide people towards sustainability. In terms of conservation of the natural environment, while using natural resources, Islam has defined this balance as the key to the relationship between people and nature. People have a responsibility towards nature that evolves from the role of man as both a user of natural resources and a preserver of the natural balance. Planning and regulating the built environment should support morals and improvement of society, according to parts of Sharia law.[58] In 2009, one Islamic group saw Medina, 'The City of the Prophet', as a possible place to launch a green campaign in neighbouring territories. Sheikh Ali Goma'a, Egypt's Grand Mufti, presented a Seven Year Plan that he had already introduced into his own city of Dar Al Iftaa.

With elaborate efforts to build eco-cities, such as Masdar, and more sustainable urban settlements in the Gulf States of the Middle East, it is unclear how far these Islamic principles are taking root among the architects, engineers and planners. Cities like Dubai seem to be emulating, and even exceeding the high energy use and car dependency of the least energy efficient North American cities. New York critic, Ouroussoff wrote in 2010:

Despite his good intentions, incorporating traditional Arab designs from ancient settlements such as Aleppo in Syria and Shibam in Yemen – both of which made living in an oven comfortable – and attempting to create an alternative to the ugliness and inefficiency of the sort of development, suburban villas slathered in superficial Islamic-style décor, gargantuan air-conditioned malls, that has been eating away the fabric of Middle Eastern cities for decades, Norman Foster has instead produced a formula for a futuristic gated-community that is exclusive rather than harmonious.[59]

Retrofitting old cities

Most urban dwellers will be affected by the retrofitting of old cities to make them more sustainable, to use renewable energy sources, to be more efficient in the use and re-use of materials, to be efficient in water management and to gain multiple benefits from urban greenspace. Much progress with some aspects of this agenda has been through European legislation and financial incentives. The European Waste Framework Directive sets the following order of priority for actions to manage waste: (a) prevention; (b) preparing for re-use; (c) recycling; (d) other recovery, e.g. energy recovery; and (e) disposal. It also requires that the re-use and the recycling of waste materials such as paper, metal, plastic and glass from households and possibly from other origins shall account for 50 per cent at least of all used materials disposed of; while at least 70 per cent of all construction and demolition waste shall be recycled by 2020. In the UK, this legislation together with a landfill tax that has risen annually from £7 per tonne in 1996 to £64 per tonne in 2012 (Table 6.2), has greatly increased recycling of materials by city authorities. Similarly, feed-in tariffs for electricity produced by householders and businesses have encouraged the installation of solar photovoltaic panels, heat pumps and wind generators. However, while such actions are all individually a step towards the eco-city ideal, they need to be brought together and combined to convert energy inefficient cities to more sustainable, more environmentally friendly places. Some cities have made good progress with this.

Freiburg, Germany

Eco-housing, car-free streets and socially conscious neighbours have made the German city of Freiburg a shining example of sustainability. Freiburg's efforts to promote sustainability initially focused on excluding private vehicular traffic from the city centre and maintaining a viable public transit system. In the mid-1970s, Freiburg began to improve the quality of life in the city centre by closing the major north–south traffic route to vehicles. This ban was soon extended to most of the city centre with a fully pedestrianized city centre, save for trams and buses. New multi-storey car parks were banned, while large bicycle parking areas were installed at the entrances to the pedestrianized area. These bike parks were connected to an extensive network of bicycle paths. These changes contributed to a doubling in the number of trips by public transport in Freiburg between 1984 and 1995, but the growth was mainly due to a cheap travel pass which gave unlimited use at zero marginal financial cost, interpersonal transferability and wide regional validity. The expansion in public transport trip demand did not produce any long-term worsening of the operating deficit of the municipal transport company.

In addition to an integrated transport policy, Freiburg has endeavoured to make its own urban redevelopments sustainable. In a former waste treatment site, a new housing development at Rieselfeld kept 30 per cent of the housing for low-income households offering about 800 subsidized rental apartments, dispersed throughout the first section of the development, along with about 600 owner-occupied units. The development uses an estimated 52 per cent less energy than normal dwellings, by using shared building walls, by building zero energy buildings, by improving the power supply (Rieselfeld is connected to a nearby district heating facility), by urging residents to buy more efficient appliances, and by encouraging the use of sustainable transport.[60]

Vancouver, British Columbia, Canada

In 2008, Vancouver, long a leader in urban sustainability adopted its EcoDensity Charter with the aim of reinforcing environmental sustainability at the heart of all decision-making.[61] Building density was increased by in-fill projects in residential areas and new developments on brownfield sites. Its Olympic Village development was the first in the world to receive LEED (Leadership in Energy and Environmental Design) Neighbourhood Development Platinum certification. The city aims to be the world's greenest city by 2020, making it the leading centre for green enterprise and reducing overall greenhouse gas emissions by 35 per cent compared to 2007 levels.[62] It sets out to achieve a zero-waste policy and to have more than 50 per cent of urban travel by public transport. These are high targets for a North American city.

CONCLUSION: EMERGING VERSUS MATURE CITIES

There are enormous contrasts between the old cities which are adapting to economic, social and environmental change and the new cities planned from the start. Emerging and mature cities have very different challenges in delivering sustainable infrastructure and place shaping, and this is related to the available land and existing land use. In cities which have evolved around historic business areas with myriad existing land rights, parks and amenity areas, business interests and protected, historic buildings, the challenge to achieve higher levels of sustainability is centred on the adaptation of the existing systems and linkages. This retrofit problem is in marked contrast to younger emerging cities which are able to adopt best practice processes of laying out whole new business, residential and industrial areas.

Internationally, we have examples of all the individual components of eco-cities in many places, but few cases of where all these components have come together. There may be a development that has wonderful eco-houses, but is still totally dependent on motor vehicle transport and has no sustainable drainage. Another city may have a wonderful greenspace plan and shady trees and good public open space. A third may have excellent public transport, but little attention to the energy efficiency of buildings. Another may have much green industry and yet be wasteful in its use of water. Thus there is value in preparing checklists and toolkits for evaluating eco-cities and urban ecosystem health, but those lists have to be both comprehensive and usable. There is still much work to do. That work will involve applying lessons from the environmental history of cities as much as thinking of new ways of doing things. On this crowded earth, urban development can seldom start on unoccupied land. It involves adapting from the past to the future, dealing with environmental legacies and entrenched human attitudes, and having great patience, tolerance and powers of persuasion.

Final Thoughts

Some three billion people now live in cities, some in great comfort, and many in great hardship. Perhaps that has always been the case. Greek civilization relied on slavery. Many modern cities rely on new migrants coming into the city to take the low-paid, but essential, work that few others wish to do. There is a huge international flow of skilled professionals moving from country to country selling their expertise to enterprises and governments offering good rewards and new challenges. Such movement is part of the character of cities, with the biggest cities consequently tending to have the greatest diversity. It also leads to change in the character of parts of cities. In some cases, old buildings become occupied by new immigrants bringing different cultures. In other cases, wealthier groups gentrify districts close to the city centre, changing the social dynamics of the area. In terms of the goals of community involvement in managing urban spaces, participating in actions to enhance sustainability, developing support systems in times of stress, this dynamic of social change poses considerable problems. The newcomers are even less likely than long-term residents to know about potential flood risks, slope instability problems, sources of noise, and issues over odours, and the use of neighbourhood open space. Urban environmental history suggests that people will come together, as did women's groups in the nineteenth century when environmental problems, such as smoke, become severe enough. Each chapter of this book, as numbered below, suggests some key lessons from environmental history that are relevant to present-day urbanites.

1. The earliest urban settlements had trade with neighbours and specialized craft workers: their urban metabolism began to reach out to other communities. The early ability to establish safe water and adequate sanitation in the Indus Valley and in Crete 4,000 years ago, suggests there is no technical reason why in the twenty-first century the millennium goals of adequate water supply and sanitation for all have not been achieved. Essentially, it is a question of political will and government priorities.
2. Cities are vulnerable to health hazards, to destruction by war, and damage by geophysical events. The impacts of such events fall unequally

305

across social groups, with the poor suffering most, and often receiving the least help in the recovery period.

3. Urban metabolism reveals a growing interdependence between cities and nations and a need to reduce the ecological footprint of the wealthy to help the poor.

4. Air pollution illustrates that problems can be overcome through combinations of legislation and technology. However, in some cases the problem is simply shifted, as happened when tall chimneys took the smoke of polluting factories away from cities to neighbouring rural areas, and in some cases to adjacent countries. Often the technology that reduced one form of air pollution introduced problems of its own. Today fine particulates from diesel engines have replaced the smoke and sulphur dioxide from fires and steam locomotives. Problem substitution and problem shifting do not solve environmental problems; they merely relocate them. The better solution is to eliminate or lower the emissions.

5. Water is essential for cities, but too much, or too little, of it, in the wrong place at the wrong time, creates great problems. Making sure that as cities grow they do not create more severe flood problems for existing residents is a key issue. Modern cities can be readily disrupted by flooding that in many areas is becoming increasingly frequent with climate change. Water supplies in many cities, on all continents, are already stretched. Increasing attention has to be paid to old techniques of rainwater harvesting, water storage and grey water re-use.

6. Experienced resources used to be well used in European cities; many still are in Asian, African and Latin American cities. The great twentieth-century landfill and land raise exercise has to cease and resource recovery needs to expand. Excessive consumption by the rich ought to decline in order for the poor to have more access to resources, and a larger share of the finite stocks of materials, and also to ensure that there are sufficient resources, including fertile soils and freshwater, for future generations.

7. The cacophony of urban noise, especially city streets full of people talking into mobile phones and tourist groups being addressed through loud hailers, makes the search for quiet more difficult. Many people acquire an ability to concentrate and shut out noise, but the poor are often unable to avoid the noise of neighbours, of traffic and of industry.

8. As cities grow, it becomes ever more important to know the ground they are expanding on to. Old excavations and sand pits are filled. Flood plains are built upon. Streams are piped and buried. Contaminated industrial sites are reclaimed. Coastal wetlands are drained and their land surfaces are raised. Hillside houses with a view are sold at a premium. All these situations may lead to problems unless the land capability and geomorphic history are understood and all the construction and foundation work is carried out to an appropriate standard.

9. Urban greenspace has a high value for a range of ecosystem services. Integrated thinking about the multiple benefits of parks, woodlands and urban nature reserves is needed in order to help cities develop accessible open spaces that future generations will enjoy. Open space and green infrastructure provision has to be an integral part of the social and economic planning for the development of cities. The experience of the great municipal parks of the nineteenth century offers many lessons for the future. Current early twenty-first century concerns, in some quarters, to deregulate urban planning risk destroying the means of achieving liveable cities with adequate urban ecosystem services.

10. The ideal eco-city is a sustainability goal to which all urban planners, developers, managers and governments ought to aspire, but the reality is that while new settlements for tens or hundreds of thousands of people may eventually be built, the retrofitting of existing megalopolis settlements for greater sustainability is an urgent task. This cannot be done piecemeal, by just working on single elements of the sustainability agenda. History shows that integrated thinking and action are required.

These individual lessons from each chapter need to form part of holistic integrated thinking about the cities of the future and their urban environments. Most of these cities will be those that exist now. They will require continuing adaptation and retrofitting as the global and their local environments change. The widespread belief that development can proceed first and the environment can be fixed later is dangerous and misguided. Designing with nature and for a healthy environment, avoiding adding to existing pollution and environmental hazards is going to save money in the medium to long term and give future generations the chance of healthier lives. History shows that this can be done by draconian, dictatorial design and decree. It also shows that it can be achieved in a prudent, participatory, peaceful manner if the people are involved at all levels and have a sense of ownership of projects in the places where they live. Initiative and leadership have to be exhibited at every level from the individual household or enterprise up to national governments and international agencies. Everyone can act to reduce emissions in their daily lives, but local authorities can use planning regulations and by-laws; national governments can legislate on emissions, from motor vehicle exhausts or factory chimneys; and international agreements, such as that on the ozone layer, can persuade governments to act.

Despite the great likelihood that the great urban megalopolises of today will continue to expand, most urban people will continue to be living in small to medium towns and cities of less than one million inhabitants. They need solutions to their environmental problems. Already many show more forward-looking attitudes than some of their larger counterparts. In China, such cities are pressing forward with eco-city programmes; in Europe, imaginative mayors and their councils are spearheading environmental initiatives; in the United States many such cities are carrying out their own policies of mitigating climate change and creating more sustainable cities. Many medium-sized cities in Africa, Asia and Latin America are showing similar leadership and such cities may continue to develop some of the most innovative ways of living more sustainably.

Nevertheless, politicians and businessmen will use the term 'sustainability' to their own advantage. All too often, developers and local governments try to convince people that a place is 'sustainable' because they have planted some trees and built some vegetated stormwater detention ponds. Sustainability goes right through the way an urban settlement operates, from its sources of water and energy; its design and construction; its management of 'experienced resources'; its adaptation to the character of the ground it is built upon; its encouragement of urban agriculture and installation of green infrastructure; its public transport system; its home heating or cooling; and its industrial ecology.

Nowadays, perhaps more than ever before in history, new thinking is required about the relative roles of government and private corporations in environmental management and supply of urban services, including utilities such as water and public transport. Urban environmental history reveals many failures of private water supply schemes, including some by modern multi-national utility corporations. While good governance is lacking in some cities, the wholesale doctrine of privatization of water and power utilities has still left the poor in many African and Asian cities almost totally dependent on private sellers of water for their daily needs. The paradox is that those most in need are most likely to be the victims of market forces.

However, in a period of human history where human rights are well protected in many countries and where the need for their further protection is emphasized internationally by the United Nations and by NGOs, urban people have to realize that with rights comes individual responsibility. The right to drive a vehicle on the city streets has to be exercised responsibly, not merely to obey traffic laws and avoid accidents, but to ensure that unnecessary pollution and noise does not occur; that vehicle parking does not obstruct others; and that excessive use of large vehicles does not lead to urban air quality deterioration that makes children and old people ill. Many urban activities tend to lead to resource overuse. A simple example is recreational walking on the hills outside industrial cities. Everyone has the right to walk along public footpaths, but the most popular ones are so well used that they become eroded and begin to degrade the surrounding areas. Eventually either use of the resource has to be restricted or considerable investment has to be made to restore the footpath and make it more resistant to trampling. The lesson here is that even though we all have rights to certain resources, we need to show individual responsibility in using them wisely and not all trying to drive down the same road or walk on the same path.

However, human nature is such that many of those who have money, including major corporations, think they can buy the right to pollute, and thus buy the right to contaminate global commons of the atmosphere and the oceans. Carbon permit trading could be accused of being a form of doing exactly that: paying to pollute. Although tree-planting or biofuel power generation may occur somewhere else as a result of the trading, the immediate environment of the polluting power plant or factory will still be affected by the continued local emissions. A sceptic might think that in the global financial casino, carbon trading is something akin to the financial derivatives that distorted the banking system after 2008. That distortion has diverted billions of public money that could have been spent on making cities better places in which to live and on assisting in the achievement of the water and sanitation millennium goals.

As a global society, we cannot isolate the urban environment from our social, cultural and economic activities. We depend on it and it depends on us. Major disasters like earthquakes and flood may affect cities, but their impact will in part depend on how we have built the cities and how we manage them and prepare for disaster. Far more loss of life occurs through what we do in cities, from the way we fail to look after ourselves properly to the way we drive motor vehicles or pollute our air, streams and soil. Throughout urban history, as hopefully this book has shown, many of these problems have been reduced by the hard work of urban people and their local governments, but all too often, new problems have arisen. The need for urban environmental improvement is still there. The present and future generations have to rise to the challenge.

Notes

INTRODUCTION

1 Mumford, 1961
2 Hall, 2002
3 Wolman, 1965
4 Melosi, 1993
5 Hays, 1996
6 Simmons, 1993 p.123
7 Sheail, 1995

8 Luckin, 2004
9 Simmons, 2001
10 Simmons, 2008
11 Rosen and Tarr, 1994
12 Melosi, 1990
13 Zimmerer, 1994
14 Head and Muir, 2006

CHAPTER 1: TRADING VILLAGE TO GLOBAL MEGALOPOLIS

1 Marean, 2010
2 Roberts and Rosen, 2009
3 Hodder, 2007
4 Roberts and Rosen, 2009
5 Hodder, 2007
6 Haas et al., 2004
7 Smith, 2002 p.7
8 Smith, 2002 p.7
9 Girardet, 1992
10 Smith, 2002 p.8
11 Teramura and Uno, 2006
12 Yu et al., 2000
13 Evans et al., 2007

14 Zhang et al., 2005
15 Morkot, 1996
16 Morkot, 1996 p.48
17 Girardet, 1992
18 Evans et al., 2007
19 Fletcher and Pottier, 2002
20 Evans et al., 2007
21 Hall, 1968 p.119
22 Hall, 1968 p.121
23 Hall, 1968 p.134
24 Groslier and Arthaud, 1957 p.30
25 Childe, 1958 p.83
26 Childe, 1958 p.83

CHAPTER 2: COMMUNITIES RESPONDING TO DISASTERS AND THREATS

1 Suhrke, 2007
2 McLeman, 2011
3 Porter, 1997 p.53
4 Achtman et al., 2004
5 Porter, 1997 p.123
6 Porter, 1997 p.125

7 Porter, 1997 p.126
8 Achtman et al., 2004
9 Achtman, 2008
10 LaFontaine, 1970 p.19
11 Swanson, 1977 p.390
12 Swanson, 1977 p.392

13 Swanson, 1977 p.393
14 Swanson, 1977 p.396
15 Ngalamulume, 2006
16 Worboys, 1988
17 La Berge, 1992
18 Elvin, 2004 p.119
19 Woodward, 1962 p.463
20 Porter, 1997 p.409
21 La Berge, 1992 p.6
22 La Berge, 1992 p.5
23 Porter, 1997 p.411
24 Woodward, 1962 p.465
25 Barrett and Higgs, 2007 p.209
26 Barrett and Higgs, 2007 p.219
27 Braudel, 1981 p.38
28 Ngalamulume, 2004 p.185
29 Ngalamulume, 2004 p.190
30 Ngalamulume, 2004 p.193
31 Barrett and Higgs, 2007 p.209
32 Curtin, 1985 p.613
33 Rose, 2004 p.771
34 Chadwick, 1842 p.369
35 cited in Bloom, 2001 p.307
36 Cassedy, 1975 p.138
37 Peterson, 2003 p.33
38 Ngalamulume, 2007
39 Massard-Guilbaud, 2002 p.30
40 Tidball and Krasny, 2007
41 Tidball and Krasny, 2007
42 Cousins et al., 2003
43 Downes et al., 2001
44 Wright, 2001
45 Jardine, 2002 p.266
46 Massard-Guilbaud, 2002 p.30
47 Pauly, 1984 p.672
48 Pauly, 1984 p.683
49 Larkham, 2005
50 Larkham, 2005
51 Mumford, 1940
52 Mason and Tiratsoo, 1990 p.98
53 Mason and Tiratsoo, 1990 p.98
54 Mason and Tiratsoo, 1990 p.112

55 Diefendorf, 1993
56 Diefendorf, 1993
57 Diefendorf, 1993
58 Paul, 1990 p.176
59 See the account of such attitudes in Poiger, 2000
60 Khalat and Khoudry, 1993
61 Davis and Weinstein, 2002
62 Brakman et al., 2003
63 Brakman et al., 2003
64 Tucker, 2004
65 Cheng and McBride, 2006 p.161
66 Petryna, 1995
67 Colten, 2005
68 Templet and Meyer-Arendt, 1988
69 Green and Bates, 2007
70 Webster, 2006
71 Hirsch and Levert, 2009 p.210
72 Hirsch and Levert, 2009 p.214
73 Hirsch and Levert, 2009 p.216
74 Hirsch and Levert, 2009 p.217
75 Allen, 2007 p.153
76 Green and Bates, 2007
77 Green and Bates, 2007
78 Chandler, 2007
79 Green and Bates, 2007
80 Comerio, 1998
81 Fothergill et al., 1999
82 Green and Bates, 2007
83 Trotter and Fernandez, 2009
84 McEvoy, 1995 p.S172
85 Engels, 1892
86 Carson and Mumford, 1979 p.150
87 European Union, 2011
88 European Union, 2011
89 Pfister, 2004 p.1176
90 Royal Commission on Environmental Pollution, 2007 p.6
91 Royal Commission on Environmental Pollution, 2007 p.7
92 Gandy, 2006 p.88

CHAPTER 3: FOODS, GOODS, MATERIALS AND ORNAMENTS

1 Brunner and Rechberger, 2002 p.55
2 Heynen et al., 2006 p.6
3 Heynen et al., 2006 p.6
4 Clement, 2010 p.298
5 Graedel and Klee, 2002 p.78
6 Gibbs and Martin, 1958

7 Clement, 2010 p.306
8 Dogan and Kasarda, 1988
9 Cooper, 2006 p.35
10 Cooper, 2006 p.57
11 Cooper, 2006 p.42
12 Cooper, 2006, p.35
13 Chew, 2001 p.23
14 Chew, 2001 p.31
15 Chew, 2001 p.47
16 Lane Fox, 2006 p.134
17 Lane Fox, 2006 p.222
18 Lane Fox, 2006 p.223
19 Salway, 1981 p.587
20 Salway, 1981 p.588
21 Morley, 2005
22 Finley, 1999
23 Mumford, 1956
24 Morley, 1996 p.24
25 Elvin, 2004 p.61
26 Elvin, 2004 p.63
27 Morley, 1996 p.25
28 Braudel, 1981 p.125
29 Roseff and Perring, 2002 p.120
30 Roseff and Perring, 2002 p.121
31 Braudel, 1981 p.226
32 Ackroyd, 2000 p.319
33 Ackroyd, 2000 p.320
34 Braudel, 1981 p.257
35 Braudel, 1981 p.193
36 Braudel, 1981 p.367
37 Baynton-Williams, 1992 pp.23 and 25
38 Tupling, 1962
39 Tupling, 1962
40 Chaloner, 1962
41 James, 2006 p.133
42 James, 2006 p.148
43 Liechty, 2002
44 Blumin, 1989 p.138
45 Laermans, 1993
46 Laermans, 1993 p.82
47 Laermans, 1993 p.83
48 Ackroyd, 2000 p.326
49 Desrochers, 2007
50 Barles, 2005
51 Barles, 2005
52 Barles, 2005
53 Morley, 1996 p.29
54 Brunner and Rechberger, 2002 p.65
55 Brunner and Rechberger, 2002 p.66
56 Liechty, 2002
57 Liechty, 2002
58 Brunner et al., 1994
59 Clement, 2010 p.307
60 OECD, 2008
61 Li, H. et al., 2010
62 Rees, 1992
63 Behrens et al., 2005
64 Pomázi and Szabó, 2008 p.366
65 Warren-Rhodes and Koenig, 2001 p.431
66 Chan and Burns, 2002
67 Sahely et al., 2003 p.468
68 Keil and Boudreau, 2006 p.44
69 Browne et al., 2009 p.2769
70 Andrén, 2009
71 Tachibanaa et al., 2008 p.1389
72 Zhang et al., 2009 p.1695
73 Guo et al., 2005 p.454
74 Zhang et al., 2008 p.1054

CHAPTER 4: SMOKE, FUMES, DUST AND SMOG

1 Chovin, 1979
2 Makra and Brimblecombe, 2004 p.643
3 Cartuffo, 1993
4 Merlin and Traisnel, 1996 p.16
5 Makra and Brimblecombe, 2004 p.645
6 Makra and Brimblecombe, 2004 p.645
7 Makra and Brimblecombe, 2004 p.644
8 Marsh, 1947 p.21
9 Marsh, 1947 p.23
10 Marsh, 1947 p.31
11 Mosley, 2001 p.122
12 Mosley, 2006
13 Mosley, 2001 p.134
14 Mosley, 2001 p.137
15 Mosley, 2001 p.138

16 Mosley, 2001 p.119
17 Mosley, 2001 p.128
18 Mosley, 2001 p.131
19 Mosley, 2001 p.139
20 Mosley, 2001 p.141
21 Mosley, 2001 p.147
22 Meyer, 2002
23 Mosley, 2001 p.160
24 Mosley, 2001 p.172
25 Mosley, 2001 p.177
26 Mosley, 2001 p.184
27 Mosley, 2001 p. 184
28 Mosley, 2003
29 Marsh, 1947 p.43
30 Marsh, 1947 p.176
31 Thorsheim, 2002
32 Cox, 1973 p.187
33 Beattie et al., 2002
34 Uekoetter, 1999
35 Uekoetter, 1999
36 Uekoetter, 1999
37 Uekoetter, 1999
38 Farrell and Keating, 2000
39 Rosen, 1995
40 Rosen, 1995
41 Rosen, 1995
42 Farrell and Keating, 2000
43 Grinder, 1980
44 Rothbard, 1974
45 Rosen, 1995
46 Platt, 1995
47 Platt, 1995
48 Rosen, 1995
49 Gugliotta, 2004
50 Gugliotta, 2004 p.497
51 Freese, 2003 p.153
52 Freese, 2003 p.156
53 Gugliotta, 2004 p.494
54 Gugliotta, 2004 p.502
55 Gugliotta, 2004 p.574
56 Gugliotta, 2004 p.582
57 Tarr et al., 1980
58 Tarr et al., 1980
59 González, 2005
60 Freese, 2003 p.149
61 Freese, 2003 p.149
62 Freese, 2003 p.150
63 Freese, 2003 p.151
64 Rosen, 1995
65 Mumford, 1940 p.193
66 Tarr and Zimring, 1997
67 Farrell and Keating, 2000
68 Farrell and Keating, 2000
69 Silbergeld, 1995
70 Harrison and Laxen, 1981 p.5
71 Lin-Fu, 1980
72 Gibson, J.L. 1904
73 Aub et al., 1926
74 Lin-Fu, 1980
75 Harrison and Laxen, 1981 p.98
76 Schoenbrod, 1980
77 Daniel et al., 1990
78 Silbergeld, 1997
79 Silbergeld, 1996
80 Day et al., 1975; Day et al., 1979
81 Douglas et al., 1993
82 Mielke et al., 1983
83 Fernández and Galarraga, 2001
84 Fernández et al., 2003
85 Miguel et al., 1997
86 Rodamilans et al., 1996
87 Harrison and Laxen, 1981 p.94
88 Harrison and Laxen, 1981 p.95
89 Gidlow, 2004
90 Thomas et al., 1999
91 Tylecote, 1976
92 Hong et al., 1996
93 Healy, 1988
94 Makra and Brimblecombe, 2004
    p.651
95 Svidén et al., 2001
96 Romo-Kroger et al., 1994
97 Gunten, 2007
98 Farrell and Keating, 2000
99 Haagen-Smit, 1970
100 Farrell and Keating, 2000
101 González, 2005
102 Haagen-Smit, 1970
103 Krier and Ursin, 1977
104 González, 2002
105 González, 2002
106 Farrell, 2005
107 Farrell and Keating, 2000
108 Leishman et al., 2004
109 Shao et al., 2006
110 Borja-Aburto et al., 1997
111 McCreanor et al., 2007
112 Briet et al., 2007; Boutouyrie, 2008
113 Goyal et al., 2006
114 Huang et al., 2010

115 Kolbe and Gilchrist, 2011
116 Levy et al., 2010
117 Wang, Y. et al., 2011
118 Wang, Y. et al., 2011
119 Pandey, Khan et al., 2012
120 Pandey, Kumar et al., 2012
121 González, 2002
122 Kolbe and Gilchrist, 2011
123 Farrell, 2001
124 Millán et al.,1984
125 Castellsague et al., 1985
126 European Commission, 2006 p.13
127 ACEA, 2010
128 Resosudarmo, 2002
129 Molina et al., 2009
130 Ghosh, 2008
131 Sun and Florig, 2002
132 China Environment Yearbook Committee, 1998
133 Edmonds, 1998
134 Chan et al., 1995
135 Sun and Florig, 2002
136 Sun and Florig, 2002
137 Sun and Florig, 2002
138 See: http://ecocentric.blogs.time.com/2011/09/27/the-10-most-air-polluted-cities-in-the-world/#ixzz1m7Ru8h1Z (accessed 11 February 2012)
139 Vernier, 1993
140 Bliese, 2001 p.72
141 Stavins, 2002
142 Drury et al., 1999
143 Stavins, 2002
144 Stavins, 2002
145 Drury et al., 1999 p.289
146 European Commission, 2011
147 Spencer and Guérin, 2012
148 González, 2005

CHAPTER 5: WATER FROM THE HILLS, THE GROUND, THE SEA, AND THE ROOF

1 Caran and Neely, 2006
2 Hibbert, 1985 p.54
3 Scarre, 1995 p.106
4 Salway, 1981 p.578
5 Wacher, 1976 p.48
6 Wacher, 1976 p.320
7 Harrigan and Doughty, 2007 p.20
8 Mumford, 1940 p.48
9 Braudel, 1981
10 Maynard and Findon, 1913 p.23
11 Willan, 1980 p.120
12 Kennedy, 1970 p.31
13 Willan, 1980 p.120
14 Willan, 1980 p.120
15 Lambert, 2007
16 Plester and Binnie, 1995
17 Corbella, 2010 p.444
18 Braudel, 1981
19 Whitfield, 2006 p.97
20 Whitfield, 2006 p.97
21 Maynard and Findon, 1913 p.23
22 Midwinter, 1971 p.103
23 Plester and Binnie, 1995
24 Braudel, 1981
25 Girard, 1812
26 Risler, 1995
27 Cited by Whitfield, 2006 p.97
28 Foxell, 2007 p.149
29 Whitfield, 2006 p.97
30 Foxell, 2007 p.149
31 Whitfield, 2006 p.97
32 Foxell, 2007 p.150
33 Adam, 1851 p.6
34 Edwards, 1962 p.190
35 Turbutt, 1999 p.1478
36 Sheail, 1986 p.48
37 Rolt, 1974 p.246
38 Binnie, 1983
39 Rolt, 1974 p.247
40 Plester and Binnie, 1995
41 Lockwood, 1995
42 Soyer and Cailleux, 1960
43 Llamas, 1983
44 Corbella, 2010 p.454
45 *New York Times*, 1904 p.6
46 *New York Times*, 1900 p.22
47 Foxell, 2007 p.150
48 Water Guide, 2007
49 Edwards, 1962 p.190
50 Edwards, 1962 p.191
51 Kitson, 1982
52 Severn Trent Water, 2006 p.7

53 Stott, 1986
54 Plester and Binnie, 1995
55 Lamont et al., 1995
56 Kalin and Roberts, 1997
57 Risler, 1995
58 Corbella, 2010 p.472
59 Garrotte et al., 2007
60 Short, 2000, p.29
61 Crabb, 1986 p.24
62 Knights and Wong, 2004
63 Sydney Water Corporation, 2008
64 Brady, 1913 p.714
65 Lowe, 2004
66 Sofoulis, 2005
67 Sofoulis, 2005
68 Hundley, 1992 p.40
69 Hundley, 1992 p.44
70 Hundley, 1992 p.49
71 Hundley, 1992 p.138
72 Hundley, 1992 p.141
73 Hundley, 1992 p.144
74 Hundley, 1992 p.160
75 Kunzig, 2008
76 Kunzig, 2008
77 Kunzig, 2008
78 Kenney et al., 2008
79 Rome, 2001 p.103
80 Hackett, 1965; Cain and Beatty, 1965
81 Rome, 2001 p.107
82 Rome, 2001 p.107
83 Jackson, 2004
84 Jackson, 2004
85 Jackson, 2004
86 Jackson, 2004
87 Jackson, 2004
88 Jackson, 2004
89 Gandy, 2006b

90 Murakami, 1995
91 Aharoni, 2006
92 Working with Water, 2010
93 Patel, 2010
94 Anon, 2007
95 VNA 2010
96 Carrera-Hernandez and Gaskin, 2007
97 Yang et al., 2009
98 Foster, n.d.
99 Kuwairi, 2006
100 Alkolibi, 2002
101 Watts, 2009
102 Syagga and Olima, 1996
103 Anon, 2010
104 Liu, 1998
105 Zhang, et al., 2009
106 Jain et al., 2007
107 Bonné et al., 2002
108 Kelly, 2006
109 Chau, 1993
110 Fernandes et al., 2006
111 Oesterholt et al., 2007
112 Karnakata Act, 2009
113 City of Tucson 2008
114 Lallana, 2003
115 Gandy, 2006b
116 Anon, 2008
117 Phienwej and Nutalaya, 2005
118 Bhatia and Falkenmark 1993
119 Hutin et al., 2003
120 Bartlett, 2003
121 Hammad et al., 2008
122 McDonald et al., 2011
123 Kimball 2005
124 Emerton et al., 1998
125 IDA 2010
126 Allan et al., 2008

CHAPTER 6: SANITATION, SEWAGE AND MOUNTAINS OF TRASH

1 Angelakis et al., 2005
2 Angelakis et al., 2005
3 Angelakis et al., 2005
4 Scarre, 1995 p.20
5 Mumford, 1961 p.216
6 Gray, 1940
7 Gray, 1940
8 Gray, 1940

9 Larkey, 1934
10 Larkey, 1934 p.1101
11 Willan, 1980 p.121
12 Mumford, 1940 p.176
13 Turbutt, 1999 p.1565
14 Royal Commission for Enquiring into the State of Large Towns and Populous Districts, 1844

15 Mumford, 1940 p.177
16 Halliday, 2001
17 Smith, 1987
18 Rolt, 1974 p.143
19 McLoughlin, 1972
20 McLoughlin, 1972
21 Special correspondent, 1894
22 Cumbler, 1995
23 Cumbler, 1995
24 Melosi, 2000 p.6
25 Schultz and McShane, 1978
26 Schaake, 1972
27 Schultz and McShane, 1978
28 Schultz and McShane, 1978
29 Schaake, 1972 p.114
30 Klingle, 2007 p.89
31 Klingle, 2007 p.92
32 Klingle, 2007 p.208
33 Klingle, 2007 p.209
34 Geiselbrecht et al., 1996
35 Malins et al., 2006
36 Myers et al., 1990
37 Krishnakumar et al., 1999
38 Johnson et al., 1998
39 Bauer, 1980
40 Stroud, 1999
41 McCracken and Curson, 2000
    p.104
42 New South Wales Department of
    Planning, 1995
43 Freestone, 2000 p.129
44 Connell and Thom, 2000 p.322
45 Walton et al., 1995
46 Walton et al., 1995
47 Baillie and Catalano, 2009 p.263
48 Baillie and Catalano, 2009 p.264
49 Loftus and McDonald, 2001 p.3
50 Alcazar et al., 2000
51 Delfino et al., 2007
52 Suez Environement, 2010
53 Midwinter, 1971 p.109
54 Burton, 2003
55 Olsen et al., 1999
56 Working Party on Sewage Disposal,
    1970
57 EEC 1975, 1976, 1978
58 Li, S.R. et al., 1995
59 Bradley and Dhanagunan, 2004
60 Hunt, 2004 p.38
61 Melosi, 2005 p.3
62 Melosi, 2005 p.4
63 Melosi, 2005 p.4
64 Petts, 1994
65 Melosi, 2005 p.5
66 Melosi, 2005 p.6
67 Barles, 2005 p.31
68 Barles, 2005
69 Barles, 2003
70 Clark, 2007
71 Meade, 1898
72 Meade, 1898 p.424
73 Clark, 2007
74 Melosi, 2005 p.39
75 Clark, 2007
76 Clark, 2007
77 Clark, 2007
78 Clark, 2007
79 Clark, 2007
80 Clark, 2007
81 Clark, 2007
82 Cooper, 2010
83 Tarr and McShane, 2005
84 Tarr and McShane, 2005
85 Melosi, 2005 p.40
86 Eliassen,1969
87 Read et al., 1998
88 Petts, 1994
89 Petts, 1994
90 Petts, 1994
91 Clark, 2007
92 Petts, 1994
93 Nichols et al., 1986
94 Takahashi, 1998 p.171
95 EEC, 1994
96 O'Meara, 1999
97 Fischer et al., 2008
98 Wong et al., 2007
99 Browne et al., 2009
100 Jeffrey, 2012
101 Asian Development Bank,
    2004
102 Kum et al., 2005
103 Seng et al., 2011
104 Seng et al., 2011
105 Henry et al., 2006
106 Oyelola and Babatunde, 2008
107 Oyelola et al., 2009
108 Melosi, 2001

CHAPTER 7: URBAN SOUNDS AND SMELLS

1   de Roo 2000
2   Glasbergen 2005
3   Classen et al., 1994
4   Stevenson, 1972 p.195
5   Miller, 1997 p.69
6   Stevenson, 1972 p.195
7   Picker, 2003 p.43
8   Ackroyd, 2000 p.366
9   Fry, Michael, 2009 p.313
10 Royston Pike,1966 p.341
11 Piccolo et al., 2005
12 Garcia, 2001a
13 Pinch and Bijsterveld, 2012 p.4
14 Stevenson, 1972 p.196
15 Brüel & Kjær, n.d.
16 Babisch, 2000
17 Picker, 2003 p.21
18 Noise Abatement Society, 1969 p.50
19 Picker, 2003 p.46
20 Picker, 2003 p.58
21 Dyos, 1982
22 Noise Abatement Society, 1969 p.51
23 Picker, 2003 p.65
24 Noise Abatement Society, 1969 p.1
25 Braun, 2012
26 Penn-Bressel, 1999
27 Schiller, 1999
28 Penn-Bressel, 1999
29 Debonnet-Lambert, 1999
30 Debonnet-Lambert, 1999
31 Debonnet-Lambert, 1999
32 Harnapp and Noble, 1987 p.222
33 Beranek, 1962
34 Coates, 2005
35 Anon, 1899
36 Bijsterveld, 2001
37 Rice, 1907
38 Smilor, 1977, 1979
39 Smilor, 1977, 1979
40 Harnapp and Noble, 1987 p.220
41 Harnapp and Noble, 1987 p.220
42 Reagan, 1987; Broder, 1988
43 Broder, 1988
44 Broder, 1988 p.307
45 Broder, 1988 p.307
46 Simo and Clearly, 2004
47 Simo and Clearly, 2004

48 Fitzgerald, 1996
49 Deepak, 1999
50 Tomkins et al., 1998
51 Tomkins et al., 1998
52 Haines et al., 2002
53 Tomkins et al., 1998
54 McMillen, 2004
55 Kranser, 2002
56 Brueckner and Girvin, 2006
57 Miami International Airport, 2000
58 Brueckner and Girvin, 2006 p.25
59 Garcia and Raichel, 2003
60 Garcia, 2001b
61 Northern Ireland Government, 2008
62 Adams et al., 2006
63 British Standards Institution, 1997
64 UK Government, 1989
65 Mumford, 1940
66 Freese, 2003
67 Classen et al., 1994
68 Ackroyd, 2000, p.367
69 Keneally, 2007 p.14
70 Carr, 2004
71 Welchman et al., 2005
72 Welchman et al., 2005
73 Engen, 1982
74 Engen, 1982 p.8
75 Engen, 1982 p.169
76 Köster, 1994 p.81
77 Köster, 1994 p.83
78 Milhau et al., 1994 p.446
79 McGinley and McGinley, 2006
80 Shi et al., 2004
81 Van Harreveld, 1998
82 Committee for European
    Normalization, 2003
83 Gandy, 1999 p.34
84 Gandy, 1999 p.26
85 Thompson, 1963 p.352
86 Van Harreveld, 2003
87 Milhau et al., 1994
88 Massard-Guilbaud, 2005
89 Massard-Guilbaud, 2005
90 Rosen, 2003
91 Rosen, 2003
92 Rosen, 2003
93 Shultz and Collar, 1993

94 Batalhone et al., 2002
95 Paillard and Martin, 1994
96 Taylor et al., 2003
97 Motsi et al., 2002

98 Lewis and Galardi, 2002
99 Koe, 2002; Koe and Yang, 2000
100 Horner, 1988
101 Kaye, 2001

CHAPTER 8: CITIES AND A DYNAMIC EARTH

1 Sbeinati et al., 2005
2 Erol and Pirazzoli, 2007
3 Reclus, 1877 p.595
4 Reclus, 1877 p.595
5 Kaplan, 1991 p.94
6 Based in part upon http://
earthquake.usgs.gov/earthquakes/
world/world_deaths_sort.php
(accessed 21 July 2012)
7 Draper, 2011
8 Corona, 2005
9 Calcaterra and Santo, 2004
10 Fiorillo and Wilson 2004
11 Brabb et al., 1972
12 Brabb et al., 1972
13 Mancini et al., 2010
14 Giraud and Shaw, 2007
15 Yi et al., 2010
16 Reclus, 1877 p.589
17 Reclus, 1877 p.639
18 Reclus, 1877 p.639
19 Brambati et al., 2003
20 Osmanoğlu et al., 2010
21 Phienwej and Nutalaya, 2005 p.368
22 Carpenter and Bradley, 1986
23 Mayuga and Allen, 1970
24 Erikson, 1976
25 Allen, 1984
26 Cooper, 1995
27 Waltham, 2005 p.670
28 Pelli et al., 1997
29 Department of Transport Local
Government and the Regions, 2002
30 Morozova, 2004
31 Reade, 1991 p.41
32 Hunt, 2004 p.109
33 Hunt, 2004 p.121
34 Gupta, 2004
35 Belcher and Belcher, 2000
36 Clift and Blusztajn, 2005
37 Staubwasser et al., 2003

38 Staubwasser et al., 2003
39 Parker et al., 2006
40 Mustafa and Wescoat, 1997
41 Akhtar, 2011
42 Zong and Chen, 2000
43 Zong and Chen, 2000
44 Ulbrich et al., 2003
45 Kreibich et al., 2005
46 Linde et al., 2011
47 Blackbourn, 2006
48 Lammersen et al., 2002
49 Disse and Engel, 2001
50 Reclus, 1877 p.386
51 Reclus, 1877 p.386
52 Reclus, 1877 p.392
56 Kates et al., 2006
54 Changnon, 1998
55 Black, 2008
56 Fink et al., 1996
57 Disse and Engel, 2001
58 Knocke and Kolivras, 2007
59 Slaymaker, 1999
60 Tooley, 2000
61 Tsuchiya and Kanata, 1986
62 Tsuchiya and Kanata, 1986
63 Donnelly et al., 2001
64 Foster & Partners, 2011
65 McRobie et al., 2005
66 Bijker, 2007
67 Matsumoto and Inoue, 2011
68 Gray, 1993
69 Douglas et al., 2002
70 James and Singer, 2008
71 Douglas, 1996
72 Hannam, 1979
73 Soil Conservation Service, 1968
74 Maynard and Findon, 1913
p.22
75 Maynard and Findon, 1913 p.23
76 Smith, 2005 p.31
77 Smith, 2005 p.32

78 Bradley, 2007 p.68
79 Deligne, 2003
80 Laconte, 2007 p.24
81 Kang and Cervero, 2009

82 Wild et al., 2011
83 Love, 2005
84 Chin and Gregory, 2009
85 Wild et al., 2011

CHAPTER 9: URBAN GREENSPACES

1   Duany et al., 2000 p.33
2   Landscape Institute, 2011
3   Miller, 1997 p.46
4   Hibbert, 1985 p.41
5   Platner, 1929 p.268
6   Masri, 1992
7   Cong and Huang, 1986 p.64
8   Miller, 1997, p.46
9   Schnefftan, 1992 p.126
10 Kimura, 1998
11 Miller, 1997 p.46
12 Miller, 1997 p.48
13 Clark, 2006
14 Clark, 2006
15 Miller, 1997 p.49
16 Miller, 1997 p.50
17 Fitter, 1945 p.56
18 Hoskins and Stamp, 1963 p.67
19 Hoskins and Stamp, 1963 p.72
20 Hoskins and Stamp, 1963 p.78
21 Goode, 1986 p.172
22 Laurie, M. 1979 p.26
23 Goode, 1986 p.172
24 Fitter, 1945 p.95
25 Clout, 1991 p.74
26 Laurie, M. 1979 p.47
27 Clout, 1991 p.142
28 Laurie, M. 1979 p.47
29 Ashworth, 1954 p.110
30 Goode, 1986 p.173
31 Goode, 1986 p.172
32 Ashworth, 1954 p.111
33 Ashworth, 1954 p.112
34 Unwin, 1929
35 Mayor of London, 2006 p.13
36 Worpole and Greenhalgh, 1995
37 Borough of Tower Hamlets, 2006
38 Borough of Haringey, 2008
39 CABE Space 2008
40 Laurie, M. 1979 p.47
41 Tan et al., 1995

42 Hough, 1984 p.15
43 Paterson, 1976 p.96
44 Cranz, 1989 p.226
45 Duany et al., 2000 p.31
46 McHarg, 1964; Rome 2001, p.125
47 Rome, 2001 p.126
48 Whyte, 1956
49 Whyte, 1968, p.199
50 Rome, 2001 p.130
51 Rome, 2001 p.140
52 Rome, 2001 p.146
53 Rome, 2001 p.147
54 Miller, 1997 p.51
55 Rome, 2001 p.151
56 O'Riordan and Davis, 1976 p.265
57 National Parks Service, 2007
58 Brubaker, 1995
59 Berry and Horton, 1974 p.368
60 Miller, 1997 p.33
61 Miller, 1997 p.34
62 Miller, 1997 p.35
63 Coles and Bussey, 2001
64 Spurr, 1976 p.317
65 Higbee, 1976 p.159
66 O'Riordan and Davis, 1976 p.274
67 Duany et al., 2000 p.62
68 Duany et al., 2000 p.143
69 Douglas and Box, 2000
70 Reid, 1961
71 Hilton, 1961
72 Victor et al., 2004
73 Ravetz, 2011 p.603
74 Ravetz, 2011 p.609
75 Houck, 2011 p.49
76 Houck, 2011 p.49
77 Clark, 2006
78 Hough, 1984 p.151
79 Frost and Hyman, 2011 p.554
80 *Manchester Guardian* 28 May 1842,
    cited in Mosley, 2001 p.37
81 Mosley, 2001 p.38

82 Mosley, 2001 p.39
83 Mosley, 2001 p.43
84 Mosley, 2001 p.44
85 Hookway, 1978 p.173
86 Friends of Birley Fields, 2008
87 Meller, 2005
88 Smit et al., 2001 p.2
89 Smit et al., 2001 p.1
90 Bowyer-Bower et al., 2004
91 Drakakis Smith et al., 1994
92 Yoyeva et al., 2002
93 Meller, 2005
94 Meller, 2005 p.84
95 Meller, 2005
96 Buczacki, 2007 p.15
97 Baynton-Williams, 1992

98 Gill at al., 2007
99 Buczacki, 2007 p.25
100 Buczacki, 2007 p.27
101 Groundwork UK, 2008
102 Karskens, 2007
103 Hough, 1984 p.21
104 Landlife, 2007
105 Hough, 1984 p.21
106 Goode, 1986 p.173
107 Hough, 1984 p.145
108 Hall and Page, 2006
109 Masai, 1998 p.69
110 Millward and Mostyn, 1988
111 Gilbert, 1989
112 Burgess et al., 1988
113 Box and Harrison, 1993

CHAPTER 10: URBAN SUSTAINABILITY

1 Dilke and Dilke, 1976 p.64
2 Veen et al., 2008
3 Mumford, 1961 p.260
4 Deelstra, 1986 p.25
5 Houck, 2011 p.55
6 Patmore, 1972 p.284
7 Hopkinson, 1941 p.4
8 Fry, Maxwell, 1941 p.19
9 Sharp, 1940 p.50
10 Sharp, 1940 p.51
11 Sharp, 1940 p.55
12 Atkinson, 1992
13 O'Neil, 1970 p.21
14 McHarg, 1969
15 Ways, 1970 p.43
16 Gans, 1972 p.81
17 Fairbrother, 1972 p.225
18 Patmore,1972 p.237
19 Mabey, 1973
20 Lovelock and Margulis, 1974
21 Carson, 1962
22 Rapoport, 1972
23 The World Conservation Strategy
    was prepared by the International
    Union for Conservation of Nature
    and Natural Resources, now called
    the World Conservation Union
    (IUCN), in cooperation with the
    World Wildlife Fund (WWF), the

    United Nations Environment
    Programme and other UN agencies,
    such as Food and Agriculture
    Organization and the United
    Nations Educational, Scientific and
    Cultural Organization (UNESCO).
24 International Union for the
    Conservation of Nature, 1980
25 World Commission on Environment
    and Development, 1987
26 Satterthwaite, 1992 p.3
27 Elkin and McLaren, 1991
28 Elkin and McLaren, 1991 p.9
29 Deelstra and Girardet, 2000 p.45
30 Keating, 1993 p.12
31 CEC, 1990
32 EU Expert Group on the Urban
    Environment, 1994
33 Ravetz, 2000
34 Fudge, 1997 p.18
35 Wang and Paulussen, 2007 p.329
36 Wang and Paulussen, 2007 p.330
37 Wang and Paulussen, 2007 p.336
38 UNCHS (Habitat), 2001 p.116
39 UNCHS (Habitat), 2001 p.117
40 World Bank, 2009
41 World Bank, 2009 p.1
42 Suzuki, et al., 2010
43 Worrall and Little, 2011

44 Head, 2008
45 Head, 2008 p.73
46 Miranda and Hordijk, 1998 p.98
47 Miranda and Hordijk, 1998
    p.101
48 Velásquez, 1998 p.27
49 Velásquez, 1998 p.35
50 Li, S. et al., 2010
51 Lafarge, 2011
52 Sseesamirembe Eco-City, 2008

53 Desert burner, 2009
54 Joss, 2010
55 Joss, 2010 p.247
56 Silverstein, 2011
57 Hassan and Cajee, 2002
58 Mortada, 2002
59 Laylin, 2010
60 Wang, R.S. et al., 2011
61 Quastel, 2009
62 Vancouver, 2011

Bibliography

ACEA 2010 *Overview of CO₂ based motor vehicle taxes in the EU.* http://www.acea.be/images/uploads/files/20100420_CO2_tax_overview.pdf [accessed 03 May 2012].

Achtman, A. 2008 Evolution, Population Structure, and Phylogeography of Genetically Monomorphic Bacterial Pathogens. *Annual Review of Microbiology,* 62, 53–70.

Achtman, M., Morelli, G., Zhu, P.X., Wirth, T., Diehl, I., Kusecek, B., Vogler, A.J., Wagner, D.N., Allender, C.J., Easterday, W.R., Chenal-Francisque, V., Worsham, P., Thomson, N.R., Parkhill, J., Lindler, L.E., Carniel, E., and Keim, P. 2004 Microevolution and history of the plague bacillus, *Yersinia pestis. Proceedings National Academy of Sciences (PNAS),* 101 (51), 17837–42.

Ackroyd, P. 2000 *London: The Biography.* London: Chatto & Windus.

Adam, W. 1851 *The Gem of the Peak; or Matlock Bath and its vicinity.* John and Charles Mozley, Derby, 5th edition (reprinted Moorland Publishing, Hartington, 1973).

Adams, M., Cox, T., Moore, G., Croxford, B., Refaee, M. and Sharples, S. 2006 Sustainable soundscapes: noise policy and the urban experience. *Urban Studies,* 43, 2385–98.

Aharoni, A. 2006 Tel Aviv's urban water system: from source to reuse. Paper presented at the SWITCH Workshop on Learning Alliance, December 10–11, 2006, Tel Aviv, Israel.

Akhtar, S. 2011 The South Asiatic Monsoon and flood hazards in the Indus River basin, Pakistan. *Journal of Basic and Applied Sciences,* 7 (20), 101–15.

Alcazar, L., Abdala, M. and Shirley, M. 2000 *The Buenos Aires water concession.* World Bank Policy Research Working Paper 2311. Washington DC: World Bank.

Alkolibi, F.M. 2002 Possible effects of Global Warming on Agriculture and Water Resources in Saudi Arabia: Impacts and Responses. *Climate Change,* 54, 225–45.

Allan, C., Curtis, C., Stankey, G. and Shindler, B. 2008 Adaptive Management and Watersheds: A Social Science Perspective. *Journal of the American Water Resources Association,* 44 (1), 166–74.

Allen, A.S. 1984 Types of land subsidence. In Poland, J.F. (ed.) *Guidebook to studies of land subsidence due to ground-water withdrawal.* Paris: UNESCO, 133–42.

Allen, B.L. 2007 Environmental justice, local knowledge, and after-disaster planning in New Orleans. *Technology in Society,* 29 (2), 153–9.

Andrén, S. 2009 The Challenge of Urban Sustainability in a Globalising Economy: Malmö as a case for an integrated sustainability policy. http://www.cityfutures2009.com/pdf/95_Andrn_Sabina.pdf [accessed 21 February 2011].

Angelakis, A.N., Koutsoyiannis, D. and Tchobanoglous, G. 2005 Urban wastewater and stormwater technologies in ancient Greece. *Water Research,* 39, 210–20.

Anon. 1899 The Horseless Carriage and Public Health. *Scientific American,* 80 (18 February 1899), 98.

Anon. 2007 Solar-powered desalination plant leads the way. *EcosMagazine*, 134 (Dec–Jan), 4. http://www.ecosmagazine.com/?act=view_file&file_id=EC134p4.pdf [accessed 22 November 2011].

Anon. 2008 Now, DJB nod must for drilling borewells in city. *The Times of India*, 3 December 2008.

Anon. 2010 Nigerian water sector embraces PSP. *Global Water Intelligence*, 11, (6). http://www.globalwaterintel.com/archive/11/6/general/nigerian-water-sector-embraces-psp.html [accessed 23 November 2011].

Ashworth, W. 1954 *The genesis of modern British town planning.* London: Routledge and Kegan Paul.

Asian Development Bank 2004 History of Waste Disposal Crisis. http://www.adb.org/documents/books/garbage-book/chap2.pdf [accessed 21 November 2011].

Atkinson, A. 1992 The Urban Bioregion as 'Sustainable Development' Paradigm. *Third World Planning Review*, 14 (4), 327–41.

Aub, J.C., Fairhall, L.T., Minot, A.S. and Resinkoff, P. 1926 Lead Poisoning. *Medicine*, 4, 1–250.

Babisch W. 2000 Traffic Noise and Cardiovascular Disease: Epidemiological Review and Synthesis. *Noise and Health*, 2, 9–32.

Baillie, C. and Catalano, G. 2009 *Engineering and Society: working towards social justice.* San Francisco: Morgan & Claypool.

Barles S. 2003 Entre artisanat et industrie: l'engrais humain XIXe siècle. Hilaire-Perez L. et Verna C. (eds) *Artisanat, industrie, nouvelles révolutions du Moyen Âge à nos jours.* Paris: ENS Éditions, 187–201.

——. 2005 A metabolic approach to the city: Nineteenth and twentieth century Paris. In: Luckin, B., Massard-Guilbaud, G. and Schott, D. (eds) *Resources of the City: Contributions to an Environmental History of Modern Europe.* Aldershot: Ashgate, 28–47.

——. 2007 Urban metabolism and river systems: an historical perspective – Paris and the Seine, 1790–1970. *Hydrol. Earth Syst. Sci. Discuss.*, 4, 1845–78.

Barrett, A.D.T. and Higgs, S. 2007 Yellow Fever: A Disease that Has Yet to be Conquered. *Annual Review of Entomology*, 52, 209–29.

Barrett J. and Scott A. 2001 *An Ecological Footprint of Liverpool: Developing Sustainable Scenarios.* York: Stockholm Environment Institute.

Bartlett, S. 2003 Water, sanitation and urban children: the need to go beyond 'improved' provision. *Environment and Urbanization*, 15 (2), 57–70.

Batalhone, S., Nogueira, J. and Mueller, B. 2002 Economics of Air Pollution: Hedonistic Price Model and Smell Consequences of Sewage Treatment Plants in Urban Areas. *Working Paper, Texto Para Discussao* 234, 1–20, Brasilia: Department of Economics, University of Brasilia, Brazil.

Bauer, W.S. 1980 A Case Analysis of Oregon's Willamette River Greenway Program. Unpublished PhD thesis. Oregon State University.

Baynton-Williams, A. 1992 *Town and City Maps of the British Isles.* London: Studio Editions.

Beattie. C.I., Longhurst, J.W.S. and Woodfield, N.K. 2002 A Comparative Analysis of the Air Quality Management Challenges and Capabilities in Urban and Rural English Local Authorities. *Urban Studies*, 39, 2469–83.

Behrens, B., Giljum, S., Kovanda, J. and Niza, S. 2005 The Material Basis of the Global Economy: Implications for Sustainable Resource Use Policies in North and South. Paper presented at the conference 'Environmental Accounting and Sustainable Development Indicators' Charles University Environmental Centre, Prague, 26–27

September, 2005. http://old.seri.at/documentuploce/pdf/seri_globalresourceuse.pdf [accessed 21 February 2011].

Belcher, W.R. and Belcher, W.R. 2000 Geologic constraints on the Harappa archaeological site, Punjab Province, Pakistan. *Geoarchaeology*, 15, 679–713.

Beranek, L.L. 1962 Noise and its control. *Encyclopaedia Britannica*, Vol. 16, Chicago: Encyclopaedia Britannica Inc., 480–480B.

Berry, B.J.L. and Horton, F.E. 1974 *Urban environmental management: planning for pollution control*. Englewood Cliffs, New Jersey: Prentice-Hall.

Best Foot Forward 2002 *City Limits: A Resource Flow and Ecological Footprint Analysis of Greater London*. Oxford: Best Foot Forward Ltd.

Bhatia, R., and M. Falkenmark. 1993. Water resource policies and the urban poor: Innovative approaches and policy imperatives. In *Water and Sanitation Currents*. Washington, DC: World Bank.

Bijker, W.E. 2007 American and Dutch Coastal Engineering: Differences in Risk Conception and Differences in Technological Culture. *Social Studies of Science*, 37 (1), 143–51.

Bijsterveld, K. 2001 The Diabolical Symphony of the Mechanical Age: Technology and Symbolism of Sound in European and North American Noise Abatement Campaigns, 1900–40. *Social Studies of Science*, 31 (1), 137–70.

Binnie, G.M. 1983 Postscript to 'The collapse of the Dale Dyke dam in retrospect'. *Quarterly Journal of Engineering Geology and Hydrogeology*, 16, 357–8.

Black, H. 2008 Unnatural Disaster: Human Factors in the Mississippi Floods. *Environmental Health Perspectives*, 116 (9), A390–3.

Blackbourn, D. 2006 *The conquest of nature: water, landscape, and the making of modern Germany*. London: Norton.

Bliese, J.R.E. 2001 *The greening of conservative America*. Boulder CO: Westview.

Bloom, M. 2001 Editorial—Primary Prevention and Public Health: An Historical Note on Dr. John Hoskins Griscom. *The Journal of Primary Prevention*, 21 (3), 305–8.

Blumin, S.M. 1989 *The emergence of the middle class: social experience in the American city, 1760-1900*. Cambridge: Cambridge University Press.

Bondesan, M., Gatti, M. and Russo, P. 2000 Subsidence in the Eastern Po Plain. In Carbognin, L., Gambolati, G. and Johnson, A.L. (eds) *Land subsidence (Proceeding of the 6th international symposium on land subsidence), Vol II*. La Garangola, Padova Italy, 193–204.

Bondesan, M. and Simeoni, U. 1983 Dinamica e analisi morfologica statistica dei litorali del delta del Po e alle foci dell'Adige e del Brenta. *Memoria società geologica d'Italia*, 36, 1–48.

Bonné, R.A.C., Hiemstra, E., Hoek, J.R. van der and Hofman, J.A.M.H. 2002 Is direct nanofiltration with air flush an alternative for household water production for Amsterdam? *Desalination*, 152, 263–9.

Borja-Aburto, V.H., Loomis, D.P., Bangdiwala, S.I., Shy, C.M. and Rascon, R.A 1997 Ozone, Suspended Particulates, and Daily Mortality in Mexico City. *American Journal of Epidemiology*, 145, 258–68.

Borough of Haringey 2008 London Borough of Haringey Open Space Strategy 'A space for everyone'. http://www.haringey.gov.uk/open_space_strategy.pdf [accessed 23 July 2012].

Borough of Tower Hamlets, 2006 An Open Spaces Strategy for the London Borough of Tower Hamlets 2006 – 2016. www.towerhamlets.gov.uk/idoc.ashx?docid=1d58706f-82c2 [accessed 23 July 2012].

Boutouyrie, P. 2008 La pollution altère la paroi des vaisseaux. *La Recherche*, 415, 24.

Bowyer-Bower, T.A.S., Mapaure, I. and Drummond, R.B. 2004 Ecological degradation in cities: Impact of urban agriculture in Harare, Zimbabwe. *Journal of Applied Science in Southern Africa*, 2 (2), 53–67.

Box, J. and Harrison, C. 1993 Natural space in urban places. *Town & Country Planning*, 62, 231–4.

Brabb, E.E., Pampeyan, E.H. and Bonilla, M.G. 1972 Landslide susceptibility in San Mateo County, California. *US Geological Survey Miscellaneous Field Studies Map* MF360.

Bradley, R.M. and Dhanagunan, G.R. 2004 Sewage sludge management in Malaysia. *International Journal of Water*, 2 (4), 267–83.

Bradley, S. 2007 *St. Pancras Station*. London: Profile Books.

Brady, E.J. 1913 *Australia Unlimited*. Melbourne: George Robertson and Company.

Brakman, S., Garretsen, H. and Schramm, M. 2003 The Strategic Bombing of German Cities during World War II and its Impact on City Growth. *Utrecht School of Economics, Tjalling C. Koopmans Research Institute*, Discussion Paper Series 03–08.

Brambati, A., Carbognin, L., Quaia, T., Teatini, P. and Tosi, L. 2003 The Lagoon of Venice: geological setting, evolution and land subsidence. *Episodes*, 26 (3), 264–8.

Braudel, F. 1981 *Civilization & Capitalism 15th-18th Century Vol.I, The Structures of Everyday Life*. London: Collins.

———. 1988 *The Identity of France, Volume One History and Environment*. London: Collins.

Braun, H-J. 2012 Turning a deaf ear? Industrial noise and noise control in Germany since the 1920s. In Pinch, T. and Bijsterveld, K. (eds) *The Oxford Handbook of Sound Studies*. Oxford: Oxford University Press, 58–77.

Briet, M., Collin, C., Laurent, S., Tan, A., Azizi, M., Agharazii, M., Jeunemaitre, X., Alhenc-Gelas, F. and Boutouyrie, P. 2007 Endothelial Function and Chronic Exposure to Air Pollution in Normal Male Subjects. *Hypertension*, 50, 970–6.

British Standards Institution 1997 *British Standard BS 4142:1997: Rating industrial noise affecting mixed residential and industrial areas*. London: British Standards Institution.

Broder, I.E. 1988 A study of the birth and death of a regulatory agenda: the case of the EPA noise program. *Evaluation Review*, 12, 291–309.

Browne, G., O'Regan, B. and Moles, R. 2009 Assessment of total urban metabolism and metabolic inefficiency in an Irish city-region. *Waste Management*, 29, 2765–71.

Brubaker, E. 1995 *Property Rights in the Defence of Nature*. London: Earthscan Publications Limited and Earthscan Canada.

Brueckner, J.K. and Girvin, R. 2006 Airport noise regulation, airline service quality, and social welfare. *CESIFO Working Paper* No. 1820.

Brüel & Kjær n.d. *Environmental Noise Measurement*. Nærum, Denmark: Brüel & Kjær. http://cafefoundation.org/v2/pdf_tech/Noise.Technologies/PAV.Environ.Noise.B&K. pdf [accessed 25 October 2011].

Brunner, P.H., Daxbeck, H. and Baccini, P. (1994) Industrial metabolism at the regional and local level: A case study on a Swiss region. In R.B. Ayres and U.E. Simonis (eds) *Industrial Metabolism – Restructuring for Sustainable Development*. Tokyo: United Nations University Press, 163–93.

Brunner, P.H. and Rechberger, H. 2002 Anthropogenic metabolism and environmental legacies. In Douglas, I. (ed.) *Causes and consequence of environmental change; Encyclopedia of Global Environmental Change* (ed. Munn, T.) Vol. 3. Chichester: Wiley, 54–72.

Buczacki, S. 2007 *Garden Natural History*. London: Collins New Naturalist.

Burgess, J., Harrison, C.M. and Limb, M. 1988 People, parks and the urban green: a study of popular meanings and values for open spaces in the city. *Urban Studies*, 25, 455–73.

Burton L.R. 2003 The Mersey Basin: an historical assessment of water quality from an anecdotal perspective. *The Science of the Total Environment*, 314–6, 53–66.

CABE Space 2008 *Public Spaces.* www.cabe.org.uk/default.aspx?contentitemid=41 [accessed 14 February 2008].

Cain, J.M. and Beatty, M.T. 1965 Disposal of septic tank effluent in soils. *Journal of Soil and Water Conservation*, 20, 101–5.

Calame, J. 2005 Post-war Reconstruction: Concerns, Models and Approaches. *Center For Macro Projects and Diplomacy, Macro Center Working Papers*. http://digitalcommons. rwu.edu/cmpd working papers/20 [accessed 21 January 2008].

Calcaterra, D. and Santo, A. 2004 The January 10, 1997 Pozzano landslide, Sorrento Peninsula, Italy. *Engineering Geology*, 75, 181–200.

Calcott, A. and Bull, J. 2007 *Ecological footprint of British City residents.* Godalming: WWF-UK.

Caputo, M., Pieri, L. and Unguendoli, M. 1970 Geometric investigation of the subsidence in the Po Delta. *Bolletino di Geofisica Teorica e Applicata*, 47, 187–207.

Caran S.C. and Neely, J.A. 2006 Hydraulic engineering in prehistoric Mexico. *Scientific American*, 295 (4), 56–63.

Carpenter, M.C. and Bradley, M.D. 1986 Legal perspectives on subsidence caused by groundwater withdrawal in Texas, California and Arizona. *Publications International Association of Hydrological Sciences*, 151, 817–28.

Carr, A. 2004 *Positive psychology: the Science of happiness and human strengths.* New York: Brunner-Routledge.

Carrera-Hernandez, J.J. and Gaskin, S.J. 2007 The Basin of Mexico aquifer system: regional groundwater level dynamics and database development. *Hydrogeology Journal*, 15 (8), 1577–90.

Carson, P.A. and Mumford, C.J. 1979 An analysis of incidents involving major hazards in the chemical industry. *Journal of Hazardous Materials*, 3, 149–65.

Carson, R. 1962 *Silent Spring.* New York: Houghton-Mifflin.

Cartuffo, D. 1993 Reconstructing the climate and the air pollution of Rome during the life of the Trajan Column. *Science of the Total Environment*, 128, 205–26.

Cassedy, J.H. (1975). The roots of American sanitary reform 1843–47: Seven letters from John H. Griscom to Lemuel Shattuck. *Journal of the History of Medicine and Allied Sciences*, 30, 136–47.

Castellsague, J., Sunyer, J., Saez, M. and J.M. Anto 1985 Short-term association of urban air pollution with emergency room visits for asthma. *Thorax*, 50, 1051–6.

CEC (Commission of the European Communities) 1990 *Green Paper on the Urban Environment.* Brussels: CEC.

Chadwick, E. 1842 Report on the Sanitary Condition of the Labouring Population. *Great Britain Parliamentary Papers, 1842*, vol. xxvi, 369–72 (reprinted as Conclusions from the Sanitary Report, 1842. In Harvie, C., Martin, G. and Scharf, A. (eds) *Industrialisation & Culture 1830-1914.* London: Macmillan and Open University Press).

Chaloner, W.H. 1962 The Birth of Manchester. In Carter C.F. (ed.) *Manchester: A survey.* Manchester: Manchester University Press.

Chan, H.S., Wong, K-K., Cheung, K.C. and Lo, J.M-K. 1995 The Implementation Gap in Environmental Management in China: The Case of Guangzhou, Zhengzhou, and Nanjing. *Public Administration Review*, 55 (4), 333–40.

Chan, J.W.K. and Burns, N.D. 2002 Benchmarking manufacturing planning and control (MPC) systems: An empirical study of Hong Kong supply chains. *Benchmarking: An International Journal*, 9 (3), 256–77.

Chandler, P.J. 2007 Environmental factors influencing the siting of temporary housing in Orleans Parish. MSc Thesis, Louisiana State University etd-04122007-133815.

Changnon, S.A. 1998 The historical struggle with floods on the Mississippi River basin: Impacts of recent floods and lessons for future flood management and policy. *Water International*, 23 (4), 263–71.

Chau, K.W. 1993 Management of limited water resources in Hong Kong. *Water Resources Development*, 9 (1), 65–73.

Cheng, S. and McBride, J.R. 2006 Restoration of the urban forests of Tokyo and Hiroshima following the Second World War. *Urban Forestry & Urban Greening*, 5, 155–68.

Chew, S.C. 2001 *World Ecological Degradation: Accumulation, urbanization, and deforestation 3000 B.C. – A.D. 2000*. Walnut Creek, CA: Altamira Press.

Childe, G. 1958 *The Prehistory of European Society*. Harmondsworth: Penguin Books.

Chin, A. and Gregory, K.J. 2009 From Research to Application: Management Implications from Studies of Urban River Channel Adjustment. *Geography Compass*, 3 (1), 297–328.

China Environment Yearbook Committee 1998 *China Environment Yearbook 1998*. Beijing: China Environment Yearbook Press.

Chovin, P. 1979 *La pollution atmosphérique*. Paris: Presses Universitaire de la France.

City of Tucson 2008. *Ordinance No. 10597*. Tucson, AZ.

Clark, J.F.M. 2007 'The incineration of refuse is beautiful': Torquay and the introduction of municipal refuse destructors. *Urban History*, 34, 255–77.

Clark, P. (ed.) 2006 *The European city and green space: London, Stockholm, Helsinki and St Petersburg, 1850–2000*. Aldershot: Ashgate.

Classen, C., Howes, D. and Synott, A. 1994 *Aroma: the cultural history of smell*. London: Routledge.

Clement, M.T. 2010 Urbanization and the Natural Environment: An Environmental Sociological Review and Synthesis. *Organization & Environment*, 23 (3), 291–314.

Clift, P.D. and Blusztajn, J. 2005 Reorganization of the western Himalayan river system after five million years ago. *Nature*, 438, 1001–3.

Clout, H. (ed.) 1991 *The Times London History Atlas*. London: Times Books.

Coates, P.A. 2005 The strange stillness of the past: towards an environmental history of sound and noise. *Environmental History*, 10, 636–65.

Coles, R.W. and Bussey, S.C. 2001 Urban forest landscapes in the UK – progressing the social agenda. *Landscape and Urban Planning*, 52, 181–8.

Colten, C.E. 2005 *An Unnatural Metropolis: Wrestling New Orleans from Nature*. Baton Rouge, LA: Louisiana State University Press.

Comerio, M. 1998 *Disaster hits home: New policy for urban housing recovery*. Berkeley, CA: University of California Press.

Committee for European Normalization 2003 *EN 13725:2003, Air Quality – Determination of Odour Concentration by Dynamic Olfactometry*. Brussels: European Committee for Standardization (CEN), Technical Committee 267.

Cong, S. and Huang, Z. (eds) 1986 *Beautiful Beijing*. Beijing: China Photographic Publishing House.

Connell, J. and Thom, B. 2000 Beyond 2000: The post-Olympic city. In Connell, J. (ed.) *Sydney: The Emergence of a World City*. South Melbourne: Oxford University Press, 319–43.

Cooper, A.H. 1995 Subsidence hazards due to the dissolution of Permian gypsum in England: Investigation and remediation. In Beck B.F., Pearson, F.M. and LaMoreaux, P.E. (eds) *Karst geohazards: engineering and environmental problems in karst terrane.* Rotterdam: Balkema, 23–9.

Cooper, L. 2006 *Early Urbanism on the Syrian Euphrates.* London: Routledge.

Cooper, T. 2010 Burying the 'refuse revolution': the rise of controlled tipping in Britain, 1920–1960. *Environment and Planning A*, 42 (5), 1033–48.

Corbella, H.M. 2010 *Urban water management and market environmentalism: A historical perspective for Barcelona and Madrid,* Tesi Doctoral, Universitat Autònoma de Barcelona.

Corona G. 2005 Sustainable Naples: the disappearance of nature as a resource in D. Schott, D., Luckin, B. and Massard-Guilbaud, G. (eds) *Resources of the City. Contributions to an Environmental History of Modern Europe.* Aldershot: Ashgate.

Cousins, W.J. 2004 Towards a first-order earthquake loss model for New Zealand. *Proceedings of the 2004 Conference of the New Zealand National Society for Earthquake Engineering.* http://db.nzsee.org.nz/2004/Paper29.pdf [accessed 22 July 2012].

Cousins, W.J., Thomas, G.C., Heron, D.W., Mazzoni, S. and Lloydd, D. 2003. Modelling the spread of postearthquake fire. *Proceedings, 2003 Pacific Conference on Earthquake Engineering*, 13–15 February 2003, Christchurch. New Zealand Society for Earthquake Engineering. Paper No. 001.

Cox, P. 1973 Air pollution, in Dawson, J.A. and Doornkamp, J.C. (eds) *Evaluating the Human Environment.* London: Edward Arnold, 184–204.

Crabb, P. 1986 *Australia's Water Resources: Their Use and Management.* Melbourne: Longman-Cheshire.

Cranz, G. 1989 *The Politics of Park Design: A History of Park Design in Urban America.* Cambridge, MA: MIT Press.

Cumbler, J.T. 1995 Whatever happened to industrial waste? Reform, compromise, and science in nineteenth century southern New England. *Journal of Social History*, 29, 149–71.

Curtin, P.D. 1985 Medical Knowledge and Urban Planning in Tropical Africa. *The American Historical Review*, 90 (3), 594–613.

Daniel K., Sedlis M.H., Polk L., Dowuona-Hammond S., McCants B., Matte T.D. 1990 Childhood lead poisoning, New York City, 1988. *Morbidity and Mortality Weekly Report CDC Surveillance Summary*, 39 (4), 1–7.

Danino, M. 2008 New insights into Harappan town-planning, proportions and units, with special reference to Dholavira. *Man and Environment*, 23 (1), 66–79.

Davis, D.R. and Weinstein, D.W. 2002 Bones, Bombs, And Break Points: The Geography Of Economic Activity. *American Economic Review*, 92 (5), 1269–89.

Day, J.P., Fergusson, J.E. and Tay Ming Chee 1979 Solubility and Potential Toxicity of Lead in Urban Street Dust. *Bulletin of Environmental Contamination and Toxicology*, 23, 497–502.

Day, J.P., Hart, M. and Robinson, M.S. 1975 Lead in Urban Street Dust. *Nature*, 253, 343–5.

de Roo G. 2000 Environmental planning and the compact city—a Dutch perspective. In de Roo G., Miller D., (eds) *Compact cities and sustainable urban development. A critical assessment of policies and plans from an international perspective.* Aldershot, UK: Ashgate, 31–41.

Debonnet-Lambert, A. 1999 Experience of demonstration projects in France. In Schwelder, H-U. (ed.) *Noise abatement in European Towns and Cities: strategies, concepts and approaches for local noise policy.* Berlin: European Academy of the Urban Environment, 23–30.

Deelstra, T. 1986 National, regional and local planning strategies for urban green areas in the Netherlands: an ecological approach. In Comité MAB Español (eds) *International Seminar on Use, Handling and Management of Urban Green Areas.* Paris: UNESCO, 23–33.

Deelstra, T. and Girardet, H. 2000 Urban agriculture and sustainable cities. In Bakker, N., Dubbeling, M., Gündel, S., Sabel-Koschella, U. and Zeeuw, H. de (eds) *Growing cities, growing food: urban agriculture on the policy agenda. A reader on urban agriculture.* Wallingford: CABI, 43–65.

Deepak, B. 1999 Issue of environmental noise and annoyance. *Noise and Health,* 1 (3), 1–2.

Delfino, J.A., Casarin, A.A. and Delfino, M.E. 2007 *How Far Does It Go? The Buenos Aires Water Concession a Decade after the Reform.* Social Policy and Development Programme Paper Number 32, Geneva: United Nations Research Institute for Social Development.

Deligne, C. 2003 *Bruxelles et sa rivière. Genese d'un territoire urbain (12ᵉ-18ᵉ siecle).* Studies in European Urban History (SEUH), Turnhout, Belgium: Brepols Publishers.

Department of Transport Local Government and the Regions, 2002 *Planning Policy Guidance Note 14 Development on Unstable Land Annex 2: Subsidence and Planning* London: The Stationery Office.

Desert burner, 2009 *MOMBASA Hacienda Eco City Under Construction.* http://www. skyscrapercity.com/showthread.php?t=915968 [accessed 31 March 2011].

Desrochers, P. 2007 How did the Invisible Hand Handle Industrial Waste? By-product Development before the Modern Environmental Era. *Enterprise and Society,* 8, 348–74.

Diefendorf, J.M. 1993 *In the wake of war: the reconstruction of German cities after World War II.* Oxford: Oxford University Press.

Dilke, O.A.W. and Dilke, M.S. 1976 Perception of the Roman World. *Progress in Geography,* 9, 39–72.

Disse, M. and Engel, H. 2001 Flood Events in the Rhine Basin: Genesis, Influences and Mitigation. *Natural Hazards,* 23, 271–90.

Dogan, M. and Kasarda, J.D. 1988, *The Metropolis Era, Volume 1, A World of Giant Cities.* Newbury Park: Sage. doi:10.1186/1476-069X-9-65 [accessed 27 January 2012].

Donnelly, J.P., Smith Bryant, S.; Butler, J., Dowling, J., Fan, L., Hausmann, N., Newby, P., Shuman, D., Stern, J. Westover, K. and Webb III, T. 2001 700 yr sedimentary record of intense hurricane landfalls in southern New England. *Bulletin Geological Society of America,* 113 (6) 714–27.

Douglas, I. 1996 The impact of land use changes, especially logging, shifting cultivation and urbanization on sediment yields in humid tropical South-East Asia: a review with special reference to Borneo. *International Association of Hydrological Sciences Publication,* 236, 463–71.

——. 2004 People-induced geophysical risks and urban sustainability. In Sparks, R.S.J. and Hawkesworth, C.J. (eds) *The State of the Planet: Frontiers and Challenges in Geophysics (American Geophysical Union Geophysical Monograph 150, IUGG Volume 19),* Washington DC: American Geophysical Union, 387–97.

Douglas, I., Ali J.A. and Clarke, M. 1993 Lead Contamination in Manchester. *Land Contamination and Reclamation,* 1 (3), 17–22.

Douglas, I. and Box, J. 2000 *The changing relationship between cities and biosphere reserves,* Newark: UK MAB Urban Forum.

Douglas, I., Hodgson, R. and Lawson, N. 2002 Industry, environment and health through 200 years in Manchester, *Ecological Economics*, 41, 235–55.

Downes, G.L., Dowrick, D.J., Van Dissen, R.J., Taber, J.J., Hancox, G.T. and Smith E.G.C. 2001 The 1942 Wairarapa, New Zealand, earthquakes: analysis of observational and instrumental data. *Bulletin of the New Zealand Society for Earthquake Engineering*, 34 (2), 125–57.

Drakakis-Smith, D., Bowyer-Bower, T. and Tevera, D. 1994 Urban poverty and urban agriculture: An overview of the linkages in Harare. *Habitat International*, 19 (2), 183–93.

Draper, R. 2011 Rift in Paradise. *National Geographic*, 220 (5), 82–117.

Drury, R.T., Belliveau, M.E., Kuhn, J.S. and Bansal, S., 1999 Pollution trading and environmental justice: Los Angeles' failed experiment in air quality policy. *Duke Environmental Law and Policy Forum*, 9, 231–89.

Duany, A., Plater-Zyberk, E. and Speck, J. 2000 *Suburban Nation: The rise of sprawl and the decline of the American Dream*. New York: North Point Press.

Dyos, H.J. 1982 *Exploring the past: essays in urban history*. Cambridge: Cambridge University Press.

Edmonds, R. L. 1998 Studies on China's Environment. *The China Quarterly*, 156, 725–73.

Edwards, K.C. 1962 *The Peak District*. London: Collins New Naturalist.

EEC 1975 Council directive of 16 June 1975 concerning the quality required of surface water intended for the abstraction of drinking water in the member states 75/440/EEC. *Official Journal of the European Communities*, 18 (L.194), 26–31.

——. 1976 Council directive of 8 December 1975 concerning the quality of bathing water 76/160/EEC. *Official Journal of the European Communities*, 19 (L.31), 1–7.

——. 1978 Council directive on the quality of freshwater needing protection or improvement in order to support fish life 78/659/EEC. *Official Journal of the European Communities*, 21 (L.222), 1–10.

——. 1994 European Parliament and Council Directive 94/62/EC of 20 December 1994 on packaging and packaging waste. *Official Journal of the European Communities*, (L.365), 10–23.

Eliassen, R. 1969 *Solid waste management: a comprehensive assessment of solid waste problems, Practices and needs*. Washington DC: Office of Science and Technology, Executive Office of the President.

Elkin, T. and McLaren, D. (with Hillman, M.) 1991 *Reviving the City: towards Sustainable Urban Development*. London: Friends of the Earth with the Policy Studies Unit.

Elvin, M. 2004 *The Retreat of the Elephants: an environmental history of China*. New Haven: Yale University Press.

Emerton, L., Iyango, L., Luwum, P. and Malinga, A. 1998. *The present economic value of Nakivubo urban wetland, Uganda*. Nairobi, Kenya: IUCN – The World Conservation Union, Eastern Africa Regional Office.

Engels, F. 1892 *The Condition of the Working Classes in England 1844*. London: Sonnenschein & Co.

Engen, T. 1982 *The perception of odors*. New York: Academic Press.

Erickson , R.C. 1976 Subsidence control and urban oil production – a case history: Beverley Hills (East) oil field, California, *Publications International Association of Hydrological Sciences*, 121, 285–97.

Erol, O. and Pirazzoli, P.A. 2007. Seleucia Pieria: an ancient harbour submitted to two successive uplifts. *International Journal of Nautical Archaeology*, 21, 317–27.

EU Expert Group on the Urban Environment 1994 *European Sustainable Cities*, 1st Annual Report to the European Conference on Sustainable Cities and Towns, Lisbon.

European Commission 2006 *EU Action against Climate Change: Reducing emissions from the energy and transport sectors*. Brussels: Directorate-General Environment.

——. 2008 *Air Quality: Existing legislation*. http://ec.europa.eu/environment/air/quality/legislation/existing_leg.htm [accessed 22 July 2012].

——. 2011 *Energy Roadmap 2050*, COM(2011) 885/2, Brussels: European Commission.

European Union 2011 *Chemical Accidents (Seveso II) – Prevention, Preparedness and Response*. ec.europa.eu/environment/seveso/legislation.htm [accessed 6 February 2011].

Evans, E., Pottier, C., Fletcher, R., Hensley, S., Tapley, I., Milne, A. and Barbetti, M. 2007 A comprehensive archaeological map of the world's largest preindustrial settlement complex at Angkor, Cambodia. *Proceedings National Academy of Sciences*, 104, 14277–82.

Fairbrother, N. 1972 *New Lives, New Landscapes*. Harmondsworth: Penguin Books.

Farrell, A. 2001 *Tensions and Linkages Between International, National and Local Pollution Control Institutions: Air Pollution in Spain*. Paper presented at the 'Smoke and Mirrors' workshop, Center for Global, International, and Regional Studies, UC Santa Cruz, Santa Cruz CA, 11–12 January 2001.

——. 2005 Learning to see the invisible: discovery and measurement of ozone. *Environmental Monitoring and Assessment*, 106, 59–80.

Farrell, A. and Keating, T.J. 2000 The globalization of smoke: Co-evolution in science and government of a commons problem. Paper presented at the Eighth Biennial Conference International Association for the Study of Common Property June, 2000, Bloomington, IN.

Fernandes, T.M.A., Schout, C., De Roda Husman, A.M., Eilander, A., Vennema, H. and van Duynhoven, Y.T.H.P. 2006 Gastroenteritis associated with accidental contamination of drinking water with partially treated water. *Epidemiology and Infection*, 135 (5), 818–26.

Fernández, R. and Galarraga, F. 2001 Lead Concentration and Composition of Organic Compounds in Settled Particles in Road Tunnels from the Caracas Valley-Venezuela. *Environmental Geochemistry and Health*, 23 (1), 17–25.

Fernández, R., Morales, F. and Benzo, Z. 2003 Lead exposure in day care centres in the Caracas Valley – Venezuela. *International Journal of Environmental Health Research*, 13, 3–9.

Fink, A., Ulbrich, U. and Engel, H. 1996 Aspects of the January 1995 flood in Germany. *Weather*, 51 (2), 34–9.

Finley, M.I. 1999 *Ancient Economy*. Berkeley CA: University of California Press.

Fiorillo, F. and Wilson, R.C. 2004 Rainfall induced debris flows in pyroclastic deposits, Campania (southern Italy). *Engineering Geology*, 75, 263–89.

Fischer, C., Hedal, N., Carlsen, R., Doujak, K., Legg, D., Oliva, J., Lüdeking Sparvath, S., Viisimaa, M., Weissenbach, T. and Werge, M. 2008 *Transboundary shipments of waste in the EU Developments 1995-2005 and possible drivers*, European Topic Centre on Resource and Waste Management, ETC/RWM Technical Report 2008/1. http://scp.eionet.europa.eu/publications/Transboundary%20shipments%20of%20waste%20in%20the%20EU/wp/tech_1_2008 [accessed 12 July 2012].

Fitter, R.S.R. 1945 *London's Natural History*. London: Collins.

Fitzgerald, B.M. 1996 The development and implementation of noise control measures on an urban railway. *Journal of Sound and Vibration*, 193, 377–85.

Fletcher, R. and Pottier, C. 2002 The Gossamer City: a new inquiry, *Museum*, 54 (1&2), 24–6.

Foster & Partners, Halcrow, Volterra 2011 *The Thames Hub: an integrated vision for Britain.* http://www.halcrow.com/Thames-Hub/ [accessed 05 November 2011].

Foster, S. n. d. *Urban water-supply security in sub-Sahjaran Africa: making the best use of groundwater.* www.worldbank.org/gwmate [accessed 12 July 2012].

Fothergill, A., Maestas, E. and Darlington, J. 1999 Race, ethnicity and disasters in the United States: A review of the literature. *Disasters*, 23 (2), 156–73.

Foxell, S. 2007 *Mapping London: Making sense of the city.* London: Black Dog Publishing.

Freese, B. 2003 *Coal: A Human History.* New York: Penguin Books.

Freestone, R. 2000 Planning Sydney: historical trajectories and contemporary debates. In Connell, J. (ed.) *Sydney: The Emergence of a World City.* South Melbourne: Oxford University Press, 319–43.

Friends of Birley Fields 2008 *Birley Fields – The Heart and Soul of Manchester.* www.fobf.org. uk/index.php/Section14.html [accessed 24 January 2008].

Frost, P. and Hyman, G. 2011 Urban areas and the biosphere reserve concept. In Douglas, I., Goode, D., Houck, M. and Wang, R.S. (eds) *Routledge Handbook of Urban Ecology*, London: Routledge, 549–60.

Fry, Maxwell 1941 The new Britain must be planned. *Picture Post*, 10 (1), 16–20.

Fry, Michael 2009 *Edinburgh: a history of the city.* London: Macmillan.

Fudge, C. 1997 Planning ahead for our multiplying megacities. *Human Ecology, Journal of the Commonwealth Human Ecology Council*, 14, 17–8.

Galloway, J.A. and Murphy, M. 1991 Feeding the city: medieval London and its agrarian hinterland. *London Journal*, 16, 3–14.

Gandy, M. 1999 The Paris sewers and the rationalization of urban space. *Transactions Institute of British Geographers*, NS 24, 23–44.

——. 2006a J.G. Ballard and the Politics of Catastrophe, *Space and Culture*, 9 (1), 86–8.

——. 2006b Planning, anti-planning and the infrastructure crisis facing Metropolitan Lagos. *Urban Studies*, 43, 371–96.

Gans, H.J. 1972 *People and Plans.* Harmondsworth: Penguin Books.

Garcia, A. 2001a Introduction. In Garcia, A. (ed.) *Environmental Urban Noise.* Southampton: WIT Press.

——. 2001b Urban Noise Control. In Garcia, A. (ed.) *Environmental Urban Noise.* Southampton: WIT Press.

Garcia, A. and Raichel, D.R. 2003 Environmental Urban Noise. *Acoustical Society of America Journal*, 114, 1199–201.

Garrote, L., Martin-Carrasco, F., Flores-Montoya, F. and Iglesias, A. 2007 Linking Drought Indicators to Policy Actions in the Tagus Basin Drought Management Plan, *Water Resources Management*, 1, 2873–82.

Geiselbrecht, A.D., Herwig, R.P., Deming, J.D. and Staley, J.T. 1996 Enumeration and Phylogenetic Analysis of Polycyclic Aromatic Hydrocarbon-Degrading Marine Bacteria from Puget Sound, *Applied and Environmental Microbiology*, 62, 3344–9

Ghosh, A. 2008 Reverse gear. *The Guardian Society*, 16 January 2008, 9.

Gibbs, J.P. and Martin, W.T. 1958 Urbanization and natural resources: A study in organizational ecology. *American Sociological Review*, 23, 266–77.

Gibson, J.L. 1904 A plea for painted railings and painted walls of rooms as the source of lead poisoning among Queensland children. *Australian Medical Gazette*, 23, 149–53.

Gidlow, D.A. 2004 Lead toxicity. *Occupational Medicine*, 54, 76–81.

Gilbert, O.L. 1989 *The Ecology of Urban Habitats.* London: Chapman & Hall.

Gill, S.E., Handley, J.F., Ennos, A.R and Pauleit, S. 2007 Adapting Cities for Climate Change: The Role of the Green Infrastructure, *Built Environment*, 33, 115–33.

Girard, P.S. 1812 *Description générale des différens ouvrages à exécuter pour la distribution des eaux du Canal de l'Ourcq dans l'intérieur de Paris, et devis détaillé des ces ouvrages*, Paris: l'Imprimerie Impériale.

Girardet, H. 1992 *Cities: new directions for sustainable living*. London and Stroud: Gaia Books.

Giraud, R.E. and Shaw, L.M. 2007 *Landslide Susceptibility Map of Utah*, Salt Lake City: Utah Geological Survey.

Glasbergen, P. 2005 Decentralized reflexive environmental regulation: Opportunities and risks based on an evaluation of Dutch experiments. *Environmental Sciences*, 2, 427–42.

González, G. A. 2002 Local Growth Coalitions and Air Pollution Controls: The Ecological Modernization of the US in Historical Perspective. *Environmental Politics*, 11 (3), 121–44.

——. 2005 *The Politics of Air Pollution: Urban Growth; Ecological Modernization; and Symbolic Inclusion*, Albany NY: State University of New York Press.

Goode, D. 1986 *Wild in London*. Michael Joseph, London.

Goyal, S.K., Ghatge, S.V., Nema, P. and Tamhane, S.M. 2006 Understanding urban vehicular pollution problem vis-à-vis ambient air quality – case study of a megacity (Delhi, India). *Environmental Monitoring and Assessment*, 119, 557–69.

Graedel, T.E. and Klee, R.J. 2002 Industrial and anthroposystem metabolism. In Douglas, I. (ed.) *Causes and consequences of environmental change; Encyclopedia of Global Environmental Change* (ed. Munn, T.) Vol. 3, Chichester: Wiley, 73–83.

Gray, E. 1993 *A hundred years of the Manchester Ship Canal*. Bolton: Aurora.

Gray, H.F. 1940 Sewerage in Ancient and Mediaeval Times. *Sewage Works Journal*, 12 (5), 939–46.

Green, R. and Bates, L. 2007 Impediments to recovery in New Orleans' Upper and Lower Ninth Ward: one year after Hurricane Katrina. *Disasters*, 31 (4), 311–35.

Grinder, R.D. 1980 The Battle for Clean Air: The Smoke Problem in Post-Civil War America. In Melosi, M.V. (ed.) *Pollution and Reform in American Cities, 1870-1930*. University of Texas Press, Austin, TX, 83–103.

Groslier, B.P. and Arthaud, J. 1957 *Angkor, Art and Civilization*. London: Praeger.

Groundwork UK 2008 *Where did Groundwork come from?* www.groundwork.org.uk [accessed 06 February 2008].

Gugliotta, A. 2004 'Hell with the lid taken off': A cultural history of air pollution – Pittsburgh. Unpublished PhD dissertation, Notre Dame University.

Gunten L. von, Eggenberger, U., Grob, P., Morales, A., Sturm, M., Urrutia, R. and Grosjean, M. 2007 Deposition of atmospheric copper and pollution history since ca. 1850 in Central Chile. Paper presented at the 5th Swiss Geoscience Meeting, Geneva, Index of /sgm2007/SGM07_abstracts/09_Geohazards_in_Lakes [accessed 03 May 2012].

Guo, X.R., Mao, X.Q., Yang, J.R. and Cheng, S.Y. 2005 An Urban Ecological Footprint Approach for Assessing the Urban Sustainability of Guangzhou City, China. *Environmental Informatics Archives*, 3, 449–55.

Gupta, A.K. 2004 Origin of agriculture and domestication of plants and animals linked to early Holocene climate amelioration. *Current Science*, 87 (1), 54–9.

Gupta, A.K., Anderson, D.M., Pandey, D.N. and Singhvi, A.K. 2006 Adaptation and human migration, and evidence of agriculture coincident with changes in the Indian summer monsoon during the Holocene. *Current Science*, 90 (8), 1082–90.

Haagen-Smit, A.J. 1970 A Lesson from the Smog Capital of the World. *Proceedings of the National Academy of Sciences*, 67, 887–97.

Haas, J., Creamer, W. and Ruiz, A. 2004 Dating the Late Archaic occupation of the Norte Chico region in Peru. *Nature*, 432, 1020–3.

Hackett, J.E. 1965 Groundwater contamination in an urban environment. *Groundwater*, 3 (3), 27–30.

Haines, M.M., Stansfeld, S.A., Head, J. and Job, R.F.S. 2002 Multilevel modelling of aircraft noise on performance tests in schools around Heathrow Airport London. *Journal of Epidemiology and Community Health*, 56, 139–44.

Hakanen, M. 1999 *Some Finnish ecological footprints at the local level*. Helsinki: The Association of Finnish Local and Regional Authorities.

Hall, C.M. and Page, S. 2006 *The geography of tourism and recreation: environment, place and space*. London: Routledge.

Hall, D.G.E. 1968 *A History of South-East Asia*, 3rd edition. London: McMillan.

Hall, P. 2002 *Cities of Tomorrow: An Intellectual History of Urban Planning and Design in the Twentieth Century*. Oxford: Blackwell.

Halliday S. 2001 Death and miasma in Victorian London: an obstinate belief. *British Medical Journal*, 323, 1469–71.

Hammad, Z. H., Ali, A. O. and Ahmed, H. H. 2008 The quality of drinking water in storage in Khartoum State. *Khartoum Medical Journal*, 1 (2), 78–80.

Hannam, I.D. 1979 Urban soil erosion: an extreme phase in the Stewart subdivision, west Bathurst. *Journal of the Soil Conservation Service of NSW*, 3, 19–25.

Harnapp, V.R. and Noble, A.G. 1987 Noise pollution. *GeoJournal*, 14, 217–26.

Harrigan, P. and Doughty, D. 2007 New pieces of Mada'in Salih's puzzle. *Saudi Aramco World*, 58 (4), 14–23.

Harrison, R.M. and Laxen, D.P.H. 1981 *Lead Pollution: Causes and Control*. London: Chapman and Hall.

Hassan, A. and Cajee, Z. 2002 Islam, Muslims and Sustainable Development. http://www. imase.org/reading/reading-list-mainmenu-34/27-islam-muslims-and-sustainable-development-the-message-from-johannesburg-2002 [accessed 17 March 2011].

Hays, S.P. 1996 The trouble with Bill Cronon's Wilderness. *Environmental History*, 1 (1), 29–32.

Head, L. and Muir, P. 2006 Edges of Connection: reconceptualising the human role in urban biogeography. *Australian Geographer*, 37 (1), 87–101.

Head, P. 2008 *Entering the Ecological Age: The Engineer's Role*. London: Institution of Civil Engineers Brunel Lecture Series. http://www.arup.com/_assets/_download/72B9BD7D-19BB-316E-40000ADE36037C13.pdf [accessed 31 March 2011].

Healy, J.F. 1988 *Mining and Metallurgy in the Greek and Roman World*. London: Thames and Hudson.

Henry, R.K., Zhao, Y. and Dong, J. 2006 Municipal solid waste management challenges in developing countries – Kenyan case study. *Waste Management*, 26, 92–100.

Heynen, N., Kaika, M. and Swyngedouw, E. 2006 Urban political ecology: politicizing the production of urban natures. In Heynen, N., Kaika, M. and Swyngedouw, E. (eds) *In the Nature of Cities: Urban political ecology and the politics of urban metabolism*. London: Routledge, 1–20.

Hibbert, C. 1985 *Rome: The Biography of a City*. London: Penguin Books.

Higbee, E. 1976 Centre Cities in Canada and the United States. In Wreford-Watson, J. and O'Riordan, T. (eds) *The American Environment: Perceptions and Policies*. London: Wiley, 145–60.

Hilton, R.N. 1961 Templer Park, Malaya. In Wyatt-Smith, J. and Wycherley, P.A. (eds) *Nature Conservation in Western Malaysia*. Kuala Lumpur: Malayan Nature Society, 100–2.

Hirsch, A.R. and Levert, A.L. 2009 The Katrina Conspiracies: The Problem of Trust in Rebuilding an American City. *Journal of Urban History*, 35 (2), 207–19.

Hodder, I. 2007 Çatalhöyük in the Context of the Middle Eastern Neolithic. *Annual Reviews of Anthropology*, 36, 105–20.

Hong, S., Candelone, J.P., Soutif, M. and Boutron, C.F. 1996 A reconstruction of changes in copper production and copper emissions to the atmosphere during the past 7000 years. *The Science of the Total Environment*, 188, 183–93.

Hookway, R. 1978 Issues in Recreation. In Davies, R. and Hall. P. (eds) *Issues in Urban Society*. Harmondsworth: Penguin Books, 161–82.

Hopkinson, T. 1941 Foreword to a Plan for Brtiain. *Picture Post*, 10 (1), 4.

Horner, G.V. 1988 Sewage treatment and odour control. *Water Services*, 92, 1113–27.

Hoskins, W.G. and Stamp, L.D. 1963 *The Common Lands of England & Wales*. London: Collins.

Houck, M. 2011 In livable cities is preservation of the wild. In Douglas, I., Goode, D., Houck, M. and Wang, R.S. (eds) *The Routledge Handbook of Urban Ecology*. London: Routledge, 48–62.

Hough, M. 1984 *City Form and Natural Process*. London: Croom Helm.

Huang, X-F., He L.Y., Hu, M. Canagratna, M.R., Sun, Y., Zhang, Q., Zhu, T., Xue, L., Zeng, L-W. Liu, X.G., Jayne, J.T., Ng, N.L. and Worsnop, D.R. 2010 Highly time-resolved chemical characterization of atmospheric submicron particles during 2008 Beijing Olympic Games using an Aerodyne High-Resolution Aerosol Mass Spectrometer. *Atmospheric Chemistry and Physics*, 10, 8933–45.

Hundley, N. Jr. 1992 *The Great Thirst: Californians and their Water 1770s-1990s*. Berkeley: University of California Press.

Hunt, N.B. 2004 *Historical Atlas of Ancient Mesopotamia*. New York: Checkmark Books.

Hutin, Y., Luby, S. and Paquet, C. 2003 A large cholera outbreak in Kano City, Nigeria: the importance of hand washing with soap and the danger of street-vended water. *Journal of Water and Health*, 01 (1), 45–52.

IDA 2010 *Sanitation and water supply: Improving services for the poor*. Washington, DC: International Development Association, World Bank.

International Union for the Conservation of Nature (IUCN) 1980 *World Conservation Strategy: Living Resource Conservation for Sustainable Development*, Gland: IUCN. http://data.iucn.org/dbtw-wpd/edocs/WCS-004.pdf [accessed 22 July 2012].

Jackson, R.E. 2004 Recognizing Emerging Environmental Problems: The Case of Chlorinated Solvents in Groundwater. *Technology and Culture*, 45, 55–79.

Jain, S.K., Agarwal, P.K. and Singh, V.P. 2007 *Hydrology and Water Resources of India*. Dordrecht: Springer Netherlands.

James, L. 2006 *The Middle Class: a history*. London: Little, Brown.

James, L.A. and Singer, M.B. 2008 Development of the Lower Sacramento Valley Flood-Control System: Historical Perspective. *Natural Hazards Review*, 125–35.

Jardine, L. 2002 *On a grander scale: the outstanding career of Sir Christopher Wren*. London: Harper Collins.

Jeffrey, S. 2012 Lengthy debate on landfill. *Armidale Express*, 25 May 2012. http://www.armidaleexpress.com.au/news/local/news/general/lengthy-debate-on-landfill/2568131.aspx [accessed 18 July 2012].

Johnson, L.L., Landahl, J.T., Kubin, L.A., Horness, B.H., Myers, M.S., Collier, T.K. and Stein, J.E. 1998 Assessing the effects of anthropogenic stressors on Puget Sound flatfish populations. *Journal of Sea Research*, 39, 125–37.

Joss, S. 2010 Eco-cities – a global survey 2009. *WIT Transactions on Ecology and The Environment*, 129, 239–50.

Kalin, R.M. and Roberts, C. 1997 Groundwater Resources in the Lagan Valley Sandstone Aquifer, Northern Ireland. *Journal of the Chartered Institution of Water and Environmental Management*, 11, 133–9.

Kang, C.D. and Cervero, R. 2009 From Elevated Freeway to Urban Greenway: Land Value Impacts of the CGC Project in Seoul, Korea. *Urban Studies*, 46, 2771–94.

Kaplan, M. 1991 *The Portuguese: the Land and its People*. London: Penguin Books.

Karnataka Act 2009 The Bangalore Water Supply and Sewerage (Amendment) Act 2009 (Karnataka Act No.19 0f 2009) KA/BG-GPO/2515/WPP-47/2009-2011. www.bwssb. org/pdf/RWH_Compulsory.pdf [accessed 23 November 2011].

Karskens, G. 2007 Water Dreams, Earthen Histories: Exploring Urban Environmental History at the Penrith Lakes Scheme and Castlereagh, Sydney. *Environment and History*, 13 (2), 115–54.

Kates, R.W., Colten, C.E., Laska, S. and S. P. Leatherman, S.R. 2006 Reconstruction of New Orleans after Hurricane Katrina: A research perspective. *Proceedings of the National Academy of Sciences of the United States of America*, 103, 14653–60.

Kaye, R. 2001 Development of odour assessment criteria in New South Wales and application of the criteria for the assessment of a major public works project. *Water Science and Technology*, 44 (9), 111–8.

Keating, M. 1993 *The Earth Summit's Agenda for Change: A plain language version of Agenda 21 and other Rio agreements*. Geneva: Centre for Our Common Future.

Keil, R. and Boudreau, J-A. 2006 Metropolitics and Metabolics: rolling out environmentalism in Toronto. In Heynen, N., Kaika, M. and Swyngedouw, E. (eds) *In the Nature of Cities: Urban political ecology and the politics of urban metabolism*. London: Routledge, 41–62.

Kelly, T. 2006 Using sustainability in urban water planning. Paper presented at the SWITCH Workshop on Learning Alliance, 10–11 December 2006, Tel Aviv, Israel.

Keneally, T. 2007 *Commonwealth of Thieves: The story of the founding of Australia*. London: Vantage Books.

Kennedy, M. 1970 *Portrait of Manchester*. London: Robert Hale.

Kenney, D.S., Goemans, G., Klein, R., Lowrey, J. and Reidy, K. 2008 Residential Water Demand Management: Lessons from Aurora, Colorado. *Journal of the American Water Resources Association*, 44 (1), 192–207.

Khalat, S. and Khoudry, P.S. (eds) 1993 *Recovering Beirut: Urban design and Post-War Reconstruction*. Leiden: Brill.

Kimball, A. 2005. Selling water instead of watermelons: Colorado's changing rural economy. *Next American City*, 3 (8) (Reprinted as: Aurora, CO, preserves and protects its water supply. In Kemp, R.L. (ed.) *Cities and water: a handbook for planning*. Jefferson NC: McFarlane, 33–5).

Kimura, K-I. 1998 Thermal comfort in Japanese urban spaces. In Golany, G.S., Hamaki, K. and Koide, O. (eds) *Japanese Urban Environment*. Oxford: Pergamon, 134–46.

Kitson, T. 1982 The allocation of water for public supply within Severn-Trent Water Authority. *International Association of Hydrological Sciences Publication*, 135, 193–202.

Klingle, M. 2007 *Emerald City: an environmental history of Seattle.* New Haven: Yale University Press.

Knights, D. and Wong, T. 2004 Strategies for achieving optimal potable water conservation outcomes – a Sydney Case Study. *Proceedings International Conference on Water Sensitive Urban Design: Cities as Catchments (WSUD 2004).* Adelaide: Stormwater Industry Association, 181–94.

Knocke E.T. and Kolivras K.N. 2007 Flash Flood Awareness in Southwest Virginia. *Risk Analysis,* 27 (1), 155–69.

Koe, L.C.C. 2002 Sewage Odour Control – The Singapore Experience. http://www.orea.or.jp/en/PDF/2004-10.pdf [accessed 12 July 2012].

Koe, L.C.C. and Yang, F., 2000. A bioscrubber for hydrogen sulfide removal. *Water Science and Technology,* 14 (6), 141–5.

Kolbe, T. and Gilchrist, K. 2011 *Particulate matter air pollution in a NSW regional centre: A review of the literature and opportunities for action.* Wagga Wagga: Centre for Inland Health, Charles Sturt University.

Köster, P. 1994 Hedonic aspects of odors and odor pollution control. In Martin, G. and Laffort, P. (eds) *Odors and deodorization in the environment.* New York: VCH Publishers, 67–84.

Kranser, L. 2002 *Chronology of the War over El Toro Airport.* San Jose: Internet for Activists, Writers Club Press.

Krausmann, F., Gingrich, S., Eisenberger, N., Erb, K-H., Haberl, H. and Fischer-Kowalski, M. 2009 Growth in global materials use, GDP and population during the 20th century. *Ecological Economics,* 68, 2696–705.

Kreibich, H., Petrow, T., Thieken, A.H., Müller, M. and Merz, B. 2005 Consequences of the extreme flood event of August 2002 in the city of Dresden, Germany. *International Association of Scientific Hydrology Publications,* 293, 164–73.

Krier, J.E. and Ursin, E. 1977 *Pollution and Policy: A Case Essay on California and Federal Experience with Motor Vehicle Air Pollution.* Los Angeles, CA: University of California Press.

Krishnakumar, P.K., Casillas, E., Snider, R.G., Kagley, A.N. and Varanasi, U. 1999 Environmental Contaminants and the Prevalence of Hemic Neoplasia (Leukemia) in the Common Mussel (Mytilus edulis Complex) from Puget Sound, Washington, U.S.A. *Journal of Invertebrate Pathology,* 73, 135–46.

Kum, V., Sharp, V. and Harnpornchai, N. 2005 Improving the solid waste management in Phnom Penh city: a strategic approach. *Waste Management,* 25, 101–9.

Kunzig, R. 2008 Drying of the West. *National Geographic,* 213 (2), 90–113.

Kuwairi, A. 2006 Water mining: the Great Man-made River, Libya. *Proceedings of the ICE – Civil Engineering,* 15 (5), 39–43.

La Berge, A.F. 1992 *Mission and Method: the early nineteenth century French public health movement.* Cambridge: Cambridge University Press.

Laconte, P. 2007 History and Perspectives on a Capital City. In Laconte P. and Hein C. (eds) Brussels: Perspectives on a European Capital. Brussels: Foundation for the Urban Environment and Éditions Aliter, 10–43.

Laermans, R. 1993 Learning to consume: early department stores and the shaping of the modern consumer culture (1860–1914). *Theory, Culture & Society,* 10, 79–102.

Lafarge 2011 *South Africa – Eco-City, an ecologically sustainable village in Johannesburg.* http://www.lafarge.com/wps/portal/2_4_4_2-SoDet?WCM_GLOBAL_CONTEXT=/wps/wcm/connect/Lafarge.com/AllCS/Cie/IH/CP1610621438/CSEN [accessed 31 March 2011].

LaFontaine, J.S. 1970 *City Politics. A Study of Leopoldville, 1962-63*. Cambridge: Cambridge University Press.

Lallana, C. 2003 *Water use efficiency (in cities): Leakage, Indicator Fact Sheet WQ06*. Copenhagen: European Environment Agency.

Lambert, T. 2007 *A Brief History of Derby*. www.localhistories.org/derby.html [accessed 22 November 2011].

Lammersen, R., Engel, H., Van den Langenheem, W., and Buiteveld, H. 2002 Impact of river training and retention measures on flood peaks along the Rhine. *Journal of Hydrology*, 267, 115–24.

Lamont, J.R., McManus, E.W. and Sutton, G.K. 1995 The sanitary administration of Belfast in the mid-1990s. *Journal of the Chartered Institution of Water and Environmental Management*, 9, 43–52.

Landlife 2007 *Annual Report 2006-7*. Court Hey Park, Liverpool: Landlife.

Landscape Institute 2011 *Local Green Infrastructure: Helping communities make the most of their landscape*. London: Landscape Institute.

Lane Fox, R. 2006 *The Classical World: an epic history of Greece and Rome*. London: Penguin Books.

Larkey, S.V. 1934 Public Health in Tudor England. *American Journal of Public Health*, 24 (11), 1099–102.

Larkham, P.J. 2005 Planning for reconstruction after the disaster of war: lessons from England in the 1940s. *Perspectivas Urbanas / Urban Perspectives*, 6, 3–14.

Laurie, M. 1979 Nature and city planning in the nineteenth century. In Laurie, I.C. (ed.) *Nature in cities*. Chichester: Wiley, 37–63.

Laylin, T. 2010 Masdar City's Just A Futuristic Playground For The Rich. *New York Times* September 29, 2010. http://www.greenprophet.com/2010/09/masdar-city-playground/ [accessed 17 March 2011].

Leishman, N.N., Killip, C., Best, P.R., Brooke, A., Jackson, L. and Quintarelli, F. 2004 *Air quality at the rural/urban interface of an expanding metropolis*. Presented at the 13th World Clean Air and Environmental Protection Congress and Exhibition, London, UK, August 2004.

Lenzen, M. and Murray, S.A. 2003 *The Ecological Footprint-Issues and Trends*. ISA Research Paper 01–03, University of Sydney: www.isa.org.usyd.edu.au [accessed 5 October 2012].

Levy, J.I., Buonocore, J.J. and von Stackelberg, K. 2010 Evaluation of the public health impacts of traffic congestion: a health risk assessment. *Environmental Health*, 9, 65, 1–12. doi:10.1186/1476-069X-9-65 [accessed 12 July 2012].

Lewis, L. and Galardi, K. 2002 Neutralizing noxious odors at Singapore's Ulu Pandan Sewage Treatment Works. *Water and Engineering Management*, January 2002, 15–17.

Li, H., Bao, W., Xiu, C., Zhang, Y. and Xu, H. 2010 Energy conservation and circular economy in China's process industries. *Energy*, 35 (11), 4273–81.

Li, S.R., Ding, T. and Wang, S. 1995 Reed-bed treatment for municipal and industrial waste waters in Beijing, China. *Journal of the Chartered Institution of Water and Environmental Management*, 9, 581–88.

Li, S., Zhang, Y., Li, Y. and Yang, N. 2010 Research on the Eco-city Index System Based on the City Classification. *4th International Conference on Bioinformatics and Biomedical Engineering, Chengdu, China*. http://ieeexplore.ieee.org/xpl/login.jsp?tp= &arnumber=5516343&url=http%3A%2F%2Fieeexplore.ieee.org%2Fxpls%2Fabs_all. jsp%3Farnumber%3D5516343 [accessed 12 July 2012].

Liechty, M. 2002 *Suitably Modern: Making Middle-Class Culture in a New Consumer Society*. Princeton NJ: Princeton University Press.

Linde, A.H. te, Bubeck, P., Dekkers, J.E.C., Moel, H. de and Aerts, J.C.J.H. 2011 Future flood risk estimates along the river Rhine. *Natural Hazards Earth System Science*, 11, 459–73.

Lin-Fu, J.S. 1980 Lead poisoning and undue lead exposure in children: history and current status. In Needleman, H.L. (ed.) *Low level lead exposure: The clinical implications of current research*. New York: Raven Press, 5–16.

Liu C. 1998. Environmental Issues and the South-North Water Transfer Scheme. *The China Quarterly*, 156, 899–910.

Llamas, M.R. 1983 The influence of the failure of groundwater supply to Madrid in the national water policy of Spain. *International Symposium on Groundwater in Water Resources Planning, Koblenz, IAHS-AISH Publication*, 142, 421–7.

Lockwood, F.W. 1995 The sanitary administration of Belfast (1898). *Journal of the Chartered Institution of Water and Environmental Management*, 9, 29–40.

Loftus, A. and McDonald, D.A. 2001 Lessons from Argentina: The Buenos Aires water concession. www.labournet.net/world/0105/arwater2.html [accessed 19 November 2011].

Love, R. 2005 Daylighting Salt Lake's City Creek: An Urban River Unentombed, 35. *Golden Gate University Law Review*. http://digitalcommons.law.ggu.edu/ggulrev/vol35/iss3/4 [accessed 02 May 2012].

Lovelock, J.E. and Margulis, L. 1974. Atmospheric homeostasis by and for the biosphere-The Gaia hypothesis. *Tellus*, 26 (1), 2–10.

Lowe, G. 2004 The Golden Pipeline [online]. *Australian Journal of Multi-disciplinary Engineering*, 2 (1), 45–53. http://search.informit.com.au/documentSummary;dn=479 500289571684;res=IELENG [accessed 5 October 2012].

Luckin, B. 2004 At the margin: continuing crisis in British environmental history? *Endeavour*, 28 (3), 97–100.

Mabey, R. 1973 *Unofficial Countryside*. London: Collins.

Madella, M. and Fuller, D.Q. 2006 Palaeoecology and the Harappan Civilisation of South Asia: a reconsideration. *Quaternary Science Reviews*, 25, 1283–301.

Makra, L. and Brimblecombe, P. 2004 Selections from the history of environmental pollution, with special attention to air pollution. Part 1. *International Journal of Environment and Pollution*, 22, 641–56.

Malins, D.C., Andersoom, K.M., Stegeman, J.J., Jaruga,P., Green, V.M., Gilamn, N.K., Dizaroglu, M. 2006 Biomarkers Signal Contaminant Effects on the Organs of English Sole (Parophrys vetulus) from Puget Sound. *Environmental Health Perspectives*, 114 (6), 823–9.

Mancini, F., Ceppi, C. and Ritrovato G. 2010 GIS and statistical analysis for landslide susceptibility mapping in the Daunia area, Italy. *Natural Hazards and Earth System Sciences*, 10, 1851–64.

Marean, C.W. 2010 When the sea saved humanity. *Scientific American*, 303 (2), 40–7.

Marsh, A. 1947 *Smoke: the problem of coal and the atmosphere*. London: Faber and Faber.

Masai, Y. 1998 The human environments of Tokyo: past, present and future – a spatial approach. In Golany, G.S., Hamaki, K. and Koide, O. (eds) *Japanese Urban Environment*. Oxford: Pergamon, 57–74.

Mason, T, and Triatsoo, N. 1990 People, politics and planning: the reconstruction of Coventry's city centre. In Diefendorf, J.M., (ed.) *Rebuilding Europe's Bombed Cities*. London: MacMillan, 94–113.

Masri, A.B.A. 1992 Islam and Ecology. In Khalid, F. and O'Brien, J. (eds) *Islam and Ecology*. New York: Cassell, 1–23.

Massard-Guilbaud, G. 2002 Introduction: the Urban Catastrophe challenge to the social, economic and cultural order of the city. In Massard-Guilbaud, G., Platt, H.L. and Schott, D. (eds) *Cities and Catastrophes*. Frankfurt-am-Main: Peter Lang, 9–42.

———. 2005 The struggle for urban space: Nantes and Clermont-Ferrand, 1830–1930. In Schott, D., Luckin, B. and Massard-Guilbaud, G. (eds) *Resources of the City: Contribution to an environmental history of modern Europe*. Aldershot: Ashgate, 113–31.

Matsumoto, M., and Inoue, K. 2011 Earthquake, tsunami, radiation leak, and crisis in rural health in Japan. *Rural and Remote Health* 11, 1759. (Online) http://www.rrh.org. au/articles/printviewnew.asp?ArticleID=1759 [accessed 05 November 2011].

Maynard, H.R. and Findon, C.J.B. 1913 Topography. In Hampstead Scientific Society, *Hampstead Heath: Its Geology and Natural History*. Unwin, London, 13–37.

Mayor of London 2006 *London Strategic Parks Project Report*. Greater London Authority, London.

Mayor of London and CABE Space 2008 *Open Space Strategies Best Practice Guidance: A Joint Consultation Draft by the Mayor of London and CABE Space*. London: Greater London Authority.

Mayuga, M.N. and Allen, D.R. 1970 Subsidence in the Wilmington Oil Field, Long Beach, California, U.S.A. In *Land Subsidence*, edited by L.J. Tison, Paris: International Association for Scientific Hydrology and UNESCO, 66–79.

McCracken, K. and Curson, P. 2000 In sickness and in health: Sydney past and present. In Connell, J. (ed.) *Sydney: The Emergence of a World City*. South Melbourne: Oxford University Press, 319–43.

McCreanor, J., Cullinan, P., Nieuwenhuijsen, M.J., Stewart-Evans, J., Malliarou, E., Jarup, L., Harrington, R., 2007 Respiratory Effects of Exposure to Diesel Traffic in Persons with Asthma. *New England Journal of Medicine*, 357, 2348–58.

McDonald R.I., Douglas, I., Revenga, C., Hale, R., Grimm, N., Grönwall, J., and Balzas, F. 2011 Global Urban Growth and the Geography of Water Availability, Quality, and Delivery. *Ambio*, 40, 437–46.

McEvoy, A.F. 1995 Working Environments: An Ecological Approach to Industrial Health and Safety. *Technology and Culture*, 36 (2), Supplement: Snapshots of a Discipline: Selected Proceedings from the Conference on Critical Problems and Research Frontiers in the History of Technology, Madison, Wisconsin, October 30–November 3, 1991, S145–S173.

McGinley, C.M. and McGinley, G.A. 2006 *An Odor Index Scale for Policy and Decision Making Using Ambient and Source Odor Concentrations*. Paper presented at the Water Environment Federation / Air & Waste Management Association Specialty Conference: Odors and Air Emissions 2006 Hartford, CT: 9–12 April 2006. www.fivesenses. com/Documents/Library/47%20Odor%20Index%20Scale%20WEF-AWMA%20 Odors2006.pdf [accessed 12 July 2012].

McHarg, I. 1964 The place of nature in the city of man. *Annals of the American Academy of Social and Political Science*, 352, 1–12.

———. 1969 *Design with nature*. Garden City, NY: The Natural History Press.

McLeman, A. 2011 Settlement abandonment in the context of global environmental change. *Global Environmental Change*, 21, Suppl. 1, S108–S120.

McLoughlin, J. 1972 *The Law Relating to Pollution*. Manchester: Manchester University Press.

McMillen, D. 2004 Airport expansions and property values: The case of Chicago O'Hare airport. *Journal of Urban Economics*, 55, 627–40.

McRobie, A., Spencer, T. and Gerritsen, H. 2005 The Big Flood: North Sea storm surge. *Philosophical Transactions Royal Society* A, 363, 1263–70.

Meade, T. de C. 1898 Presidential Address to the Conference of Municipal and County Engineers, Birmingham. *Journal of the Royal Society for the Promotion of Health*, 19, 420–5.

Meller, H. 2005 Citizens in pursuit of nature: gardens, allotments and private space in European cities, 1880–2000. In Luckin, B., Massard-Guilbaud, G. and Schott, D. (eds) *Resources of the City: Contributions to an Environmental History of Modern Europe.* Aldershot: Ashgate, 80–96.

Melosi, M.V. 1990 Cities, Technical Systems and the Environment. *Environmental History Review*, 14, 45–64.

——. 1993 The Place of the City in Environmental History. *Environmental History Review*, 17 (1), 1–23.

——. 2000 *The Sanitary City: Urban Infrastructure in America from Colonial Times to the Present.* Baltimore: Johns Hopkins University Press, Baltimore.

——. 2001 *Effluent America: Cities, Industry, Energy, and the Environment.* Pittsburgh: University of Pittsburgh Press.

——. 2005 *Garbage in the Cities: Refuse, Reform and the Environment*, Pittsburgh: University of Pittsburgh Press.

Merlin, P. and Traisnel, J-P. 1996 *Énergie, environnement et urbanisme.* Paris: Presses Universitaires de France.

Meyer, A.D. 2002 Class, Consumption, and the Environment. *International Labor and Working-Class History*, 61, 173–6.

Miami International Airport 2000 *Plane facts about aircraft noise.* http://www.miami-airport.com/pdfdoc/noisepub.pdf [accessed 17 August 2007].

Midwinter, E. 1971 *Old Liverpool.* Newton Abbot: David and Charles.

Mielke, H.W., Anderson, J.C., Berry, K.J., Mielke, P.W., Chaney, R.L., and Leech, M. 1983 Lead Concentrations in Inner-City Soils As a Factor in the Child Lead Problem. *American Journal of Public Health*, 73, 1366–69.

Miguel, E. de, Llamas, J.F., Chacon, E., Berg, T., Larssen, S., Royset, O. and Vadset M., 1997 Origin and patterns of distribution of trace elements in street dust: unleaded petrol and urban lead. *Atmospheric Environment* 31, 2733–40.

Milhau, A., Hamelin, M. and Tary, V. 1994 Regulations concerning odors. In Martin, G. and Laffort, P. (eds) *Odors and deodorization in the environment.* New York: VCH Publishers, 445–63.

Millán, M.A, Alonso, L.A., Legarreta, J.A., de Torrontegui, L.L.J., Albizu, M.V., Ureta, I. and Egusquiaguirre, C. 1984 A fumigation episode in an industrialized estuary: Bilbao, November 1981. *Atmospheric Environment*, 18, 563–72.

Miller, R.W. 1997 *Urban forestry: planning and managing urban greenspaces.* Second edition, Upper Saddle River, NJ: Prentice-Hall.

Millward, A. and Mostyn, B. 1988 People and nature in cities: the social aspects of managing and planning natural parks in urban areas. *Urban Wildlife Now*, 2, Nature Conservancy Council.

Miner, J.R. 1997 Nuisance Concerns and Odor Control. *Journal of Dairy Science*, 80, 2667–72.

Miranda, L. and Hordijk, M. 1998 Let us build cities for life: the national campaign of Local Agenda 21s in Peru. *Environment and Urbanization*, 10 (2), 69–102.

Molina, L.T., De Foy, B., Martinez, O.V. and Figueroa, V.H.P. 2009 Temps, climat et qualité de l'air à Mexico. *Bulletin de l'OMM*, 58 (1), 8–53.

Morkot, R. 1996 *The Penguin Historical Atlas of Ancient Greece.* London: Penguin Books.

Morley, N. 1996 *Metropolis and Hinterland: The City of Rome and the Italian Economy 200 B.C - 200 A.D.* Cambridge, Cambridge University Press.

———. 2005 Feeding ancient Rome. *Proceedings of the Bath Royal Literary and Scientific Institution*, 9. www.brlsi.org/proCEed05/antiquity0105.htm [accessed 11 February 2008].

Morozova, G.S. 2004 A review of Holocene avulsions of the Tigris and Euphrates rivers and possible effects on the evolution of civilizations in lower Mesopotamia. *Geoarchaeology*, 20, 401–23.

Mortada, H. 2002 Urban sustainability in the tradition of Islam. In Brebbia, C.A., Martin-Duque, F. and Wadhwa, L.C. (eds) *The Sustainable City II: Urban Regeneration and Sustainability*. Southampton: WIT Press, 720–47.

Mosley, S. 2001 *The Chimney of the World: A history of Smoke Pollution in Victorian and Edwardian Manchester*. Cambridge: The White Horse Press.

———. 2003 Fresh Air and Foul: The Role of the Open Fireplace in Ventilating the British Home, 1837–1910. *Planning Perspectives*, 18, 1–21.

———. 2006 Common ground: integrating social and environmental history. *Journal of Social History*, 40, 915–33.

Motsi, K.E., Mangwayana, E. and Giller, K.E. 2002 Conflicts and problems with water quality in the upper catchment of the Manyame River, Zimbabwe. In Haygarth, P. and Jarvis, S. (eds) *Agriculture, Hydrology and Water Quality*. Wallingford: CABI, 481–90.

Mumford, L. 1940 *The Culture of Cities*. London: Secker & Warburg.

———. 1956 The Natural History of Urbanization. In Thomas, W.L. Jr (ed.) *Man's Role in the Changing the Face of the Earth*. Chicago and London: University of Chicago Press, 391–402.

———. 1961 *The City in History*. London: Secker & Warburg.

Murakami, M. 1995. *Managing water for peace in the Middle East: Alternative strategies*. Tokyo: United Nations University Press.

Mustafa, D. and Wescoat, J.L. 1997 Development of flood hazards policy in the Indus River Basin of Pakistan, 1947–1996. *Water International*, 22 (4), 238–44.

Myers, M.S., Landahl, J.T., Krahn, M.M., Johnson, L.L. and McCain, B.B. 1990 Overview of studies on liver carcinogenesis in English Sole from Puget Sound: Evidence for a xenobiotic chemical etiology I: Pathology and epizoology. *The Science of the Total Environment*, 94, 33–50.

Nakagoshi N., Watanabe, S. and Kim, J-E., 2006 Recovery of greenery resources in Hiroshima City after World War II. *Landscape and Ecological Engineering*, 2, 111–8.

National Parks Service 2007 *Land and Water Conservation Fund State Assistance Program 2007 Annual Report*. www.nps.gov/lwcf/lwcf_annual_rpt2007_wils.pdf [accessed 04 February 2008].

New South Wales Department of Planning 1995 *Cities for the 21st Century*. Sydney: The Department.

New York Times 1900 London and New York Water Supply. 15 April, 22. query.nytimes.com/gst/abstract.html?res=F50812F8385D12738DDDAC0994DC405B808CF1D3 [accessed 28 December 2007].

New York Times 1904 London's Water Experience. 25 July, 6. query.nytimes.com/gst/abstract.html?res=F70D12FD3A5913738DDDAC0A94DF405B848CF1D3 [accessed 28 December 2007].

Ngalamulume, K. 2004 Keeping the City Totally Clean: Yellow Fever and the Politics of Prevention in Colonial Saint-Louis-du-Sénégal, 1850–1914. *The Journal of African History*, 45 (2), 183–202.

———. 2006 Plague and Violence in Saint-Louis-du-Sénégal, 1917–1920. *Cahiers d'études africaines*, 2006/3 (183), 196.

———. 2007 Smallpox and social control in colonial Saint-Louis-du-Sénégal, 1850–1915. In Falola, T, and Heaton, M.M. (eds) *HIV/AIDS, illness and African Well-being*. Rochester, NY: Rochester University Press, 62–78.

Nichols, F.H., Cloern, J.E., Luoma, S.N. and Peterson, D.H. 1986 The Modification of an Estuary. *Science*, 231, 567–73.

Noise Abatement Society, 1969 *The Law on Noise*.

Northern Ireland Government 2008 Noise Complaints on the Decrease. http://www. northernireland.gov.uk/news/news-doe/news-doe-december-2008/news-doe-171208-noise-complaints-on.htm [accessed 4 October 2012].

Nossiter, A. 2007 Largely Alone, Pioneers Reclaim New Orleans. *New York Times*, 2 July 2007. www.nytimes.com/2007/07/02/us/nationalspecial/02orleans.html [accessed 23 January 2008].

O'Meara, M. 1999 *Reinventing Cities for People and the Planet*. Worldwatch Paper 147, Washington, DC: Worldwatch Institute.

O'Neil, P. 1970 Kill that Hill! Pave that Grass! *Life*, 49 (3), 20–3.

O'Riordan, T. and Davis, J. 1976 Outdoor Recreation and the American Environment. In Wreford-Watson, J. and O'Riordan, T. (eds) *The American Environment: Perceptions and Policies*. London: Wiley, 259–76.

OECD. 2008 *Measuring material flows and resource productivity: Synthesis report*. Paris: OECD.

Oesterholt, F., Martijnse, G., Medema, G. and Van Der Kooij, D. 2007 Health risk assessment of non-potable domestic water supplies in the Netherlands. *Journal of water supply: research and technology, AQUA*, 56, 171–9.

Olsen, G.N., Danbury, M.F. and Leatherbarrow, B. 1999 The Mersey Estuary Pollution Alleviation Scheme: Liverpool interceptor sewers. *Proceedings Institution of Civil Engineers Water, Maritime & Energy*, 136, 171–83.

Osmanöglu, B, Dixon T.H., Wdowinski, S., Cabral-Cano, E. and Jiang, Y. 2010 Mexico City Subsidence Observed with Persistent Scatterer InSAR. www.geodesy.miami.edu/articles/2010/MexicoCitySubsidence.pdf [accessed 28 October 2011].

Oyelola, O.T. and Babatunde, A.I. 2008 Effect of Municipal Solid Waste on the Levels of Heavy Metals In Olusosun Dumpsite Soil, Lagos State, Nigeria. *International Journal of Pure and Applied Sciences*, 2 (1), 17–21.

Oyelola, O.T., Babatunde, A.I. and Odunlade, A. K. 2009 Health Implications Of Solid Waste Disposal: Case Study Of Olusosun Dumpsite, Lagos, Nigeria. *International Journal of Pure and Applied Sciences*, 3 (2), 1–8.

Pacholsky, J. 2003 *The ecological footprint of Berlin (Germany) for the year 2000: Technical Report*. Nairobi: UNEP and IETC.

Paillard, H. and Martin, G. 1994 Odor elimination in wastewater treatments plants and sewage networks. In Martin, G. and Laffort, P. (eds) *Odors and deodorization in the environment*. New York: VCH Publishers, 415–44.

Pandey, P., Khan, A.H., Verma, A.K., Singh, K.A., Mathur, N., Kisku, G.C. and Barman, S.C. 2012 Seasonal Trends of PM (2.5) and PM (10) in Ambient Air and Their Correlation in Ambient Air of Lucknow City, India. *Bulletin of Environmental Contamination and Toxicology*, 88 (2), 265–70.

Pandey, P., Kumar, D., Prakash, A., Masih, J., Singh, M., Kumar, S. Jain, V.K.and Kumar. K. 2012 A study of urban heat island and its association with particulate matter during winter months over Delhi. *Science of the Total Environment*, 414, 494–507.

Parker, A.G., Goudie, A.S., Stokes, S., White, K., Hodson, M.J., Manning, M. and Kennet, D. 2006 A record of Holocene climate change from lake geochemical analyses in southeastern Arabia. *Quaternary Research*, 66, 465–76.

Passchier-Vermeer, W. and Passchier, W.F. 2000 Noise Exposure and Public Health. *Environmental Health Perspectives*, 108 (suppl. 1), 123–31.

Patel, P. 2010 Solar-Powered Desalination: Saudi Arabia's newest purification plant will use state-of-the-art solar technology. *MIT Technology Review*. http://www.technologyreview.com/energy/25010/?a=f [accessed 5 October 20112].

Paterson, J. 1976 The Poet and the Metropolis. In Wreford-Watson, J. and O'Riordan, T. (eds) *The American Environment: Perceptions and Policies*. London: Wiley, 93–108.

Patmore, J.A. 1972 *Land and Leisure*. Harmondsworth: Penguin Books.

Paul, J. 1990 Reconstruction of Dresden: Planning and Building during the 1950s. In Diefendorf, J.M. (ed.) *Rebuilding Europe's Bombed Cities*. London: MacMillan, 170–89.

Pauly, J.J. 1984 The Great Chicago Fire as a National Event. *American Quarterly*, 36, (5), 668–83.

Peacock, W., Morrow, B.H. and Gladwin, H. 1997 *Hurricane Andrew: ethnicity, gender and the sociology of disasters*. New York & London: Routledge.

Pelli, C., Thornton, C. and Joseph, L. 1997 The world's tallest buildings. *Scientific American*, 277 (6), 65–73.

Penn-Bressel, G. 1999 Noise abatement plans and environmentally compatible urban traffic and transport in Germany. In Schwelder, H-U. (ed.) *Noise abatement in European Towns and Cities: strategies, concepts and approaches for local noise policy*. European Academy of the Urban Environment, Berlin, 39–42.

Peterson, J.A. 2003 *The Birth of Sanitary reform in the United States 1840-1917*. Baltimore: Johns Hopkins University Press.

Petryna, A. 1995 Chernobyl in Historical Light. *Cultural Anthropology*, 10 (2), 196–220.

Petts, J. 1994 Incineration as a Waste Management Option. In Hester, R.E. and Harrison, R.M. (eds) *Waste Incineration and the Environment*. London: Royal Society of Chemistry, 1–25.

Pfister, C. 2004 Switzerland. In Krech, S. III, McNeill, J.R. and Merchant, C. (eds) *Encyclopaedia of World Environmental History Volume 3*. New York: Routledge, 1175–7.

Phienwej, N, and P. Nutalaya. 2005 Subsidence and flooding in Bangkok. In Gupta, A. (ed.) *The Physical Geography of Southeast Asia*. Oxford: Oxford University Press, 358–78.

Piccolo, A., Plutino, D., and Cannistraro, G. 2005 Evaluation and analysis of the environmental noise of Messina, Italy. *Applied Acoustics* 66, 447–65.

Picker, J.M. 2003 *Victorian Soundscapes*. New York: Oxford University Press.

Pinch, T. and Bijsterveld, K. 2012 New Keys to the World of Sound. In Pinch, T. and Bijsterveld, K. (eds) *The Oxford Handbook of Sound Studies*. Oxford: Oxford University Press, 3–35.

Platner, S.B. 1929 (as completed and revised by Thomas Ashby) *A Topographical Dictionary of Ancient Rome*. London: Oxford University Press.

Platt, H.L. 1995 Invisible gases: smoke, gender, and the redefinition of environmental policy in Chicago, 1900–1920. *Planning Perspectives*, 10, (1995) 67–97.

Plester, H.R.F. and Binnie, C.J.A. 1995 The evolution of water resource development in Northern Ireland. *Journal Chartered Institution of Water and Environmental Management*, 9, 272–80.

Poiger, U.G. 2000 *Jazz, Rock, and Rebels: Cold War Politics and American Culture in a Divided Germany*. Berkeley: University of California Press.

Pomázi, I. and Szabó, E. 2008 Urban metabolism: The case of Budapest. In Havránek, M. (ed.) *ConAccount 2008: Urban metabolism: measuring the ecological city*. Prague: Charles University Environment Center, 351–74.

Porter, R. 1997 *The Greatest Benefit to Mankind: A medical history of humanity from antiquity to the present*. London: Harper Collins.

Quastel, N. 2009 Political Ecologies of Gentrification. *Urban geography*, 30, 694–725.

Rapoport, A. (ed.) 1972 *Australia as human setting: Approaches to the designed environment*. Sydney: Angus & Robertson.

Ravetz, J. 2000 *City Region 2020: Integrated planning for a sustainable environment*. London: Earthscan.

—. 2011 Peri-urban ecology: Green infrastructure in the twenty-first century metroscape. In Douglas, I., Goode, D., Houck, M. and Wang, R.S. (eds) *Routledge Handbook of Urban Ecology*. London: Routledge, 599–620.

Read, A.D., Phillips, P. and Robinson, G. 1998 Landfill as a Future Waste Management Option in England: The View of Landfill Operators, *Geographical Journal*, 164, 55–66.

Reade, J. 1991 *Mesopotamia*. London: The British Museum.

Reagan, M. 1987 *Regulation: The Politics of Policy*. Boston: Little Brown.

Reclus, E. 1877 *The Earth: A descriptive history of the phenomena of the life of the globe, Section II*. London: Bickers and Son.

Rees, W.E. 1992 Ecological footprints and appropriated carrying capacity: what urban economics leaves out. *Environment and Urbanisation*, 4 (2), 121–30.

Reid, J.A. 1961 Conservation and the quartz ridges. In Wyatt-Smith, J. and Wycherley, P.A. (eds) *Nature Conservation in Western Malaysia*. Malayan Nature Society, Kuala Lumpur, 66–7.

Resosudarmo, B.P. 2002 Indonesia's Clean Air Program. *Bulletin of Indonesian Economic Studies*, 38, 343–65.

Rice, L. 1907 Our Most Abused Sense—The Sense of Hearing. *Forum*, 38 (April), 560–3.

Risler, J.J. 1995 Groundwater Management in France. *Journal Chartered Institution of Water and Environmental Management*, 9, 264–71.

Roberts, N. and Rosen, A. 2009 Diversity and Complexity in Early Farming Communities of Southwest Asia: New Insights into the Economic and Environmental Basis of Neolithic Catalhöyük. *Current Anthropology*, 50 (3), 393–402.

Rodamilans, M., Torra, M. To-Figueras, J., Corbella J., López, B., Sánchez, C. and Mazzara, R. 1996 Effect of the Reduction of Petrol Lead on Blood Lead Levels of the Population of Barcelona (Spain). *Bulletin of Environmental Contamination and Toxicology*, 56, 717–21.

Rolt, L.T.C. 1974 *Victorian Engineering*. Harmondsworth: Penguin Books.

Rome, A. 2001 *The Bulldozer in the Countryside: suburban sprawl and the rise of American Environmentalism*. Cambridge: Cambridge University Press.

Romo-Kroger, C.M., Morales, J.R., Dinator, M.I. and Llona, F. 1994 Heavy metals in the atmosphere coming from a copper smelter in Chile. *Atmospheric Environment*, 28 (4), 705–11.

Rose, M.H. 2004 Technology and Politics: the scholarship of two generations of urban-environmental scholars. *Journal of Urban History*, 30 (5), 769–85.

Roseff, R. and Perring, D. 2002 Towns and the Environment, in Perring, D. (ed.) *Town and Country in England: frameworks for ecological research*, (CBA Research Report 134), York: Council for British Archaeology, 116–26.

Rosen, C.M. 1995 Businessmen against Pollution in Late Nineteenth Century Chicago. *Business History Review*, 69, 351–97.

——. 2003 'Knowing' Industrial Pollution: Nuisance Law and the Power of Tradition in a Time of Rapid Economic Change, 1840–1864. *Environmental History*, 8. http://www.historycooperative.org/journals/eh/8.4/rosen.html [accessed 4 October 2007].

Rosen, C.M. and Tarr, J. 1994 The Importance of an Urban Perspective in Environmental History. *Journal of Urban History*, 20 (3), 299–310.

Rosenbaum, M.S., McMillan, A.A., Powell, J.H., Cooper, A.H., Culshaw, M.G. and Northmore, K.J. 2003 Classification of artificial (man-made) ground. *Engineering Geology*, 69, 399–409.

Rothbard, M.N. 1974 Conservation in the Free Market. In Rothbard, M. N. (ed.) *Egalitarianism as a Revolt Against Nature and Other Essays*. Washington, DC: Libertarian Review Press, 175–89.

Royal Commission for Enquiring into the State of Large Towns and Populous Districts. *Parliamentary Papers* 1844; 17:50.

Royal Commission on Environmental Pollution. 2007 *The Urban Environment: Summary of the Royal Commission on Environmental Pollution's Report*. London: The Royal Commission on Environmental Pollution.

Royston Pike, E. 1966 *Human Documents of the Industrial Revolution*. London: George Allen and Unwin.

Sahely, H.A., Dudding, S. and Kennedy, C.A. 2003 Estimating the urban metabolism of Canadian cities: Greater Toronto Area case study. *Canadian Journal of Civil Engineering*, 30 (2), 468–83.

Salway, P. 1981 *Roman Britain*. Oxford: Clarendon Press.

Satterthwaite, D. 1992 Sustainable Cities: Introduction. *Environment and Urbanization*, 4 (2), 3–8.

Sbeinati, M.R., Darawcheh, R. and Mouty, M. 2005. The historical earthquakes of Syria: an analysis of large and moderate earthquakes from 1365 B.C. to 1900 A.D. *Annals of Geophysics*, 48, 347–435.

Scarre, C. 1995 *The Penguin Historical Atlas of Ancient Rome*. London: Penguin Books.

Schaake, J.C. Jr., 1972 Water and the City. In Detwyler, T.R. and Marcus, M.G. (eds) *Urbanization and Environment*. Belmont, CA: Wadsworth, 97–133.

Schiller, N. 1999 Practical financing and implementation of noise abatement measures in Celle. In Schwelder, H-U. (ed.) *Noise abatement in European Towns and Cities: strategies, concepts and approaches for local noise policy*. European Academy of the Urban Environment, Berlin, 69–73.

Schnefftan, K. 1992 Architecture and gardens: a unique sense of space. In Davis, M.B. (ed.) *Insight Guides Japan*, Hong Kong: APA Publications, 121–8.

Schoenbrod, D. 1980 Why regulation of lead has failed. In Needleman, H.L. (ed.) *Low level lead exposure: The clinical implications of current research*. Raven Press, New York, 259–66.

Schultz, S.K. and McShane, C. 1978 To engineer the metropolis: sewers, sanitation, and city planning in late-nineteenth-century America. *Journal of American History*, 65 (2), 389–411.

Seng, B., Kaneko, H., Hirayama K. and Katayama-Hirayama.K. 2011 Municipal solid waste management in Phnom Penh, capital city of Cambodia, *Waste Management Research*, 29, 491–500.

Severn Trent Water 2006 *Water Resources Plan: Overview 2005 – 2010*. Birmingham: Severn Trent Water.

Shao, M., Tang, X., Zhang, Y. and Li, W. 2006. City clusters in China: air and surface water pollution. *Frontiers in Ecology and the Environment* 4, 353–361. http://dx.doi.org/10.1890/1540-9295(2006)004[0353:CCICAA]2.0.CO;2 [accessed 12 July 2012].

Sharp. T. 1940 *Town Planning*. Harmondsworth: Penguin Books.

Sheail, J. 1986 Government and the perception of reservoir development in Britain: an historical perspective. *Planning Perspectives*, 1, 45–60.

———. 1995 Guest Editorial: The Ecologist and Environmental History – a British Perspective. *Journal of Biogeography*, 22 (6), 953–66.

Shi, L., Geng, J., Xu, J-F., Ning, X-Y. and Liu, Y. 2004 Odor Regulation and Progress of Odor Measurement in Europe. *Urban Environment & Urban Ecology*, 17, 20–1.

Short, A. 2000 Sydney's dynamic landscape. In Connell, J. (ed.) *Sydney: The Emergence of a World City*. South Melbourne: Oxford University Press, 19–36.

Shultz, T. and Collar, C. 1993 Dairying and Air Emissions. Davis CA: *University of California Cooperative Extension Dairy Manure Management Series*, UCCE-DMMS-4 10/93.

Silbergeld, E.K. 1995 The International Dimensions of Lead Exposure. *International Journal of Occupational and Environmental Health*, 1, 336–48.

———. 1996 Lead poisoning: the implications of current biomedical knowledge for public policy. *Maryland Medical Journal*, 45 (3), 209–17.

———. 1997 Preventing lead poisoning in children. *Annual Reviews of Public Health*, 18, 187–210.

Silverstein, Y. 2011 Green Judaism – balancing sustainability and tradition. *Haaretz*, 12 September 2011. http://www.haaretz.com/jewish-world/the-jewish-thinker/green-judaism-balancing-sustainability-and-tradition-1.383959 [accessed 22 July 2012].

Simkhovich, B.Z., Kleinman, M.T. and Kloner, R.A. 2008 Air Pollution and Cardiovascular Injury: Epidemiology, Toxicology, and Mechanisms. *Journal of the American College of Cardiology*, 52, 719–26.

Simmons, I.G. 1993 *Environmental History: a concise introduction*. Oxford: Blackwell.

———. 2001 *An environmental history of Great Britain: from 10,000 years ago to the present*. Edinburgh: Edinburgh University Press.

———. 2008 *Global Environmental History 10.000 BC to AD 2000*. Edinburgh: Edinburgh University Press.

Simo, A. and Clearly, M.A. 2004 Intrusive Community Noise Impacts South Florida Residents. coeweb.fiu.edu/research_conference/2004_COERC_Proceedings.pdf [accessed 17 August 2007].

Slaymaker, O. 1999 Natural hazards in British Columbia: an interdisciplinary and inter-institutional challenge. *International Journal of Earth Sciences*, 88, 317–24.

Smilor, R.W. 1977 Cacophony at 34th and 6th: the noise problem in America 1900–1930. *American Studies*, 18, 23–38.

———. 1979 Personal Boundaries in the Urban Environment. *Environmental Review*, 3, Spring, 25–36.

Smit, J.C., Nasr, J. and Ratta, A. 2001 *Urban Agriculture: Food, Jobs and Sustainable Cities* The Urban Agriculture Network, Inc. (2001 edition, published with permission from the United Nations Development Programme). http://jacsmit.com/book/Chap02.pdf [accessed 04 May 2012].

Smith, D.P. 1987 Sir Joseph William Bazalgette and The Big Stink. *Transactions of the Newcomen Society*, 58, 89–112.

Smith, M.E. 2002 The Earliest Cities. In Gmelch, G. and Zenner, W.P. (eds) *Urban Life: Readings in the Anthropology of the City*, (4th edn). Prospect Heights, IL: Waveland Press, 3–19.

Smith, S. 2005 *Undergound London: Travels Beneath the City Streets*. London: Abacus.

Sofoulis, Z. 2005 Big Water, Everyday Water: A Sociotechnical Perspective. *Continuum: Journal of Media & Cultural Studies*, 19 (4), 445–63.

Soil Conservation Service (US) 1968 *Standards and Specifications for Soil Erosion and Sediment Control in Urbanizing Areas*. Washington, DC: US Dept. of Agriculture.

Soyer, R. and Cailleux, A. 1960 *Géologie de la région parisienne*. Collection: Que sais-je? Paris: Presses Universitaires de la France.

Special correspondent 1894 The official report of the Paris cholera epidemic of 1892. *The Lancet*, 3 February, 293–4.

Spencer, T. and Guérin, E. 2012 Time to reform the EU Emission Trading Scheme. *European Energy Review*, 23 January 2012. http://www.europeanenergyreview.eu/site/pagina.php?id=3478 [accessed 11 February 2012].

Spurr, P. 1976 *Land and Urban Development*. Toronto: James Lorimer.

Sseesamirembe Eco-City 2008 The Signing of a Memorandum of Understanding. http://www.sseesamirembe.com/article.php?title=The%20Signing%20of%20a%20Memorandum%20of%20Understanding%20&content_page=article_08_14_2008_1 [accessed 31 March 2011].

St. Croix Sensory, Inc. 2005 *A Review of The Science and Technology of Odor Measurement*. St. Elmo: St. Croix Sensory.

Staubwasser, M., Sirocko, F. Grootes, P.M. and Segl, M. 2003 Climate change at the 4.2 ka BP termination of the Indus valley civilization and Holocene south Asian monsoon variability. *Geophysical Research Letters*, 30 (8), 1425, doi:10.1029/2002GL016822 [accessed 5 October 2012].

Stavins, R.N. 2002 Experience with Market-Based Environmental Policy Instruments *Fondazione Eni Enrico Mattei, Nota di Lavoro* 52.2002. http://www.feem.it/userfiles/attach/Publication/NDL2002/NDL2002-052.pdf [accessed 28 January 2012].

Stenseth, N.C., Atshabar, B.B., Begon, M., Belmain, S.R., Bertherat, E., et al. 2008 Plague: Past, Present, and Future. *PLoS Med*, 5 (1), e3. doi:10.1371/journal.pmed.0050003 [accessed 5 October 2012].

Stevenson, G.M. 1972 Noise and the urban environment. In Detwyler, T. and Marcus, M.G. (eds) *Urbanization and Environment*. Belmont CA; Duxbury Press, 195–228.

Stott, A.P. 1986 Sediment tracing in a reservoir-catchment system using a magnetic mixing model. *Physics of the earth and planetary interiors*, 42, 105–12.

Stroud, E. 1999 Troubled Waters in Ecotopia: Environmental Racism in Portland, Oregon. *Radical History Review*, 74: (Special Issue on Environmental Politics, Geography and the Left), 65–95. Reprinted in Warren, L.S. ed., 2003 *American Environmental History*, Blackwell Readers in American Social and Cultural History Series, Oxford: Blackwell.

Suez Environnement 2010 *The ICSID confirms Argentina's liability for terminating the water and wastewater contracts for the City of Buenos Aires and the State of Santa Fe*. Press Release 2 August 2010. http://www.suez-environnement.com/en/news/press-releases/press-releases/?communique_id=771 [accessed 21 November 2011].

Suhrke, A. 2007 Reconstruction as Modernisation: the 'post-conflict' project in Afghanistan. *Third World Quarterly*, 28 (7), 1291–308.

Sun, G. and Florig, H.K. 2002 *Determinants of air pollution management in urban China*. Paper presented at the workshop 'Smoke and Mirrors: Air Pollution as a Social and Political Artifact'. Center for Global, International, and Regional Studies, UC Santa Cruz, Santa Cruz, CA, 11–12 January 2002.

Suzuki, H., Dastur, A. Sebastian Moffatt, M.Yabuki, N. and Maruyama, H. (eds) 2010 *Eco2 Cities: Ecological Cities as Economic Cities*. Washington DC: The World Bank.

Svidén, J., Hedbrandt, J., Lohm, U. and Tarr, J. 2001 Copper emissions from fuel combustion, consumption and industry in two urban areas, 1900-1980. *Water, Air, and Soil Pollution: Focus*, 1, 167–77.

Swanson, M.W. 1977 The sanitation syndrome: Bubonic Plague and Urban Native Policy in the Cape Colony, 1900-1909. *The Journal of African History*, 18, 387–410.

Syagga, P.M. and Olima, W.H.A. 1996 The impact of compulsory land acquisition on displaced households: the case of the Third Nairobi Water Supply Project, Kenya. *Habitat International*, 20, 61–75.

Sydney Water Corporation 2008 *Sydney's Desalination Project*. http://www.sydneywater. com.au/Water4Life/Desalination/ [accessed 12 July 2012].

Tachibanaa, J., Hirotab, K., Gotoc, N. and Fujie, K. 2008 A method for regional-scale material flow and decoupling analysis: A demonstration case study of Aichi prefecture, Japan. *Resources, Conservation and Recycling*, 52, 1382–90.

Takahashi, N. 1998 Changes in Tokyo's waterfront environment. In Golany, G.S., Hamaki, K. and Koide, O. (eds) *Japanese Urban Environment*. Oxford: Pergamon, 147–77.

Tan, W.K., Lee, S.K., Wee, Y.C. and Foong, T.W. 1995 Urbanization and Nature Conservation. In Ooi, G.L. (ed.) *Environment and the City: sharing Singapore's experience and future challenges*. Singapore: Times Academic Press, 185–99.

Tarr, J.A., Goodman, D.G. and Koons, K. 1980 Coal and Natural Gas: Fuel and Environmental Policy in Pittsburgh and Allegheny County, Pennsylvania, 1940–1960. *Science, Technology, & Human Values*, 5, (32), 19–21.

Tarr, J.A. and Lamperes, B. C. 1981 Changing Fuel Use Behavior and Energy Transitions: The Pittsburgh Smoke Control Movement, 1940–1950: A Case Study in Historical Analogy. *Journal of Social History*, 14, 561–88.

Tarr, J. and McShane, C. 2005 Urban Horses and Changing City-Hinterland Relationships. In Luckin, B., Massard-Guilbaud, G. and Schott, D. (eds) *Resources of the City: Contributions to an Environmental History of Modern Europe*. Aldershot: Ashgate, 48–62.

Tarr, J. and Zimring, C. 1997 The Struggle for Smoke Control in St. Louis. In Hurley, A. (ed.) *Common Fields: an environmental history of St. Louis*. St. Louis: Missouri Historical Society Press, 199–220.

Taylor, K.G., Boyd, N.A. and Boult, S. 2003 Sediments, porewaters and diagenesis in an urban water body, Salford, UK: impacts of remediation. *Hydrological Processes*, 17, 2049–61.

Templet, P.H. and Meyer-Arendt, K.J. 1988 Louisiana Wetland Loss: A Regional Water Management Approach to the Problem. *Environmental Management*, 12 (2), 181–92.

Teramura, H. and Uno, T. 2006 Spatial Analyses of Harappan Urban Settlements. *Ancient Asia*, 1, 73–9.

Thomas, V.M., Socolow, R., Fanelli, J.J. and Spiro, T.G. 1999 Effects of Reducing Lead in Gasoline: An Analysis of the International Experience. *Environmental Science and Technology*, 33, 3942–8.

Thompson, E.P. 1963 The Making of the English Working Class. London: Gollancz.

Thorsheim, P. 2002 The paradox of smokeless fuels: gas, coke and the environment in Britain, 1813–1949. *Environment and History*, 8, 381–401.

Tidball, K.G. and Krasny, M.E. 2007 From Risk to Resilience: What Role for Community Greening and Civic Ecology in Cities? In Wals, A. (ed.) *Social Learning Towards a more Sustainable World*. Wageningen: Wageningen Academic Publishers, 149–64.

Tomkins, J., Topham, N. Twomey, J. and Ward, R. 1998 Noise versus Access: The Impact of an Airport in an Urban Property Market. *Urban Studies*, 35, 243–58.

Tooley, M.J. 2000 Storm surges. In Hancock, P.L. and Skinner, B.J. (eds) *The Earth*. Oxford: Oxford University Press, 999–1001.

Trotter, J.W. and Fernandez, J. 2009 Hurricane Katrina: Urban History from the Eye of the Storm. *Journal of Urban History*, 32 (2), 607–13.

Tsuchiya, Y. and Kanata, Y. 1986 Historical study of changes in storm surge disasters in the Osaka area. *Natural Disaster Science*, 8, 1–18.

Tucker, R.P. 2004 War. In Krech, S. III, McNeill, J.R. and Merchant, C. (eds) *Encyclopaedia of World Environmental History Volume 3*. New York: Routledge, 1284–91.

Tupling, G.H. 1962 Mediaeval and early modern Manchester. In Carter, C.F. (ed.) *Manchester and its Region*. Manchester University Press, Manchester, 115–30.

Turbutt, G. 1999 *A History of Derbyshire* (4 vols). Cardiff: Merton Priory Press.

Tylecote, R.F. 1976 *A History of Metallurgy*. London: Mid-County.

Uekoetter, F. 1999 Divergent Responses to Identical Problems: Businessmen and the Smoke Nuisance in Germany and the United States, 1880-1917. *The Business History Review*, 73, 641–76.

UK Government 1989 *The Noise at Work Regulations 1989 No. 1790* Regulation 6. http://www.legislation.gov.uk/uksi/1989/1790/regulation/6/made [accessed 26 October 2011].

Ulbrich, U., Brücher, T., Fink, A.H., Leckebusch, G.C., Krüger, A. and Pinto, J.G. 2003 The central European floods of August 2002: Part 1 – Rainfall periods and flood development. *Weather*, 58, 371–7.

UNCHS (Habitat) 2001 *The State of the World's Cities 2001*. Nairobi: United Nations Centre for Human Settlements.

Unwin, R. 1929 *Memorandum No. 1 Open Spaces. Greater London Regional Planning Committee First Report December 1929*. London: Knapp and Drewett.

US Government Interagency Working Group 2000 International Crime Threat Assessment. http://clinton4.nara.gov/WH/EOP/NSC/html/documents/pub45270/pub 45270chap2.html#6 [accessed 05 September 2011].

Van Harreveld, A.Ph. 1998 A review of 20 years of standardization of odour concentration measurement by dynamic olfactometery in Europe. *Journal of the Air and Waste Management Association*, 49, 705–15.

——. 2003 Odor regulation and the history of odor measurement in Europe. In N. a. V. Office of Odor (ed.) *State of the art of odour measurement*. Tokyo: Environmental Management Bureau, Ministry of the Environment, Government of Japan, 54–61.

Vancouver 2011 *Greenest City 2020 Action Plan*. Vancouver: City of Vancouver. http://vancouver.ca/greenestcity/PDF/GC2020ActionPlan.pdf [accessed 21 July 2012].

Veen, M. Van de, Livarda, A. and Hill, A. 2008 New Plant Foods in Roman Britain: Dispersal and Social Access. *Environmental Archaeology*, 13 (1), 11–36.

Velásquez, L.S.B. 1998 Agenda 21; a form of joint environmental management in Manizales, Colombia. *Environment and Urbanization*, 10 (2), 9–36.

Vernier, J. 1993 *L'Environnement*. Paris: Presses Universitaires de France.

Victor, R.A.B.M., Neto, J. de B.C., Ab'Saber, A.N., Serrano, O., Domingos, M., Pires, B.C.C., Amazonas, M. and Victor, M.A.M. 2004 Application of the Biosphere Reserve Concept to Urban Areas: The Case of São Paulo City Green Belt Biosphere Reserve, Brazil—São Paulo Forest Institute: A Case Study for UNESCO. *Annals of the New York Academy of Sciences*, 1023, Urban Biosphere and Society: Partnership of Cities, 237–81.

VNA. 2010. Hanoi suburbs stricken by drought. *Vietnamese News Agency*, 18 May.

351

Wacher, J. 1976 *The Towns of Roman Britain*. London: Book Club Associates.

Walsh, C., McLoone, A., O'Regan, B., Moles, R. and Curry, R. 2006 The application of the ecological footprint in two Irish urban areas: Limerick and Belfast, *Irish Geography*, 39 (1), 1–21.

Waltham, T. 2005 Karst terrains. In Fookes, P.G., Lee, E.M., and Milligan, G. (eds) *Geomorphology for Engineers*. Dunbeath, Caithness: Whittles Publishing, 662–87.

Walton, B., Bateman, J.S. and Heinrich, M. 1995 Water supply franchising in Buenos Aires. *Journal of the Chartered Institution of Water and Environmental Management*, 9, 369–75.

Wang, R.S., Downton, P. and Douglas, I. 2011 Towards Ecopolis: New Technologies, new philosophies and new developments. In Douglas, I. Goode, D., Houck, M. and Wang, R.S. (eds) *Routledge Handbook of Urban Ecology*. London: Routledge, 636–51.

Wang, R.S. and Paulussen, J. 2007 Sustainability Assessment Indicators: Development and practice in China. In Hak, T., Moldan, B. and Dahl, A.L. (eds) *Sustainability Indicators: A Scientific Assessment*, (SCOPE 67). Washington, DC: Island Press, 329–41.

Wang, Y., Hopke, P.K. and Utell, M.J. 2011 Urban-Scale Seasonal and Spatial Variability of Ultrafine Particle Number Concentrations. *Aerosol and Air Quality Research*, 11, 473–81.

Warren-Rhodes, R. and Koenig, A. 2001 Escalating Trends in the Urban Metabolism of Hong Kong: 1971–1997. *Ambio*, 30 (7), 429–38.

Water Guide 2007 *Three Valleys Water*. www.water-guide.org.uk/three-valleys-water.html [accessed 28 December 2007].

Watts, J. 2009 China plans 59 reservoirs to collect meltwater from its shrinking glaciers. *The Guardian*, 2 March 2009.

Ways, M. 1970 How to think about the environment. *Life*, 49 (3), 36–44.

Webster, Richard A. 2006. Outline of New Orleans ninth ward's progress and challenges. *CityBusiness*, 4 September 2006.

Welchman, S., Brooke. A.S. and Best, P.R. 2005 Is odour intensity all it's cracked up to be? Paper presented at the 17th International Clean Air & Environmental Conference, Tasmania, Australia, May 2005.

Whitfield, P. 2006 *London in Maps*. London: The British Library.

Whyte, W. 1956 *The Organization Man*. New York: Simon & Schuster.

———. 1968 *The Last Landscape*. New York: Doubleday.

Wild, T.C., Bernet, J.F., Westling, E.L. and Lerner, D.N. 2011 Deculverting: reviewing the evidence on the 'daylighting' and restoration of culverted rivers. *Water and Environment Journal*, 25 (3), 412–21.

Willan, T.S. 1980 *Elizabethan Manchester*. Manchester: Chetham Society and Manchester University Press.

Wilson, J. 2001 *The Alberta GPI Accounts: Ecological Footprint, Pembina Institute for Aprropriate Development Report No. 28*. Drayton Valley, Alberta: Pembina Insitute.

Wolman, A. 1965 The metabolism of cities. *Scientific American*, 213 (3), 179–90.

Wong, M.H., Wu, S.C., Deng, W.J., Yu, X.Z., Luo, Q., Leung, A.O.W., Wong, C.S.C., Luksemburg, W.J. and Wong, A.S. 2007 Export of toxic chemicals: A review of the case of uncontrolled electronic-waste recycling. *Environmental Pollution*, 149, 131–40.

Woodward, E.L.1962 *The Age of Reform 1815-1870*. Oxford: Oxford University Press.

Worboys, M. 1988 Manson, Ross and Colonial Medical Policy: tropical medicine in London and Liverpool 1899-1914. In McLeod, R. and Lewis, M. (eds) *Disease, Medicine and Empire: Perspectives on Western Medicine and the Experience of European Expansion*. London: Routledge, 21–37.

Working Party on Sewage Disposal 1970 *Taken for Granted*. London: Her Majesty's Stationery Office.

Working with Water 2010 *Windesal could provide solution for Kangaroo Island's power and water needs*. http://www.workingwithwater.net/view/7851/windesal-could-provide-solution-for-kangaroo-islands-power-and-water-needs/ [accessed 03 May 2012].

World Bank 2009 *Systems of Cities: Harnessing urbanization for growth and poverty alleviation*. Washington DC: World Bank.

World Commission on Environment and Development (WCED) 1987 *Our Common Future*. New York: Oxford University Press.

Worpole, K. and Greenhalgh, L. 1995 *Park Life: Urban Parks and Social Renewal*. London: Comedia-Demos.

Worrall, P. and Little, S. 2011 Urban ecology and sustainable urban drainage. In Douglas, I., Goode, D., Houck, M. and Wang, R.S. (eds) *The Routledge Handbook of Urban Ecology*. London: Routledge, 561–70.

Wright, M. 2001 *Quake – Hawke's Bay 1931*. Auckland: Reid Publishing (NZ) Ltd.

Yang, M., Kang, Y. and Zhang, Q. 2009 Decline of groundwater table in Beijing and recognition of seismic precursory information. *Earthquake Science*, 22, 301–6.

Yi, L., Wang, J., Shao, C., Guo, J.W., Jiang, Y., and Bo, L. 2010 Land Subsidence Disaster Survey and Its Economic Loss Assessment in Tianjin, China. *Natural Hazards Review*, 11, 35–42. doi:10.1061/(ASCE)1527-6988(2010)11:1 (35). http://ascelibrary.org/doi/abs/10.1061/(ASCE)1527-6988(2010)11%3A1(35) [accessed 5 October 2012].

Yoyeva, A., de Zeeuw, H. and Teubner, W. (eds) 2002 *Urban agriculture and cities in transition. Proceedings of the regional workshop, 20-22 June 2002, Sofia, Bulgaria*, SWF-ETC-ICLEI-Europe, Leusden, Netherlands.

Yu, S., Zhu, C., Song, J. and Qu, W. 2000 Role of climate in the rise and fall of Neolithic cultures on the Yangtze Delta. *Boreas*, 29, 157–165.

Zhang, H., Wang, X., Ho, H.H. and Yon, Y. 2008 Eco-health evaluation for the Shanghai metropolitan area during the recent industrial transformation (1990–2003). *Journal of Environmental Management*, 88, 1047–55.

Zhang, Q., Xu, Z., Shen, Z., Li S. and Wang, S. 2009 The Han River watershed management initiative for the South-to-North Water Transfer project (Middle Route) of China. *Environmental Monitoring and Assessment*, 148, 369–77.

Zhang, Q., Zhu, C., Liu, C.L. and Jiang. T. 2005 Environmental change and its impacts on human settlement in the Yangtze Delta, P.R. China. *Catena*, 60, 267–77.

Zhang, Y., Yang, Z. and Yu, X. 2009 Evaluation of urban metabolism based on energy synthesis: A case study for Beijing (China). *Ecological Modelling*, 220, 1690–6.

Zhao, X., Zhang, X., Xu, X., Xu, J., Meng, W. and Pu, W. 2009 Seasonal and diurnal variations of ambient PM2.5 concentration in urban and rural environments in Beijing. *Atmospheric Environment*, 43, 2893–900.

Zimmerer, K.S. 1994 Human Geography and the 'New Ecology': The Prospect and Promise of Integration. *Annals Association of American Geographers*, 84 (1), 108–25.

Zong, Y. and Chen, X. 2000 The 1998 Flood on the Yangtze, China. *Natural Hazards*, 22, 165–84.

Index

CPSIA information can be obtained
at www.ICGtesting.com
Printed in the USA
LVHW050050080121
675998LV00004B/111